Twentieth-Century Spain

D0873142

This is a much-needed new overview of Spanish social and political history, which sets developments in twentieth-century Spain within a broader European context. Julián Casanova, one of Spain's leading historians, and Carlos Gil Andrés chart the country's experience of democracy, dictatorship and civil war, and its dramatic transformation from an agricultural and rural society to an industrial and urban society fully integrated into Europe. They address key questions and issues that continue to be discussed and debated in contemporary historiography, such as why the Republic was defeated, why Franco's dictatorship lasted so long and what mark it has left on contemporary Spain. This is an essential book for students as well as for anyone interested in Spain's turbulent twentieth century.

Julián Casanova is Professor of Contemporary History at the University of Zaragoza and visiting Professor at Central European University, Budapest.

Carlos Gil Andrés teaches history at Rey Don García of Nájera.

Twentieth-Century Spain

A History

Julián Casanova
Carlos Gil Andrés

Translated by
Martin Douch

CAMBRIDGE
UNIVERSITY PRESS

University Printing House, Cambridge CB2 8BS, United Kingdom

Cambridge University Press is part of the University of Cambridge.

It furthers the University's mission by disseminating knowledge in the pursuit of education, learning and research at the highest international levels of excellence.

www.cambridge.org
Information on this title: www.cambridge.org/9781107602670

© Julián Casanova 2014

Originally published in Spanish as *Historia de España en el siglo XX* by Ariel, 2009 © Ariel 2009

First published 2014

Printed in the United Kingdom by Clays, St Ives plc

A catalogue record for this publication is available from the British Library

Library of Congress Cataloguing in Publication data
Casanova, Julián.
[Historia de Espana en el siglo XX. English]
Twentieth-century Spain : a history / Julián Casanova, Carlos Gil Andrés; translated by Martin Douch.
  pages   cm
ISBN 978-1-107-01696-5 (hardback) – ISBN 978-1-107-60267-0 (paperback)
1. Spain – History – 20th century.   I. Gil Andrés, Carlos.   II. Title.
DP233.C3813   2014
946.08–dc23

ISBN 978-1-107-01696-5 Hardback
ISBN 978-1-107-60267-0 Paperback

Contents

Illustrations

Key figures

Alcalá Zamora, Niceto (1877–1949). A liberal politician during the Restoration. In 1930, following the fall of Primo de Rivera's dictatorship, he declared himself to be anti-monarchist and took part in the San Sebastián Pact. After the municipal elections of 14 April 1931 he headed the first provisional government of the Republic. He was president of the Second Republic between 1931 and April 1936. At the end of the Civil War, he was forced to go into exile, firstly in France and then in Argentina, where he died.

Alfonso XIII (1886–1941). King of Spain between May 1902 and April 1931. He was the posthumous son of Alfonso XII and María Cristina von Habsburg, who was regent on his behalf until he reached the age of majority. He was a monarch who played an active role in politics, favouring the interests of the privileged classes and the army, and incapable of guiding the political regime of the Restoration towards a true democracy. In 1923 he acknowledged Primo de Rivera's *coup d'état* and backed the dictator. In 1931, disapproval of the monarchy became clear in the municipal elections, in what was an unquestionable plebiscite in favour of a republic. The king was forced to accept the situation and go into exile.

Arana, Sabino (1865–1903). A nationalist politician who founded the Partido Nacionalista Vasco (PNV) in 1895. The basic idea behind its ideology, 'God and the old laws', demonstrated its identification with the *fueros* (regional law codes and privileges), traditional Catholicism and anti-liberalism. The movement called for the independence of *Euskalerria*, a group of Basque territories united by language, race and faith. The development of Basque nationalism is linked to the defence of tradition within the conflictive context of industrialisation in Vizcaya.

Azaña, Manuel (1880–1940). Intellectual, writer and main republican leader in the 1930s, minister of war, prime minister (October 1931 to September 1933) and president of the Republic from May 1936. Crossed into France when the defeat of the Republic was imminent, resigned and died in Montauban in November 1940.

Aznar, José María (1953–). Conservative prime minister of Spain for two terms (1996–2004). In 1989 he refounded the right-wing party Alianza Popular under the name of Partido Popular (PP). During the next few years, as secretary general of the PP, he was able to improve the party's election results. He came to power in 1996 with the support of the nationalist parties. In 2000, in the midst of an economic boom, he won an absolute majority and directed Spanish politics in the first four years of the twenty-first century.

Calvo Sotelo, Leopoldo (1926–2008). Prime minister between February 1981 and October 1982. He came from a traditional Catholic and monarchist family. In the early years of the transition to democracy he was a member of the Unión de Centro Democrático (UCD) governments led by Adolfo Suárez. Following Suárez's resignation and Lieutenant Colonel Antonio Tejero's attempted coup (*el 23-F*), he became prime minister until Felipe González's socialists won the elections.

Canalejas, José (1854–1912). A liberal politician and prime minister between 1910 and 1912. He was the foremost leader of the Partido Liberal in the early years of the twentieth century. His political and social reforms, which aimed to lead the Restoration regime towards a system of democracy, met many obstacles. He was assassinated in a terrorist attack.

Carrillo, Santiago (1915–2012). Historic leader of the Partido Comunista de España (PCE). His political activism began in the final years of the Second Republic, when he became president of the Juventudes Socialistas Unificadas (United Socialist Youth). During the Civil War he was a councillor on the Junta de Defensa de Madrid. After the war, he went into exile, first in France and then in the USSR. In 1960 he became the secretary general of the PCE, a post he held until 1982, the final moment in the transition to democracy, and a period when he played an important role.

Companys, Lluís (1886–1940). A republican Catalan nationalist politician, very active in the early decades of the twentieth century for his opposition to the political regime of the Restoration and Primo de Rivera's dictatorship. In April 1931 he was elected as a councillor of the Esquerra Republicana de Catalunya. In October 1934, as president of the Generalitat de Catalunya, he proclaimed the Catalan state. In the spring of 1936, after a time in prison, he once again took on the presidency of the Generalitat, holding the post until the end of the Civil War. In 1940 he was arrested by the Gestapo in France and handed over to the Nationalist authorities. He was executed by firing squad in October the same year.

Dato, Eduardo (1856–1921). A Spanish politician and member of the Partido Conservador during the Restoration. He was a member of various governments until, in 1913, Alfonso XIII appointed him prime minister. He occupied this post on three occasions (1913–15, 1917 and 1920–1). He displayed a predisposition towards social and political reform, but he was unable to avoid the crisis of the monarchist–parliamentary regime. He was assassinated by Catalan anarchists in March 1921.

Franco, Francisco (1892–1975). An army general, he plotted and rose against the Republic, and on 1 October 1936 his fellow officers designated him head of the three branches of the armed forces, Generalísimo, and principal leader of Nationalist Spain against the Republic. He won the war and became dictator of Spain until his death on 20 November 1975.

Gil Robles, José María (1898–1980). Lawyer, Catholic politician and founder of the Confederación Española de Derechas Autónomas (CEDA). An advocate of a corporative and authoritarian state, he was the Republic's minister of war in 1935; he supported the military coup of 1936 and, once the war had started, Franco's cause, although from Portugal and without taking active part in the war.

González, Felipe (1942–). Prime minister (1982–96). He joined the Partido Socialista Obrero Español (PSOE) in 1966, became a member of its executive four years later and in 1974 was elected its secretary general. The undisputed leader of Spanish socialism in the two previous decades, he became prime minister following the landslide victory obtained in October 1982. He renewed his mandate in the three subsequent parliamentary terms, a long period which enabled him to advance his social democratic political programme.

Iglesias, Pablo (1850–1925). Historic Spanish socialist leader. Founder of the Partido Socialista Obrero Español in 1879 together with a group of Madrid printers. At the beginning of the twentieth century he was also president of the Unión General de Trabajadores (UGT). He was elected a councillor for Madrid in 1905. And in 1910, standing for the republican–socialist alliance, he won a seat in the Cortes. As the years went by, his name became a near-mythical symbol of socialism.

Juan Carlos I (1938–). King of Spain since 22 November 1975, proclaimed by the Francoist Cortes following the death of the dictator. Born in exile, but educated in Spain. Franco appointed him his successor in 1969. He took on dynastic rights in 1977, after they had been renounced by his father, Don Juan de Borbón. A year later, the referendum to approve the Constitution ratified parliamentary monarchy as the state political system. Juan Carlos I's action in the unsuccessful 23-F 1981 *coup d'état* gave him legitimacy and popularity.

Largo Caballero, Francisco (1869–1946). Principal leader of the Partido Socialista Obrero Español and its trade union organisation UGT, he was minister of labour (1931–3) and wartime prime minister of the Republic between September 1936 and May 1937.

Lerroux, Alejandro (1864–1949). Republican leader, he was part of the republican–socialist coalition which took power in April 1931, but broke with this coalition in December of that year, and was prime minister during 1934 and 1935 together with the non-republican right-ist party CEDA. He took no part in the Civil War.

Martínez Barrio, Diego (1883–1962). A republican leader and prime minister after the dismissal of Azaña in September 1933, he was Speaker of the Cortes in the spring of 1936 and throughout the Civil War.

Maura, Antonio (1853–1925). Leader of the Partido Conservador in the first two decades of the twentieth century. He was prime minister in 1903 and again between 1907 and 1909. He unsuccessfully tried to bring about reform of the political system from above. He was prime minister three more times (1918, 1919 and 1921), in much shorter and less stable terms of office, during the final years of the Restoration crisis.

Mola, Emilio (1887–1937). An army general and principal organiser of the July 1936 uprising, which he co-ordinated under the alias of 'El Director'. He accepted Franco as leader and died in a plane accident in June 1937.

Montseny, Federica (1905–94). An anarchist leader, she was minister of health in Largo Caballero's government, between November 1936 and May 1937, thus becoming the first female minister in Spain's history.

Negrín, Juan (1892–1956). A socialist leader and distinguished professor of physiology in the University of Madrid, having studied in Leipzig, Germany. Leader of the republican government from May 1937 onwards, he preached discipline and order on the home front and resistance to the end.

***Pasionaria, la*, Dolores Ibárruri (1895–1989).** A communist leader, she became famous during the Civil War for her speeches defending the Republic and for her slogan '*No pasarán*' when Franco's troops were trying to take Madrid in the autumn of 1936.

Prieto, Indalecio (1883–1962). Reformist socialist political leader during the first third of the twentieth century. He was the driving force behind collaboration with the PSOE in the process that led to the proclamation of the Second Republic. He was minister of finance and public works in 1931, and during the Civil War he held two ministries in Largo Caballero's governments. When the war was over, he went into exile and was the principal socialist and republican leader.

Primo de Rivera, José Antonio (1903–1936). A prominent leader of the Spanish fascist movement. He was the eldest son of the dictator Miguel Primo de Rivera. In 1933 he founded the Falange. When the Civil War broke out, he was being held prisoner in Alicante, accused of promoting violence and preaching armed rebellion against the republican regime. He was shot on 20 November 1936. After the war, José Antonio became a mythical figure of the Francoist regime, and his name could be seen in squares and on church walls all over Spain.

Primo de Rivera, Miguel (1870–1930). A Spanish army officer who forged his career in military campaigns in Cuba, the Philippines and Morocco. In 1919 he attained the rank of lieutenant general. In September 1923, as captain general of Catalonia, he led the *coup d'état* that, with the support of the king, put an end to the parliamentary regime of the Restoration. In the following years he headed a military dictatorship which lasted until January 1930, when he left power as a result of his poor health and growing political and social opposition. Shortly afterwards, he died in Paris.

Rodríguez Zapatero, José Luis (1960–). Leader of the Partido Socialista Obrero Español (PSOE) and a socialist deputy in 1986. He was secretary general of the PSOE from 2000 onwards. After the socialist victory in the March 2004 elections he was appointed prime minister, a post he repeated for a second term until November 2011, when his position was weakened by the harsh effects of the international financial crisis.

Romanones, Conde de (1863–1950). Don Álvaro de Figueroa y Torres, Count of Romanones, was one of the foremost leaders of the Partido Liberal throughout the first third of the twentieth century. He was prime minister on three occasions (1912–13, 1915–17 and 1918–19). Mention of his name represents all the main characteristics of political cronyism and Spanish monarchic liberalism.

Serrano Súñer, Ramón (1901–2003). Leader of the Catholic right during the Republic, he managed to escape from prison in Madrid at the beginning of 1937 and became the principal champion of fascism in the zone ruled by Francisco Franco, his brother-in-law. It was he who was responsible for bringing together various factions into the unified FET y de las JONS, founded in April 1937.

Suárez, Adolfo (1932–). Prime minister (1976–81). His political career began under Franco with the general secretariat of the Movimiento.

From 1969 to 1973 he was director general of Radiotelevisión Española. After the death of Franco, he was a member of Arias Navarro's cabinet. In 1976 he was appointed prime minister by the king. He directed the political transition process at the head of the Unión de Centro Democrático (UCD), the party that won the 1977 and 1979 elections. He resigned in January 1981, shortly before the unsuccessful 23-F *coup d'état*.

Abbreviations

AC	Acción Católica
ACNP	Asociación Católica Nacional de Propagandistas
AIT	Asociación Internacional de los Trabajadores
AP	Alianza Popular
AVE	Alta Velocidad Española
CAMPSA	Compañía Arrendataria del Monopolio de Petróleos, SA
CC.OO.	Comisiones Obreras
CDS	Centro Democrático y Social
CEDA	Confederación Española de Derechas Autónomas
CEOE	Confederación Española de Organizaciones Empresariales
CESID	Centro Superior de Información de la Defensa
CiU	Convergència i Unió
CNT	Confederación Nacional del Trabajo
COAG	Coordinadora de Agricultores y Ganaderos
CSIC	Consejo Superior de Investigaciones Científicas
CTNE	Compañía Telefónica Nacional de España
CTV	Corpo di Truppe Volontarie
EA	Eusko Alkartasuna
ENCASO	Empresa Nacional Calvo Sotelo
ENDESA	Empresa Nacional de Electricidad, SA
ERC	Esquerra Republicana de Catalunya
ETA	Euskadi Ta Askatasuna
FAI	Federación Anarquista Ibérica
FE	Falange Española
FET y de las JONS	Falange Española Tradicionalista de las Juntas de Ofensiva Nacional Sindicalista
FNTT	Federación Nacional de Trabajadores de la Tierra
FRAP	Frente Revolucionario Antifascista Patriótico

xiv

FUE   Federación Universitaria Escolar
GAL   Grupos Antiterroristas de Liberación
GRAPO   Grupos de Resistencia Antifascista Primero
            de Octubre
HB   Herri Batasuna
HOAC   Hermandad Obrera de Acción Católica
INI   Instituto Nacional de Industria
IR   Izquierda Republicana
IRPF   Impuesto sobre la Renta de las Personas Físicas
IU   Izquierda Unida
JAP   Juventudes de Acción Popular
JOC   Juventud Obrera Católica
JONS   Juntas de Ofensiva Nacional Sindicalista
JSU   Juventudes Socialistas Unificadas
LOAPA   Ley Orgánica de Armonización del Proceso
            Autonómico
LODE   Ley Orgánica del Derecho a la Educación
MCE   Movimiento Comunista de España
ONU   Organización de Naciones Unidas
ORT   Organización Revolucionaria de Trabajadores
OSE   Organización Sindical Española
PCE   Partido Comunista de España
PNV   Partido Nacionalista Vasco
POUM   Partido Obrero de Unificación Marxista
PP   Partido Popular
PSE   Partido Socialista de Euskadi
PSOE   Partido Socialista Obrero Español
PSP   Partido Socialista Popular
PSUC   Partit Socialista Unificat de Catalunya
PTE   Partido del Trabajo de España
RENFE   Red Nacional de los Ferrocarriles Españoles
SEU   Sindicato Español Universitario
TOP   Tribunal de Orden Público
TVE   Televisión Española
UCD   Unión de Centro Democrático
UGT   Unión General de Trabajadores
UMD   Unión Militar Democrática
UME   Unión Militar Española
UR   Unión Republicana
ZEN   Zona Especial Norte

Twentieth-century Spain timeline

10 December 1898 Treaty of Paris between Spain and the United States. Handover of Cuba, the Philippines and Puerto Rico, the last vestiges of the colonial empire.

February 1902 First general strike in Spain.

May 1902 Alfonso XIII comes of age and accedes to the throne.

January 1903 Death of Práxedes Mateo Sagasta.

January–April 1906 Algeciras Conference. Advance of Franco-Spanish colonialism in Morocco.

July 1907 Foundation of Solidaridad Obrera.

July 1909 *Semana Trágica* in Barcelona. The Lobo Gulley massacre.

October 1909 Antonio Maura resigns as prime minister.

November 1910 Foundation of the Confederación Nacional del Trabajo (CNT) in Barcelona.

April 1912 Founding of the Partido Reformista.

November 1912 Assassination of José Canalejas. Establishment of the Spanish protectorate in Morocco.

April 1914 The Mancomunitat (Federation) of Catalonia is established.

August 1914 Spain declares its neutrality in the First World War.

February–March 1917 Strike at La Canadiense in Barcelona, which evolves into a general strike.

July 1921 The Annual and Monte Arruit disasters.

November 1921 Foundation of the Partido Comunista de España.

September 1923 A *coup d'état* led by Miguel Primo de Rivera and the setting up of the Military Directorate.

December 1925 Foundation of the Civil Directorate. Death of Pablo Iglesias.

May 1926 End of the Moroccan war. Abd-el-Krim surrenders to France.

July 1927 Foundation of the Federación Anarquista Ibérica (FAI) in Valencia.

January 1930 The dictator Miguel Primo de Rivera resigns.

17 August 1930 Signing of the San Sebastián Pact.

12 December 1930 Republican uprising in Jaca led by the army officers Fermín Galán and Ángel García Hernández. Both are executed.

17 February 1931 Appointment of Admiral Juan Bautista Aznar as prime minister.

12 April 1931 Municipal elections which turn into a plebiscite between the monarchy and a republic.

14 April 1931 Republican candidates win in the large cities. Proclamation of the Republic in various parts of the country.

14 April 1931 Francesc Macià proclaims the Catalan Republic.

28 June 1931 Elections for the Constituent Cortes, with a majority for the republican–socialist coalition.

9 December 1931 The Republic's Constitution is passed by the Cortes.

10 December 1931 Niceto Alcalá Zamora is chosen as president of the Republic by the Cortes.

10 August 1932 Failure of an attempted *coup d'état* by General José Sanjurjo.

9 September 1932 The Cortes pass the Statute of Autonomy of Catalonia and the Agrarian Reform Act.

4 March 1933 Founding of the Confederación Española de Derechas Autónomas (Spanish Confederation of the Autonomous Right – CEDA).

7 September 1933 Niceto Alcalá Zamora dismisses Manuel Azaña and Alejandro Lerroux is commissioned by the president of the Republic to form a new government.

19 November 1933 New parliamentary elections with a majority for the CEDA and the Partido Radical.

27 April 1934 Alejandro Lerroux resigns as prime minister and Ricardo Samper is appointed to the post the following day.

4 October 1934 Alejandro Lerroux forms a new government.

5 October 1934 A general strike in Catalonia which unleashes the events of October 1934.

5–18 October 1934 Workers' uprising in Asturias which is crushed with harsh repression from the Africa Army.

17 May 1935 The Cortes pass the appointment of General Francisco Franco as chief of the General Staff.

16 February 1936 General election held in the Republic for the third time. Election won by the Frente Popular.

21 February 1936 Granting of amnesty to political prisoners.

8 March 1936 Generals opposing the Republic meet in Madrid. They decide to launch a military coup.

10 May 1936 Manuel Azaña is appointed president of the Republic.

13 July 1936 Assassination of José Calvo Sotelo.

18 July 1936 Franco declares a state of war and pronounces himself in opposition to the government.

19 July 1936 Franco arrives in Tetuán and some of the peninsular garrisons join the coup. Formation of the José Giral government.

4 September 1936 Francisco Largo Caballero is appointed prime minister.

21 September 1936 Franco is named Generalísimo by the National Defence Council.

20 November 1936 José Antonio Primo de Rivera is executed by firing squad.

26 April 1937 Bombing of Guernica by the Condor Legion.

16 June 1937 POUM is declared illegal and its leader, Andreu Nin, is arrested and transferred to Madrid.

21 October 1937 Gijón and Aviles fall to Franco's troops, and the Republic loses control of the whole of northern Spain.

6 April 1938 Formation of the new Juan Negrín government.

25 July 1938 to 16 November 1938 Battle of the Ebro.

26 January 1939 Barcelona falls to the Nationalist forces.

29 March 1939 Madrid falls to the Nationalist forces.

1 April 1939 Franco announces the end of the war.

23 October 1940 Meeting between Franco and Hitler in Hendaye.

28 February 1941 Death of Alfonso XIII.

25 August 1948 Don Juan (Alfonso XIII's son) and Franco agree to bring Juan Carlos de Borbón to live in Madrid.

26 September 1953 Signing of the Pact with the United States.

14 December 1955 Spain admitted to the UN.

25 February 1957 Formation of a new government with 'technocrats'.

17 May 1958 A law governing the Fundamental Principles of the Movimiento.

February 1959 Foundation of Euskadi Ta Askatasuna (ETA).

9 May 1963 Setting up of the Public Order Tribunal (TOP).

28 December 1963 First Development Plan.

10 September 1968 Second Development Plan.

12 October 1968 Independence of Spanish Guinea.

22 July 1969 Franco nominates Juan Carlos de Borbón as his successor.

23 March 1972 Third Development Plan.

8 June 1973 Luis Carrero Blanco appointed prime minister.

20 December 1973 Assassination of Luis Carrero Blanco by ETA.

3 January 1974 Carlos Arias Navarro forms a government.

20 November 1975 Death of Franco.

1 July 1976 Carlos Arias Navarro resigns.

5 July 1976 A new government led by Adolfo Suárez.

15 December 1976 The Political Reform Act passed by referendum.

9 April 1977 Legalisation of the Partido Comunista de España (PCE).

15 June 1977 First general election won by the Unión de Centro Democrático (UCD).

25 October 1977 Signing of the Moncloa Pacts.

6 December 1978 The Spanish Constitution is passed by referendum.

1 March 1979 New elections again won by the UCD.

29 January 1981 Resignation of Adolfo Suárez.

23 February 1981 The 23-F *coup d'état*.

25 February 1981 Leopoldo Calvo Sotelo appointed prime minister.

30 May 1982 Spain joins NATO.

28 October 1982 The Partido Socialista Obrera Español (PSOE) wins the general election.

2 December 1982 First government of Felipe González.

1 January 1986 Spain admitted into the European Community.

12 March 1986 Spain's permanent membership of NATO approved by referendum.

22 June 1986 The PSOE wins general election again.

14 December 1988 General strike against the government's economic policy.

29 October 1989 The PSOE re-elected.

20 April 1992 The Universal Exposition in Seville.

25 July 1992 The Barcelona Olympic Games begin.

6 June 1993 Fourth victory of Felipe González with an absolute majority.

3 March 1996 The Partido Popular (PP), under Aznar, wins the general election.

12 March 2000 Aznar and the PP re-elected.

22 July 2000 José Luís Rodríguez Zapatero elected secretary general of the PSOE.

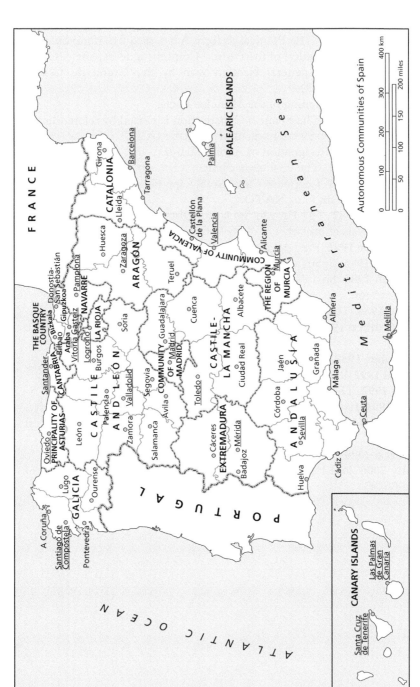

Map 1 Spain and its autonomous regions

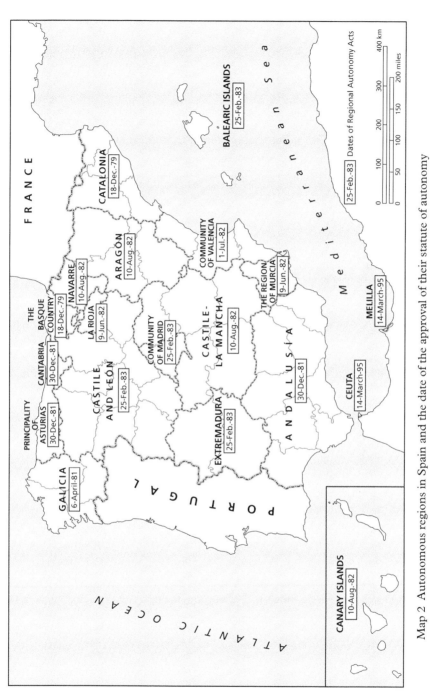

Map 2 Autonomous regions in Spain and the date of the approval of their statute of autonomy

FRANCE

THE BASQUE COUNTRY
18-Dec.-79

NAVARRE
10-Aug.-82

CATALONIA
18-Dec.-79

ARAGÓN
10-Aug.-82

LA RIOJA
9-Jun.-82

PRINCIPALITY OF ASTURIAS
30-Dec.-81

CANTABRIA
30-Dec.-81

GALICIA
6-April-81

CASTILE AND LEÓN
25-Feb.-83

COMMUNITY OF MADRID
25-Feb.-83

CASTILE-LA MANCHA
10-Aug.-82

COMMUNITY OF VALENCIA
1-Jul.-82

BALEARIC ISLANDS
25-Feb.-83

EXTREMADURA
25-Feb.-83

THE REGION OF MURCIA
9-Jun.-82

ANDALUSIA
30-Dec.-81

MELILLA
14-March-95

CEUTA
14-March-95

PORTUGAL

ATLANTIC OCEAN

Mediterranean Sea

CANARY ISLANDS
10-Aug.-82

25-Feb.-83 Dates of Regional Autonomy Acts

0 100 200 300 400 km
0 50 100 150 200 miles

Introduction

'In all their affairs, nothing is ever quite what it seems. We grope in a sort of fog when we try to understand them.' The quote comes from *The Spanish Labyrinth*, the book that Gerald Brenan began writing in Great Britain while Spain was steeped in the blood of a civil war. The author was almost sick with worry and shock, horrified as he was by the 'hysterical frenzy of killing and destruction' that he had seen with his own eyes in the summer of 1936, before he left the peninsula. Spain was his intellectual passion. In 1919 he had crossed the 'whole yellow ox hide' travelling in dirty third-class train carriages overflowing with peasants with their chickens and bundles of vegetables; he had slept in humble inns with their straw mattresses crawling with bedbugs and fleas, until he found the retreat he had been looking for, a small village lost in the Alpujarras, a landscape that seemed more like the mountains of Afghanistan or the Berber villages of North Africa than the heavily populated Europe he had come from, overshadowed by the devastating experience of the Great War.

Brenan saw Spain as being the country of a glorified feeling of 'the homeland', eastern thought, hunger and supply shortages, vast agricultural injustice, the almost religious fervour of popular anarchism, permanent calls to revolution, a country difficult to govern even at the best of times. In his opinion, the Civil War had been the explosion in the powder magazine that had slowly been accumulating, the scene of a drama in which the fortunes of the civilised world were being played out in miniature. Spain was not isolated from events in Europe, but its inhabitants were confronting very different social and economic situations which mirrored the political trends of the great powers only superficially and belatedly. 'Everything to be found in Spain is *sui generis*.'[1] In 1949 Brenan went back and found a society held back by hardship, overcome by the worst sort of hangover, 'the type that follows a civil war and reign of terror'. In the 1950s he returned for good to live in a country 'in the

---

[1] Gerald Brenan, *The Spanish Labyrinth* (Cambridge University Press, 1943), p. xvii.

disguise of modern European customs which it does not fit in with, and against which it offers a constant and not entirely conscious resistance', a territory which he still defined as 'enigmatic and disconcerting'.[2]

One might say that, more than anything else, the British Hispanicist's account symbolises the history of the twentieth century. In 1894, the year of his birth, Spain was a decrepit old empire on the eve of its final 'disaster'. The average lifespan of the population was no more than thirty-five years. Most Spaniards remained aloof from the political system, and many of them had to cross the Atlantic to former colonies to earn the bread they lacked in their own communities. It was a country of emigrants, victims of persecution and exile. And it was in exile that Alfonso XIII died, the king crowned at the beginning of the century, as did Primo de Rivera, the dictator who brought him down with him in his fall. Also to die in exile were the two presidents of the Second Republic, Alcalá Zamora and Azaña, and most of their prime ministers, as well as hundreds of thousands of others who at the end of the Civil War joined a mass exodus to escape from repression. Under Franco's regime, many Spaniards experienced internal exile imposed by silence and the struggle for survival, and several million men and women once more went abroad to look for work. Someone who never had to do this was Franco, who died in a hospital bed after nearly four decades of authoritarian power.

Brenan belonged to the same generation as Franco, being barely two years younger than the dictator. He died when he was nearly 93 years old, a long lifespan that was also a product of the change of centuries. By then Spain was a modern society fully integrated in the European community, a consolidated democracy that was growing and evolving at a remarkable rate. He was finally laid to rest, in the land that he had loved and studied so much, in January 2001, barely twenty days after the turn of the century, in a country that bore little resemblance to the one he had discovered eighty years previously. It was no longer an exotic, romantic destination for inquiring travellers looking for new sensations but a welcoming location chosen by waves of immigrants who had been displaced from their countries through poverty and insecurity.

Brenan's fame as a writer has survived him, but not his vision of the history of the peninsula: that has been overtaken by the analyses of younger Hispanicists and a generation of Spanish historians who, since the 1980s,

---

[2] Gerald Brenan, prologue from John Haycraft, *Babel in Spain* (London: Hamish Hamilton, 1958), p. 17. Details and comments on the life and work of the British Hispanicist are from his memoirs, *Autobiografía: una vida propia. Memoria personal (1920–1975)* (Barcelona: Península, 2003), and from the biography written by Jonathan Gathorne-Hardy, *Gerald Brenan: The Interior Castle* (London: Sinclair-Stevenson Ltd, 1994).

have been broadening their research topics, renewing their methods and also their ways of tackling and interpreting the past, to revise and take apart the most common clichés and misrepresentations. Today we know that the history of Spain in the first third of the twentieth century was not the chronicle of a secular frustration foretold, which of necessity was to finish up as a collective tragedy; an accumulation of failures and defects – of industry and agriculture, the bourgeoisie and the middle class, the state and civil society – which prevented the country from following the European path to progress and modernisation. The Restoration era was not a stagnant pool in which nothing moved; neither was the brief democratic experiment of the Second Republic the inevitable prologue to the Civil War; nor was the long-drawn-out Francoist dictatorship a parenthesis which, at the end of the day, favoured economic development and the advent of freedom; and the transition to democracy was never a perfect script previously written from the upper echelons of power.

The history of Spain did not run its course independently of the rest of Europe, nor was it any stranger to the social, economic, political and cultural transformations experienced by the rest of the continent. There were many more similarities than differences, particularly with its southern European neighbours. We historians also know that there is no 'normal' model of modernisation with which Spain could be contrasted as being an anomalous exception. Hardly any country in Europe resolved the conflicts of the 1930s and 1940s – the century's dividing line – by peaceful means. In the subsequent 'golden' age, there was economic growth, and the welfare state expanded in monarchist as well as in republican countries, under social-democratic governments as well as Christian Democrat coalitions. Outside western Europe, the outlook is still bleak. The inequality gap has been growing instead of closing. One of the lessons that the twentieth century has taught us is that there was no direct path to progress, no single pattern that all the countries in the world could follow to achieve development and collective well-being.

Events followed their particular course but they could have been very different. The history of this century was pervaded by splits and regression, by violent revolutions and acrimonious conflicts between opposing ideologies, by totalitarian states and dictatorships of all colours, by world wars and unprecedented human disasters that have overshadowed the shining light of scientific discoveries and material improvements. One hundred years of brutality and civilisation, of civil victims and citizen conquests: the twentieth century also witnessed the most accelerated social changes in the history of mankind. This was a time that for Spain has meant the end of demographic transition, the disappearance of the traditional peasant world, the spread of education, the emancipation of women, the transport and communications revolution, the creation of public opinion and the extension of citizens' rights. At the beginning of the century there had been writers who spoke of the 'age of the masses', an almost pejorative concept that masked the fear of crowds taking to the streets to demand their rights, of majorities that were capable of bringing down governments at the polls. Now that the 1900s have passed into history, a more correct reading might be to talk of the century of the citizen, when ordinary people were given individual freedoms, political and employment rights, and the new social rights demanded by civil society. We have been all too quick to forget that these rights were not always within our reach, that they were not gratuitous concessions from the people in power but the collective achievements of entire generations and remarkable figures who were determined to improve the world they had been born into.

There are too many names, too many events for all of them to appear in a book that aims to encompass the history of the twentieth century in under four hundred pages. Some readers may miss a remark about a specific fact, mention of a relevant name or an account of a noteworthy event. A work of synthesis is always a limited selection. As historians, we select and classify the traces left by the past to construct overall interpretations that will help us to understand the most important historical issues. Anyone who is looking for a more detailed chronicle of events, a more thorough study of the economic variables, political events, social structures and cultural changes may do so with the aid of encyclopaedias, multi-volume collections and the most comprehensive works available in bookshops and libraries. Many works on twentieth-century Spain have been published in the last decade, some of them extremely good. But a non-specialist reader, a university student and a foreigner interested in learning about Spain's most recent history will all have problems in finding a compact book that relates the essential facts and explains the fundamental changes and processes of an intense, controversial and extraordinarily complex century.

This is the gap that this book aims to fill. The narrative follows the unifying thread of political history and the rhythm of conventional chronological divisions; later, at the end of each part and in the epilogue, it takes a more measured look at some of the more interesting thoughts and arguments of current Spanish historiography. Did the end of the Restoration clear the way for democracy? What was the significance of Primo de Rivera's dictatorship? What brought on the Civil War? What were the reasons for the Republic's defeat? Why did Franco's dictatorship last so long, and what mark did it make? What assessment can we make of the Transition after a quarter of a century of democracy? Questions, issues and problems that continue to occupy the minds of experts in contemporary history.

The book also aspires to be an invitation to read other books, such as those appearing in the annotated bibliography at the end. Historical knowledge needs to break out from the academic sphere and reach a broader public, a new generation of Spaniards with no first-hand experience of this past century, a generation that needs to understand the complexity of past events to address the problems of the future. We historians are not antiquarians buried in archives, mindless of the world we live in. We are committed to society, writing from the present and aware that research is just part of our work. We have the obligation to teach and disseminate the long tortuous process that has brought us democracy, tolerance and peaceful coexistence. There is still work to be done. As Azaña said in the bull ring in Madrid, in a speech given in September 1930, 'freedom does not make men free; it just makes them men'.[3] The rest is up to us.

JULIÁN CASANOVA AND CARLOS GIL ANDRÉS
July 2009

[3] Manuel Azaña, *Discursos políticos* (Barcelona: Crítica, 2004), p. 83.

Part I

The monarchy of Alfonso XIII

1   The legacy of a century

The beginning of the twentieth century was not the start of a new historical period for Spain. The political regime of the Restoration, inaugurated
on the return to the throne of the Bourbon dynasty and the approval of
the 1876 Constitution, survived basically unchanged until 1923. Some
texts take 1902, the year Alfonso XIII reached the age of majority, as the
start of their history of the century; others begin with 1898, the year
forever associated with the loss of the last colonies; and still others prefer
to talk in a broader sense about the end-of-century or inter-century crisis,
to place events in Spain at that time within the European context and to
emphasise Spain's problems, plain to see in the 1890s, that were to provide
the framework for the long political crisis in the first decades of the new
century.

At any event, the change of century seems a good time to pause a moment
and present a general overview of Spanish society; to explain, albeit briefly,
the bases of the political system, the roots of the anti-dynastic opposition,
the principal features of the social and economic structures and the
evolution of the social movements, on the eve of what was to be called
the century of the masses. With a snapshot taken around 1900 we can
look back rather than forward, to show some of the basic problems and
most important conflicts that would be bequeathed to the twentieth
century. Among these problems were the insufficient nationalisation
of the state, the limits of political representation, the weight of institutions such as the army or the Church, and the lack of legal channels to
incorporate the demands of the populace. This chapter will give a rapid
summary that, despite these problems, aims to quell the myth of failure
as an explanatory model: a failure of industrialisation, the non-existence
of a bourgeois revolution, the absence of agrarian modernisation, an
archaic *cacique* system, mass demobilisation. In fact, as recent historiography has shown, the society that experienced the *Desastre* of '98 was
more dynamic, modern and complex than portrayed by contemporaries
who so successfully disseminated the clichéd image of decadence and
stagnation.

The *Desastre del '98*

'Surrender is unavoidable.' So wrote General Arsenio Linares, under siege by the North Americans in Santiago de Cuba on 12 July 1898, in an official cable describing the harrowing situation being suffered by the city's defenders, who had been decimated by the battles of San Juan and El Caney, and were exhausted, sick and starving: 'We have been suffering constant rainfall in the trenches for twenty hours; the men have no shelter, and they have only rice to eat and cannot change or wash their clothes.' More than a week had passed since the sinking of Admiral Pascual Cervera's squadron, outside the bay, and few doubted that the US flag would soon be flying in the city's Plaza de Armas. If the struggle went on, said the general, 'we would only be prolonging the agony; sacrifice is futile'. His note went beyond an analysis of the military situation. The final lines, devoted to describing the morale of the troops, were almost a summary of the characteristics of the conflict and, to a certain extent, also a harbinger of the critical pens that were to portray the defeat as a *Desastre* with a capital D: 'These defenders are no longer beginning a campaign full of enthusiasm and energy: for three years they have been battling against the climate, deprivation and fatigue, and these critical circumstances have come about when they no longer have any stamina or physical strength, nor the means to regain them. They lack idealism, because they are defending the property of those who, in their presence, have abandoned it, and of those who they are up against, allied to the American forces.'[1]

Four days later the act of capitulation – in reality an unconditional surrender – was signed which, in practice, was to mean the end of the war. The ceremonial laying down of arms took place on the morning of 17 July, on the outskirts of Santiago de Cuba. The march past of the Spanish troops in front of the United States leaders symbolised, perhaps more than any other image, the end of one era and the beginning of another. It was the Spanish empire's final significant display of force of arms, before the uniforms of the army that, in the following century, was to impose its supremacy all over the world. As Lord Salisbury had said previously that year, in his famous speech at the Albert Hall in London on 4 May, three days after the naval defeat at Cavite, in Philippine waters: 'You may roughly divide the nations of the world as the living and dying.' On the one hand, explained the British prime minister, you had great countries that year after year were growing in power, wealth and military strength; on the

---

[1]   Letter from General Arsenio Linares to the Captain General of the Island of Cuba, General Ramón Blanco, 12 Jul. 1898, Archivo General Militar de Madrid, Fondo de Ultramar, Caja 5.798.

other, states in which disorganisation and decadence were swiftly taking over: 'Decade after decade, they are weaker, poorer and less provided with leading men or institutions in which they can trust.' Decadence, poverty, poor administration and corruption formed a 'terrible picture' that the press were describing 'with darker and more conspicuous lineaments'. This was the tone that filled the pages of the Spanish newspapers when they learnt the harsh reality of a defeat that, although foreseen, no one expected to be so swift, humiliating or embarrassing.

The war in Cuba had begun in February 1895 with the famous *Grito de Baire*, an insurrection well organised by leaders such as Máximo Gómez, Antonio Maceo and José Martí. At the end of March, Práxedes Mateo Sagasta's government, which had declared its intention to defend Spanish sovereignty to the last peseta and the last man, handed over the reins to Antonio Cánovas del Castillo, who was also intent on sending ship after ship from the peninsula to put down the rebellion. The 15,000 soldiers present on the island at the beginning of spring grew to more than 100,000 at the end of the year, to reach more than 200,000 in subsequent years. It was, as Manuel Moreno points out, the biggest military operation ever undertaken by a colonial power in America, a deployment that was to be surpassed only by the American entry into the Second World War.[2] For the time being, in 1895, the accumulation of troops did not achieve the desired result. News arriving from Cuba spoke of the encounters with the *mambises* (Cuban insurgents) as being victories, but the insurrection, far from being smothered, was growing. The rebels rejected open combat and wore down the Spanish units with their greater mobility, their knowledge of the terrain and the support they received from the civilian population.

The captain general, Arsenio Martínez Campos, labelled as weak, was replaced in January 1896 by Valeriano Weyler, a soldier with a reputation for harshness which he was soon to show with his decision to wage 'war with war'. The Spanish columns, in gruelling advances and setbacks, relentlessly harassed the rebels who were isolated by the *trochas*, the fortified lines crossing the island from north to south to cut off the nuclei of rebellion. Concentrating the rural population around the towns and garrisons, destroying crops and peasant dwellings, and banning harvesting activities were examples of the scorched earth policy designed to eradicate the social and economic foundations of the independence movement. This extreme war strategy, which harmed Spain's external image and was denounced as being cruel and inhumane, provided the United States with the argument it needed to justify its belligerence and a possible military

---

[2] Manuel Moreno Fraginals, *Cuba/España, España/Cuba* (Barcelona: Crítica, 1995).

intervention, not just in the islands of Cuba and Puerto Rico, which were near its coast, but also in the Philippines; it was there, in August 1896, that there had been an independence rebellion which forced the Spanish government to send 30,000 troops to the faraway archipelago under the command of General Camilo Polavieja, another inflexible officer who wasted no time in having the nationalist leader, José Rizal, shot.

Before the end of the year, the death of one of the rebel leaders, Antonio Maceo, was received with jubilation by the Spanish public, and it seemed to augur a change of direction in the conflict. But the popular celebrations were merely a mirage that disappeared in the early months of 1897, revealing a reality that did not match the optimistic tone of Weyler's reports. The truth was that neither the destruction of crops and dwellings nor the large concentrations of troops, costly in men and resources, succeeded in eliminating the rebel bands, who moved around unhindered in the centre and east of the island and relentlessly harassed the supply detachments and convoys. Despite the fact that all the major towns remained in Spanish hands, the insurgents were masters of the countryside, a situation that was maintained, basically unchanged, until the end of the war. The arrival of the new summer, in the middle of the dreaded rainy season, became the expeditionary force's worst enemy. Barely 4% of the more than 50,000 soldiers who died in Cuba were victims of war wounds. Most of them died from yellow fever, malaria, dysentery, typhoid and other tropical diseases that fed on bodies that were exhausted, ill fed and ill equipped. It is no wonder that Máximo Gómez claimed that his best generals were called June, July and August.

It was while this was going on that the Spanish prime minister, Antonio Cánovas, was assassinated by an Italian-born anarchist, Michele Angiolillo, at the Santa Águeda spa resort in the Basque region of Guipúzcoa. The death of the conservative leader was also the end of Weyler. The new Liberal government, with Práxedes Sagasta once more directing the war, sent General Ramón Blanco to Cuba, with orders that included the repeal of the exceptional measures, a comprehensive pardon for prisoners and exiles, and a wide-ranging programme of self-government reforms. But it was too late. The rebels had gone too far to consider any outcome other than independence from Spain. During the first few months of 1898 the Army of Independence continued its offensive in the eastern half of the island, forcing the Spanish to abandon their most exposed positions and retreat to their strongholds, a strategy that was also reinforced by the intervention of the United States in the conflict and the fear of a possible landing near the major towns.

The blowing up of the battleship USS *Maine* in Havana harbour, probably due to an accident, was the excuse for which the Americans had been waiting. On 18 April, the Senate and House of Representatives authorised President William McKinley to send an ultimatum to Spain which, reading between the lines, was a declaration of war. Five days later in Spain, the Regent, María Cristina of Austria, signed the Royal Decree that acknowledged the state of war, giving rise to a wave of patriotic fervour that spread throughout the country. The jingoistic atmosphere at demonstrations, protests, bullfights and poetry-reading sessions was mirrored in the headlines of most of the newspapers, with their constant reminders of the Spanish 'lion' against the Yankee 'pig'. Corpus Barga, a witness of these days in the streets of Madrid, recalled the fervour caused by the patriotic march from the operetta *Cádiz* among a people 'that was exultant'. But this fever of patriotism was short-lived. After the loss of Cervera's squadron and the surrender of Santiago came the occupation of Puerto Rico on 25 July, and the beginning of peace talks. The peace preliminaries were accepted on 12 August, almost at the same time as the capitulation of Manila in the Philippines and, although the signing of the Treaty of Paris was postponed until 10 December, the end of the summer saw the arrival at ports and railway stations in the peninsula of repatriated troops dressed in rags, a pathetic sight that became the most inescapable and visible image of the defeat.

Overnight, as if the nation had suddenly woken from a century-long sleep, unfounded and vocal triumphalism gave way to disillusion, disappointment, protest and the demand that those responsible be held to account. As Manuel Azaña wrote many years later, 'the Spanish seemed to be vomiting up the lies and half-truths that they had been swallowing for centuries'. The former prime minister and historian Francisco Silvela spoke of a Spain 'without a pulse' which needed a change of regime; General Polavieja criticised its policy as being old and decrepit; Ricardo Macías Picavea denounced the 'gangrene' of the Cortes and the sterility of the Crown; in the Senate, the Count of Almenas said that there was a need to 'rip many crosses off chests and raise many sashes from the waist to the neck'; and Joaquín Costa, the leading critic of the oligarchy and *caciquismo*, called on the 'neutral masses' of the country to participate in a 'far-reaching revolution'. In his opinion, there was only one way of dealing with the 'knot': 'cut it'. The government suspended constitutional guarantees as a result of rumours of a Carlist uprising,[3] a republican *pronunciamiento* and even a military *coup d'état*. But none of this happened.

[3] Carlism was an extreme right monarchist popular movement born in the 1830s, amid a dynastic dispute. On the death of Fernando VII, in September 1833, there was a succession problem. Fernando VII only had a daughter and, in order for her to be able to reign, he abolished the Salic Law (established by the Bourbons in Spain to prevent women from

The leading Spanish politicians had accepted the war against the United States as the lesser evil, convinced that the granting of independence to the Cubans or the sale of the island to the Americans would have been extremely dangerous for the Restoration and the very survival of the monarchy. The events that followed the *Desastre* were to prove them right. The Liberals continued in government with no problems until, in February 1899, they 'handed over the baton' to a conservative cabinet led by Silvela, with Polavieja as minister of war. One part of the regenerationist movement was thus included in the dynastic system and the rest, such as the protests of the Chambers of Agriculture and of Commerce, the 'life force' of the country, faded into the background during the subsequent months without managing to put forward a political alternative. As *El Imparcial* rightly pointed out, the revolution that had failed to emerge from the barracks or the barricades was even less likely to come from 'shuttered shops'. And as the journalist José Francos Rodríguez said later: 'we had to content ourselves with venting our spleen in writing'.

There was not even an economic crisis after '98. Despite the high cost of the war, in both human lives and resources, the repatriation of capital from the colonies, the maintaining of exports, the arrival of foreign investments and tax reforms favoured an economic situation that bore little or no resemblance to the catastrophist diagnoses of the regenerationists who were preaching that the country was on the edge of an abyss. And the criticisms of the *noventayochistas* (writers of the generation of '98) regarding the fraud and corruption of the political system were not original either. In previous years, writers such as Valentí Almirall, Gumersindo de Azcárate, Lucas Mallada, Ángel Gavinet, and even Miguel de Unamuno had savagely denounced the scourge of *caciquismo* and the decadence of an anaemic and backward nation. The far-reaching impact of this regenerationist literature, with its marked tone of moral indignation, contributed considerably to the subsequent success of the theory of 'failure' as an explanation for everything that had happened in Restoration Spain, a stereotyped view that historians in recent years have revised by proposing a more complex and varied analysis, enriched by the contributions from other social sciences and by a comparative perspective that places the study of the Spanish case within a general European context.

ascending the throne). His brother Carlos María Isidro used this law to claim the throne and, on the death of Fernando VII, he began a war between his supporters (Carlists), who defended a radical absolutism, and the supporters of the future queen, Isabella II, who defended a constitutional, liberal monarchy. After three civil wars in the nineteenth century, the defeated Carlists became a marginal movement.

The Restoration structure and its cracks

In the nineteenth century it was difficult to find any other European state that had undergone so many military *pronunciamientos*, popular uprisings, revolutions or civil wars as Spain had between the Peninsular War of 1807–14 and the end of the First Republic in December 1874. No other country with a similar profile, as Josep Fontana has pointed out, had to overcome so many major obstacles to the consolidation of Liberalism, such a high number of proclaimed and abolished constitutions, so many advances on the road towards democracy frustrated by setbacks and counter-revolutionary movements.[4] Antonio Cánovas del Castillo was aware of this contentious history when he advocated the return of the Bourbons to Spain in the person of the young prince, Alfonso. The 1876 Constitution was the cornerstone of a doctrinal regime that aspired to surmount this stormy past by constructing around itself, as Melchor Fernández Almagro wrote, a secure and long-lasting 'atmosphere of moderation', which would give 'the public room to breathe', away from the ups and downs caused by military plots, republican and Carlist uprisings, and the growing danger of protest movements among the popular classes. From this viewpoint, there is no denying the success of the Restoration. It survived, almost unchanged, for half a century, with a prudent capacity for adapting to the circumstances of each situation, and showed no visible signs of fatigue until at least the First World War, when it revealed its basic limitations and lack of a true commitment between the governing parties and the Crown to turn an elitist political system, typical of the nineteenth century, into the public participation democracy that was being demanded by the mass society of the twentieth century.

One of the main reasons for the exceptional duration of the Restoration lay, as Jover Zamora affirmed, in the eclectic nature of the 1876 Constitution, with its solid conservative but ambiguous aspects in the drafting of many of its articles.[5] The text did not try to hide the doctrinal roots of Cánovas' ideology, which could be seen, for example, in the return of census suffrage, the defence of a militarised public order system, the reappearance of the confessional nature of the state and the limits on Parliament's legislative power, in the well-known form of shared sovereignty between the Cortes and the king. Naturally, these measures drew on the 1845 Constitution much more than on the democratising proposals of 1869. But once the monarchy had been firmly established, and the Carlist War and the

---

[4] Josep Fontana, *La época del liberalismo* (Barcelona: Crítica/Marcial Pons, 2007), vol. VI of the *Historia de España*, series editors, Josep Fontana and Ramón Villares.

[5] José María Jover Zamora, Guadalupe Gómez Ferrer Morant and Juan Pablo Fusi Aizpurúa, *España: sociedad, política y civilización* (Madrid: Debate, 2001).

Cuban rebellion successfully concluded, the regime implemented the British-style two-party system which involved the distribution of power between the conservative and liberal elites and the gradual inclusion, outside the system, of Carlist splinter groups and republicanism that would cause them to abandon any insurrectional tendencies. The alternation of political power between two groups was a tacit agreement that was not formalised until 1885, in what was known as the Pardo Pact, an official endorsement that was forced by circumstances, the early death of Alfonso XII and the beginning of María Cristina's regency. The Liberals had already governed from 1881 to 1884, with progressive measures such as the right of assembly or freedom of the press, and it was in what was called the 'long parliament', between 1885 and 1890, that their leader, Práxedes Mateo Sagasta, promoted a series of reforms which, while not straying from the Constitution, brought about a certain modernisation of the administration and, particularly, the reform of the most restrictive aspects of Cánovas' legislation. In this respect, the laws governing free assembly in 1887 and jury trial in 1888, the Civil Code passed in 1889 and the granting of universal male suffrage in 1890 represented undeniable steps forward. But anyone expecting that the broadening of suffrage would represent a threat to the regime, or at least a change in the composition of Parliament, was in for a long wait. It was not, as Cánovas feared, incompatible with 'individual ownership' and 'inequality of wealth', let alone the first step towards a 'frenzied and anarchic socialism'. Rather, as Manuel Suárez Cortina has pointed out, it represented a false trail on the road to the democratisation of institutions.[6]

In fact, it is safe to say that no one wanted to take this road. The way the political system worked was familiar to all those who experienced it and has been described in great detail by historians, but is worth revisiting in order to emphasise how the theoretical principle of national sovereignty was reversed. It was not the number of votes cast that determined the composition of Parliament, and thus the political colour of the executive power; it was royal prerogative that decided the government, that 'fabricated' a favourable legislative chamber. Indeed, whenever there was a crisis or the government's action was considered to have caused the cabinet to outlive its usefulness, it was then that the *turno* system came into play. The king would then appoint as prime minister the leader of the party not in power and issue a decree for the dissolution of the Cortes. Before the elections were called, the operation known as *encasillado* (allotting) would take place. This involved the Interior Ministry agreeing on a share-out

[6] Manuel Suárez Cortina, *La España liberal (1868–1917): política y sociedad* (Madrid: Síntesis, 2006).

of parliamentary seats that would be acceptable to the opposition, and instructing the civil governors to negotiate rigged elections with the provincial elites and local dignitaries that would ensure the 'right' result. In this way, the government was always guaranteed a comfortable majority of more than two hundred deputies, leaving fewer than a hundred seats for the dynastic minority and a bare handful for parties not included in the pact. In 1891, after the first elections with universal suffrage, Cánovas breathed easily with the 253 seats obtained by the conservatives compared to 84 for the liberals, 39 for the republicans and 7 in the hands of the Carlists. And he had no problem two years later, when it was Sagasta's turn, in accepting that his group was reduced to 61 deputies and the new governing party held no fewer than 281 seats. '*Panes prestados*' (literally, 'loaves that have been lent' – i.e. 'one good turn deserves another'), as Clarín wrote in *La Regenta*, his 1880s novel.

It should be remembered that both liberals and conservatives belonged to parties made up of regional leaders and their beneficiaries within a parliamentary group but without any independent legal status. They had their own newspapers and a large number of political centres and associations, but there was no register of adherents nor any structure capable of mobilising public opinion other than banquets, speeches and electoral visits prior to polling. In the larger cities, with closed-list ballots, there was at least a small chance for the anti-dynastic parties to win representation. But in the small provincial capitals and rural districts, all with uninomial representation, there was no potential for any surprise result. In most cases, the rotation of liberals and conservatives was respected, sometimes with the introduction of outside candidates, known as *cuneros*, but there was also a large number of districts, known as *propios*, in which the same names always appeared.

This was the setting for the *cacique*, a fundamental component in the local political structure and the target of regenerationist critics, the 'foreign body' of the nation, said Costa, which needed to be rooted out in order to produce the impending revolution. However, for years historians seem to have been of one mind in an interpretation that sees *caciquismo* not as a parasite feeding off a healthy society organism, alien to the 'real Spain', nor as the automatic drive belt of a monolithic 'power block' over an apathetic and illiterate population, but as an essential component for understanding the political culture of the Restoration and the social roots of power. Firstly, it was not a new phenomenon in the history of Spain, but a practice that had existed from the beginning of the liberal state, and had been firmly entrenched during the reign of Isabella II. Secondly, it was not a feature peculiar to Spanish society either, but an example of political interference and patronage found, to a greater or lesser extent, in

other countries, particularly in the Mediterranean region, as borne out by
the cases of Italy and Portugal and even, albeit at a different level, of France.
It was a client model, as pointed out by José Álvarez Junco, developed in
centralised and urban states, with modern but under-resourced administrations, that had yet to complete the process of nationalisation and which
coexisted with predominantly agrarian societies in which power was fragmented into local plots, political spaces where previous community identities and traditional loyalties of a corporative nature survived.[7]

It was, in short, a complex phenomenon, which can begin to be under-
stood only if one leaves aside the traditional view that used to study the
political system from the top downwards, and observes it more closely,
from the bottom upwards, starting with the concrete reality of the local
powers and the social and economic structure of the rural communities.
From this viewpoint, *caciquismo* was much more than a tally of electoral
trickery, bribes, fraud, vote-rigging and pay-offs that bought votes and
minds in a passive and demobilised rural environment. The peasants'
attitude of conformity and deference was part of a strategy with the basic
aim of the reproduction of the family unit and access to the resources of
the land and service of the local community. To achieve this, the villagers,
aware of what they could expect from official politics and a state perceived
as something that was distant and unfamiliar, used the means they had
at their disposal. Via a network of personal relationships, within a barely
literate culture, the *cliente*, in exchange for his loyalty, would expect his
patrón to provide benefits involving land tenure, rent, capital loans, stable
employment and fair distribution of working hours. They also expected a
set of administrative advantages, used arbitrarily, which were summed up
in a famous slogan: a favour for a friend; for an enemy, the law.

This is why political control of the town and city councils was so important. They were responsible for keeping a register of the census and collecting property taxes, establishing the conditions for the use of communal
property, issuing tree-felling licences and business and trading permits,
drawing up lists of the poor and the electoral roll, and providing primary
education, charitable assistance, access to grain stores, control of rural
security, and public works and the wages of labourers employed in them.
Client relationships also extended to the municipal courts, provincial
assemblies and, of course, to civil governors: a veritable local and provincial
mediation structure that was continued in the daily life of the Cortes.
There, deputies and senators acted as mediators between the demands of

[7] José Álvarez Junco, 'Redes locales, lealtades tradicionales y nuevas identidades colectivas en
la España del siglo XIX', in Antonio Robles Ejea (comp.), *Política en penumbra: patronazgo y
clientelismo políticos en la España contemporánea* (Madrid: Siglo XXI, 1996), pp. 71–94.

their constituents and the state budget, fully aware that their continuity depended partly on their success in acquiring collective concessions such as a bridge, a road, a stretch of railway line, a school, a Civil Guard post or aid to soften the adverse effects of a natural disaster. This is borne out by the complaints of the 'orphan' districts, those that did not have a well-known influential champion.

In this Parliament, held together by client lobbying, local interests and private businesses, with intermittent activity due to constant suspensions and early dissolutions, there was little scope for political activity from the anti-dynastic opposition. Following its military defeat in 1876, Carlism had become a dispersed and disorganised movement that caused little concern to the early governments of the Restoration. The hopelessness of the Carlist cause was evident in 1885, on the death of Alfonso XII, when the Vatican and the Spanish Church hierarchy expressed their virtually unanimous backing for the regency. This led to internal division three years later with the schism of the fundamentalists, led by Ramón Nocedal, although they were never more than a minority group. In the final decade of the century, Carlism, under the personal leadership of the pretender Carlos VII from his exile in Venice, attempted to improve its public profile and take part in the political struggle by creating a more solid and modern structure. The Marquis of Cerralbo was the key figure during the years of intensive propaganda work, with new newspapers and an extensive network of associations and traditionalist youth wings, although they were unable to resurrect their insurrectional political culture. In October 1900, following the expectation created by the *Desastre* of '98, there was one last attempt at armed insurrection, a resounding failure which ended up by persuading the most recalcitrant of Carlists that, in the new century that was about to begin, they needed to abandon the path of conspiracy, hang up their arms and uniforms, and become involved in mainstream politics.

A similar process occurred in the ranks of republicanism, fragmented by leadership struggles and debate on progressive doctrinal principles, split into groups of leading figures and small parties ranging from the federalism of Francesc Pi y Margall, the radicalism of Manuel Ruiz Zorrilla and the reformist tendencies of Gumersindo de Azcárate and Nicolás Salmerón, right up to the Possibilism of Emilio Castelar, who resolved to turn the 'complexion of revolution' into a 'peaceful and legal' alternative. The tentative uprising of 1883 and General Manuel Villacampa's unsuccessful *pronunciamiento* three years later marked the military's final attempts to bring about revolution. The barricade and plotting became things of the past, to be replaced by social mobilisation in the streets and participation in mainstream politics. One of the consequences of this was the experience of the Unión Republicana (UR) in 1893. The movement needed to be reorganised and modernised; it was, as Vicente Blasco Ibáñez wrote, no use waiting for the commemoration of the First Republic to come round every 11 February to talk about revolution and then 'go home, just like that, to put the words into storage until the following year'. However, the importance of republicanism at the end of the century went much further than its meagre election results, except in certain municipal polls. It played an unmistakeable role in the realm of cultural and educational renovation, in the wake of the Institución Libre de Enseñanza, and a marked presence in urban community life, with an extensive network of political centres, clubs and associations. It was a broad and diverse social movement, with solid foundations within the *petite bourgeoisie* and middle classes, but also in the world of labour, where it competed with anarchists and socialists in representing popular discontent with restricted suffrage.

Some of the first cracks in the hitherto solid Canovist edifice began to appear away from Parliament and the capital. Only the short-sighted, said Damián Isern in 1901, could fail to foresee that the 'poison of separatism' would appear in the country's most prosperous cities, Barcelona and Bilbao. The so-called national question, the emergence of peripheral nationalist movements in Catalonia and the Basque Country, had cultural and social roots that had been apparent since the mid nineteenth century, but it was in the final decade, during an extensive process of industrial growth and economic transformation, that these movements became politicised and developed into a threat for the centralist regime of the Restoration.

In the case of the Basque Country, the final years of the century marked the leap from the persistence of rural traditionalism and the cause of regional privileges to what was to become a fully fledged nationalist ideology. In 1892, Sabino Arana published *Bizkaya por su independencia*, one year before his famous speech in Larrazábal given to a group of dignitaries who laid the foundations for a social club, which finally in 1895 was established as the first Bizkai-Buru-Batzar (Regional Council of Vizcaya), the forerunner of the Basque Nationalist Party. As Antonio Elorza has written, the original independence proposal for Vizcaya, subsequently extended to the territories where *euskera* (the Basque language) was spoken, should be seen as a response to the rapid demographic, economic and urban transformation experienced in the industrial and mining districts, as well as the two-fold threat to the middle classes and self-employed posed not only by the capitalist *grande bourgeoisie* but also by socialist organisations that were gaining ground in the urban areas with a high concentration of immigrant workers from rural districts.[8] This was

---

[8] Antonio Elorza, *Un pueblo escogido: génesis, definición y desarrollo del nacionalismo vasco* (Barcelona: Crítica, 2001).

the setting for the ideology of Arana, the motto 'God and the old law' built around a set of concepts based on the difference of language, Catholic fundamentalism, the mythification of the history of *Euzkadi* – later *Euskadi* – and the racial superiority of the Basques over the Spanish. However, by the turn of the century Arana's ideology had eased towards more autonomistic tendencies; social support for it grew, and it emerged as a conservative and Christian political alternative to the monopoly of the dynastic parties and the threat of the workers' movement. His early death in 1903 left a movement that was divided into two tendencies, one a nationalist independence line and the other following reformist and regionalist paths.

The emergence of Catalan nationalism occurred roughly at the same time as that in the Basque Country, but it had different characteristics. Since the middle of the century, the Catalan bourgeois elite's discontent with the centralism of one Spanish government after another had been building a Catalan nationalist identity around the romantic *Renaixença* movement, a series of literary and cultural initiatives that aimed to recover and preserve its own language, history and customs: literary salons, poetry competitions, day centres, concerts, organised excursions, and local and regional associations which, from 1880 onwards, disseminated the idea of a national community outside the political system of the Restoration. The possibility of a progressive federal Catalanism, similar to the Centre Català founded in 1882 by Valentí Almirall, was swept aside by the success of a movement with conservative roots, the Unió Catalanista, whose programme was established in the *Bases de Manresa* passed in 1892, a linguistic and cultural demand that also sought the creation of independent institutions within Catalonia. In the final years of the century, informal Catalanism evolved into the construction of a nationalist political movement, from which there was no going back after the defeat of '98 and the loss of the colonial market, when a large section of the commercial and industrial bourgeoisie could no longer find any reasons to support the parties that represented the Spanish liberal state. This resulted, in 1901, in the creation of the Lliga Regionalista, a conservative autonomist party, with leaders such as Enric Prat de la Riba and Francesc Cambó, which very soon figured strongly in the polls, foreshadowing a hegemony that was to last throughout the first quarter of the twentieth century.

The roots of Galician nationalism are to be found in a cultural movement known as O Rexurdimento and in the birth, at the close of the century, of a liberal-style regionalism, represented by Manuel Murguía, and a more traditionalist variant, formulated by Alfredo Brañas, although these were minority tendencies within a mostly rural society that had nothing in common with Basque and Catalan industrial development. It

was not until 1907, with the appearance of Solidaridad Gallega, an echo
of the Catalan model, that the first signs of a political movement could be
discerned. The belated Galician model shows, as Justo Beramendi has
pointed out, that the consolidation of an alternative national identity to
that of the Spanish state could only come about wherever there was a class
or set of social groups with certain power, who believed in nationalism as
a political project that would serve their interests. They were social groups
of various sizes and types, depending on each case, but with a noteworthy
ability to construct a social movement that would enable their particular
features, autochthonous language and pre-national values to be accepted
by increasingly larger sectors of the population as components of a national
identity. The fact that these circumstances came about in Spain at the end
of the nineteenth century to a greater degree than in other multi-ethnic
countries in Europe was due, Beramendi goes on, to failings in the process
of nationalisation undertaken by the liberal state, the 'factory defect' of a
'chronically ill patient in sound health'.[9]

Historians have been discussing the 'weakness' of the Spanish state for
some years now. Borja de Riquer places the hub of the question within an
interpretation of peripheral nationalist movements not as a reaction to
the pressure of centralism, but as being due to the state's ineffectiveness
in forging a national identity, the administration's inability to achieve
cultural and linguistic unification and foster economic and social modernisation, and finally to bring together and politically integrate the
majority of the population.[10] Nevertheless, this is not a question of once
more propagating the theory of failure as a standard explanation of all
the shortcomings of Spain's twentieth-century history. By the end of the
century, the basis of the liberal state had been constructed; it had territorial limits that no one questioned, a homogeneous administrative body
suitably organised into ministries, a modern legal system, a unified fiscal
structure and a political regime of limited representation, the Restoration,
yet one cannot deny the success of its stability and noteworthy ability to
link the interests of the local elites with the power of the government.

Thus, it was a centralised state that aimed to be enduring, following the
French model, but was incapable of reaching all corners of the country,
except to collect taxes and recruits, let alone extending a process of
nationalisation that displayed significant shortcomings to the majority of
the population. Among the factors explaining these limitations, say

[9] Justo Beramendi, José Luis de la Granja and Pere Anguera, *La España de los nacionalismos y las autonomías* (Madrid: Síntesis, 2001), pp. 43, 103.
[10] Borja de Riquer, 'La débil nacionalización española en el siglo XIX', *Historia Social*, 20 (1994), pp. 97–114.

authors such as Xosé Manuel Núñez Seixas, special emphasis should be placed on the political divisions and violent confrontations that accompanied the building of the liberal state, the chronic debt of the Treasury, the lack of resources to provide public services and belated industrial development, which was concentrated in the peripheral regions that were not centres of political decision.[11] Furthermore, the Spanish state had to contend with the opposition of the Catholic Church to any secularising measure that diminished its privileges, with the army's constant interference in civil life, and with an oligarchic and influence-peddling system that was opposed to reforms of a democratic nature, with a highly limited potential for social penetration because of the continuity of local powers that acted with a fair amount of autonomy. In short, it was a state that showed no interest in promoting the national identity of its citizens, nor did it have the necessary means. The rickety education system was unable to impose a single language or extend the patriotic and symbolic values of the nation, a unifying measure that was absent from the barracks as well, with a military service that was abhorred by the popular classes.

And in the final quarter of the nineteenth century, the age of imperialism, of the glorification of nationalism in other European states, Spain lacked a defined external enemy. It had no prestigious foreign schemes or activities in progress at the time, unlike the big powers, nor did it have to worry about a possible foreign invasion, as smaller countries did. What it did have was the *Desastre* of '98, a series of events that had been, as Rafael Altamira wrote then, 'merely the effect' of other more 'intimate', deeper effects that were linked to the idea that 'we ourselves have of the social entity that we live in and are part of'. The unease of the intellectuals was a symptom, an external sign, wrote Carlos Serrano, of a more serious internal disease that was affecting Spanish society on the threshold of the twentieth century.[12]

Society, change and continuity

In 1900, average life expectancy in Spain was under 35, an extremely low figure, much lower than the European average, showing, perhaps more than any other figure, the harsh conditions of life that most of the 18.6 million inhabitants had to endure. The high mortality rate, 29 per 1,000 and the

[11] Xosé Manoel Núñez Seixas, *Los nacionalismos en la España contemporánea, siglos XIX y XX* (Barcelona: Hipòtesi, 1999).
[12] Rafael Altamira, *Psicología del pueblo español* (Madrid: Biblioteca Nueva, 1997 [1902]), p. 53; Carlos Serrano, *El turno del pueblo: crisis nacional, movimientos populares y populismo en España (1890–1910)* (Barcelona: Península, 2000); and Serrano, with Serge Salaün, *1900 en España* (Madrid: Espasa-Calpe, 1991).

extremely high infant mortality rate – of every thousand births, 186 babies died before reaching the age of 1 – were linked, above all, to poor hygiene and sanitation, an unhealthy diet, ignorance of the causes of diseases and how they were passed on, and the apathy of the administration. At the turn of the century, the Spanish still had fresh in their minds the last major subsistence crisis, in 1868, the years of severe shortages, such as 1898, and the effects of the cholera epidemic of 1885. As well as food shortages and periodic epidemics, there was also the high death rate caused by endemic diseases such as smallpox, measles, dysentery, typhus, tuberculosis and dangerous intestinal infections that traditionally devastated working-class families. And in the working-class districts of the cities, the situation was no better, with crowded housing, sewage problems and dreadful conditions in the workplace leading to a high rate of industrial injury and disease linked to unhealthy and unhygienic surroundings. The demographic transition process had barely begun.

Another significant indicator of Spain's backwardness compared to more advanced countries was illiteracy, an alarmingly widespread failing in the eyes of any foreign observer. In 1900, the year of the creation of the Ministerio de Instrucción Pública, of every 100 Spanish adults, 56 could neither read nor write, a percentage that was even higher in the case of women or in agricultural regions where intensive labour in the fields bound children to the land without their having reached a basic level of education. The rural schools were poorly equipped, teachers had little training and even worse salaries – 'as poorly nourished as a schoolmaster' went the saying – education in the cities was run by the Church, with a precarious network of provincial secondary schools and a limited number of universities in which scientific and technological innovation had been ignored.

The third phenomenon that should be emphasised, if we compare Spain's case with the general European context at the turn of the century, is its belated process of urbanisation. At the end of the century, Madrid and Barcelona had just over half a million inhabitants, and the number of cities with a population of 100,000, practically all of them on the edges of the peninsula, could be counted on one hand. Spain was a mostly rural country: 80% of the population still lived in locations of fewer than 10,000 inhabitants, a figure that stresses the predominance of the primary sector in the national economy. Agriculture produced more than 40% of the country's wealth and employed 68% of the active population, a percentage which would certainly be even higher if the official statistics had taken into account the number of women working on the land.

The continuance of a rural and peasant way of life, the high illiteracy rate and the long shadow cast by an old demographic regime, still marked

by past food shortages and epidemics, look like typical features of a
country that was backward and inert. But the snapshot of the turn of the
century that we have presented does not show the full picture: the changes
that were occurring. As David Ringrose has pointed out, turn-of-the-
century Spain, although clearly lagging behind more advanced countries,
such as Britain, France or Germany, had followed a familiar variant of
the European path to development.[13] In the words of Gabriel Tortella,
this was a 'Latin pattern' of modernisation with similar characteristics
and phases to those of Italy, Portugal and even Greece.[14] So, instead of a
century of failure, this period might be spoken of as being marked by
relatively slow development and moderate growth, particularly in the
final third of the nineteenth century. José Luis García Delgado has capa-
bly summarised the appreciable signs of material progress and economic
dynamism. Per capita output had grown by almost two-thirds in the second
half of the nineteenth century, the basic railway network had been practically completed, and the industrial structure, although still held back by
its belated beginnings and the predominance of sectors such as foodstuffs
and textiles, was showing the first signs of production diversification in
fields such as the steel industry, construction, electricity and the manufac-
ture of fertilisers and explosives. New sectors were emerging, coinciding
with the second industrial revolution, and new techniques were applied
to traditional preparations, such as canned vegetables and fish, footwear,
paper, olive oil, wine and flour. Barcelona and its environs continued to be
the leading industrial area, followed by Vizcaya and the mining areas of
Asturias, but other centres were emerging, such as Madrid and Valencia,
with constantly improving connections thanks to the railways, the telegraph, the early telephones and the gradual spread of electricity. The
number of company registrations and the growing banking system, helped
by the return of capital from Central and South America, were further
good examples of a production sector that was ready to exploit the growth
opportunities provided by the twentieth century, a train that Spain made
certain it was on, albeit not in the first-class section.[15]

Something similar might be said of Spain's primary sector, traditionally
accused of being 'the source of all ills', a phrase used as the title of a
collective work edited by Josep Puyol, in which several experts give the lie
to the hackneyed idea of semi-feudal stagnation, archaic practices and

---

[13] David Ringrose, *Spain, Europe and the 'Spanish Miracle'* (Cambridge University Press, 1998).
[14] Gabriel Tortella, *El desarrollo de la España contemporánea: historia económica de los siglos XIX y XX* (Madrid: Alianza, 1994).
[15] José Luis García Delgado and Juan Carlos Jiménez, *La historia de España del siglo XX: la economía* (Madrid: Marcial Pons, 2007), p. 357.

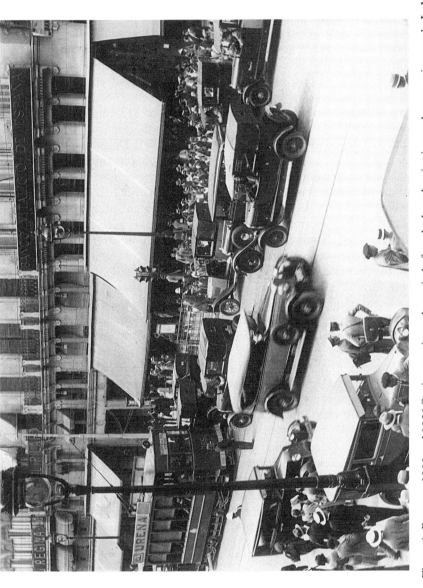

Figure 1 Between 1900 and 1930 Spain experienced a period of marked modernisation and economic growth. In Madrid, shown here in 1930, the population grew from half a million inhabitants in 1900 to 1 million three decades later. © Agencia EFE

absenteeism, to express a completely different state of affairs, much more dynamic and complex. Spanish agriculture was no stranger, at least from the mid nineteenth century onwards, to the major transformations engendered by the liberal revolution and the broadening of capitalist economic relationships. While we have previously cited the metaphor of a train to illustrate Europe's march towards modernity, a route that Spain was taking as well, albeit towards the rear of the column, we now have the image of a large tree with a common trunk and several distinctive branches. What occurred in the Spanish case, according to these authors, is that the European model, when deployed in the biological and environmental conditions of the peninsula, generated lower growth rates, marked social inequality and a long series of conflicts and confrontations.[16]

According to this interpretation, the new techniques of intensive cultivation in western Europe were of little use in the predominantly cereal-growing centre and south of the country, where there was little water or organic fertiliser as a suitable technological provision. Added to the scant use of agricultural machinery were the limitations of traditional irrigation and the existence of large areas that were unproductive because the land was either left fallow or earmarked for pasture. The environmental and technological restraints would explain a lower productivity per hectare and reduced ability to contribute foodstuffs, capital and human resources to economic activities. The situation was different in the damper regions in the north, where stock and crop farming coexisted, and in the irrigation zones along the Mediterranean coast, which specialised in fruit and vegetable growing, with closer links to foreign trade. But the important transformation was yet to come. Intensive mineral and chemical fertiliser usage, technological renovation and state intervention through hydro schemes to extend irrigation were processes that belong to the history of the twentieth century and which had barely got off the ground at the end of the previous century.

At any event, Spanish agriculture did experience growth, albeit modest, in the nineteenth century and showed a marked ability to adapt to the changes and challenges of the market. The crisis at the end of the century was one of these challenges. As we know, the transport revolution also took in the international agricultural produce market and brought about a widespread fall in prices, a fall that particularly affected Spanish cereals, which were unable to compete with foreign grain. The first response was the introduction of trade barriers to restrict the home market to national

---

[16] Josep Puyol, Manuel González De Molina, Lourenzo Fernández Prieto, Domingo Gallego and Ramón Garrabou, *El pozo de todos los males: sobre el atraso en la agricultura española contemporánea* (Barcelona: Crítica, 2001).

production, a protectionist policy that was neither solely a Spanish anomaly nor an insurmountable obstacle to agricultural development. It is true to say that, in the absence of other possibilities, increased cereal production could be achieved only by extending cropping areas, which would be reclaimed from common land and woodland, with considerable social cost, particularly for smallholders. Something different could be said about the wine sector, which was affected by an overproduction crisis and which had to meet the challenge of the reconstruction of the vineyards when the phylloxera plague, the scourge of the French vineyards, also came to Spain.

If one aspect underlined the state of Spanish agriculture at the end of the nineteenth century, it was the survival potential of the rural population. In the northern part of the peninsula, peasant families survived by reducing their level of consumption, if necessary, and by intensifying their labour, obtaining complementary resources thanks to temporary emigration, establishing co-operatives and gaining access to local markets through customer and neighbourhood networks. In the large estate areas, the cultivation of cereals, together with vines and olives, and extensive grazing enabled production to be diversified and estates to be maintained, albeit at the expense of serious social conflict, particularly in areas where the large landowners had accumulated all the resources, and the day-labourers had no access to the land. In short, it was a rural society that adapted to change and displayed a marked ability for self-reproduction but, at the same time, preserved deep social inequalities.

It was the harsh existence of the farmworkers in the south that was denounced by Azorín in his essay, *Andalucía trágica*. He was referring to the precarious living conditions of the 'buttresses of the fatherland', the malnourished and the exhausted, unprotected by the state and also by the bosses, the same bosses who called for urgent measures from those who filled 'the chambers and the ministries' if they did not want 'those who live in the factories and fields to see you as being the cause of their woes'. Although the macro-economic indicators at the turn of the century displayed a moderately positive picture, as we have pointed out, what the public perceived was far removed from what official statistics and comparison with the situation abroad demonstrated. What the lower classes saw was the deprivation to be found in many rural communities and the working-class *barrios* of the cities. They did not feel that they had a better life than their parents, as Juan Pan-Montojo has rightly pointed out, nor that they had abandoned the daily struggle for survival.[17]

[17] Juan Pan-Montojo, 'El atraso económico y la regeneración', in Pan-Montojo (ed.), *Más se perdió en Cuba: España, 1898 y la crisis de fin de siglo* (Madrid: Alianza, 1998), pp. 261–334. For a general analysis, see also Ringrose, *Spain, Europe and the 'Spanish Miracle'*.

In fact, the labourers' average daily wage at the time barely amounted to two pesetas, almost certainly much less for women but somewhat higher for skilled labourers. Even so, sex, trade and geographical differences do not detract from the overall picture of insecurity and precariousness. Pedro Carasa lists these insecurities as being, firstly, economic – covering basic necessities such as food, clothing and housing; labour insecurity, for the discontinuity of employment and the whims of the bosses; legal insecurity with the employer, landlord or money-lender; social insecurity when any emergency, illness or accident occurred; and, finally, material insecurity, because of supply shortages or higher taxes. Carasa maintains that poverty was a widespread, permanent problem that afflicted three-quarters of the Spanish population. He calculates that the charity institutions of the Church and town and village councils provided permanent assistance to barely 2 or 3% of the inhabitants. These would have been the 'sustained'. A second group, the 'pauperised', around 20%, would have included families who were trapped by need and were seeking public assistance and benefits provided by their employers. The largest sector, some 60% of the population, the 'potentially pauperised', were on the edge of subsistence, in danger of falling into poverty when an unfavourable set of circumstances arose, such as a family problem, a poor harvest or a harsh winter.[18]

Looked at thus, it is hardly surprising that the people perceived with fear and hostility the rise of a few centimos in the price of bread, the announcement of a surcharge in the hateful *consumos* tax (a tax on food-stuffs and other consumer goods brought into a town or village for sale or consumption), the disappearance of a common resource or the draft for military service, which carried off the sons of the poor who could not afford to buy their way out. The most visible manifestation of this unrest was the regular outbreak of riots and public uproar, in which the leading role was played by women as a consequence of the responsibilities they had to take on within the family and the community. They were responsible for social and biological reproduction and for preserving life.

The calls for cheap bread and against consumer taxes and military service could be heard everywhere in Spain in the nineteenth century and still, with even more vehemence, towards the end of the century. These were neither isolated cases nor anachronistic practices. In the summer of 1892, the Spanish daily *El País* declared that, after some fifty riots against the consumer tax, if things carried on in this manner, 'all-out civil war' might be a possibility. And, in spite of press censorship, we have reports of more than

---

[18] Pedro Carasa Soto, 'La Restauración monárquica', in Ángel Bahamonde (ed.), *Historia de España siglo XX: 1875–1939* (Madrid: Cátedra, 2000), pp. 252–3.

eighty riots against the price of bread in May 1898. Apparently, more hatred
was directed towards grain-hoarders and speculative traders than against
the United States troops. And the people used the resources, strategies and
experience of community action to put pressure on local authorities and
protest to the representatives of the state, a distant and unintelligible body
that was to be seen in daily life through the presence of secretaries, judges,
bailiffs and military recruiting agents.

And then there is the Civil Guard. In Spain, with no police force, the
maintenance of public order and the repression of any type of disturbance,
however small, was entrusted to the military. The unsatisfactory use of
the Civil Guard, armed with Mauser rifles, and the constant calling on
the army, 'the solid buttress of the present social order' in the words of
Cánovas, provoked a disproportionate degree of violence, the submission
of arrested civilians to military jurisdiction and the hostility of the population towards the armed forces. 'Hostility and animosity', said an editorial in the military publication *El Ejército Español* in 1892, 'which show this
army in society's eyes as being somewhat unpleasant'.

To escape the risk of repression, there were other forms of 'minor'
protest, anonymous, silent actions, usually by individuals, which were
considered to be common misdemeanours but with an evident social
undercurrent. These were illegal acts such as the evasion of military
service – deserters and those who obtained exemption through fraud –
non-payment of taxes or a whole series of examples of peasant resistance,
the 'weapons of the weak' as James Scott termed them: tree-felling, stealing timber for fuel, overgrazing, poaching, land clearing, vandalism to
property, pollarding, arson and so on. This wide range of expressions of
dissidence demonstrated, together with collective actions, the will of the
most vulnerable sectors of society, rendered so by the management of
community resources and public affairs. It was the politics of the people
without power.[19]

But on the threshold of the twentieth century these 'traditional' public
protests, while still effective at a local level, began to coexist with new
forms of social mobilisation, with new ideas, demands and expectations
ever more closely linked to the world of employment and the realm of
national politics. The spread of capitalist economic relationships and
the gradual ability of the state institutions to reach every town and village
produced greater fragmentation and social inequality within communities
and enabled the construction of other identities such as the working class.
And, ever since E. P. Thompson described it, we know that the making

[19] James Scott, *Weapons of the Weak: The Everyday Forms of Peasant Resistance* (New Haven:
Yale University Press, 1985).

of the working class has been a cultural progress of discovery and self-definition, forged by the common experiences of workers, who acknowledged and articulated their concerns as being their own and, at the same time, opposed to the interests of the economic and political elites. The workers began to take up new stances with regard to other social groups, with a different discourse and with a perception that they were firmly linked to a movement that allowed them to stand up to employers and the authorities.[20] They were helped in this by growing urbanisation, improved transport, the development of the mass media, such as the press, the opening up of political opportunities and the example of the successes of new forms of collective action, such as strikes, rallies or demonstrations.

However, the repressive measures implemented by the early governments of the Restoration ended with the workers' mobilisations that had emerged during the Democratic Sexennium, launched by the Spanish Regional Federation of the AIT (Asociación Internacional de los Trabajadores, the Spanish incarnation of the International Workers' Association), the first such organisation on a national scale. It was not until the beginning of the 1880s, with a more permissive liberal policy, that Spain saw the return of isolated strikes in Barcelona and Madrid and examples of severe conflicts such as those that occurred in the Río Tinto (1888) or Vizcaya (1890) mining areas. Even so, at the close of the nineteenth century the majority of federated workers were not from the pits, large estates or modern mechanised industrial centres. In the provincial towns and cities, as well as the environs of Barcelona, there was still a predominance of small factories and workshops belonging to skilled workers, who had greater resources, more supportive relationships and better organisational capacity than unskilled workers and women, who came late to the world of industry. Those engaged in traditional trades, such as typesetters, cobblers, carpenters and coopers, were fully integrated into their places of residence, had better access to information, a higher salary and previous experience in forming associations.

In this respect, mutual aid societies, set up in the 1840s, still bearing vestiges of the traditional tradesmen's guilds, were an important factor. They were associations that afforded aid in cases of illness, unemployment or accident, but over time many of them evolved into the seed of associations of resistance devoted to the improvement of working conditions. They created internal and community links which, as Jorge Uría points out, represented genuine schools of democracy, a process of learning

---

[20] E. P. Thompson, *The Making of the English Working Class* (London: Victor Gollancz, 1963).

and public clamour on the road towards political awareness.[21] The 1887
Associations Act was one more step in this direction because it provided
workers' associations with a stable legal framework, requiring them to
present statutes, yearly accounts, membership lists and minutes of meetings. Around this environment of trade associations arose a workers' culture of austerity, morality and solidarity relationships, a microcosm in
which class awareness was gradually constructed, with material demands,
naturally, but also with symbolic objectives, and its own rituals and celebrations, such as May Day, first celebrated in 1890. The first May Day
highlighted the ability of workers' associations and centres to take to the
streets and demonstrate their 'tremendous energy', as one regional newspaper commented at the time, but also the limitations to their mobilisation
and the divisions between the two principal ideological doctrines that
sought the emancipation of the proletariat: anarchism and socialism.

In Spain, the first phase of expansion of anarchism, within the AIT,
had concluded with the Cantonal insurgency and the end of the First
Republic. The movement reappeared in 1881 with the founding of the
Federación Regional de Trabajadores de la Región Española (Spanish
Regional Workers' Federation), an association whose membership was
split between Catalonia and Andalucía and which already in its first year
claimed to have 70,000 workers on its lists. But internal divisions and the
indiscriminate repression suffered by its members put an end to its hopes
of forging an extensive grass-roots organisation. Firstly, it was persecution
in 1883 for events related to the Mano Negra.[22] This was followed a
decade later, in 1892, by arrests and trials after peasant rioting in Jerez
de la Frontera. The movement became split between the associations that
defended trade union struggle, labour demands and participation in
mobilisations, such as the eight-hour day or May Day celebrations, and
those anarchist collectives that were committed to secret organisations,
doctrinal purity and violent reprisals, 'propaganda by deed'. Among the
terrorist acts in those years were the assassination attempt against General
Martínez Campos and the Liceo bombing in Barcelona in 1893, the bomb
attack on the Corpus Christi procession in 1896, and the assassination of
Cánovas in 1897. This terrorism was not an original feature of Hispanic
anarchism but an international phenomenon, with much-publicised attacks

---

[21] Jorge Uría, *La España liberal (1868–1917): cultura y vida cotidiana* (Madrid: Síntesis,
2008).
[22] As the anarchist movement gradually took root in Andalucía, at the beginning of the
1880s, it was accused of felonies allegedly committed by an anarchist organisation that
signed itself 'Mano Negra' (Black Hand). The Federación Regional de Trabajadores de
la Región Española always denied any connection, but these events led to all anarchist
workers' associations being outlawed.

in France, Austria, Italy and elsewhere. What was unique about terrorism in Spain was the brutality of the repression, the torture and the condemnation of innocent people that gave such sad notoriety to the 'accursed castle' in Barcelona, Montjuïc.

In 1898, in a campaign for a review of the Montjuïc trials, socialist leaders took part in rallies and demonstrations alongside republican and liberal politicians. It was the first time they had done so, the first opportunity to see them emerge from the isolation in which they had remained since the founding of the Partido Socialista Obrero Español (PSOE) in 1879. The origins of the party could be found in a group of typesetters in Madrid, members of the Asociación General del Arte de Imprimir, the 'cradle of a giant', as Juan José Morato called it. It championed the emancipation of the working class, transfer of ownership and acquisition of power. It was a doctrinal line established by its leader, Pablo Iglesias, who in time was to become a symbol of the moral virtues of socialism, an apostle and master of the movement. But in order to achieve their objectives, they would have to work on strengthening a fully independent organisation before any talk of revolution was possible. In 1886 they had their own media mouthpiece, *El Socialista*, and two years later a union base, the Unión General de Trabajadores (UGT), which aimed to be a federation bringing together workers' organisations from all over Spain. Its isolation strategy, hostility towards anarchists, refusal to work with the republican 'bourgeoisie' and its scant understanding of the agricultural world severely restricted its potential for growth, in number not only of groups and affiliates but also of votes. In the closing stages of the nineteenth century, while Italian and French socialists could boast large contingents of parliamentary groups and the British and German trade unions had hundreds of thousands of affiliates, Spanish socialism painted a sorry picture. Santos Juliá has counted some twenty city councillors and no more than 20,000 votes in the whole of Spain. Meanwhile, the UGT had sixty-nine sections and just over 14,000 members, clear proof of how slow it was to get off the ground and its limited presence in society.[23] At the height of the Cuban war, the campaign against the injustice of the draft, 'every one or no one', and the mobilisation against the excesses of government repression saw the beginning of a new period in the history of Spanish socialism, the start of a mass movement with parliamentary aspirations and a rapprochement with the republicans. It was a struggle for the democratisation of the institutions which would form part of the history of the twentieth century.

[23] Santos Juliá, *Los socialistas en la política española, 1879–1982* (Madrid: Taurus, 1996).

So said Luis Morote in *La moral de la derrota*, the book he published in 1900, one of the texts that may be salvaged from the mass of regenerationist writings in the immediate aftermath of the *Desastre*: the most urgent task of the new century was to preserve and enhance 'the substance and reality of democracy'. In order to avoid a revolution that would settle the 'formidable' struggle between labour and capital by force, the political system needed to be provided with a true 'social content'. Morote was not as pessimistic as his contemporaries about Spain's future. He compared the history of the nineteenth century with 'an insect that has undergone a major metamorphosis, which we are not fully aware of, since we are both actors and audience, simultaneously in the auditorium and on the stage'. In his opinion, the indications of this metamorphosis were the Carlist wars, civil confrontations and the harsh battles between theocratic principle and civil power, between individual rights and the remains of the *ancien régime*, between federalism and nationality. And since it was aware of this major metamorphosis in its interior, Spain was gradually letting go of the remnants of its exterior empire, its fundamentally rotten 'offal', destined to disappear. It was not the new Spain that had suffered the effects of the *Desastre*, but the old Spain, the Spain which at the beginning of the century was beginning to crumble away: 'It is true that we have been reduced to the same peninsular boundaries that we had the day after Granada was taken back from the Moors. But even if after such a tough battle against the elements only the hull has been saved, at least it is unscathed and still seaworthy.'[24]

[24] Luis Morote, *La moral de la derrota* (Madrid: Biblioteca Nueva, 1997).

2   The 'revolution from above'

Upon reaching the age of majority in the spring of 1902, Alfonso XIII ascended to the throne of Spain, after swearing to uphold the Constitution, a text that had been in force for twenty-five years. He was a new king for a new century. Here was an opportunity to adapt the political system of the Restoration to the new challenges and problems posed by society, to repair the cracks formed by the *Desastre* of 1898 before they threatened its existence – in short, to begin a programme of national 'regeneration', the word on everyone's lips, repeated in the corridors of the Cortes and all the provincial community centres.

With the help of the Crown, the political elites aimed to lead a reform from above, a nationalising mobilisation that would broaden the social bases of the regime without putting its hegemony at risk, thus avoiding a revolution. The political history of Spain between 1902 and 1917 bears witness to this failure. The reasons for this are complex and diverse. The first reason was the attitude of Alfonso XIII himself, who from the outset insisted on intervening in political life and refused to renounce any of his prerogatives. The second was the crisis of the traditional parties, which were incapable of maintaining undisputed leaders and converting their roll-call of worthies into modern organisations. The internal division of liberals and conservatives, with factions, cronies and *caciques* at loggerheads over the distribution of power, undermined the stability of the governments and put a brake on Parliament's legislative initiatives. The chance for the conservatives arrived with Antonio Maura, between 1904 and 1909; the Liberals' effort, under José Canalejas, was frustrated by his assassination in 1912.

As well as the problems inherited from the nineteenth century, such as clericalism and militarism, there were others such as the war in Morocco, Catalan nationalism, radical republicanism and the growth of the workers' movement which was able to channel people's demands and move beyond the local context of early actions and promote nationwide campaigns. The first episode of crisis in the political system came in 1909, with the news of the *Semana Trágica* (Tragic Week) in Barcelona. After 1913, there was no

35

Figure 2 In the Spanish court, the customs and practices of the *ancien régime* still prevailed. Alfonso XIII was born king and was educated as such in an aristocratic, clerical and military atmosphere. © Time & Life Pictures/Getty Images

longer any talk of a peaceful sharing of power by the two main dynastic parties. And in subsequent years, with increasingly unstable governments, the political, economic and social impact of the Great War led the country to the revolutionary summer of 1917, a point of no return on the road towards the final decomposition of the regime.

Regenerating the nation

A jubilant crowd filled the streets on that light spring morning. It was 17 May 1902, the day that the young king, now sixteen, was to swear to uphold the Constitution and assume his powers and responsibilities as monarch. The reports of the time spared no detail in describing the public enthusiasm unleashed by the royal procession through the main streets of Madrid, from the Royal Palace to the Congress of Deputies. And it was hardly surprising. The people of Madrid had not witnessed such a spectacle in a long time. The Crown deployed all the pomp of its majestic ceremonial along a route full of arches, banners and streamers 'all under a flight of doves and a hail of flowers'. At the head of the procession were groups of grooms and mace-bearers, with kettledrums and bugles, and a line of plumed horses with brightly coloured saddlecloths embroidered with silver and gold. They were followed by decorated carriages, twelve Berlines with the grandees of Spain, the coaches of the Infantas, the Queen Regent, the Prince and Princess of Asturias and, finally, the carriage bearing the emblem of the royal crown, with a smiling Alfonso XIII acknowledging the cheers of the crowds. Among the carriages were trumpeters and escort squadrons. Along with them were mounted escorts, ladies-in-waiting, footmen and other members of the royal household. Inside Congress the flamboyant tunics of the knights, the pelisses of the Hussars of Pavia and the robes of the prelates stood out. A grandiose display, said Fernández Almagro, of the 'traditional and alluring world of pomp and ceremonial'.[1] It would prove to be an image from another time.

In the Spanish court, the customs and practices of the *ancien régime* still prevailed. Alfonso XIII was born to be king and was educated as such in an aristocratic, clerical and military atmosphere, in sombre and deeply religious surroundings recreated by his mother, María Cristina, away from outside influences. It was 'a highly reclusive life', wrote the politician and writer Fernando Soldevilla in his account, 'entirely cut off from the people'. His playmates had been the children of nobles; his instructors, except for the liberal Santamaría de Paredes, were courtiers who were

---

[1] Melchor Fernández Almagro, *Historia del reinado de D. Alfonso XIII* (Madrid: Montaner y Simón, 1933).

known for their religious devotion, together with traditional military men who had a military conception of public life. This training gave him his Catholic convictions, his love of uniforms and parades, and the pleasure with which he represented his role as soldier-king, always attentive to the welfare of the army. Naturally, this was not the most suitable preparation for the head of state of a parliamentary monarchy that was trying to deal with the wave of modernity being ushered in by the twentieth century.

Nor were the royal prerogatives that were normal for a mid-nineteenth-century monarch the best tools for opening up the social bases of the regime and following the road towards a democratic system. Alfonso XIII was commander-in-chief of the armed forces, with power to appoint, dismiss and decorate members of the army, as he made quite clear in the first Council of Ministers meeting he presided over. The powers granted to him by the 1876 Constitution did not stop there. His person was 'sacred and inviolable', and he was not answerable to Parliament. He chose the prime minister; he could hire and fire ministers and designate life senators; he shared legislative power with the Cortes, which he could call and dissolve; he looked after the administration of justice and directed diplomatic relations. Aware of his wide-ranging prerogatives, he soon made clear that he had no intention of renouncing them, and that he would intervene in politics as a governing king, not as a monarch relegated to a mere moderating and representative role.

This much can be ascertained from the entries he had made months earlier in his diary with a certain criticism of public opinion: 'This year I shall be taking up the reins of the state, something that is very important the way things are at the moment; because whether the Bourbon monarchy survives or a republic is proclaimed will depend on me. Because I find the country broken by our past wars, longing for someone to lead it out of this situation; social reform in favour of the needy; the army, with an organisation that is lagging behind modern trends; the navy, without ships; the flag desecrated; governors and mayors who do not implement laws, and so on.' He felt that he could be a king who would cover himself in glory 'regenerating' the Fatherland, but also one who did not 'govern', one that would be led by his ministers and finally banished.[2] In writing these words he was probably recalling the hurried exit from Spain of his grandmother, Isabella II. But for today's reader, it would be hard not to relate them to the monarch's own future, with his abandoning of the Royal Palace into exile, almost twenty-nine years later on the night of 14 April 1931.

---

[2] Private diary of Alfonso XIII, in Melchor Fernández Almagro, *Historia política de la España contemporánea, 1897–1902* (Madrid: Alianza, 1972), p. 300.

Nevertheless, in May 1902 there was nothing to portend the end of his reign in this fashion. The monarchy had emerged unscathed from the *Desastre* of '98 and the *turno* system was working with its customary precision, although the system did have a serious problem, the leadership succession in the Conservative Party, following the assassination of Cánovas, as well as in the Liberal Party. After the swearing of the Constitution, during the *Te Deum* celebrated in the Church of San Francisco, Sagasta fainted, something the doctors attributed to the excitement of the day and the heat in the building. He was 76 years old. His death, in January 1903, marked the end of a generation.

The first person who had a chance to implement change and renovation was Francisco Silvela in March 1899. He was not exactly a politician divorced from the defects of the system he was denouncing – he had been a minister several times, the first in 1879 – but, as leader of the Unión Conservadora, he was able to separate the most stubborn historical factions from power and present a cabinet that was willing to implement the regenerationist ambitions of the nation. Hence initiatives such as the new Ministry of Public Instruction and Fine Arts, and proposals from Eduardo Dato's Interior Ministry for the first measures of social reform, such as the regulating of working hours for women and children, the Workplace Accidents Act and the studies that preceded the founding of the Social Reforms Institute, an organisation that did not see the light of day until 1903. The high spot was provided by Raimundo Fernández Villaverde, the minister of finance, who managed to put the Treasury in order and modernise fiscal policy by creating the Contribución de Utilidades (utilities tax). But it was only a fleeting success. The deficit reduction measures caused the resignation, firstly, of the minister of war, the controversial General Polavieja, and then Antonio Durán y Bas, who was influenced by the protests of the Catalan bourgeoisie against the new taxes. Catalan nationalist discontent became a political movement in 1901 with the founding of the Lliga Regionalista, which obtained resounding electoral success in Barcelona that same year.

Problems were growing for the conservative government as the turn of the century drew near. In the summer of 1899, the tax protests in Barcelona were joined by the closing of shops as agreed by the Chambers of Commerce, directed by Basilio Paraíso, and the mobilisation of the Chambers of Agriculture that Joaquín Costa had brought together in the Liga Nacional de Productores. In the first few months of 1900, the two organisations came together to form the Unión Nacional, a body that was prepared to challenge official politics with a new shutdown of shops and a national campaign to promote fiscal disobedience. But the closing of shops, the first repossessions, the shortage of resources and the lack of wider support soon put an end to the revolt of what were known as the 'productive classes' and their regenerationist programme. In fact, when the Unión Nacional stood as a political party in the 1901 elections, it won just four seats. It was a predictable failure for a party that the Count of Romanones described as 'a lot of noise and palaver, and then nothing'. There was no fresh path to regeneration, no short-cut outside the system. Anyone who wanted to combat the defects of the regime would have to do so within the traditional parties that they had criticised so much or, as Costa did, find themselves a niche within the ranks of republicanism.

Other voices of protest were of deeper concern to the conservative government. In the June 1899 closing-of-shops incident, the press made great play of the fact that the Zaragoza demonstration ended up with an attack on the Company of Jesus college and residence. And it was no isolated incident. In several locations in Andalucía, Valencia and Catalonia mobs carried out similar actions against Jesuit buildings or images of the Sacred Heart of Jesus, a symbol loaded with anti-liberal and reactionary connotations. Anti-clericalism was returning to the forefront of national politics. It was not a new phenomenon; people still remembered the wave of rioting, burning of convents and murdering of monks in 1822, 1834 and 1835. Modern anti-clericalism went far beyond the popular criticisms of the enriching and immorality of the clergy that had existed since the Middle Ages. It was a traditionally liberal political movement, to be found also in neighbouring countries such as Portugal, France and Italy, which called for secularisation, in other words, freedom of worship, separation of civil society from Church dominance and the creation of a secular state. As Gumersindo de Azcárate said, it was not about the exclusion of God, but 'the exclusion of the priest from a sphere of influence that was never his'.

At the turn of the century, this political movement was publicly expressing itself as a reaction against the excesses of clericalism, while the Church hierarchy was doing all it could to maintain its political, legal, economic and social privileges. In fact, the arrival of the Restoration had ensured the positive recovery of the Church's power and influence, thanks to the confessional nature of the 1876 Constitution. As well as its predominance in education – particularly in secondary education – and its traditional control of charity and social welfare institutions, there was the re-establishment of the Religious Orders and Congregations Act, with a spectacular rise in the number of religious, more than 50,000, and a more active presence in people's daily lives. This was accompanied by a rise in the number of public missions, processions, pilgrimages to sanctuaries and other mass religious practices, such as Marian devotions or the veneration of the Sacred Heart of Jesus. There was also an upsurge in the number of Catholic workers' circles, confessional associations, catechism classes and courses of adult education, and the publication of Catholic propaganda books, leaflets and newspapers. In the press, the predominant line was still anti-liberal and counter-revolutionary. There was very little theological renovation, due to the belated arrival in Spain of Leo XIII's examination of social problems in his encyclical *Rerum Novarum*. But it was more a question of pastoral strategy than of content, of making a stand against secularisation, using more modern methods of mobilisation. If it was a political battle, said Cardinal Antonio María Cascajares in 1898, 'then it is to politics that we must go in order to fight revolution inch by inch',[3] a cause that was blessed by the assembled bishops at the Catholic Congress in Burgos in 1899.

Thus clericalism and anti-clericalism were, in the first decade of the twentieth century, two complex, dynamic and almost complementary phenomena that fed off each other. The *Desastre* of '98 provided the first motives for anti-clerical protest. The republican press had criticised the Church for exalting belligerent patriotism and blamed the religious orders for the Philippine revolution and the loss of the Philippines. And this 'discontent', as Sagasta acknowledged, was aggravated by a series of 'coincidences'. Among these coincidences, in the context of government policy, were the religious convictions of members of the government, such as General Polavieja and Luis Pidal y Mon, and the maintaining of state religious subsidies amidst a profusion of 'sacrifices' and cuts in public expenditure. Then, in the autumn of 1900, came news of the unsuccessful Carlist uprising and the announcement of the wedding of the Princess of Asturias to the Italian son of the Count of Caserta. Finally, in the first few weeks of 1901, there was the Ubao trial, concerning a young girl confined in a convent without her parents' permission, and the uproar surrounding the premiere of *Electra*, the well-known play by Benito Pérez Galdós about the religious question, dubbed by the Archbishop of Burgos as 'the battle flag of the rabid persecution of Catholicism'.

It was a 'flag', acknowledged Romanones, 'that brought us back to power'.[4] The Liberal Party justified its anti-clerical postures as being part of a broader regenerationist programme, as an obstacle that had to be cleared in order to open up the path to the modernisation of Spain. But, deep down, it was also a question of political expediency, a resource with a remarkable capacity for social mobilisation. José Canalejas became leader of this movement, particularly after his famous speech in Congress in December 1899, when he proclaimed that it was necessary to 'wage war on clericalism'. The religious question was to be found in Parliament, the press and the streets, and isolated riots evolved into orderly demonstrations

[3] *La Rioja*, 12 Mar. 1898.
[4] Conde de Romanones, *Notas de una vida I* (Madrid: Marcial Pons, 1999), p. 122.

and organised campaigns that demonstrated the success of new forms of collective action, such as meetings, assemblies, the boycotting of Catholic demonstrations or the profaning of religious rites, such as the 'promiscuation meals' (the audacious eating of meat on Good Friday).

The major role in anti-clerical protest was played by radical republicanism with a populist base, the clearest examples being Vicente Blasco Ibáñez in Valencia and Alejandro Lerroux, *el emperador del Paralelo* (the Paralelo was a sector of Barcelona with a rich night life). On a basis of an extensive network of centres, and a hot-headed and aggressive ideology, with references drawn from progressive liberalism and popular culture, republicanism became a mass movement that was able to confront the dynastic parties successfully in local elections, dominate the public stage, with constant recourse to mobilisation in the streets, and to maintain its hegemony among urban workers at least until the years of the Great War.[5] Without that background, one cannot understand the events of the Tragic Week in 1909, or the survival of an anti-clerical collective identity which, although losing ground in the second decade of the twentieth century, remained latent and once more unleashed itself during the years of the Second Republic.

But for the time being, in March 1901, the most visible consequence of the wave of anti-clerical protests was the fall of the conservatives and the return to power of Sagasta. In his last government, the 'old shepherd' gave some ministries to new leaders in the party, such as José Canalejas and Álvaro de Figueroa y Torres, the Count of Romanones, who were needed to implement measures against clericalism, prepare Alfonso XIII's ascent to the throne and ensure the unity of the various factions in the party. When a sick and exhausted Sagasta resigned in December 1902, a few weeks before his death, a battle for the Liberal leadership opened up among clients grouped around historical leaders such as Segismundo Moret, Eugenio Montero Ríos and General José López Domínguez.

A look at the list of governments over the next year or two reveals to what extent the internal crisis of the dynastic parties hampered any serious attempt at regeneration. Between December 1902 and June 1905 there was only one general election, in April 1903, and yet there were five conservative governments in succession: those of Francisco Silvela, Raimundo Fernández Villaverde, Antonio Maura, Marcelo de Azcárraga and once again Fernández Villaverde. The Cortes, suspended six times during this span, only opened for brief periods, barely twelve months of parliamentary activity in more than two and a half years. That was when the expression

---

[5] José Álvarez Junco, *El emperador del Paralelo: Lerroux y la demagogia populista* (Madrid: Alianza, 1990).

'*crisis oriental*' was coined, linking the cabinet reshuffles to the visits the political leaders made to the Oriente Palace (the royal residence).

The return of the Liberals to power in June 1905 did not bring with it greater government stability. None of the conservative and liberal governments of that period had the strength or will to implement a programme of reform that, as Juan Pro has pointed out, was needed to tackle basic issues: to put an end to the arbitrary power of the Crown so that governments would depend on parliamentary majorities, not the other way round; to get rid of systematic electoral manipulation, an essential requirement for integrating broad sectors of society into political life; and to transform political parties of worthies into modern grass-roots formations that truly represented and channelled the demands of public opinion.[6] No government, that is, except perhaps for the one led by Antonio Maura.

Maura and the *Semana Trágica*

In his parliamentary reports, Azorín described Antonio Maura as the best orator of the time, one of the few men 'with a truly modern outlook'. As well as acknowledging his gift of eloquence, few failed to recognise him as the most important conservative politician of the first quarter of the twentieth century. Born in Mallorca, he entered political life as a member of the Liberal Party through his brother-in-law, Germán Gamazo, and served Sagasta as a minister in 1892. Following Gamazo's death, in 1901, Maura assumed leadership of his faction, the 'Gamazists', which crossed over en masse to the conservative ranks one year later. It was then that he delivered his famous speech on the need for a 'revolution from above'. He had previously referred to this in his reply to the survey on *Oligarquía y Caciquismo* sponsored by Costa in the Madrid Athenaeum. Maura agreed with almost all the regenerationists when it came to identifying the roots of decay. In Spain, none of the lower, middle, more educated and entrenched classes felt any 'encouragement to assume the obligations of citizenship'. And this was because the government was a 'device', a 'perennial spoil' disputed by the two camps in a minor skirmish, who exercised arbitrariness when they could and craved it when they were on the receiving end. But the remedy for this 'deviation', explained Maura, could not be the 'annihilation' of the system, the 'unsettling' of the *cacique* oligarchy, because then 'Spain would descend into anarchy.' In his opinion, one could not hope for the overnight transformation of an entire nation that had 'turned its back on the scaffolding of the Constitution'. And so, where were the fulcrum and

---

[6] Juan Pro Ruiz, 'La política en tiempos del Desastre', in Pan-Montojo (ed.), *Más se perdió en Cuba*, pp. 151–260.

force for reform to be found? In the 'most accessible' part, the government. This would ensure that 'the necessary works for remedying the discredit into which words have fallen' would be undertaken as soon as possible.[7]

Words and actions. His first opportunity to put his ideas into practice came after the 1903 elections, when Silvela appointed him interior minister. His decision not to intervene in the processing of the results produced, according to some authors, one of the least manipulated polls of the entire Restoration. Proof of this was the advance of the republicans, who won thirty-six seats, almost twice the number they had previously had. However, we should not exaggerate the extent of this measure. The republican urban vote at that time had reached a ceiling that it would never surpass, always less than 10% of the votes cast, and the client structure showed that it could function even without the relative intervention of the ministry. The conservatives won 240 seats, only 5 fewer than the previous Liberal government had held.

In December 1903, with a conservative majority in the Cortes, Maura was appointed prime minister for the first time. His government lasted only a year, not long enough to implement legislative reforms but enough to show his intentions, the bases of his plan for 'revolution from above'. Alfonso XIII's tour of the provinces and his presence in Barcelona were part of Maura's personal effort to reinforce the image of the Crown and, at the same time, to broaden the social bases of the regime without jeopardising its survival. The same motive was behind his protectionist economic policy, which satisfied the economic elites, and his proposals for social reform, a 'prophylactic', Maura wrote, to forestall a dreaded revolution 'from below' with resources other than just the constant deployment of the forces of public order.[8] The spring of 1904 saw the setting up of the Institute of Social Reforms and the tackling of measures relating to the physical and moral protection of children, workplace inspections, the promotion of co-operatives and the six-day working week. These initiatives, as well as others relating to the reform of the civil administration, were hampered by bureaucratic obstacles, parliamentary delays and the resistance of conservative interest groups.

As well as the internal opposition, there were criticisms from liberals and republicans. Anti-clerical protests intensified over the appointment of Archbishop Bernardino Nozaleda, from the Philippines, as archbishop of Valencia and the signing of an agreement with the Vatican recognising

---

[7] Antonio Maura, *Oligarquía y caciquismo como la forma actual de gobierno en España: urgencia y modo de cambiarla. Información en el Ateneo de Madrid, 1901* (Madrid: Ediciones de la Revista de Trabajo, 1975), vol. II, pp. 12, 15.

[8] Antonio Maura, *Nuestro Tiempo: revista mensual ilustrada* (Madrid), Aug. 1904, no. 44.

the legal status of the religious orders in Spain. Telegrams complaining
of public disorder piled up on the interior minister's desk: street fighting
between clericalists and anti-clericalists, riots over taxes and food shortages, and a hitherto unprecedented wave of strikes. UGT membership
went up from 14,737 in 1900, divided into 69 associations, to the 56,905
listed in its proceedings at the beginning of 1905, from 373 local branches.
The growth of the organised labour movement, particularly its spread
outside the urban environment, was spectacular. Silvela's old fears were
being realised and the 'firebrand of discord' was also reaching the rural
environment, to districts with no previous history of organised unity. In
the autumn of 1904, the economist Adolfo Álvarez Buylla remarked,
from the field, that agricultural workers, 'fully aware of the advantages
of unity, although at times exaggerating them, are welcoming with the
desperation of a shipwrecked sailor the lifebelt of association, which is
spreading and propagating throughout the Castilian countryside in
miraculous fashion'. It was a 'sign of the times'.[9] Equally spectacular,
as the daily *El País* remarked, was the evolution of how discontent was
being expressed. The Andalucian peasants had often rioted in bad years
to the battle cry of 'bread and jobs', but 'the novelty is that they have now
called for a general strike out of solidarity'. The example of the 1902
general strike in Barcelona was repeated in the mining areas of Vizcaya
in the autumn of 1903. The military governor of Bilbao called out
the troops and declared a state of emergency, but he did remark in his
report that the strike had spread from the miners to the dockworkers
and railwaymen, and from them to the rest of the workers, in the firm
conviction 'that only through solidarity with others can their objectives
be fulfilled'.

  However, the rise of associationism and the escalation of labour conflicts began to diminish in the autumn of 1904, before the fall of Maura's
government. The labour crisis and food shortages swept through the ranks
of the workers' associations, and the results of collective actions began
to favour the employers, who started to use the weapons of association and
boycott as well. *La Unión Obrera* recommended socialists not to call
strikes that were bound to fail, and that, although the workers were always
'right to ask, what they should study is whether they have the strength to
succeed'. As Fernández Almagro said in just a few words: 'Poverty and
exhaustion are allies of authority.' In fact, what hunger and deprivation
were doing was diminishing confidence and resources in the protest

---

[9] Adolfo Álvarez Buylla, *Memoria acerca de la Información Agraria en ambas Castillas*, in
   Julio Aróstegui (ed.), *Miseria y conciencia del campesino castellano* (Madrid: Narcea, 1977).

movement instead of mobilising it. The failure of the general strike called by the socialists in July 1905 was proof that the workers' movement was not yet able to make the leap from local actions to national campaigns.

Therefore, the fall of Maura's government in December 1904 was not caused by the voices of public protest nor the climate of social conflict. Nor was it the result of campaigns in the republican press or a loss of confidence in the parliamentary majority. The crisis was caused by Alfonso XIII's insistence on appointing the chief of the General Staff against the wishes of the minister of war, yet another example of the young monarch's meddling. On this occasion Maura was not prepared to give in to the king's wishes and he tendered his resignation. On learning of this, Azorín commented that the reaction of parliamentarians and the press was unanimous: 'Maura has come out of this as a decent, strong, honourable and proud man.'[10] It was one step back to gather momentum to move forward. In the following months, during a succession of weak Liberal governments, his status was gradually enhanced.

Meanwhile, the military question and the controversial behaviour of the king remained in the foreground of national politics. In November 1905, the Catalan satirical weekly *Cu-Cut!* published a cartoon about the army that outraged the Barcelona garrison. Several groups of non-commissioned officers attacked the offices and printing works of the magazine, as well as the headquarters of *La Veu de Catalunya*, the principal Catalan nationalist newspaper. The captain general of Catalonia did not condemn the violent action of his subordinates, who had also received the support of the army authorities in Seville and Madrid. The military press immediately called for the suspension of constitutional guarantees in Barcelona as well as a law to give military tribunals power to try and punish any offence against the army. Montero Ríos' government agreed to the first request but not the second. The intervention of the king, on the side of the aggrieved military personnel, caused the prime minister to resign. His successor, Moret, in spite of Congress' firm opposition, acceded to the wishes of the Crown and the demands of the army. March 1906 saw the passing of the Repression of Crimes Against the Fatherland and the Army Act, known as the Law of Jurisdictions, which included any attacks by the press on the military. Carolyn Boyd has seen the incidents of 1905 as being a return to praetorianism, the blight of the nineteenth century that the architects of the Restoration wished to remove from public life. These events demonstrated to the most recalcitrant officers that violence was a successful strategy for achieving their ends, a lesson that they would not forget

[10] Azorín, 'La caída', 16 Dec. 1904, *Parlamentarismo español* (Barcelona, 1968), p. 152.

in the future whenever they felt that their corporative interests were at risk or thought that, as guardians of patriotic values, the integrity of the nation was under threat.[11] Furthermore, the distance grew between the army and civil society, with the anti-militarism of a major sector of the population inflamed, particularly after 1898, by the maintaining of an unfair call-up system and the constant use of the troops whenever public order was threatened.

This anti-militarist feeling was one of the features that brought about the unity of all the opposition forces in Catalonia for the 1907 elections. It was an unqualified success. Solidaritat Catalana won forty-one of the forty-four seats that it contested. This was a spectacular result although it did not affect the absolute majority achieved by the Conservative Party: 253 seats compared to the 78 of the liberals, almost as many as the total of all the anti-dynastic groups. According to Romanones, Alfonso XIII was led to declare that the Cortes were now full 'of the friends of the government and enemies of the Regime'.[12] Now Antonio Maura did have a united block, without any divisions or families, that was well disciplined around an undisputable leader. His turn had come. It was the opportunity for a long-term stable government to 'weed out' the *cacique* system and clean up politics. But it has to be said that, despite the sincerity of his statements, the elections clearly showed the limitations of a genuine reform of the system. For that, he needed a strong government with an overwhelming parliamentary majority. And the only way of ensuring that was for him to exploit the 'repertoire' of manipulation, corruption and fraud that he had so often denounced, a job that was undertaken with great skill by his interior minister, Juan de la Cierva.

The deputies elected in April 1907 had much more work than their predecessors. In the two subsequent years, up to the troubled summer of 1909, more than 200 bills went through Congress. They were all part of a comprehensive state project that María Jesús González has called 'conservative socialisation', a non-revolutionary public mobilisation.[13] Without abandoning his solid Catholic and monarchist beliefs, Maura was convinced that a gradual reform, from a strong government but one that abided by parliamentary formalities – '*luz y taquígrafos*' (transparency) was his famous expression – could convert the 'neutral masses' of the country, who he believed were essentially conservative, into active

---

[11] Carolyn P. Boyd, *La política pretoriana en el reinado de Alfonso XIII* (Madrid: Alianza, 1990).

[12] Romanones, *Notas de una vida I*, p. 122.

[13] María Jesús González, *El universo conservador de Antonio Maura: biografía y proyecto de Estado* (Madrid: Biblioteca Nueva, 1997).

citizens. To do this, the government needed to legitimise the public institutions and bring them closer to society, and create a civic and participatory
structure for the Spanish population to abandon the distant and negative
perception it had of the state.

His project centred around three basic reforms: municipal justice, the
electoral system and local administration. The Municipal Justice Act
aimed to provide independence and stability to the municipal judges,
thereby breaking up the client structure. A frontal attack against fraud
and corruption was the purpose of the Electoral Reform Act, which
removed from political power the drawing up of censuses and the composition of electoral boards and decisions on recounts, and among many
other measures dealt with controversial issues such as compulsory voting
or the famous Article 29, which allowed for direct election in constituencies with only one candidate. Finally, the 'weeding out' of the *cacique*
system was the remit of the Local Administration Bill, probably the most
ambitious initiative of all, which broadened the powers of the town and
city councils and provided them with legal autonomy and independent
political status.

The second legislative front of Maura's 'long' government was social
reform, a series of projects with a paternalistic tone which aimed, above
all, to reduce social conflict and 'class egotism', representing, nevertheless, notable progress in almost uncharted territory. The setting up in
1908 of the National Social Security Institute, industrial tribunals, conciliation and arbitration committees, and the employment inspection
corps, as well as the April 1909 Strikes Act, were the most outstanding
results of this protectionist and conciliatory policy. However, this series of
provisions, some soon to be obsolete or only half-finished, failed to open
up the way to a peaceful solution to conflicts between employers and workers. Maura's feeling, when the upheaval of the summer of 1909 destroyed
all he had worked for, must have been one of frustration. The plans for
reorganising the army and reforming the call-up system remained on the
drawing board, as did the Local Administration Bill which, after countless
debates and amendments, never passed into law. Nor did the electoral
reforms meet their objectives. Electoral lists of candidates were hand-
picked by the government, vulnerable when faced by republican and
Catalan nationalist campaigns, and were exposed in the big cities, but
they were still effective in the rural single-seat constituencies. Years later,
the poet Antonio Machado recalled the failure of the revolution from
above, 'from the top of the greasy pole', a period that had been 'a kingdom of shadows paved with good intentions', shadows that were 'Spain's
directionless aspirations'. Maura, with a mentality that was 'archaic and
empty, but with honest intentions', was remembered for his 'attitude of

an important man who wanders through a gypsy fair without selling or buying anything'.[14]

The beginning of the end came in May 1908, when Maura brought the Repression of Terrorism Bill before Congress, a law designed to put an end to anarchist bombings using exceptional measures such as the suppression of newspapers and associations, banishment orders and prison sentences in order to prevent the spread of anarchistic ideas. The proposal, which put the rights of free association and expression at risk, immediately attracted the criticism of liberals and republicans, united in a 'Leftist Block'. For the first time since the beginning of the Restoration, a dynastic party, the Liberals, distanced itself from the *turno* pact and moved to the left, inspired by the slogan 'against Maura and his works', the phrase that was written on the banner hanging above the rally in the Teatro de la Princesa, with speeches from Moret and Canalejas as well as Melquíades Álvarez, Gumersindo de Azcárate and Juan Sol Ortega. The propaganda campaign against the government, run by the Madrid press group made up of *El Imparcial*, *El Liberal* and *Heraldo de Madrid*, was without precedent in Spain. And the mobilisation did not end with the withdrawing of the bill. On the contrary, it gained new followers when news of what was happening in Morocco began to arrive. Political criticism was transformed, from that moment on, into a general outcry against Maura.

The Spanish presence in North Africa had been established by the secret accord signed with France in 1904 and by the 1906 Algeciras Conference. It consisted of an area of influence, with very little significance in the international context, limited to the mountainous region of the Rif. Spain's interest in this territory was motivated more by a question of national prestige, tarnished since the loss of its colonies, than by its strategic situation or potential economic benefits. Skirmishes and confrontations with neighbouring Berber tribesmen, beginning in 1908, became more frequent in 1909, particularly around the mining areas near Melilla. On 9 June, an attack by Rif tribesmen caused six deaths, and the government decided to send reinforcements to the region to protect Spanish interests. According to the official version, it was a simple 'border policing operation' to ensure the safety of the area. But it was not seen as such by a large sector of public opinion. Still in people's minds was the *Desastre*, and the most critical anti-government press underlined that only the assets of certain businessmen and the ambition of the army were at stake on African soil. The people, said *La Correspondencia de España*, wanted nothing to do with a venture that would only extract 'blood from the poor and money from the taxpayers'.

---

[14] Antonio Machado, 'Los complementarios', in *Poesía y prosa*, vol. III, *Prosas completas (1893–1936)* (Madrid: Espasa-Calpe, 1989), p. 1175.

The socialists began a 'campaign of upheaval', and the rallies that were held in many cities were repeated in the streets, with demonstrations that ended in concentrations outside barracks and occasional riots on station platforms. The call-up of the reservists on 12 July, seen as a two-fold injustice, amplified the voices of protest. Starting on 14 July, there were incidents over the embarkation of troops, scenes similar to those seen on subsequent days in the stations of Madrid and other cities.

News of the first skirmishes outside Melilla showed that this was not just going to be a brisk punishment operation. The attack on Mount Gugurú on 23 July ended with a large number of casualties, amidst chaos and general confusion, and 27 July saw the massacre of a column cut off in the Lobo Gulley: 150 dead in one day and more than 1,000 casualties before the end of the month. The PSOE and UGT called a general strike in the whole of Spain for 2 August. But events were precipitated in Barcelona, starting on 26 July. The strike called for that day by Solidaridad Obrera, the anarchist-leaning trade union founded in 1907 with the participation of socialists and republicans, spread throughout the city and marked the beginning of a week of armed confrontations, barricades, and attacks on trams and *fielatos* (a type of urban customs post), as well as anti-clerical violence. The columns of smoke rising from burning churches, convents and schools traced the most recognisable image of this 'infernal week in July', as one Catholic newspaper commented. Responsibility for the burning of eighty religious buildings, and the sacrilegious acts committed in some of them, was attributed to radical republican groups inspired by Lerroux. At any event, the notably heterogeneous social composition of the riots showed the range of anti-clerical feeling in the culture of the popular classes. When the army regained control of all the city's districts, on Friday 30 July, the casualty count showed 104 civilians and 8 police dead, as well as several hundred injured.

The events of the *Semana Trágica* went beyond the Barcelona city limits. Protests and violent confrontations spread to at least nineteen provinces, as Andre Bachoud has related.[15] The suspension of constitutional guarantees in the whole of Spain was announced on 28 July, and the same day saw the beginning of preventive arrests, the closing of associations and the implantation of rigid press censorship. The harshness of the subsequent repression, with more than a thousand arrests and military trials, resulting in seventeen death sentences, has been linked to one name, Francisco Ferrer y Guardia, an anarchist ideologue and founder of the Escuela Moderna, who was one of the five condemned people to be finally executed.

[15] Andre Bachoud, *Los españoles ante las campañas de Marruecos* (Madrid: Espasa-Calpe, 1988).

His summary trial became an internationally publicised event and the outcry from the European left provided even more fuel for the '¡Maura no!' campaign at home. On 13 October, the 'martyr of Montjüich', as the left-wing journalist Antonio Fabra Rivas called him, was executed. Two days later the Cortes opened and criticism rained down on a government that was already condemned. As Maura himself explained, he could not prevail 'against half Spain and more than half of Europe'.[16] Alfonso XIII was the last to abandon him. On 21 October he obliged him to resign and entrusted Moret with forming a new Liberal government.

From Canalejas to the Great War

The change of government was not the only consequence of the grim events of 1909. The republicans, workers' parties and trade unions had seen for themselves the potential of pressure from crowds, the power of taking over the streets and the possibility of launching national movements, an experience that they would not fail to exploit in the future. Furthermore, the discontent generated by the war and the hostility towards the unfair call-up system showed that they were useful instruments for stirring up the people. At a time when nationalist imperialism was inciting the popular masses of the European powers to identify with the state, in Spain the opposite phenomenon was occurring. The country, which not long before had lost the last remnants of its colonial empire, was incapable of defeating an insignificant enemy located on its own doorstep. The memory of the *Desastre* of '98 and the events of the summer of 1909 revealed cracks in the legitimacy of the Restoration system and inaugurated the crisis of the hegemony of the state, a process that was unstoppable from 1917 onwards. Military operations were terminated in January 1910, after securing the area of Melilla, but the end of the fighting was merely a brief spell of calm in a conflict, the Moroccan war, that was to define Spain's history for two decades. Probably no other European country devoted so many resources over such a long period of time in an attempt to secure such an insignificant territory. And of course, bearing in mind the enormity of the events that followed, from the open conflict in 1921 because of the Annual disaster to the rebellion of July 1936, with the *Africanista* officers as the main players, no other country paid such a high price.

For the time being, in January 1910, peace in the Rif provided little respite for Moret, the Liberal leader who, as the historian Pabón wrote,

---

[16] Gabriel Maura and Melchor Fernández Almagro, *Por qué cayó Alfonso XIII: evolución y disolución de los partidos políticos durante su reinado* (Madrid: Ambos Mundos, 1948), p. 155.

ended up as castaway in the storm that he himself had unleashed. The short span of his government was due not so much to the hostility shown by some of the army, the boycott of the conservative opposition or the threat to the alliance between republicans and socialists, ratified in November of the previous year, as to the lack of support in his own party. The leaders of the rival factions schemed against him and in February 1910 persuaded the king, in what was known as the Ash Wednesday crisis, to withdraw his confidence and appoint José Canalejas in his place. His arrival in office showed how little the dynastic political parties had changed, parties that were more akin to upper-class families and cliques of the nineteenth century than to the mass organisations of the twentieth century.

However, once in power, Canalejas displayed his genuine willingness to change, his resolute pledge to implement a comprehensive programme of liberal renovation and social reform. And he was to use an approach very different from Maura's. While the conservative leader, nervous about the participation of the masses, based his project on the purging of the electoral system and public institutions, and on raising ethical standards in the administration, Canalejas' reformist drive was grounded on the social and cultural regeneration of the people, on the role of the state as the leading player in the modernisation of society. The nearly three years that he led the government, until his assassination in November 1912, represented the most serious and encouraging attempt yet to open a path to democracy from within the political system of the Restoration, albeit without jeopardising the foundations of the constitutional monarchy.

José Canalejas y Méndez was then 55 years old, with a long political career in the radical wing of the Liberal Party behind him. Elected for Soria in 1881 and a minister in Sagasta's governments of 1885 and 1894, he stood out for his innovative approach, within the bounds of the dynastic left. As Salvador Forner has pointed out, the figure of Canalejas embodied in Spain the new social direction taken by European liberalism during the early years of the twentieth century, inspired by the experience of countries such as Belgium, France and Great Britain. This new-style liberalism championed state intervention in social and economic relationships, with a view to improving the condition of the working classes. It was a social innovation that, in the long term, was to enable the political integration of the workers, an indispensable requirement for securing the democratisation of the regime, deep down a 'crowned Republic', as he often said with regard to the British example.[17] Among the most important labour reforms passed during his mandate were the laws governing a nine-hour

---

[17] Salvador Forner Muñoz, *Canalejas y el Partido Liberal Democrático (1900–1910)* (Madrid: Cátedra, 1993).

working day in the mines, apprenticeship, rest days for women working in shops and the law regulating women's night shifts. There were also a considerable number of proposals concerning employment contracts, collective negotiation, control of hazardous industries and compulsory social security, most of them still being discussed in Parliament when he was assassinated.

Also pending was one of his most striking proposals, legislation governing provincial federations, the first step to state decentralisation and a response to demands by regionalists. A year after his death, in December 1913, the Senate authorised the Mancomunidad (Federation) of Catalonia, presided over by Enric Prat de la Riba, who united the administration of the four provincial governments, although this decision did not mean that new powers were granted.

All this was an example of a moderate opening up, the principle that also guided the government's policy on the 'religious question'. Despite his reputation as an anti-clerical agitator, Canalejas displayed a conciliatory attitude and always looked for formulas that would represent a compromise between the pre-eminence of the Catholic religion as laid down in the Constitution and a gradual separation of Church and State. These secularising measures were intended to establish the supremacy of civil power in the face of threats of conservative reaction to any type of democratising proposal. Debate over the Ley del Candado, passed at the end of 1910, had given rise in preceding months to a wave of anti-clerical demonstrations, Catholic rallies, threats from traditionalist groups and even the first steps being taken to break off diplomatic relations with the Vatican. But it was in fact a tentative proposal and only temporary, a modification of the Associations Act, which limited itself to banning the establishing of new religious orders in Spain for two years, until a subsequent law finally defined the question, something that never came to fruition. The most significant legislation, exemption from religious instruction for children of non-Catholic parents, was not even Canalejas' idea, and was passed by Romanones' government in 1913.

The achievements and limitations of the liberal reformist programme could be seen in the two laws that were most eagerly awaited by 'certain sectors of Spanish society', as Canalejas acknowledged in Congress in the spring of 1911: the removal of the unpopular and abusive consumer tax, and the reform of the call-up system, detested for its arduous conditions of service and the continuity of the buy-out clause. The former did not entirely meet its objective because many town councils, stifled by the lack of resources of their own, extended the collection of the tax for two years. The second measure also only went halfway. The Compulsory Military Service Act, passed in February 1912, allowed for '*cuota*' soldiers:

draftees who contributed to the cost of their kit and paid 1,000 pesetas spent only ten months in the ranks, reduced to five months if they paid 2,000 pesetas; at all times they carried out the duties destined for first-class or outstanding soldiers.

El Socialista called this a 'cruel joke' that was being played on 'the working people', because no *cuota* soldiers were being sent to the 'slaughter-house' of Africa. Once more, we see the impact of the Moroccan war. In the spring of 1911 military operations were resumed and there were protests all over Spain. In the first week of May alone there were anti-war demonstrations in twenty-seven provinces. As the philosopher and essayist José Ortega y Gasset said at the time, it was a popular hostility that needed to be 'tamed' if one wanted to flatten 'the mountain of hatred that has arisen between the two halves of Spain in 1909'. *El País* wrote that those who resisted the advance of the proletariat were the same people who were spurring on the troops in the Rif mountains, and for this reason the people linked 'the social issues that concerned them with the war effort'. And so it was. In the wave of rallies, demonstrations and strikes of the summer of 1911, the social and economic demands were very often linked to a rejection of the war in Morocco, an opposition to the conflict that influenced the calling of a general strike and the almost rebellious climate that reigned in most of the country during the month of September.

The protest movement began on 11 September with partial strikes in Vizcaya, Asturias and Málaga which over the next few days, in the midst of the general confusion and disorganisation, spread to Zaragoza, Valencia and other points of Spain. A few days before that, the first congress of the Confederación Nacional del Trabajo (CNT), the anarchist-leaning trade union constituted the previous year in Barcelona on the foundations of Solidaridad Obrera, was held. The PSOE and UGT were late in joining the general strike, when the workers had already called off their action in many areas. The most serious incidents took place in Cullera on 18 September, when some strikers killed three public employees. The death sentence imposed on seven of the accused unleashed a press campaign in support of the condemned which, deep down, was a confrontation with the government and the constitutional monarchy. Alfonso XIII and Canalejas, wishing to avoid a repetition of the Ferrer case, managed to commute the penalties. But the repressive measures were particularly harsh on the organised labour movement. The CNT was banned, community centres and UGT premises were closed down for months, and multiple arrests were made. The firm hand of the prime minister was exercised once more the following year, in September 1912, when the railway strike closed down all the lines in Spain, with more than 70,000 workers involved. Canalejas did not hesitate to follow the example of

Aristide Briand in France, calling up the reservist employees, thereby militarising the service.

The general strikes, the threat of outbreaks of revolution and the failure of peaceful negotiation methods thwarted Canalejas' hopes of a reformist evolution of the labour movement within the framework of a constitutional monarchy. He himself was to be a further victim of this conflict. On 12 November 1912 he was assassinated in the Puerta del Sol, outside a bookshop, by the anarchist Manuel Pardiñas, who had in fact thought of assassinating the king. It took three close-range pistol shots, the same number that had decided the fate of another prime minister, Cánovas del Castillo, fifteen years earlier. To a certain extent, the two magnicides opened and closed the central period of Restoration Spain, from the all-out war in Cuba under the command of Weyler to the signing of the Spanish protectorate in Morocco, from the first cracks in the political system at the end of the great reformist plan, to the beginning of the regime that Galdós defined in 1910 as 'a useless mass of propped-up ruins'.[18]

It was not as bad as that – at least, not yet. Galdós made his pronouncement in Congress as a deputy for the Conjunción Republican-Socialista, which had been notably successful in that year's elections, obtaining thirty-seven seats in the Cortes, one of them occupied by Pablo Iglesias, the first socialist to sit in Parliament. But the Conjunción held barely 9% of seats in that Parliament. And Galdós was one of the moderate republicans who, in the spring of 1912, joined Melquíades Álvarez and Gumersindo de Azcárate in the founding of the Partido Reformista. Among its ranks was a young Manuel Azaña, chairman of the Athenaeum, who sought to transform the structure of Spain 'without surrendering to the ghost of a bloody revolution'.[19] It was a question of uniting within one political project the intellectual elites prepared to push the form of government into the background to concentrate on educating and nationalising the masses and opening the doors to democracy within the monarchy. It was a lukewarm reform because progress, wrote Felipe Trigo in the prologue of *Jarrapellejos*, the novel he dedicated to Melquíades Álvarez in 1914, 'is not a speeding train but a growing tree'.

But very little regenerating sap ran through the cracked trunk of the constitutional political system. The regime continued to rely on the foundational pact of the dynastic parties, on oligarchical roots that were ever more fragmented and contentious. The following years saw rotations of power between liberals and conservatives, but now there was no leadership

[18] Benito Pérez Galdós, *La fe nacional y otros escritos sobre España* (Madrid: Rey Lear, 2012), p. 69.
[19] Azaña, *Discursos políticos*, p. 38.

that was not disputed, nor a solid Congress, nor a stable government with the time and energy for anything other than circumventing problems and conflicts. Government instability was plain to see because of the constant recourse to closure of the Cortes, an exceptional measure that became the norm. The truth is that during these years very few laws were passed, and this legislative vacuum created ever closer links between the fate of the executive power and the confidence of the Crown and the intervention of the king, thereby eroding the legitimacy of the parliamentary system.

It was precisely when this legitimacy was needed most. In the summer of 1914, the controversy over the Catalan question, social conflicts and military operations in Morocco were relegated to the background with the news of a military escalation of hitherto unknown dimensions: the Great War. Spain's initial stance could only be neutrality. On that point there were no great differences between liberals and conservatives. Both Dato and Romanones were aware of the army's limited potential and the country's marginal position on the European stage, outside the great international alliances that defined the blocks facing each other in the trenches. However, as the months passed, the declaration of neutrality did not save Spain from intense debate in the press and public opinion, which ended up involving the institutions, associations and political parties.

It was a 'civil war of words', as Gerald Meaker put it.[20] Among the Allies' supporters were almost all the liberals, with restrained sympathies for France and Great Britain, sympathies that were much more openly expressed by the reformists, republicans and even socialists. Their public statements, more belligerent against the central European empires, hailed the Allied victories as advances in the cause of progress, democracy and freedom. Among the supporters of Germany were the Carlists, the young *Mauristas* and broad sectors of the army, the Church and the nobility, who were much more sympathetic to the ideal that the German Empire represented as guardian of traditional values, militarism and the defence of social order against any attempt at revolution. The debate began to sour and intensify after 1915 with the incorporation of Italy on the Allied side, with propaganda campaigns directed and financed by the embassies of the great powers and the torpedoes launched by German submarines against Spanish shipping. The controversy over a suitable response to these attacks caused a split in the Liberals and the final crisis of the Romanones government in April 1917.

The impact of the First World War in Spain went much further than disagreements over diplomatic policy or diatribes in the media. Most of

---

[20] Gerald H. Meaker, *The Revolutionary Left in Spain, 1914–1923* (Stanford University Press, 1974).

the population was not involved in this debate, concerned as it was over more basic issues such as labour conditions or the shortage of staple food-stuffs. It is well known that during the war the upswing in external demand generated a spectacular process in the Spanish economy of industrial and commercial expansion, with huge business profits. But the other side of this productive euphoria was the high inflation that caused a sharp increase in food prices, with wage rises always lagging behind. Bread shortages began to be evident in the early months of 1915. Spaniards, said Acción Socialista, might not be destined to die as victims of the bloody conflict in Europe, but they would succumb just like the warring nations: 'They, from the cause; we, from the effects. In other words, just the same.' The first Subsistence Act froze exports and reduced import tariffs on wheat and flour, but the measure failed to have the desired effect. Throughout 1916 there were riots against the bread shortage and rising taxes, with women in the vanguard of the crowds. Nor did the second Subsistence Act stop the protests, attacks on flour mills and bakeries, and confrontations with the forces of order.

Traditional rioting coexisted with strikes and demonstrations promoted by the organised labour movement, resolved to channel popular indignation. The national railworkers' strike in the summer of 1916 was followed by the agreement reached by the two majority trade unions, the UGT and CNT, to organise a 24-hour general strike throughout Spain calling on the government to reduce food costs and to solve the employment crisis. The strike manifesto, directed towards citizens and the people in general, declared that this action would be the final warning to the authorities. If suitable measures were not taken, it would be plain to see 'that what our country is suffering can only be remedied by seizing power and handing it over to others who are less hidebound by private concerns'. The general strike of 18 December was, without a doubt, the biggest social mobilisation that Spain had ever seen. It was a warning from the new social army of the workers, wrote Luis Araquistáin in *El Socialista*, of what they were capable of doing; some military exercises, proletarian manoeuvres that were an invitation to a major strike 'on the day that rehearsals are over and battle is joined'. And it was not long in coming. In March 1917, a few weeks after the Russian revolutionary movement had brought about the abdication of Tsar Nicholas II, the UGT and the CNT agreed on an indefinite general strike to be called within three months.

Wenceslao Fernández Flórez had already written about the leading role played in politics by the working class in one of his parliamentary chronicles published at the beginning of the Great War. In his opinion, the characteristics of the traditional parties had disappeared, the interests of all those involved in party politics had melded together, and the only victims were the workers, the target of trials and persecutions. Within the large 'governed' party, it was the workers who had 'more nerve and less submission, more courage to protest'. For this reason, 'the instrument of former struggles and all its reprisals' were saved 'for wielding between the two camps'. His account of the Great War years, of a neutrality with 'flashes of nervousness', arrived at a point of no return in April 1917, with the fall of Romanones. 'To be frank, the Constitution has been devalued in our eyes. It is like having a counterfeit coin: you can "flaunt" it in front of your friends, but if you have to pay for something with it, you will end up in gaol. We no longer love this fickle tome.'[21] It was no longer loved by those who talked of revolution, those sceptics of the liberal parliamentary regime, nor by the voices of those who were beginning to think about a radically different solution, leaning towards nationalism, authoritarianism and militarism.

[21] Wenceslao Fernández Flórez, *Impresiones de un hombre de buena fe (1914–1919)* (Madrid: Espasa-Calpe, 1964).

3 The crisis of the Liberal regime

Most experts are in agreement, in general terms, that the 1917 crisis represented a watershed for the legitimacy of the political system of the Restoration. The praetorian threat of the secret Juntas de Defensa, the demands of the *Asamblea de Parlamentarios* (a series of unofficial meetings between Catalan and national deputies and senators to discuss political problems) and calls for revolutionary strikes by the workers posed a serious challenge to the state. The regime survived, but it was incapable of undertaking the reforms needed to broaden its social and political base and successfully tackle an orderly transition to democracy. The governments of those years were weak and unstable, sustained by parties split into factions and interests that occupied a fragmented Parliament, and they were incapable of getting ambitious projects off the ground such as those that had been tackled by Maura and Canalejas in the previous decade.

They failed because, as well as the economic and social impact of the Great War, there were problems deriving from the corporativism of the army, the authoritarianism of the Crown, escalation of the Moroccan conflict, the intensity of trade union mobilisation and public protests, reminiscent of the Russian revolution, nationalist demands and the defection of conservative sectors, Catholic associations and employers' groups, which were increasingly in favour of anti-parliamentary solutions. This situation went on until September 1923, when Miguel Primo de Rivera, the captain general of Catalonia, declared a state of emergency and demanded that power be handed over to him. There was hardly any opposition. The *coup d'état* saw the overthrow of the Constitution and the beginning of a military dictatorship.

Summer 1917

A 'seditious, unpatriotic, revolutionary and anti-social movement of a turbulent minority, cruelly deceived by another even smaller minority, made up of a few rogues with no conscience, no honour and no manliness who, in exchange for a meagre sum, do not hesitate to destroy their Fatherland, spill their brothers' blood and incite them to perpetrate such horrendous and savage crimes': so wrote *El Debate* to describe the revolutionary general strike of August 1917. The Catholic and conservative newspaper was amazed at the simple way in which 'such a dangerous and harmful device' occurred. An assembly of railway workers agreed on a partial strike and, out of solidarity, 'as the most natural and inoffensive thing in the world, with magnificent skill, it has led to a general strike. And an indefinite general strike, called for no apparent reason, is always revolutionary in nature.' The national economy was paralysed, the 'orderly process of social life' was interrupted, economic development was halted and large fortunes destroyed, all of which was accompanied by outbreaks of violence that aroused and stirred 'loutish instincts'. The origin of this 'disastrous situation', the newspaper went on, was nothing but the 'pseudo-democratic spirit imported from decadent countries', which had relaxed 'the mainsprings of the state, of authority and social discipline in our community. One of the most urgent things to be done is to react against this and place the classic concepts back onto the fundamental bases of society.'[1]

In fact, as we know, the political and social storm of the summer of 1917 did not begin with the general strike. The first to transcend the bounds of constitutional legality were those responsible for defending it, the army. The Juntas de Defensa movement, as Carolyn Boyd has explained, represented the return of praetorianism to public life and the beginning of the end of the supremacy of civil power.[2] The spring of 1917 saw the forming of many Juntas in Spain, made up of officers who were annoyed at the economic problems created by the Great War, and at government measures designed to modernise the army and pension off surplus officers as well as to eliminate the policy of arbitrary promotions that gave greater weight to the merits of those who were serving in Morocco, the *Africanistas*, than to the principle of length of service. In practice, it was a case of attempted unionisation, a clear breach of military discipline, but orders to disband fell on deaf ears.

The leaders of the Junta de Infantería in Barcelona were arrested and held in Montjuïc castle, which lead to the publication, on 1 June, of a manifesto in which the officers demanded not only the release of those detained and recognition of the Juntas, but also the opening of a process of political reform; this declaration, with its regenerationist overtones, deep down hid the corporativist interests behind the protest. The

---

[1] *El Debate*, 23 Aug. 1917.   [2] Boyd, *La política pretoriana en el reinado de Alfonso XIII*.

peninsula-based officers threatened to disobey their commanders and in view of the worrying turn that the situation was taking, which included rumours of a *coup d'état*, the captain general of Catalonia, José Marina, ordered the release of the detainees. The showdown, in which the insubordinate officers came out on top, ended with the resignation of the government led by Manuel García Prieto, the Liberal leader who had replaced Romanones in April that year, and with the acceptance of the statutes of the Juntas. In the words of Fernández Almagro, once again the 'sword' held sway in the state, and it was not 'brandished in the shade, as on other occasions, but out in the open, with more hope than scandal for the expectant citizens'. The army received 'stimulus and submission' instead of punishment, but the Juntas de Defensa could not avoid 'the consequences of their call for a different policy: it has never been easy to predict history nor measure out events. Europe was providing our crisis with a stormy background. The Great War, which was fragmenting peoples and institutions, made all type of subversion viable.' The Russian empire had already fallen and other places could easily be set alight by 'sparks from this conflagration'.[3]

To prevent this, the new Conservative government, led by Dato since 9 June, decreed the suspension of constitutional guarantees and press censorship that was so harsh that Fernández Flórez stated that the list of things that could be talked about was much shorter than the banned topics list. But the official silence could not gag the expectation created by the military movement and the discontent of the political class. At least, that was what the socialists thought, and they rekindled their contacts with the republicans in the conviction that, as Santos Juliá has explained, the conditions required for revolution had duly ripened. There were bourgeois parties ready to take power, fractious officers tempted to mobilise the troops, and strong, disciplined workers' organisations, united for months by the joint promise of the UGT and the CNT to call an indefinite general strike. They could not afford to let this long-awaited chance slip by. Julián Besteiro, a PSOE intellectual, recalled that at that time 'people of all classes, except the uppermost', believed that 'this was it, revolution would be an effortless undertaking'.[4]

On 16 June, after several meetings between Pablo Iglesias, Melquíades Álvarez and Lerroux, a left-wing alliance was agreed with the purpose of heading a general movement of political reform. They were joined by the

[3] Fernández Almagro, *Historia del reinado de D. Alfonso XIII*.
[4] Santos Juliá, 'Preparados para cuando la ocasión se presente: los socialistas y la revolución', in Juliá (ed.), *Violencia política en la España del siglo XX* (Madrid: Taurus, 2000), pp. 145–90.

Catalan deputies and senators as well as by certain liberals who asked the government to open the Cortes in order to deal with the most pressing problems and discuss, without delay, a revision of the Constitution. Their demands included the concession of full national sovereignty, without the intervention of the Crown, a greater separation of legislative and judicial power, and the beginning of a decentralising policy that would grant progressive allocation of regional autonomy.

The cabinet refused to repeal the exceptional measures, much less to open the Cortes under pressure from a group of politicians whose activities, in its opinion, were verging on sedition. In Barcelona, Cambó led the unrest and called an Assembly of Parliamentarians to debate a basic programme with two underlying principles: the formation of a provisional government and the setting up of a constituent Cortes after clean elections that would embody 'the sovereign will of the country'. The Assembly was held on 19 July, with a smaller attendance than expected, barely 70 parliamentarians – regionalists, reformists and republicans – of the more than 700 that made up the two chambers. But the forces of order dissolved the meeting without too many problems, with the symbolic arrest of the principal promoters. For the moment, it seemed that the involved parties were not willing to take their challenge to the government further. And with no political leaders conspiring or military chiefs anxious to deploy the troops, the workers' leaders were left to face the calling of a revolution alone.

But they answered the call, although it has to be said that it was more a case of being swept up by events than leading a movement. While certain members of the PSOE and UGT national committees, such as Besteiro and Pablo Iglesias, were negotiating with the anti-dynastic parties, others, such as Francisco Largo Caballero, attended secret meetings in Barcelona with the CNT leadership in an attempt to contain the more impatient trade unionists. In the midst of an escalation of conflicts, such as took place with the Bilbao metalworkers, employees of the arsenal in Cartagena, and various mining areas, the catalyst was the railway and tram strike in Valencia from 16 to 24 July. In the opinion of many historians, including Manuel Tuñón de Lara, the harshness of the repression and the sacking of the strikers were part of a deliberate government strategy to provoke the workers' movement before it was ready to take action.[5]

Whatever the reason, it is true to say that in the early days of August railway workers throughout Spain agreed to go on strike in solidarity with their sacked Valencian comrades, and the joint PSOE and UGT

---

[5] Manuel Tuñón de Lara, *Poder y sociedad en España, 1900–1931* (Madrid: Espasa-Calpe, 1992), p. 262.

leadership, with Besteiro, Andrés Saborit, Daniel Anguiano and Largo Caballero at the head, believed there was no alternative but to call an indefinite strike from 13 August onwards. Their manifesto, aimed at 'the workers and public opinion' was not much different from the reformist programme of the Assembly of Parliamentarians: a provisional government, clean elections and constituent Cortes that would tackle the fundamental problems of the country. Until these objectives were met, 'the workers' movement is resolved to stay on strike'.

Practically every sector went on strike in Asturias, the Basque Country, Madrid, the industrial areas of Catalonia and the Valencian coast, the Andalucian mining areas, such as Linares, Peñarroya and Río Tinto, and several provincial capitals. But little interest was aroused in the remaining regions and hardly any in the rural areas. Furthermore, the swift arrest of the strike committee left the movement with no central leadership or co-ordinated strategy, and the most active regions were isolated from each other, to face the troops that were heavily deployed against the pickets occupying the streets and stations and at factory gates. After several days of confrontation, during which there were almost 100 deaths and 2,000 workers were arrested, most strikers admitted defeat. The Asturian miners were the last to go back to work, in the middle of September, by which time courts martial were in full swing handing down harsh sentences to those most committed. Before the end of the month, Besteiro, Largo Caballero, Anguiano and Saborit, the main leaders of the socialist trade union UGT, were in prison in Cartagena, sentenced to life imprisonment. The government was able to breathe a sigh of relief. The 'great advent' announced by *El Socialista* had failed; the 'crowning of the biggest battle of all' had been reduced to isolated skirmishes. To the great relief of the king, Spain was not a second Russia, for the moment.

The situation in Russia in February 1917 had some similarities to Spain's in the summer of that year: an escalation of strikes, public order conflicts and food riots, the closing of Parliament, political parties prepared to head a regime change, the discontent of the army and the presence of a workers' movement resolved to take to the streets and paralyse the economy. But Spain was not at war; it did not have thousands of soldiers in the trenches; and, furthermore, when the time came for revolution, the barracks did not open their gates to welcome the workers, and the army was firmly on the government side.

However, the failure of the revolutionary movement of the summer of 1917 did not mean that the regime emerged unscathed. Pressure wielded by the Juntas de Defensa, which in June had brought about the fall of García Prieto's Liberal government, overthrew the Conservative government of Eduardo Dato in October. Civil power came out worst from the interventionism of the army, which from then on enjoyed the firm backing of Alfonso XIII, who was convinced that the army was the best guarantee for the survival of the throne. Between that date and the *coup d'état* of September 1923 – a period of barely six years – four general elections were held and twelve prime ministers formed governments. There were so-called concentration and national governments, disunited cabinets without the backing of the majority, and also multi-party coalitions. But government instability was the dominant trend. And the improvised solutions and emergency agreements that attempted to restore the two-party rotation system were unable to clear the obstacles of parliamentary fragmentation, the unbreachable wall of rural *cacique* domains, the growing demands of Catalan and Basque nationalism, setbacks in the colonial war in Morocco, and the wave of social unrest and violent confrontations that spread throughout Spain.

The Bolshevik triennium

The failure of the political objectives set by the August 1917 general strike did not lead to the defeat of the workers' movement. On the contrary, it demonstrated a remarkable ability to organise and channel workers of all sectors and to put pressure on the oligarchic system of the Restoration, which was reluctant to admit the participation of the masses into political life. The movement wielded a social and political influence that a few years earlier would have been unthinkable. The social mobilisation of the summer was kept dormant thanks to the pro-amnesty campaign of the prisoners, and this aroused a current of sympathy in a large section of public opinion, leading to the consolidation of workers' organisations and trade union infrastructures. Subsequent months saw the beginning of a rapid rise in the number of both affiliates and organisations set up in the main cities and many rural areas in the interior. The backdrop was the economic situation of the Great War years, which accelerated social and structural changes that had people talking about a nationwide working class for the first time. And the indisputable leading players on this stage were the two main trade unions, the UGT and the CNT.

In the second decade of the twentieth century the UGT underwent a profound transformation. The 40,000 members of 1910 went on to become almost 100,000 in 1917 and more than 200,000 in 1920. And it was not just a question of numbers. Throughout those years, the flimsy union of artisan associations became a nationwide trade union federation which started incorporating industrial workers, particularly miners and metal and railway workers as well as, albeit to a lesser extent, farmworkers. The artisan associations regrouped as trade unions and industrial federations and their leaders wielded greater influence, with Largo Caballero gradually coming to the fore. Little by little, local labour conflicts gave way to national campaigns and mobilisations which involved entire sectors of industry or services. In this way, the UGT became a modern mass trade union, well organised and with a strong leadership structure, which was able to channel workers' demands, co-ordinate the collective actions of its members and enter negotiations at the highest level with employers' federations and with the state to represent all workers.

Its leadership, chastened by the failure of the 1917 general strike, refused to take part in the political struggle, leaving that role to the PSOE parliamentary group, with six seats in the Cortes in 1918, and instead concentrated on trade union issues. They did not believe that the proletarian revolution would come about as a result of a violent outbreak on a given day; on the contrary, they believed that it would be the result of an evolutionary process, a gradual growth and consolidation of the organisation. As Pere Gabriel has explained, it was a unionism based on pressure and negotiation that aimed to obtain improved labour conditions and social reforms by taking part in state institutions. Thus it fostered the growth of large industrial federations and relegated to the background the territorial structure, distancing itself from the trade union pattern of confrontation, local protests, strikes and direct confrontation with the employers. With this strategy, the UGT was undeniably successful in the mining and metal-working areas in the north and in key sectors such as the railways, but it was unable to implant itself in the country's most industrial region, Catalonia. There it was seen as a remote, centralist organisation, at odds with a federal-style popular Catalan nationalism.[6] Furthermore, its hierarchical structure was incompatible with the large variety of labour traditions and local social relationships, and it did not have influential leaders capable of building a stable, efficient organisation around them. In Catalonia, the leading role in worker representation was played by the CNT.

The Confederación Nacional del Trabajo was undoubtedly the most important Spanish labour organisation in the first decades of the twentieth century. In its initial launch phase, in 1910–11, it claimed to have a membership of 26,000 workers from more than 100 associations, most of them based in Catalonia. But it was during the First World War, after several years of repression and underground activity, that the CNT became a mass trade union, with a meteoric growth that saw it go from the 100,000 registered affiliates in 1918 to the more than 700,000 workers who, it claimed, were represented in the congress held in the Teatro de la Comedia in Madrid at the end of 1919. More than half the delegates and

[6] Pere Gabriel, 'El ugetismo socialista catalán, 1888–1923', *Ayer*, 54 (2004), pp. 165–97.

adherents came from Catalonia, with a noteworthy intake from the Levant, Andalucía and Aragón and smaller delegations from the remaining regions. The construction of the anarcho-syndicalist structure was closely linked to the Great War, with the economic boom caused by Spanish neutrality, the transformation of production systems and labour relations, the growth of the cities, with a large intake of immigrant workers, and the appearance of a new generation of militants who had little to do with the world of traditional crafts. Among the latter were Ángel Pestaña, Salvador Seguí, Joan Peiró and Manuel Buenacasa, who disseminated their anarchist and libertarian ideas from the pages of *Tierra y Libertad* and *Solidaridad Obrera*, and young revolutionaries who were not averse to armed activism, such as Buenaventura Durruti, Joaquín Ascaso and Juan García Oliver.

At any event, there was a clear difference between, firstly, the leadership structure and propagandists related to the anarchist press, the athenaeums and lay schools, with little trade union experience, that kept theoretical concepts and revolutionary slogans alive; secondly, the militants who actually concerned themselves with the day-to-day struggle and the internal organisation of craft associations and *sindicatos únicos* (single unions), imposed since 1918; and, finally, the great majority of affiliates, workers unconcerned with doctrinal debates who paid their dues and joined labour disputes because they felt that this was the way to improve their salaries and working conditions. Deep down, the daily workings and political culture of the CNT workers were not so different from those of the socialist workers. Although the former advocated independent direct action against the employers, outside the legal framework in force, and the latter defended the discipline of the organisation and participation in arbitration committees, both shared, as Santos Juliá has noted, a rejection of politics, anti-parliamentarianism, the repudiation of social order and belief in the proletarian revolution as a fact that was both natural and inevitable.[7] This is why the history of relationships between the two main trade union structures was marked by mutual suspicion and acrimonious confrontations, but also by basic agreements and joint action. And it is also why it is easy to see why many workers' associations throughout Spanish territory changed their allegiance from one structure to the other, without generating many problems, and took joint action when conditions were favourable, as was the case in the second decade of the twentieth century.

At a time of a general increase in prices and large company profits, workers discovered the advantages of union organisation and constant

---

[7] Juliá, *Los socialistas en la política española, 1879–1982*.

pressure on employers to win salary increases and improve their lifestyles. As long as the economy kept growing, the employers were prepared to yield to the workers' demands in a bid to avoid any prolonged conflict. And the success of the early strikes, which were short, with the workers coming out on top, encouraged the spirit of association, 'societal zeal' in the words of Fernández Almagro, an 'atmosphere of discontent' which, said the interior minister in February 1918, could lead to 'an atmosphere likely to end in revolution'.

The winds of revolution were coming from Russia, where the Bolsheviks, who had put an end to the tsarist dynasty, were preparing to install a proletarian regime. According to Juan Díaz del Moral, news of the events in Russia caused a stir among the Spanish proletarian militants. In the cities and villages of Andalucía the clarion call was sent out by propagandists and leaders of the workers' movement in a bid to spread the enthusiasm and launch the struggle. He felt there were two elements that came together to feed 'this formidable groundswell': on the one hand, Russia, the 'evocative word', and on the other, the organisation as 'a well-tempered weapon'. He used the term '*Trienio bolchevista*' ('Bolshevik triennium') – an expression that has become famous in Spanish histor-iography – to refer to the most crucial period of strikes and social conflict between the early months of 1918 and the end of 1920. His comments gave a very clear picture of the fear and unease felt by employers and landowners, alarmed by the preaching of orators invoking the example of the 'red dawn' in the east and by the climate of insecurity caused by the burning of crops, sabotage and attacks on estates.[8] However, the concrete demands from workers' associations were in most cases limited to wage claims and improvements in working conditions.

The importance of this cycle of social conflicts was registered in the statistics of the Institute of Social Reforms. According to its calculations, the 306 strikes noted in 1917 rose to 463 in 1918, 895 in 1919 and 1,060 in 1920. From that moment, the trend was reversed. The conclusion of the war in Europe brought to an end the mirage of inflated profits, as prices fell, personnel levels were reduced and wages frozen. Strikes were intensi-fied and the initiative began to pass to the employers, now better organised, who frequently used the lock-out as their weapon to counter the attack of the trade unions and undermine their organisations. The governments of those years, which brought in major reforms such as the eight-hour day and which tried out conciliation formulas and modest attempts at negotiation, always ended up with the abusive deployment of the Civil Guard and the

[8] Juan Díaz del Moral, *Historia de las agitaciones campesinas andaluzas* (Madrid: Alianza, 1984), pp. 265–9.

army, repression of workers' organisations and the adoption of exceptional measures such as declaring a state of emergency or the suspension of constitutional guarantees, in force from 1919 to spring 1922.

And, during those years, if there was one place where confrontation was visible between the union power of the organised working class, employers' fear of the overturning of the established order, the authorities' concern over the spiral of strikes and social violence, and the presence of military uniforms in the streets, that place was undoubtedly Barcelona. A significant city and date, February 1919, the beginning of the strike in La Canadiense, 'a memorable event' according to the militant anarchist writer Diego Abad de Santillán, 'which demonstrated the combative spirit and resistance of the workers'.[9] The strike in this hydro-electric company, which supplied water and power to the city, began with a protest over the dismissal of some administrative staff and later spread to all the sections of the group. The city was blacked out, the economy was brought to a standstill and the CNT displayed a trade union might that impressed all who witnessed it, a hitherto unseen capacity for mobilisation. After a strike lasting forty-four days, the conflict ended with victory for the CNT. But the captain general of Catalonia, General Joaquín Milans del Bosch, refused to release his prisoners subject to martial law, one of the demands that the strikers had negotiated with the government. Once more the army, resolved to impose the harshness of martial law over any solution involving conciliation, was defying civil power.

The CNT reacted by calling a general strike. The more restrained viewpoints were overruled by groups favouring more radical action, which were prepared to employ violent confrontation and solutions of force. That moment saw 'the beginning of the inferno', in the words of Tuñón de Lara.[10] The military chiefs, outside the influence of the civilian authorities, created a repressive climate aimed at occupying the streets, closing down trade unions, arresting their leadership and blocking any type of negotiation, with the complicity of the employers and sectors of order. The most radical business-owners, leading figures in the Barcelona Employers' Federation, went on the offensive, and in the autumn they declared a lock-out that brought commerce and industry to a standstill for three months, until the end of January 1920, leaving several hundred thousand workers idle. Furthermore, they financed private security corps, some of which turned into armed gangs; they organised non-revolutionary workers' associations, the so-called *Sindicato Libre*, with Carlist leanings,

---

[9] Diego Abad de Santillán, *Alfonso XIII, la II República, Franco* (Madrid: Júcar, 1979), p. 81.
[10] Tuñón de Lara, *Poder y sociedad en España, 1900–1931*.

which declared outright war on the CNT; and they resurrected the traditional *somatén*, a network of neighbourhood self-defence forces which came to consist of more than 60,000 armed men.

Employer lock-outs, the setting up of civic guards, and the violent practices of the trade unions were also experienced in other Spanish cities. But the intensity of the violence and the growing number of shootings, bombings and assaults meant that all eyes turned to what was happening in Barcelona. The most violent period coincided with the arrival of General Severiano Martínez Anido, the civil governor of Barcelona from November 1920 to October 1922, remembered for the brutality of his repressive measures and for having implemented what was known as the *ley de fugas*, the direct shooting of prisoners under the pretext of an escape attempt. The wave of violence, on both sides, did not come to an end until the *coup d'état* of Primo de Rivera. Fernando del Rey Reguillo has calculated that, in the province of Barcelona alone, there was a total of 981 victims of labour-related violence between 1917 and 1923, 267 of whom died.[11] Many of them were anarcho-syndicalist militants and leaders, and many more were employers, supervisors, gunmen and anti-union workers. The extreme harshness of the repression and the intervention of paramilitary groups under the auspices of the employers do nothing to lessen the CNT's responsibility in the spiral of violence during those years. The most extreme anarchists replaced the more moderate leaders and fostered social war, the action of the 'kings of the working-class pistol', often common murderers and assailants from the criminal class, with nothing heroic or commendably militant about them.

It is hardly surprising that in September 1923 the *coup d'état* of Primo de Rivera, proclaimed in Barcelona, was welcomed with considerable satisfaction and relief by the employers, owners and conservative sectors of Catalonia and the rest of Spain, who for some time had been pining for a return to order and the removal of the spectre of Bolshevism, a nightmare that had lasted for six years. It did not matter that this longed-for 'social peace' was imposed by the bayonet.

From the Annual disaster to the *coup d'état*

Between 1917 and 1923, Spanish governments had to face several challenges, too many perhaps to be able to formulate a firm political plan and devote themselves to anything other than the mere survival of the regime,

[11] Fernando del Rey Reguillo, 'El empresario, el sindicalista y el miedo', in Rafael Cruz and Manuel Pérez Ledesma (eds.), *Cultura y movilización en la España contemporánea* (Madrid: Alianza, 1997), pp. 235–72.

which was being constantly eroded by military intervention, social conflicts, regionalist demands, anti-parliamentary criticisms from both the left and right wings, and the fragmentation of the dynastic parties. García Prieto's 'concentration' government lasted four months, right up to the day the Cortes opened after the February 1918 elections had left a Parliament split into factions. To the right of the conservatives were the followers of Maura and de la Cierva; around the Liberals were the democrats and the followers of Santiago Alba and Ortega y Gasset. Facing them were twenty Catalan nationalist deputies, a similar number of reformists and republicans, eight Carlists, seven Basque nationalists and six socialists. It was a highly complex situation, leaving little room for any of these groups to be able to govern with any guarantee.

The intervention of Alfonso XIII broke this deadlock with the formula of a 'national' government headed by Maura, with Dato, Romanones, García Prieto, Alba and Cambó around him as ministers. It was an emergency solution that lifted the hopes of some sectors. Members of La Lliga (Catalan nationalists) entered the Madrid government, and the faction leaders laid aside their differences with legislative initiatives such as the Civil Service Act, which put an end to the status of the *cesante* (a laid-off government employee), or the reform of parliamentary regulations, which reduced legislative obstructions by limiting the time for parliamentary debates and procedures, the famous 'guillotine'. But this national government only lasted six months, until internal differences made it impossible to carry on.

The governments that followed, sustained by just one parliamentary group, occasionally backed by a particular faction, weakened the political system even more. First there was the Liberal government of García Prieto, lasting barely a month; then, from December 1918 to April 1919, Romanones, who had to face the explosive social situation in Barcelona over the La Canadiense strike and the autonomist movements that had been stirred up in Catalonia, the Basque Country and in Galicia by the expectations created all over Europe by the end of the war and the triumph of the principle of nationhood as declared by President Woodrow Wilson. There were too many problems at once. Romanones was succeeded by Maura for three months, supported only by the most authoritarian faction headed by de la Cierva. Then came the conservative governments of Joaquín Sánchez de Toca, from July to December 1919; Manuel Allendesalazar, until May 1920; and Eduardo Dato, the theoretical leader of parliamentary conservatism, whose government came to a tragic end on 8 March 1921, when three anarchists gunned him down in the Plaza de la Independencia in Madrid for having passed the *ley de fugas*. After this assassination, the king once again called on Allendesalazar, the prime minister who was to be held responsible for the military disaster at Annual, to form a government.

In the history of colonial warfare, there are plenty of examples of military disaster suffered by the European powers, such as the setbacks suffered by the British at Khartoum and in South Africa, or the Italians in Abyssinia, but as Sebastian Balfour has noted, none of these disasters was so devastating or had such deep national repercussions as the debacle suffered by the Spanish army in North Africa in the summer of 1921.[12] In the spring of that year the French, after a pause made necessary by the Great War, resumed their activity in Morocco, which revived Spanish plans for military intervention. The conservative governments of Maura and Sánchez de Toca ordered the high commissioner, General Dámaso Berenguer, to begin operations against the tribes that were not subject to his authority, an ambitious plan which aimed to complete the military occupation of the entire protectorate. Successful early ventures, due in part to the deployment of native troops and elite units such as the Legion, formed in 1920, encouraged General Manuel Fernández Silvestre – a personal friend of Alfonso XIII, famous for his despotic nature and temerity – to undertake an offensive from Melilla to Alhucemas. It was a risky campaign for the size of the terrain, the shortage of arms and supplies, and their ignorance of the enemy. He was up against Abd-el-Krim, the chief of the Beni Urriaguel tribe, a former employee of the colonial administration, who had toured the mountains of the region to recruit the tribesmen and organise a *harka* against Spanish rule.

The swift advance of the troops brought Silvestre to the military camp at Annual, an exposed position that ended up by turning into a rat-trap, target-shooting practice for the rifles of the Rif tribesmen firing from the nearby hills. On 21 July, cut off and with no defences, the general decided to begin a withdrawal, in fact a headlong flight which ended in general panic and absolute chaos, leaving corpses strewn along the more than 100 kilometres that separated Annual and the walls of Melilla. The indigenous troops deserted and discipline fell to pieces. The disaster was completed on 9 August with the surrender of General Felipe Navarro and the massacre of his troops on Mount Arruit.

The overwhelming victory of Abd-el-Krim, who with barely 4,000 warriors virtually managed to exterminate a modern army of 15,000 men, over time became a mythical reference for the leaders of anti-colonial movements all over the world. Spain did not take long to react, particularly when people first learnt of the real dimension of the disaster, the

[12] Sebastian Balfour, *The End of the Spanish Empire, 1898–1923* (Oxford University Press, 1997).

Figure 3 In 1921, Spanish troops faced Moroccan political and military leader Abd-el-Krim, who, with barely 4,000 warriors, virtually exterminated a modern army of 15,000 men. It was the most bloody and humiliating tragedy ever suffered by the Spanish army overseas. © Agencia EFE

horror stories of the soldiers who survived and the shame of the 10,000 unburied bodies, among them Silvestre, strewn around Annual, Dar Drius, Mount Arruit, Zeluan or Nador, names that would forever be associated with the most bloody and humiliating tragedy ever suffered by the Spanish army overseas. In the autumn, the first witnesses to return to the scene found the air charged 'with foulness and tragedy' and trod 'macabre landscapes of implausible reality'. 'Dante had never seen anything like this', said Fernández Almagro.[13] The harrowing account by Ramón J. Sender in *Imán* described the flight as an awesome nightmare that lifted the veil on the horrors of war: 'It is war. This is war. The flag on the school flagpole, the "*Marcha Real*", history, defence of the nation, the deputy's speech and the *zarzuela* of the moment. All that, surrounded by medals, brings this. If that is the Fatherland, this is war: a man fleeing among mutilated, desecrated corpses, his feet destroyed by the stones and his head by bullets.'[14]

The hostile attitude towards the war in Morocco from certain sectors of the public, visible from 1909 onwards, was present in protest campaigns from the workers' movement, in numerous rallies and demonstrations, and in nearly all the demands made on May Day. The draft-dodging percentages were overwhelming: 11% in 1910, 20% in 1915 and 17% in 1920. That year Romanones acknowledged that the phenomenon could not be explained simply by emigration, that the fundamental cause was of 'an ethical nature', the injustice and inequality that people perceived in the barracks, 'an underlying discontent, a tendency towards rebellion that was not favourable for military discipline and the security of the state'.[15]

And yet, as Pablo de la La Porte pointed out, the magnitude of the Annual disaster, with its accounts of the cruelty and savagery of the Rifs, engendered a wave of patriotism among the Spanish people that had never been seen before.[16] In the autumn of 1921, Maura, prime minister of the government that had replaced Allendesalazar's after the *Desastre*, had no problem in sending reinforcements across the strait, including *cuota* recruits, who usually served only in the peninsula. Large crowds assembled to see the troops off, and many people donated money. But it was a mirage that lasted only a few months. The lost positions were not recaptured, the liberation of prisoners was delayed for almost two years, and promises of an early end to the conflict came to naught. Morocco,

---

[13] Fernández Almagro, *Historia del reinado de D. Alfonso XIII*, vol. II, p. 90.
[14] Ramón J. Sender, *Imán* (Barcelona: Destino, 1994).
[15] Conde de Romanones, *El Ejército y la política* (Madrid: Renacimiento, 1920), p. 147.
[16] Pablo La Porte, 'Marruecos y la crisis de la Restauración, 1917–1923', *Ayer*, 63 (2006), pp. 53–74.

stated Besteiro in Parliament, warranted 'not one drop of blood from a son of Spain'. As far as the public was concerned, once the brouhaha was over, the colonial venture benefited only 'the officers and the contractors', as one of Arturo Barea's characters said in *La forja de un rebelde*.[17] One government followed another in Madrid, with José Sánchez Guerra's Conservative administration in March 1922, and then García Prieto's Liberal coalition in December the same year, and 'each one left the Moroccan case to his successor, as if it were a will awaiting probate'.

Debate raged on the responsibilities for the Annual disaster during this period, the last of the Restoration political system, and the question had yet to be resolved in September 1923 when the *coup d'état* came. Initially, Maura's government limited itself to talking about military blame and so commissioned an official report from General Juan Picasso, who was a model of impeccable thoroughness and efficiency. But towards the end of October 1921, when the Cortes opened, the opposition also demanded to talk about political responsibilities, and debate followed debate on this issue. What became apparent was military incompetence, the principal cause of the disaster, and also officer absenteeism, the corruption and inefficiency that reigned in the Africa Army, and the enormous hole that its maintenance was leaving in the public purse. And the protests went further, to the government and also the monarch. In this respect, there were the famous speeches of the socialist Indalecio Prieto, denouncing the 'heaps of human rubble' strewn over Moroccan soil, thousands of corpses 'which it seems have assembled around the base of the throne demanding justice'.[18] Public criticism of the role played by the king, a firm defender of colonial interventionism, notably impaired his prestige and undermined even more the foundations of the regime, widening the breach that separated it from a major sector of society.

To the left were the socialists who, after the defeat of the 1917 general strike, had stopped believing in the possibility of reform of the Restoration system. This posture had been reinforced following strenuous debate over the nature of the Bolshevik revolution and possible membership of the Third International. This internal controversy gave rise to a split by one section of the Juventudes Socialistas (Socialist Youth) and the creation in 1920 of the Spanish Communist Party. The PSOE and UGT still defined themselves as revolutionary organisations, but they believed that the revolution would come via evolution, a fruit ripened by a future crisis in the capitalist economic system. For this reason they declared that they

---

[17] Arturo Barea, *La forja de un rebelde*, II, *La Ruta* (Madrid: Turner, 1977).
[18] Indalecio Prieto, *Con el Rey o contra el Rey: guerra de Marruecos (1ª parte). Crónicas, artículos y discursos sobre la campaña africana de 1921* (Barcelona: Planeta, 1980).

were interested only in issues to do with workers' problems, and that they were indifferent as regards political change and the future of the parliamentary regime, as proved by their passive reaction to the military coup in September 1923.

The socialists' refusal to collaborate with the bourgeois parties was closely linked to the drift of Melquíades Álvarez's reformists to the fringes of the Liberal Party and the decay of historical republicanism, which had won ten seats in the 1920 elections. The republicans continued to believe that, rather than a gradual transition of liberalism to democracy, the only way to attain power was through insurrection involving members of the military committed to the cause. Although the crisis caused by the debate over responsibilities for the Annual disaster had given a second wind to Parliament, this revitalisation did not change the perception held by a majority of the public that it was an institution that had been discredited by electoral fraud, constant changes of government and disputes over access to power of the various factions and families that populated the ranks of the traditional dynastic parties. This opinion was neatly summed up by Antonio Machado in 1922: 'The elements that form the tableau depicting the monarchy are all old politicians ... A constant stream of cliques and coteries of various persuasions who, bowl in hand, await their turn at the palace gate. All of them are prisoners of their old age, and they believe in the inevitability of the collapse of Spain, but they all hope to satisfy once more their mercenary ambitions.' The regime was in ruins, under attack from the outside and undermined from within, and nobody supported it when Primo de Rivera overthrew it in September 1923. The poet then summed it up with these words: 'Spain is on all fours. Will she get up? She'll probably find the posture comfortable and stay down for a long time.'[19]

Against the passive reaction of the republicans, socialists and workers' organisations to the military coup, right-wingers and the sectors 'of order' showed that they were prepared to support it from the very start. The rejection of liberalism was a long-standing hallmark of Carlists and extremists, who had never accepted the regime constructed by Cánovas. But in the years following the Great War, as Fernando del Rey has explained, new conservative currents had come to the fore, evolving from the discrediting of parliamentarianism to ideas that were increasingly closer to authoritarian radicalism.[20] A leading sector of these forces were

---

[19] Machado, *Prosas completas, 1893–1936*, pp. 1221 and 1289.

[20] Fernando del Rey Reguillo, 'Las voces del antiparlamentarismo conservador', in Mercedes Cabrera (ed.), *Con luz y taquígrafos: el Parlamento en la Restauración (1913–1923)* (Madrid: Taurus, 1998), pp. 273–328.

the 'Maurists' (followers of Maura), who openly opposed left-wing organ-
isations, with new leading lights such as José Calvo Sotelo and Antonio
Goicoechea, who were increasingly leaning towards the extreme right.
Their defence of clericalism, dating from Spain's devotion to the Sacred
Heart of Jesus in 1919, brought them closer to the opinions of social
Catholicism, a reactionary movement against secularism and the dangers
of social revolution.

The political organisation of the Catholic movement arrived late,
embodied in 1922 with the founding of the Partido Social Popular. But
its strength lay in a broad network of associations that ran the gamut from
the Catholic Leagues and young people's and women's confessional
associations to workers' circles and agricultural trade unions, with little
support in the urban environment but widely accepted by rural smallholders. In 1920 the Confederación Nacional Católica Agraria had an
official membership of 52 federations, 5,000 unions and 600,000 affiliates.
It was a powerful dam built, as Severino Aznar, one of the Confederation's
most active propagandists acknowledged, to prevent 'the waters of
secularism, indifference and revolution from weakening, collapsing and
engulfing the old legacy of Spanish faith'. Following the message of its
motto, 'God, Fatherland and Agriculture', no possible harm could be
visited on the social Catholics by a regime such as Primo de Rivera's
which, through its most representative political institution, the Unión
Patriótica, would underline the principles of 'Nation, Church and King'.
Thus it was hardly surprising to see the support of the Catholic organisations and the Church hierarchy, clearly reactionary and anti-democratic,
for a dictatorship that would enable them to maintain their privileges and
recover their influence in the civil and cultural sphere.

Along with the traditionalists, Maurists and the Catholic sectors, there
were many other players and social organisations that welcomed, as
the author and diplomat Ramiro de Maeztu said in the spring of 1923,
the firm intervention of 'a handful of men who would be unyielding yet
capable'.[21] They included the nobility, employers' confederations and
professional associations, all of them disenchanted with the political
class, and well disposed towards a solution of a technical and corporative
nature, an 'iron-willed surgeon' with carte blanche to resolve the country's problems without going through unnecessary parliamentary procedure. Also included were the supporters of Spanish nationalism, who in
previous years had mobilised the trade and industrial circles in various
cities, the Castilian regional governments and cross-party coalitions such

---

[21] Ramiro de Maeztu, 'El millón de Larache', *El Sol*, 12 Mar. 1923.

as the Liga de Acción Monárquica, set up in the Basque Country, and the
Unión Monárquica Nacional, founded in Catalonia, against the Catalan
and Basque 'separatists'. Even Cambó's Lliga Regionalista, prepared to
leave aside its political claims in the hope of safeguarding economic
protectionism and recovering its social hegemony within the principality,
joined in.

And – naturally – the army did also. After Annual, the professional
officer class was obsessed with the feeling of revenge, with a deep hostility
towards the state and increasingly open scorn for the alleged supremacy of
the civil institutions. Ortega y Gasset accurately pointed this out in comments written at the beginning of 1921, before the disaster, and published
later in *España invertebrada*: 'Resentment and antipathy brewed towards
all other social classes among the armed forces, and their organisation
became ever more tightly sealed, less porous to the society that surrounded it. That's when the army started to live – in ideas, objectives,
feelings – on its own resources.' Ortega felt that the colonial venture in
Morocco had turned 'the unfocused soul of our army into a closed fist,
morally ready for attack. From that moment on, the armed forces have
been a loaded rifle with no target to shoot at.' The inevitable consequence
of that process was that the army would turn against the nation and aspire
to conquer it: 'How can we prevent their thirst for campaigning from
being repressed, and they refuse to take some prime minister as if he were
a hill?'[22]

First it was Maura's government of concentration that fell, in March
1922, pressured by the corporative demands of the Juntas de Defensa,
officially dissolved but which continued running under the name of
Information Commissions. Then, the end of the year saw the resignation
of the cabinet led by José Sánchez, who had promoted the trial of the
officers denounced in the Picasso Report for being reckless or negligent,
but no agreement was reached in Parliament as to the extent of political
responsibilities. The unease of the high command increased with the
coming to power of the Liberal coalition led by García Prieto, especially
when the minister of state, Santiago Alba, appointed a civilian as high
commissioner for Morocco, and stated his intention to cut costs and scale
down the army. Tension grew even further in the summer of 1923.
Fighting intensified and more reinforcements were sent. On 23 August
a group of recruits mutinied in the port of Málaga, refusing to be transferred to Melilla. The death penalty imposed on the corporal accused of
heading the mutiny was revoked by the government, a decision which the

military authorities considered to be an intolerable slight and proof of the weakness of civil power.

In the summer of 1923, various military plots were hatched. The most visible of these was led by General Francisco Aguilera, another was devised by a group of generals with connections to the Royal Palace and a third was being prepared by officers in the Barcelona garrison. This last one involved Miguel Primo de Rivera, the captain general of Catalonia. Throughout the spring he had seen how social violence was escalating in the streets of Barcelona and the number of terrorist attacks was increasing without the government allowing him to declare a state of emergency. During the summer he attended the assembly of the Nationalist Triple Alliance, an initiative of Acció Catalana, the radical splinter group from the Lliga that supported the right to self-determination. On 11 September, the *Diada* (Catalan national holiday, commemorating the fall of Barcelona during the War of the Spanish Succession in 1714) was attended by the Catalan independence movement together with representatives from the Basque Nationalist Communion and the Galician Nationalist Brotherhood. It was a genuine anti-Spanish nationalist provocation. As if that were not enough, one week later the Parliamentary Responsibilities Commission was due to present its report to the chamber before the opening of the Cortes, set for 1 October. But they were not to open. In the early hours of 13 September Primo de Rivera declared a state of emergency in the four provinces of Catalonia. The *coup d'état* was under way. The Fatherland would finally be rid of 'professional politicians, men who for one reason or another provide us with a set of misfortunes and immorality that began in '98 and threaten Spain with an imminent tragic and dishonourable end'.[23]

The Restoration: a fledgling democracy?

Did Primo de Rivera kill off a sick body, as he himself saw it, or did he strangle a newborn baby? This was the imagery used by Raymond Carr to declare that the coup against the parliamentary system came just when the progressive liberals who made up the last government were managing the transition from oligarchy to democracy.[24] Shlomo Ben-Ami shares this opinion. Both authors see the programme of reforms under García Prieto as being proof that all was not lost for the Restoration regime in 1923; that it was the clearest evidence that the crisis of the liberal system did not

[23] 'Al país y al ejército españoles', proclamation by Miguel Primo De Rivera, *La Vanguardia*, 13 Sep. 1923.
[24] Raymond Carr, *Spain, 1808–1939* (Oxford University Press, 1966).

inevitably lead to its decomposition and final destruction; that, in short, despite the magnitude of the problems and conflicts that existed, there was a way to democracy, a clear path for a constitutionally approved gradual transition.[25]

Indeed, García Prieto's Liberal government had come to power, in December 1922, with an ambitious programme packed with progressive promises of a democratic nature. Its principal promoter was Santiago Alba, a sympathiser of Melquíades Álvarez's reformists, who at last managed to form part of a monarchist government. Among the measures proposed by the government were the promotion of education and public works, a proportional tax system, a reduction of the treasury deficit, agricultural legislation, new electoral rules, the democratisation of the Senate and the broadening of municipal autonomy. There were also other proposals that were particularly controversial, such as a revision of Article 11 of the Constitution – concerning the official status of Catholicism as the state religion; the first steps towards a new social policy, based on recognition of the trade unions and compulsory negotiation of labour disputes; and the reinforcing of civil power over the army, with a peace-making policy in Morocco, a reduction in military costs and a drive to set up a parliamentary commission to examine who was responsible for the Annual disaster.

The historians Miguel Martorell and Fernando del Rey claim that these 'symptoms of deepening democracy' show that 'no door was ever fully closed'. The Liberal government was put down 'just when it was displaying a more pluralist facade, when public opinion was beginning to perceive a more responsible attitude'. In their opinion, had it not been overthrown by force, the liberal system's political culture of transaction and understanding 'might well have been the breeding ground for a gradual establishing of full democracy with no upheavals or exclusions', a liberal regime that 'could have saved Spain from the brutal confrontations in the 1930s that developed into a bloody civil war and an equally cruel dictatorship under Franco'.[26]

And del Rey, together with Mercedes Cabrera, has suggested a new interpretation of the crisis of the Restoration regime, placing it among the moderately optimistic viewpoints that reject the predominant theories of the failure of the liberal state, the damning regenerationist legacy that came to place the blame 'for the impossible coexistence within a republican

---

[25] Shlomo Ben-Ami, *La dictadura de Primo de Rivera, 1923–1930* (Barcelona: Planeta, 1983).

[26] Miguel Martorell and Fernando del Rey Reguillo, 'El parlamentarismo liberal y sus impugnadores', *Ayer*, 63 (2006), pp. 23–52.

context and the looming war' on the past. Del Rey and Cabrera are in no doubt that economic interests did have a part to play in politics, but not structurally, in terms of class domination exclusively. In their opinion, it was a question not of a monolithic oligarchy, a 'power block' with no cracks, but an 'extraordinarily complex jigsaw puzzle' that was constantly changing and variable throughout the whole period. In the final years of the Restoration, Parliament not only did not lose its powers: it even reinforced them. And the governments, despite all the problems and conflicts, tried to keep politics above pressures exerted by certain regional bourgeoisies, large industrial and agricultural groups, a section of the army, the radical workers' movement and the republican and socialist opposition, with flaws and limitations that could not be ascribed solely to the perverseness of the regime.[27]

In general, the historians of this period, writing from widely divergent viewpoints, have in recent years presented an analysis of the Restoration that is less simplistic and deterministic than the views that have prevailed until recently. Assessments such as those presented by María Ángeles Barrio, Manuel Suárez Cortina and Javier Moreno Luzón, among others, have emphasised the complexity of factors governing the final crisis of the regime, just one more episode in the crisis of the European liberal states between the wars, with shared general characteristics and unique features specific to the Spanish case.[28]

However, many experts still doubt whether there was any potential for progress towards democracy within the Restoration state. They feel that the gap between proposals and achievements of the final Liberal government was further proof of the political system's inability to escape the process of decomposition in which it found itself in 1923. Javier Tusell argues, for example, that the 23 April elections that gave the liberal groups their parliamentary majority were no different to previous ones, with no glimmer of electoral regeneration in a poll with a high abstention rate and no fewer than 145 uncontested seats, under the auspices of the famous Article 29. The government gave no impression of unity, with personal internal divisions, mini-crises and constant cabinet reshuffles. Nor did it keep its promises of reform, and it was incapable of keeping the dangers that beset the parliamentary regime at bay. What there was in Spain 'was

[27] Mercedes Cabrera and Fernando del Rey Reguillo, 'De la oligarquía y el caciquismo a la política de intereses: por una relectura de la Restauración', in Manuel Suárez Cortina (ed.), *Las máscaras de la libertad: el liberalismo español 1808–1950* (Madrid: Marcial Pons, 2003), pp. 289–325.
[28] María Ángeles Barrio Alonso, *La modernización de España (1917–1939): política y sociedad* (Madrid: Síntesis, 2004); Javier Moreno Luzón (ed.), *Alfonso XIII: un político en el trono* (Madrid: Marcial Pons, 2003).

not a democracy in crisis, nor even the dawning of a new political system, but a growing sense of being in a vacuum'.[29]

Meanwhile, María Teresa González Calbet has remarked on the government's ineffectiveness and how door after door was being slammed on García Prieto's government's proposals. First it was the Church, which halted the planned reform of Article 11 of the Constitution. Then it was their speculative initiatives regarding social intervention and employment conciliation, boycotted by the employers' organisations and military authorities. And, in particular, the army, with the backing of the king, opposed the shrinking of its powers in the matter of public order as well as a change of policy in the protectorate in Morocco, by plotting openly and publicly, with the government just looking on. In González Calbet's opinion, at this stage, there was no political party, either on the right or the left, that was capable of unblocking the system and undertaking a reform from within.[30]

Teresa Carnero Arbat, for her part, does not feel that the regime overthrown by the *coup d'état* could be seen as being a 'fledgling' democracy either. What disappeared in 1923 was 'a doctrinaire parliamentary democracy' which in addition was reinforced 'with new regressive profiles as regards its non-democratic originating features'. She is referring to the persistent lack of concern of the political elite in putting an end to electoral fraud, its inability to turn the dynastic parties into mass organisations and government interference in parliamentary life, which was evident particularly in the light of the atmosphere of war present in Europe, when for a vast majority of the population the Cortes had ceased to have any legitimacy. This loss of credibility was accentuated by the brevity of parliamentary sessions, the repeated suspending of constitutional guarantees as a remedy, and the abuse of government decrees. Anyone who tried to restore parliamentary power, such as the reformist deputy José Manuel Pedregal, a minister in the last Liberal government, was met with nothing but general repudiation and the door being held open for his resignation: 'Thus, there was no movement whatsoever in the supply of democracy, despite the perceptible increase in demand.'[31]

Carnero does not disregard the responsibility of the radicalisation of the workers' left wing, the destabilising impact of social conflict in a context dominated by the turbulence over events in Russia. But, in her opinion,

[29] Javier Tusell, *Historia de España: la edad contemporánea* (Madrid: Taurus, 2002).
[30] María Teresa González Calbet, *La dictadura de Primo de Rivera: el Directorio Militar* (Madrid: Ediciones El Arquero, 1987).
[31] María Teresa Carnero Arbat, 'Política sin democracia en España: 1874–1923', *Revista de Occidente*, 83 (1988), pp. 43–58.

the revolutionary spiral was not the most important socio-political problem for understanding the decline that led to Primo de Rivera's coup.
More significant was the regressive movement of those on the extreme
right of the political spectrum, those not forming part of the Conservative
Party founded by Cánovas, and therefore outside parliamentary politics,
who were willing to support the revolt that was being prepared by the
military.

The growing influence of authoritarian and anti-parliamentary attitudes was not a feature peculiar to the political culture of Spanish society
in the 1920s. It was a general phenomenon, evident all over Europe,
forming part of the general crisis affecting the liberal states between the
two world wars. All historians seem to be in agreement over this.
Paradoxically, the end of the Great War seemed to suggest otherwise.
As Mark Mazower has noted, the victory of the Allied powers and the
collapse of the Russian, Austro-Hungarian, German and Ottoman
empires brought representative parliamentary systems to the whole of
Europe. But the triumph of liberalism was short-lived. The impact of
the Russian revolution and the shadows of communist subversion spread
throughout the continent, and in just a few years political polarisation
forced democratic values into a corner. Although the threat of revolution
in 1918 and 1919 did not materialise, and any attempts were easily
squashed, anti-liberal and anti-democratic beliefs spread rapidly and
twenty years later the parliamentary governments that did survive were
few and far between. It was the age of authoritarian dictatorships, such as
Primo de Rivera's in Spain, and fascist regimes.[32]

Similarly, Eric Hobsbawm maintains that the right-wing reaction was a
response not to Bolshevism as such, but to all movements, particularly
those of the organised working class, that threatened the established social
order, which had been shaken up by the emergence of the society of the
masses. 'Parliamentary democracy was a weak plant growing on stony
ground.'[33] For this plant to grow on firm roots, what was needed was a
context of economic prosperity, a broad consensus on democratic values,
where citizens' votes went beyond national, ethnic or religious divisions,
and a willingness of social forces to negotiate, reach compromises and
deactivate internal conflicts. Juan José Linz adds two more conditions: the
absence of any crisis regarding the legitimacy of the state and the efforts of
the political players to defend democracy – 'the lack of will of political
leaders is an important part of history'. And this circumstance was absent

---

[32] Mark Mazower, *Dark Continent: Europe's Twentieth Century* (London: Penguin, 1999).
[33] Eric J. Hobsbawm, *Age of Extremes: The Short Twentieth Century, 1914–1991* (London:
      Random House, 1994).

from Restoration Spain as well. The governing elites failed to confront the challenges of social and economic modernisation, and they also failed to promote the reform of the institutions and the integration of most of the population into the system. Neither the political elites nor the head of state, the king, showed any interest in doing so.[34]

The figure of Alfonso XIII has generated a great deal of literature ranging from hagiography and justification to more or less balanced criticism or outright condemnation. However, most historians believe that his performance as sovereign and his constant political interventions were obstacles to a possible conversion of the regime into a representative democracy. The most relevant issue, in this respect, is not the direct role he might have played in the plotting of the *coup d'état* in 1923, whether or not he was aware of the managing of the conspiracy or whether he encouraged it with his public and private declarations or with his inaction at the decisive moments. The fundamental factor, says Mercedes Cabrera, is that he received Primo de Rivera's oath as president of the Directorate which immediately proceeded to suspend the Constitution. This decision tied in well with his authoritarian and anti-democratic beliefs.[35] From the beginning of his reign, Carolyn Boyd tells us, he had constantly furthered the notion of the weakness of civil power and the military's readiness to intervene in politics.[36] What he had not thought when he counted on the army to safeguard the Crown was that the dictatorship that he inaugurated would not be a mere 'parenthesis' of circumstances, but the beginning of the irreversible liquidation of the constitutional monarchy.

---

[34] Juan José Linz, 'La crisis de las democracias', in Mercedes Cabrera, Santos Juliá and Pablo Martín Aceña (comps.), *Europa en crisis, 1919–1939* (Madrid: Pablo Iglesias, 1991), pp. 231–80.

[35] Mercedes Cabrera, 'El rey constitucional', in Moreno Luzón (ed.), *Alfonso XIII: un político en el trono*, pp. 83–110.

[36] Carolyn P. Boyd, 'El rey-soldado: Alfonso XIII y el ejercito', in Moreno Luzón (ed.), *Alfonso XIII: un político en el trono*, pp. 213–38.

4   The Primo de Rivera years

On 13 September 1923, Miguel Primo de Rivera, the captain general of Catalonia, led a military uprising to put an end to the constitutional government; he came to power with the blessing of the king, the support of the army as well as employers' and Catholic organisations, and the indifference and apathy of most of the population. In the early stages, up to the spring of 1924, the dictator aimed to quash public disorder, the threat of regional nationalism, the affair of the 'responsibility' for the Morocco disaster and the blight of *caciquismo*, which were, in his view, the main evils affecting Spain. His was a firm hand in an iron glove.

From then on, exceptional measures implemented by decree gave way to a process of institutionalisation. If the regime wanted to survive, it had to tackle social and economic problems and embark on the mobilisation of its social support, basically the *somatén* and the Unión Patriótica. In the autumn of 1925, capitalising on the success of the military campaign in Morocco, the dictator began thinking of a political solution that would give his regime legitimacy and stability. Before the year was out, the Military Directorate gave way to a civilian-style government that promoted administrative reforms and legislation of a social nature that played a big part in reducing labour conflicts. The summer of 1926 saw the beginning of a plan to set up a corporate parliament, the National Assembly, which opened its doors a year later with the mission of drawing up a new constitution.

But it was too late. From the end of 1928, Primo de Rivera began losing support at the same time as the list of his enemies started to swell. The opposition of part of the army, student unrest, the series of plots and conspiracies, the disaffection of the employers and the UGT, the distancing of the king, and the organisation of political opposition in the form of republicanism caused the decomposition of the regime and the isolation of the dictator, and he was forced to resign in January 1930. Alfonso XIII's hope of closing a seven-year parenthesis and returning to the previous situation as if nothing had happened was an illusion which was to last barely a year. The fate of the monarchy was linked to that of the dictatorship that he had indulged and approved.

The military arm

At half past one in the morning of 13 September 1923 the *Capitanía General* contacted the newsdesks of all the newspapers in Barcelona by telephone. Primo de Rivera wished to announce an 'extremely important' document to the press. One hour later reporters filled the office of the dictator. The general, with a resolute air, amiable but with a solemn voice, handed over some leaflets with the request – or the order – that they be inserted in all the newspapers. The manifesto, directed to 'the country and the army', declared that the time had come to save the Fatherland, to launch 'on behalf of Spain and the king' a mobilisation that had been demanded by the 'rational population'. Someone had to put an end to the 'social indiscipline' created by murders, terrorist attacks, the impunity for those disseminating communist propaganda, the effrontery of separatism and the 'despicable political intrigues' that used 'the Morocco tragedy' as a justification. In other words, the country faced a set of 'disgraceful and shameful' situations that needed to be 'remedied swiftly and radically'. To achieve this, and until the country could provide 'men who were upright, wise, industrious and honest', a 'temporary military directorate' was to be set up in Madrid, charged with the running of the institutions and maintenance of public order, a 'peace' based on 'healthy action and fair punishment'. Military personnel committed to the movement resolved to avoid the 'spilling of blood', convinced that 'no clean, pure or patriotic blood will be against us'. However, he did announce 'that faith in the ideal and the survival instinct of our regime will lead us to be extremely strict with those that fight it'.[1]

At three in the morning, when there were still stragglers on the Ramblas, several military pickets took over telegraph and telephone buildings. Two hours later, when it was still dark, troops spread out through the streets of Barcelona and proceeded to display, as stipulated by the regulations, the decree that declared a state of emergency in the four provinces of Catalonia. During the day that followed, the rebel captain general attended the opening of the International Furniture Exhibition as if nothing had happened. That night he was seen off at the station by a crowd cheering Spain and the army. He was on his way to Madrid to receive from the king the request to form a new government. And thus, as Manuel Rubio Cabeza said in his account of the dictatorship, was solemnised 'the triumph of the military arm'.[2]

---

[1] 'Al país y al ejército españoles', proclamation by Miguel Primo de Rivera, *La Vanguardia*, 13 Sep. 1923.

[2] Manuel Rubio Cabeza, *Crónica de la Dictadura de Primo de Rivera* (Madrid: Sarpe, 1986), p. 20.

A few months later, Unamuno wrote that Primo de Rivera's coup was more of a 'push' than a putsch. In fact, his action was following the classic example of the military *pronunciamientos* of the nineteenth century. The commander of a unit, claiming to be the spokesman of the will of the nation, would take up arms against the civil power in the hope that his rebellious gesture would be followed by the rest of the army and the civil forces. But unlike previous uprisings, as Eduardo González Calleja has pointed out, the September 1923 action was the first corporate intervention of the army, which had no intention of ceding power to a party or political leader, instead planning the construction of a military regime.[3]

Miguel Primo de Rivera was 53 at the time. His professional career was mapped by his family's military and aristocratic roots and by his war record in colonial conflicts. A lieutenant in the Melilla campaign in 1893, with swift promotions to captain and major after his service in Cuba and the Philippines, he became a colonel in the 1909 operations, general in 1911 and lieutenant general in 1919. On the death of his uncle, General Fernando Primo de Rivera, he inherited the title of Marquis of Estella. In subsequent years he served in the captain general's headquarters in Valencia, Madrid and Barcelona, where he headed the insurrection that put an end to the last Liberal government of the monarchy. His calculated ambiguity enabled him to evade any confrontation between *junteros* (supporters of a junta) and *Africanistas* and offer himself as a stopgap solution for the military commanders who were plotting against the regime.

In essence, when he published his manifesto, Primo de Rivera could only count on the support of the military governor of Zaragoza, General José Sanjurjo, and the circle of generals close to the court, the so-called Madrid *cuadrilátero*. The rest of the captains general and military governors did not support the rebellion, but they were not prepared to confront their brothers-in-arms either. In the crucial hours of 13 to 14 September the uprising clearly benefited from the abstention of most of the army, from the weakness of the government, confused and hesitant, from the apathy of the public and, above all, from the steps taken by the king. These last included, firstly, his deliberate delay in returning from San Sebastián to Madrid; then his decision, on the morning of 14 September, to consult his military advisers before taking any steps, which provoked the resignation of García Prieto; and finally the voluntary handing over of power to Primo de Rivera, even when he declared, after being sworn in as prime minister, that he had no intention of forming a civil government, more or less abiding by the Constitution, but a Military Directorate.

---

[3] Eduardo González Calleja, *La España de Primo de Rivera: la modernización autoritaria* (Madrid: Alianza, 2005).

Hardly any objections were raised. The firm backing of the employers' organisations, the Chambers of Commerce and Industry, farmers' associations and Catholic sectors was to be expected, but not the silence of the dynastic parties and the apathy of the republicans, waiting to see the true intentions of the rebellion, which contrasted with the open support, albeit with internal divisions, shown by the Maurists, the traditionalists, the Lliga and the Partido Social Popular. The PSOE and UGT called for calm from their members and recommended that they take no part in 'sterile movements' such as the tentative outbreaks of protest encouraged by the CNT and the communists. Primo de Rivera had threatened the use of force against any attempt at opposition. But he did not need to. As Arturo Barea wrote, 'the man in the street was spellbound by what was happening, like a chicken looking at a piece of chalk; and when he tried to recover his balance, events had passed him by: the government had resigned, some of its members had fled abroad, the king had given his approval to a *fait accompli* and Spain had a new government called the Directorate'.[4]

In his first declarations the dictator repeated that his sole purpose was to carry out emergency surgery which would amount to a 'short-term promissory note', a 'brief parenthesis', as the *Gaceta* of 16 September said, 'in the constitutional progress of Spain, to re-establish it, with the country providing us with men uncontaminated by the vices that we attribute to politics, as soon we can provide them to Your Majesty so that normality can be resumed'. On 12 November, Melquíades Álvarez and the Count of Romanones, as Speakers of the Congress and the Senate respectively, went to visit the king to remind him that this 'parenthesis' could not be extended any longer. Article 32 of the Constitution clearly stipulated that the king had to convene the Cortes within three months of its dissolution. The written note that they handed to him emphasised that this article was the only one in the entire Constitution that, in referring to the person of the king, used the word 'obligation'. Annoyed by this visit, he replied coldly that this was no time for the Cortes or the Constitution but for imposing 'Peace and Order on the Country'. And he had no problem, two days later, in signing the royal decree that dismissed the two Speakers and dissolved the previous government's commissions. The official note from the Directorate stated that 'the country is no longer impressed by liberal and democratic play-acting. It wants order, work and economy.' The mask of legitimacy had finally disappeared.

---

[4] Barea, *La forja de un rebelde*, II, *La Ruta*, p. 255.

But at that time, both the king and the dictator were more interested in the preparations for the official visit to Italy, to be made between 19 and 24 November. In Rome, in an audience with the Pope, Alfonso XIII stated that if there was another crusade against the enemies of his country's sacrosanct religion, 'Spain and her faithful king under your mandate will never desert the place of honour that its glorious traditions have marked out for it for victory and the glory of the Cross.' Primo de Rivera praised Mussolini as 'an apostle of the campaign directed against the dissoluteness and anarchy that is about to begin in Europe'. Il Duce replied by displaying his optimism 'regarding the strength and duration of your government'. There was no need to worry about a handful of idle, miserable politicians: 'Try to last, day by day, month by month, year by year, as we have done and must continue to do. You also will endure, since your government responded to a need that was deeply felt by the best part of your people.' Back in Spain, with these words echoing in his ears, Primo de Rivera declared that 'the second part of our mission' had begun, 'for which it would be rash and absurd to fix a timetable'.[5]

The first part had begun on 14 September with the declaration of a state of emergency, in force throughout Spain until 15 May 1925. The Military Directorate was made up of eight generals and a rear admiral who represented the various wings of the armed forces and all the military regions, but in fact they had no powers. Primo de Rivera exercised total power as 'sole minister', aided by Severiano Martínez Anido as under-secretary of the interior and another general, Miguel Arlegui, as director general of public order. Crimes against the security and unity of the Fatherland were heard by military courts, constitutional guarantees were suspended and severe press censorship was imposed, banning criticism of the government and the Church, news on social conflicts, and comments on court judgements or the situation of the army in Morocco.

The repressive measures were particularly harsh on anarcho-syndicalists and communists. Most of the CNT centres were searched and closed down, and its leaders underwent arbitrary arrest and exile. The persecution of communist activists left the PCE with fewer than 500 militants throughout Spain. The nationalist parties were similarly affected. The royal decree of 18 September ordered the persecution of separatism. No flag other than the Spanish flag could be flown; in official acts, street name-plates and advertisements, the only language would be Castilian Spanish, and the same went for schools and liturgical services; and most of the cultural centres and self-employed professional associations were closed down. In

[5] Rubio Cabeza, *Crónica de la Dictadura de Primo de Rivera*, pp. 100–1.

the Basque Country the Partido Nacionalista Vasco (PNV) was outlawed, and all the *batzokis* (PNV social clubs) closed their doors. In Catalonia the repression was directed mainly against Estat Català and Acció Catalana, and they went underground. There was no tolerance whatsoever for those who openly or covertly acted against the unity of Spain. The dictator coined the motto of 'one Spain, great and indivisible', and went so far as to say in a rally that it was better to see the Fatherland 'red rather than broken'.

The centralism of the Military Directorate was constructed by the issuing of decrees. On 20 September 1923 the civil governors were replaced by the army. Ten days later town and city councils in Spain, more than 9,000 of them, were dissolved, to be occupied by associate members, chosen from the highest tax-payers, and in January 1924 it was the turn of the provincial governments, who left their powers in the hands of administrators. All these measures were justified as being part of a regenerationist programme that aimed to eradicate *caciquismo*, demolish the 'old politics' and rid the administration of vice and corruption. 'Clean-up operations' was how the newspaper *El Sol* benevolently described this. The same euphemism applied to the suppression of the Jury Court and all the municipal courts, and the disciplinary measures against public servants accused of absenteeism, corruption and anti-patriotism.

Deep down, the campaign of administrative ethics was a facade that hid the gradual institutionalisation of military control of civil society. The most obvious evidence of this was the figure of the government delegate. These were army officers, one for each judicial district, whose mission was to oversee the running of town and city councils, intervene in local problems and promote 'the currents of a new civic life'. In October 1923, 486 delegates were appointed, an extensive network that transmitted to towns and villages the spirit and letter of the guidelines that Primo de Rivera and Martínez Anido issued to the provincial governors. As well as monitoring administrations and public order, the delegates had an educational undertaking: to foster nationalist-type ceremonies and rituals and disseminate patriotic values.

Another of the missions of the government delegates was to stimulate the local *somatén*, one of Primo de Rivera's personal endeavours and one of his first initiatives. The royal decree of 17 September 1923 extended throughout Spain the *somatén*, a traditional Catalan institution that had served to mobilise 'people of order' during the harsh years of *pistolerismo* (the 'gun-law' period of the early 1920s). This was an armed militia that at certain times could be used as an auxiliary force for the police and army and which, secondly, would serve to 'organise law-abiding people', 'healthy' citizens prepared to collaborate with the authorities of the regime, under military supervision. In the spring of 1924 there were more than

100,000 *somatenistas* in Spain, a number that gradually increased until it was double that in 1928, when it began its decline. The *somatén* certainly never came to be the civil organisation that Primo de Rivera had hoped it would be. It did not gain the popular support that was expected and was relegated to supplementary duties of vigilance and policing, and to taking part in official parades and ceremonies, lending them an almost 'folksy' note. But in the early months of the dictatorship it seemed it could have been the seed of a mobilisation of the masses, the nucleus of the social support that Primo de Rivera needed to convert a temporary state of emergency into a stable and long-lasting authoritarian regime.

Unamuno accused the Directorate of being no longer an 'inter-regnum', an 'interim situation', a 'treaty' or a 'political armistice'. In his opinion, it was very clear what the final objective of the *'pronunciamiento* of itinerant generals' was. The initial proclamations were merely a smoke-screen: 'It was not about carrying out a cleaning-up revolution from the top; it was about trying to avoid the revolution that could be seen coming from below.' The regenerating promises of 'weeding out *caciquismo* and re-establishing authority' were no more than 'diversionary tactics, and a way of attracting poor deluded fools who dream of the horrors of communism and trade unionism'. In January 1924 Unamuno was exiled to Fuerteventura and dismissed as professor and vice-rector of the University of Salamanca. He was accompanied by Rodrigo Soriano, a republican politician and jour-nalist who had severely criticised the Directorate in the athenaeum in Madrid. The subsequent closure of the athenaeum and the news of the punishment imposed on Unamuno provoked the first protests of intel-lectuals against the regime. Ortega y Gasset, who had made no secret of his sympathy for Primo de Rivera's coup, soon went from his initial support to the concern and unease he felt with every new decree and official notice: 'In fact, I fear that the old system that is the butt of the Directorate's attacks is a very different entity to that which I wanted to see eliminated.' Writers such as Fernández Flórez – who had asked the 'discharged politicians' to take 'that great pile of copies of the Daily Parliamentary Proceedings' with them – gradually changed their attitude as 1924 progressed: 'As for the present . . . you know full well that silence has become liberal.'[6]

The process of institutionalisation of the regime gathered momentum in the spring of 1924. March saw the setting up of the National Economy Council, a corporate body that was charged with channelling the interests of

---

[6] Genoveva García Queipo De Llano, *Los intelectuales y la Dictadura de Primo de Rivera* (Madrid: Alianza, 1988).

pressure groups, regulating protection measures for the national economy and establishing the bases of a paternalistic interventionist policy. Social policy was put into the hands of the under-secretary of labour, Eduardo Aunós, a former deputy of La Lliga, who launched the Higher Labour, Commerce and Industry Council, finally integrating the Institute of Social Reforms into the Ministry of Labour. Its job was to regulate labour relations and develop social legislation through arbitration organisations and joint worker–employer committees that would put an end to strikes and social conflicts. The reform of the local and provincial administration was the responsibility of José Calvo Sotelo, a young lawyer from the Maurist ranks. The promulgation on 8 April of the Municipal Statute was the precursor of the Provincial Statute passed a year later. City councils and provincial governments won more financial independence and prerogatives which enabled them to improve their services and promote infrastructure and city planning. Their establishment was regulated by a mixed system of corporate election and universal suffrage which, in the case of the city councils, permitted men over 23 years old and women who were heads of family to vote.

But these elections were never held. The appointment of the provincial deputies and elected municipal councillors remained in the hands of the civil governors, who accumulated almost total power over the local corporations and absolute control over provincial politics. On 5 April 1924, after seven months of exclusively military rule, the Directorate published a note to announce the gradual separation of the posts of civil and military governor. The dictatorship was firmly entrenched, there were no serious public order problems and, moreover, the regime was preparing a political organisation that would provide all the men needed to fill a public administration: the Unión Patriótica.

Its precursor was the Unión Patriótica Castellana, an association set up by the leaders of social Catholicism, with roots among the owners of small and medium-sized farms in the Castilian provinces. Sections were being set up in many provinces of the interior between November 1923 and spring 1924. On 5 April, Primo de Rivera called on the government delegates to join forces in local initiatives in a major movement based on the principles of 'Religion, Fatherland and Monarchy'. It was to be a 'great party' which, under the name of Unión Patriótica would bring together Spaniards 'of good faith', following the hierarchical and organic line from the individual to the state via the family, the municipality and the province, the foundations of the Fatherland. During its first year of existence, the Unión Patriótica did not manage to establish a national structure, but very soon the new town and city councils and the demilitarised civil governments began to draw on Unión members from the local committees and boards. In the summer of 1924 the organisation claimed to have almost 2 million affiliates, who formed a bulwark to defend order, ownership and authority to ensure the continuity of the dictatorship.

The president of the Military Directorate could be satisfied with the result. In less than two years he had dealt with the problem of Catalonia, eradicating any manifestation of nationalism; social unrest, free from any revolutionary hazards, had been reduced to the lowest level for many years; and the basic institutions of the new regime were becoming consolidated with the help of the *somatén* and the Unión Patriótica. Admittedly, there was still the Morocco problem, one of the arguments used to justify the *coup d'état*. The situation had barely changed since then. In fact, it could be said to have worsened. Attacks by Abd-el-Krim's forces in the eastern zone of the protectorate had caused a great many losses among the Spanish troops, who were forced to redeploy around the main cities, Ceuta, Melilla, Tetuán and Larache, with the significant loss of the city of Chefchaouen in November 1924.

Buoyed by his successes, Abd-el-Krim decided to attack the north of the French protectorate, reaching the outskirts of Fez. This venture was to cost the Rifian warlord dear. The French authorities responded by sending reinforcements and beginning discussions with Spain to negotiate the conditions for a joint military campaign. Primo de Rivera, who had been undecided until then, was forced by events to abandon his policy of reducing troop strength and military expenditure. In July 1925, the two powers signed a military co-operation agreement that established a French offensive at the same time as a Spanish landing in the Bay of Alhucemas. On 6 September, after several days of firing on the tribal positions nearby, the Spanish units took the beach at La Cebadilla and began a swift advance inland. On 2 October they conquered Ajdir, Abd-el-Krim's capital, and a week later they joined up with the French columns in the souk at Telata. The rebel tribes surrendered one after the other, and the recently created 'Rif Republic' fell like a house of cards.

It was not until a few months later, in early spring 1926, that Abd-el-Krim surrendered to the French authorities and handed over the last enemy redoubts. In fact, the military operations continued until the summer of 1927, when the pacification of the entire protectorate, from Larache to the other side of Melilla, was completed. But in November 1925, when he returned from Morocco, Primo de Rivera was able to claim victory and almost certainly enjoy his moment of prestige and popularity. He said then that within a very short time Spain would see 'the coming to power of the Unión Patriótica'. On 2 December he notified the king of his intention to replace 'a military dictatorship with a civil and economic one, with a more suitable, yet no less rigorous, organisation'. Alfonso XIII replied that he was 'convinced of the need to continue the work of salvation in which the Directorate had made great strides'.

The Civilian Directorate

On 3 December 1925, Primo de Rivera reintroduced the concept of the Council of Ministers and appointed a civilian cabinet that operated basically unchanged until January 1930. This change was due to the dictator's wish to sideline the army and fill the main posts of the administration with politicians who could tackle problems 'of a purely civil or economic nature'. The government featured two heavyweights from the previous administrative structure, Eduardo Aunós and José Calvo Sotelo, with the labour and finance portfolios respectively, and a prominent engineer, the Count of Guadalhorce, in development. With strong connections in the industrial, financial and agricultural sectors, they ran the three departments responsible for spurring the economic development, public investment and social reforms required for consolidating the regime.

But the presence of experts and public servants in the government did not mean a change of direction or an opening up of the dictatorship. Executive power remained in the hands of Primo de Rivera, and he exercised it fully. Political problems were not handled by the Council of Ministers, but resolved directly by the dictator or his right-hand man, General Martínez Anido, who was at the same time deputy prime minister and minister of cabinet affairs, and it was he who dealt with questions of public order and appointed civil governors. There were two other high-ranking officers in the cabinet, the ministers of war and the navy, whose jurisdictions were the only ones that had powers to act in all crimes related to interior security, including theft and other common crimes. This government, with its strong military influence, took on unlimited executive and legislative powers and totally controlled judicial power. The Council of Ministers could overrule the verdicts of the administrative dispute tribunals, appoint special judges and punish any inappropriate conduct of magistrates. Furthermore, there was no appeal against their resolutions. The public was totally defenceless, with no civil rights or constitutional safeguards.

Nevertheless, a regime that aspired to be long-lasting and make a clean break with the liberal parliamentary system needed a political pretext, a legal facade to give it legitimacy and social backing. The idea of a corporate parliament gathered steam in July 1926, after the National Assembly of Uniones Patrióticas. In September, coinciding with the third anniversary of the *coup d'état*, a national plebiscite was held that was open to male and female voters aged 18 or older. The propagandists of the Unión Patriótica, with the support of the Church, conducted an intense campaign to persuade the people to place their confidence in the *caudillo de Alhucemas*. In the end, with marked inconsistencies – no surprise to anybody, nor was it anything new – the authorities secured the signatures of 7 million of the 13 million Spaniards who had the right to vote.

The next step, once the king's misgivings had been overcome, was the preparation of a National Assembly. The Royal Decree that called it clearly emphasised that it was 'not necessarily a Parliament, it [would] not be legislating or sharing sovereignty'. It was an advisory body of representation of interests made up of senior state officials, the army, the Church and justice, delegates from the municipalities, regional assemblies and provincial organisations of the Unión Patriótica and, finally, representatives of 'activities in national life', from the academic world, production sectors, and employer and trade associations. From the moment it opened, in September 1927, the government exercised absolute control over the Assembly, including the appointment of its members, the internal operation of the chamber, the order of sessions and the content of the debates.

The Directorate charged the Assembly with the drawing up of a draft constitution. The text was not handed over to the government until the spring of 1928, the complementary laws not until a year later; the final draft was not published until July 1929. The draft that was passed combined the corporate and organic natures of the dictatorship with the traditional principles of doctrinaire liberalism: the indissoluble unity of the Fatherland, a confessional state, shared sovereignty between the Cortes and the king, who was head of the executive, extraordinary powers for the government to defend public order, a single chamber made up in equal proportions of representatives from the corporations and those appointed by direct suffrage, and broad powers for a Council of the Kingdom made up of representatives from the nobility and upper echelons of the state, the Church and the army. But in the end, all the work done on Section I of the Assembly was fruitless. As Calvo Sotelo wrote, the project was abandoned. It was too late. By the summer of 1929, Primo de Rivera had lost a large part of the credit with which he had begun the Civil Directorate. Neither the king nor the army, his two staunchest bastions, were willing to give their unconditional backing. The failure of the Unión Patriótica and the *somatén* was no secret to anyone, and there was a growing number of opponents prepared to plot against and overthrow the dictatorship.

The external image of the regime seemed to indicate the opposite. In June 1929 there was a meeting in Madrid of the League of Nations Security Council and the following month saw the opening of the Ibero-American Exhibition in Seville, the finest example of spiritual and cultural Hispano-Americanism to be backed by the dictator, and the International Expo in Barcelona, a showcase for the economic and technological progress of the age. The country was not left out of the international economic boom, the 'Golden Twenties'. Spanish industry was experiencing an annual growth rate of more than 5%, helped by the promotion of national production and restriction on competition. The most active sectors, steel, building, cement and chemicals, were driven by the acceleration of city development, the spread of electricity, companies' need for machinery, the arrival of foreign investment and increased exports. These were years of industrial diversification and business concentration, with state backing for the establishment of oligopolies and monopolies, such as the Compañía Arrendataria del Monopolio de Petróleos, SA (CAMPSA) and the Compañía Telefónica Nacional de España (CTNE), and the implementation of an ambitious plan for the modernisation of infrastructures which gave rise to an extension of the road and rail networks, the Ports Act and the establishment of River Boards.

And, while employees' working conditions saw no substantial improvement, it is fair to say that, in general, workers felt greater security and well-being thanks to the high employment rate, the stability of basic foodstuff prices and an improvement in labour relations. This was, to a great extent, possible because of social protection measures (including cheap housing, retirement, social assistance for urban migrants, health services and the six-day week) and because of paternalistic employment legislation that allowed reformist workers' societies if they accepted the corporate framework. August 1926 saw the promulgation of the Labour Code, which regulated industrial and agricultural contracts, and the birth, in November of the same year, of the Organización Nacional Corporativa, the sphere of action of the workers' and employers' Joint Committees, the Corporation Councils, which represented each trade on a national basis, and the Higher Labour Council, a ministry advisory body. The success of the Organización Nacional Corporativa could be seen in the reduction of social conflict, in terms of both the number and duration of strikes, and in the fact that it drew the UGT into the corporate system.

The socialist trade union clearly benefited from its legalist strategy, managing to corner most of the worker representation posts. Largo Caballero was a member of the Council of State, the UGT increased the number of affiliated trades and total membership, reaching 235,000 in 1928, and it saw its rural presence improved with the setting up of the Federación Nacional de Trabajadores de la Tierra (FNTT). However, collaboration had its drawbacks. The socialists refused to attend the National Assembly and in 1928 began to distance themselves from the regime. In August 1929 the PSOE and UGT leadership signed a joint manifesto rejecting the dictatorship, in which they stated their intention to fight for a 'republican state of freedom and democracy'.

Until then, any attempts to overthrow the regime were met with simple police operations. Firstly, there was an attempted anarchist action in Vera de Bidasoa, in November 1924, a raid from France made by several hundred armed militants, which was dispersed after a shoot-out with the Civil Guard and the Carabineros. It marked the beginning of an insurrectional strategy that was to last an entire decade. The closing down of CNT premises and the banning of their trade union activities opened the way for the predominance of 'pure' anarchists, who were adherents of 'direct action' and 'revolutionary gymnastics'. In July 1927, the most radical anarchist groups founded the Federación Anarquista Ibérica (FAI) in Valencia, a libertarian organisation that sought to become the front line of the CNT and the driving force for rebellion against the dictatorship.

This line was also taken by the Catalan nationalists of Estat Català, led by Francesc Macià, who tried to penetrate via Prats de Mollo in November 1926. The strategy of these small groups was to create a ripple effect in subversive activities. Hardliners would issue the first blow, and this would be followed by a general strike, the collaboration of other revolutionary sectors and the insurrection of a sector of the army. And it would all look as if it were something spontaneous, as if the people were prepared at all times to take to the streets, waiting for a spark, a hand that would light the fuse.

Another more serious plot was hatched in Valencia in June 1926, the *Sanjuanada*. This was a civil–military conspiracy led by Generals Aguilera and Weyler, and by the former Speakers of the parliamentary chambers, Melquíades Álvarez and the Count of Romanones. The idea was to issue a manifesto threatening division and confrontation within the army unless Alfonso XIII dismissed Primo de Rivera and appointed a provisional government charged with returning to the situation that existed in Spain prior to the September 1923 coup. The *pronunciamiento* was thwarted because of discrepancies between the officers in the plot and leaks that had reached the press and the police. It was all over in a couple of days with the arrest of General Aguilera and the imposing of heavy fines on the ringleaders. Any serious insurrectional movement would need to have public support and the involvement of a major part of the armed forces, two elements that were missing at the time.

Things began to change shortly afterwards. On 4 September 1926, the officers of the Artillery Corps staged a collective protest and shut themselves within their barracks. Their action was a continuation of the old dispute between *junteros* and *Africanistas* over the issue of promotions and awards. The Directorate's decrees that did away with promotions by strict seniority and allowed discretional promotions had infuriated the Artillery Corps and others such as the Engineers and Medical Corps. Primo de Rivera responded to this defiance by ordering the dissolution of the Artillery Corps, the taking over of their barracks, the suspension of the employment and salary of more than 1,000 officers, and the establishment of martial law throughout Spain. A few months later the officers who had been punished returned to their posts and the dictator tried to restore the unity of the army with conciliatory measures. But the open wounds refused to heal, and the number of dissatisfied officers began to grow. In this respect, the personal squabbles and frustrations, the comparative grievances and internal frictions among officers and corps, were more important than the ideological approaches or reactions against reforms such as the cut-backs in expenditure and personnel, the reduction of military service to two years or the re-establishment of the Military Academy in Zaragoza, under the direction of General Franco.

Another unexpected conflict for the dictator was the one that arose in university classrooms. The number of students in Spanish universities had risen from fewer than 20,000 in 1922 to almost 60,000 in 1929, a sure sign of the improved economic situation of the urban middle classes and the importance of social and cultural changes. The first student protests, arising in the spring of 1925, took shape in late 1926 with the founding of the Federación Universitaria Escolar (FUE), created to counteract the primacy of the Catholic associations. After March 1928, with the strike called to protest against the dismissal of Professor Luis Jiménez de Asúa, demands of an academic and professional nature turned into mobilisations opposing the regime. The unrest moved up a notch with the passing of a law that granted privileges to confessional establishments. In March 1929, following a wave of assemblies, strikes and demonstrations, Primo de Rivera ordered the military occupation of the establishments, the expulsion of the strikers from university and the closing down of various universities, among them Central University in Madrid and Barcelona University. Youth unrest did not stop until the end of the dictatorship, spurring on protest by intellectuals and resistance movements against the regime, increasingly identified with the cause of democracy and the Republic.

Republicanism, which had lost its direction and was divided after the *coup d'état*, found a common denominator in late 1926 in the Alianza Republicana, an aggregation of the radical forces of Lerroux, Catalan republicans led by Marcelino Domingo and the most reformist sectors, such as Acción Republicana, the group driven by intellectuals such as Manuel Azaña, Ramón Pérez de Ayala and Luis Araquistáin. The republicans took an active part in the civil–military plot headed by José Sánchez Guerra in January 1929. Directing it from voluntary exile in Paris, the conservative politician tried to unite into one single party the monarchists who were yearning for a return to the 1876 Constitution, the republicans who were asking for Cortes Constituyentes and officers dissatisfied with the dictator, basically artillery officers and generals such as Miguel Cabanellas, Gonzalo Queipo de Llano, Eduardo López de Ochoa and Alberto Castro Girona. But on 29 January, when Sánchez Guerra arrived in Valencia, the insurrection had been aborted because of a premature uprising, a few hours earlier, in the Artillery Barracks in Ciudad Real.

Once again, Primo de Rivera had survived an attempt to overthrow his regime. But it was becoming clear that he was being increasingly isolated. Alfonso XIII had withdrawn his confidence in him and was trying, unsuccessfully, to gather support that would enable him to go back to a pre-*coup d'état* situation and, *en passant*, save the Crown. By mid 1929 the economic situation had markedly deteriorated, the number of strikes was increasing monthly and the Directorate responded to the rise in social conflict with repressive measures such as random arrests and the closure of workers' centres. Furthermore, landowners' associations, Catholic trade unions and employers' associations, which were opposed to the development of agricultural Joint Committees, labour arbitration laws and Calvo Sotelo's plans for fiscal reform, reversed the unconditional membership that they had pledged in 1923 and distanced themselves from the regime. The dream of a corporate authoritarian state was rapidly fading. What Maeztu called the 'spiritual project', based 'on Religion, the family, the state and ownership' was rapidly falling apart. In its final days, the *somatén* and the Unión Patriótica, far from being the mass organisations that they were expected to be, had become the refuge for *caciques* and upstarts, and their most active militants acted as if they were an auxiliary para-police force in tasks of repression. Spain, wrote Unamuno at the time, was a 'cemetery of the living', a 'gaol full of released prisoners'.[7]

In the last few weeks of 1929, Primo de Rivera, disillusioned and increasingly weakened by his diabetes, told his ministers of his intention to transfer power to a transition government. In January 1930, amid insistent rumours of a military plot hatched by General Goded, the military governor of Cádiz, Primo de Rivera turned his eye to the army, his regime's only real buttress. Unknown to the king, he consulted the captains general in what was a sort of motion of confidence. The support he received from Sanjurjo was the solitary exception to the inhibition and ambiguity received from the rest of the military leaders. There was no other solution than to go to the Palacio Real to tender his resignation, which he did on 27 December, and to leave the country. He died in Paris two months later.

---

[7] Ramiro de Maeztu, *Defensa de la Hispanidad* (Madrid: RIALP, 1934), p. 293, cited by Rafael Núñez Florencio, *El peso del pesimismo: del '98 al desencanto* (Madrid: Marcial Pons, 2010), p. 239.

Meanwhile, Alfonso XIII ignored those who wanted Cortes Constituyentes to be called and appointed General Dámaso Berenguer as prime minister in the vain hope that it would close a parenthesis, as if nothing had happened, and thus restore the political 'normality' that existed prior to 1923. But, as Miguel Maura wrote, the Constitution, 'in shreds' after six years of constant violation of all of its precepts, was just a distant memory. 'To pretend, in 1930, to resurrect the text of this fundamental law, as well as being the height of stupidity, was a mockery that the country could not forgive, and it was perhaps the main cause of the rejection of the person of the monarch, which a traditionally monarchist public displayed in the elections of 12 April 1931.' The regime of the Restoration, judged Azaña, 'forced to choose between being submissive or tyrannical, chose tyranny, deciding to bet all it had. Well, it did, and lost everything.'[8]

What was the dictatorship?

'Was it just another *pronunciamiento* or the beginning of something totally new in the country? Was it a last-century-style revolution or a this-century-style revolution?' Eugenio D'Ors asked himself these questions in March 1924, when Primo de Rivera's dictatorship was still a strictly military government that had yet to begin its institutionalisation process. D'Ors was one of the Spanish intellectuals who was most familiar with the authoritarian currents of the European right, one of the thinkers who kept most abreast of the trends that were to be found 'in all orders, the need to think hierarchically', the echo of a song that came from beyond the Pyrenees and which he called 'the *Marseillaise* of authority'.[9]

The *Marseillaise* of authority was no less than the rise of the anti-parliamentary radical right. Primo de Rivera's coup was not a unique incident, an original solution to the crisis of the liberal system or an event peculiar to Spanish contemporary history, but just another of the authoritarian military or semi-military regimes to arise in inter-war Europe. As José Luis Gómez Navarro has stated in his detailed research, the dictatorships that were imposed in those years in the countries of Mediterranean and eastern Europe were a consequence of the processes of economic development, social modernisation and political mobilisation that took place at the end of the nineteenth century and the early decades of the twentieth in countries that were late in becoming industrialised and had to face the challenge of joining the mass agrarian and industrial political stage.

[8] Miguel Maura, *Así cayó Alfonso XIII: de una dictadura a otra* (Barcelona: Ariel, 1966).
[9] García Queipo De Llano, *Los intelectuales y la Dictadura de Primo de Rivera*, pp. 88–93.

Portugal, Greece, Poland, Romania, Bulgaria, Hungary and Yugoslavia all underwent this process. In all these examples, the dictatorial regimes were a solution to the failure of political systems to integrate emerging social sectors and advance to a new legitimacy based on popular sovereignty and the extension of human rights. As against the loss of the parties' credibility, and inability or lack of political will of the elites to bring about this change, the army and the bureaucracy, with the backing of the monarch, were the institutions that were able to take power and safeguard the public order that had been threatened with the spectre of worker revolution.[10]

Fascism was a different phenomenon. It is true to say that the triumph of the 'blackshirts' in Italy occurred the year before Primo de Rivera's coup, and he made no secret of his admiration for the figure of Mussolini. Soon afterwards, during his official visit to Italy, the Spanish dictator admitted that his *pronunciamiento* had a lot to do with the 'electrifying of the atmosphere' caused by the fascist movement. On the same visit, Alfonso XIII introduced Primo de Rivera as his own Mussolini. Both dictators rejected democracy and parliamentarianism, called for the use of force and coercion to put an end to revolutionary 'chaos' and committed themselves to a corporate state to regulate social relationships. They had the same enemies and similar objectives. But the historical context and the similarities in style or language do not blur the differences between authoritarian dictatorships and fascist regimes.

Where the latter were successful, in Italy and Germany, more developed countries with a higher level of social and political organisation, there had previously been democratic governments which, while being fragile and unstable, had allowed broad sectors of the population to become involved and workers' organisations to become stronger. The nature and depth of these social changes called for a different, much more radical response, a modern counter-revolutionary-style movement that came from civil society. Fascism, with its comprehensive ideology, mythical thinking and charismatic leadership cult, displayed an impressive ability to generate mass nationalisation and organisation not only among the upper and middle classes and the *petite bourgeoisie* but also in certain workers' sectors and among a good number of young people. Neither Mussolini nor Hitler needed a military coup to come to power. And once they were in power, they established single-party totalitarian regimes, with a new governing elite, supported by the ruling classes, that tried to control the minds of all citizens using terror to suppress any attempt at opposition.

[10] José Luis Gómez Navarro, *El régimen de Primo de Rivera: reyes, Dictaduras y dictadores* (Madrid: Cátedra, 1991).

Military dictators did not come to power through a mobilisation of the masses. They led defensive reactions, based on traditional values which, in principle, did not pretend to build a new society. But they all, as Shlomo Ben-Ami has pointed out, very soon realised that the use of force and issuing of decrees were not enough as exclusive government instruments. And so, while still considering the army as a basic pillar of the government, they created political parties conceived as a means to broaden their social bases and cloak themselves in some semblance of popular approval. However, these government parties, such as the Unión Patriótica, never managed to garner the mass support that they were meant to, and they did not survive the regimes that formed them. Primo de Rivera, this author goes on to say, failed in his attempt at civil institutionalisation and simply 'put into deep freeze' certain problems that he believed to have been solved, such as the purported disappearance of anarchism, the elimination of the Catalan nationalism issue, the restoration of social peace and the recomposition of army unity. In addition, his social reform policy, although it might have been controlled and limited, cost him the support of the traditional conservative sectors and employers' organisations, those who in theory should have been his strongest support. And that is why, with the foundations of the old regime destroyed without being replaced with a new state, the dictator 'left a dangerous power vacuum behind him'.[11]

Comparative perspective research by historians such as Ben-Ami or Gómez Navarro represents an undeniable advance in the study of Primo de Rivera's dictatorship. Before that, up until the mid 1980s, historians took various approaches, from Marxist-inspired analysis to studies of a more liberal orientation. Among the former was Manuel Tuñon de Lara, who defined the dictatorship as a reaction to the dominant 'power bloc' to restore the balance of power and resolve the crisis of state primacy. Among the latter were authors such as Carlos Seco Serrano, Javier Tusell and even Raymond Carr, who played down socio-economic factors in order to stress the importance of the political crisis of the parliamentary system as the origin of the military coup. In their opinion, what happened in Spain between 1923 and 1930 was the final test for regenerationism, a constitutional 'parenthesis' which produced no significant transformation in the political climate.

On the other hand, María Teresa González Calbet maintains that the dictatorship did produce fundamental and irreversible changes. These included the crisis and destruction of the dynastic parties, the disappearance of projects that addressed options for reform within the system, the

---

[11] Ben-Ami, *La dictadura de Primo de Rivera, 1923–1930.*

conclusive discrediting of the monarchy and the appearance of new theoretical and political options, on both left and right. Similarly, Eduardo
González Calleja believes that Primo de Rivera's dictatorship should not
be interpreted as an 'emergency' parenthesis, but as a completely new
political experiment which, at least from 1925 onwards, clearly set out to
'liquidate' the Restoration system and consolidate and perpetuate a new
corporate, nationalist and 'fascistising' regime. Its failure had far-reaching
consequences for the Spanish political scene: 'In the short, medium and
long term, the dictatorship played a decisive role not only in the spread of
a public comportment in favour of democracy, but also in the redefinition
of an authoritarian alternative to it.'[12]

The country saw political change as well as structural transformation.
Between 1900 and 1930 Spain experienced a period of marked modernisation and economic growth. In these three decades, the total population
rose from 18.6 million to 23.5 million inhabitants, and average life expectancy went from 35 to 50, with a sharp decline in the infant mortality rate.
At the same time, the illiteracy rate went down from 60% to 35%, due to
a considerable advance in primary education coupled to the impulse
given to scientific and university training. These educational and cultural
improvements went hand in hand with the upswing in urban development, which doubled the size of the most important cities and brought
10 million Spaniards into towns and cities of more than 10,000 inhabitants, a process accompanied by substantial immigration from agricultural regions. Around 1930, the rural world was still predominant in
many areas of Spain, but the agricultural labour force amounted to less
than 50% of the total working population. The agricultural sector grew
in productivity, area sown and crop diversity, and the use of fertilisers,
although it was losing ground to the secondary sector. Industry, with a
million new workers since the beginning of the century, doubled its
production and was no stranger to the technological changes of the second
industrial revolution, the development of chemical, electrical and equipment firms, or the upswing in construction. The tertiary sector, albeit
belatedly, also showed clear signs of growth and renovation both in the
transport and communications system and in financial services, trade and
administration.

In the years between Alfonso XIII's ascension to the throne and the eve
of his overthrow, the national income doubled and Spain, while experiencing major regional disparities, in general narrowed the gap between
itself and other European countries. But the cycle of economic prosperity

---

[12] The nature of the dictatorship is discussed in González Calleja, *La España de Primo de
Rivera*, pp. 392–405.

was about to come to an end. As José Luis García Delgado and Juan Carlos Jiménez have pointed out, the waves of the 1929 global crisis, an international recession of hitherto unknown dimensions, crossed the Atlantic during 1930 and soon reached the heart of Europe. The crisis arrived at the worst moment for Spain, at least for the governments of the Republic established in April 1931, which had to confront two situations that did not make good bedfellows, economic crisis and political change.[13]

[13] García Delgado and Jiménez, *La historia de España del siglo XX: la economía*, pp. 403–8.

Part II

The Second Republic

5   A parliamentary and constitutional republic

The municipal elections of 12 April 1931 became a plebiscite between a monarchy and a republic. The republicans won in most of the provincial capitals, and King Alfonso XIII was forced to leave Spain. He did so from Cartagena, and when he arrived in Paris he declared that the Republic was 'a storm that will soon blow over'.[1] However, it lasted longer than the dethroned king thought or hoped. This Republic was to experience more than five years of peace, until a military uprising and a war destroyed it by force of arms.

In the first two years of the Republic, the republican and socialist governments introduced sweeping reforms that affected the state, the Church, the army and almost every sector of society. These reforms opened a chasm between Church and State, employers and workers, defenders of traditional order and supporters of the Republic. Almost from the beginning there were serious public order problems, demonstrations, agricultural worker revolts and sabre rattling, including the first attempt at a military coup against the legitimate Republic. This mixture of great hopes, reforms, conflicts and resistance was what marked the Republic during its first two years.[2]

Winds of change

After the fall of General Miguel Primo de Rivera's dictatorship, on 26 January 1930, hostility towards the monarchy spread unchecked via the medium of meetings and demonstrations throughout Spain. Firstly, more and more monarchists were beginning to lose their confidence in Alfonso XIII. The year 1930 was one of high-profile resignations of politicians who had hitherto been loyal to the Crown. Distinguished

---

[1] Quoted in Eduardo González Calleja, 'El ex rey', in Moreno Luzón (ed.), *Alfonso XIII: un político en el trono*, p. 406.

[2] A more detailed analysis of the republican period and the Civil War may be found in Julián Casanova, *The Spanish Republic and Civil War* (Cambridge University Press, 2010).

monarchists such as Miguel Maura, son of Antonio Maura, the former leader of the conservatives, and Niceto Alcalá Zamora, the Liberal ex-minister, felt at the time that it was better to defend, from inside a republic, 'legitimate conservative principles', than to 'leave the way open' to the parties of the left and workers' organisations.[3]

This was because the fall of the dictatorship caused a sudden process of politicisation and a surge in republicanism, which had hitherto been weak, incapable as it was of breaking the stranglehold of *caciquismo* and of suggesting real alternatives. Various republican sectors had already joined to form a Republican Alliance in 1926, which took its lead from Alejandro Lerroux's old Partido Radical, and from a new group, Acción Republicana, led by Manuel Azaña, which had broken with Melquíades Álvarez's reformists in 1923. The extreme left wing of this new republican initiative was occupied by the Partido Republicano Radical Socialista, founded in 1929 by two Alianza Republicana dissidents, Marcelino Domingo and Álvaro de Albornoz. The most conservative faction was the Derecha Liberal Republicana, set up in July 1930 by Alcalá Zamora and Miguel Maura.

In just a few months, the old form of republicanism, made up of small discussion groups, transformed into a movement of various political parties, with recognised leaders and new social foundations. Among these names were conservatives and Catholics, such as Maura and Alcalá Zamora, passionate defenders of anti-clericalism, such as Álvaro de Albornoz, and nationalists in Esquerra Republicana de Catalunya (ERC), such as Francesc Macià and Lluís Companys, or the Galician Organización Republicana Gallega Autónoma, led by Santiago Casares Quiroga. Together, despite their noticeable differences in ideology and principles, they formed a comprehensive republican coalition which came into being on 17 August 1930 in San Sebastián.

From what was known as the San Sebastián Pact emerged the revolutionary committee that made a commitment to channel the demands for autonomy by the Catalans, to prepare an uprising against the monarchy and to proclaim a republic. A few weeks later the socialist movement, whose leaders did not attend this meeting, although one of them, Indalecio Prieto, did so 'on a personal basis', agreed at a PSOE executive commission meeting held on 20 October to accept the three posts that the republicans offered them on the committee. An essential factor in reaching this decision, thereby avoiding the choice of whether to ignore or subscribe to action by the Republic, was the attitude of Largo Caballero, who ended

---

[3] Miguel Maura, *Así cayó Alfonso XIII*, p. 48.

up convinced that the socialists had to help the republicans 'to exert an influence' from within 'on the orientation of the revolution' and thus enable a peaceful and gradual move towards socialism.[4]

Furthermore, during that year, 1930, distinguished writers and university professors 'defined themselves', as their contemporaries put it, to express their rejection of the monarchy and support for a republic. This unrest began just a few days after the fall of the dictator, with the return from exile of Miguel de Unamuno, who was acclaimed by crowds at every stage of his journey from Irún to Madrid, and it ended with the famous article by the philosopher José Ortega y Gasset, published in *El Sol* on 15 November. 'The Berenguer Error', as the article was entitled, was the idea that everything would return to normal after seven years of dictatorship, as if nothing had happened, which is what General Dámaso Berenguer, Primo de Rivera's replacement appointed by the king was supposed to be ensuring. But the monarchy was beyond hope of salvation. '*Delenda est monarchia*', concluded Ortega in a phrase that summed up the anti-monarchist feeling that was rife among politicians, intellectuals and the common people at that time.

Barely a month later, the union of republicans and socialists tried to destroy the monarchy by force, although with very little preparation and fewer resources. The military uprising, which had a long tradition in contemporary Spanish society, was organised in this case by the revolutionary committee and would be supported in the streets by a general strike called by the workers' organisations. Those in charge of the plan, Captains Fermín Galán and Ángel García Hernández, led the troops in revolt in Jaca, in the province of Huesca, in the early hours of 12 December 1930, three days prior to the date that the revolutionary committee had apparently set. The revolt failed because of the lack of support for revolutionary actions in the army and because the strike received limited support in Zaragoza, the stronghold of anarchists, and Huesca. On Sunday 14 December, a summary court martial found the two ringleaders guilty and condemned them to face the firing squad. Even before its birth, the Republic already had its first martyrs, and King Alfonso XIII was held responsible for failing to grant them a pardon. 'The monarchy committed an outrage in executing Galán and García Hernández, an outrage which in no small way led to its overthrow', wrote Manuel Azaña.[5]

---

[4] Santos Juliá, *Los socialistas en la política española, 1879–1982* (Madrid: Taurus, 1996), pp. 147–53.
[5] Manuel Azaña, *Diarios 1932–1933 (los 'Cuadernos robados')* (Barcelona: Crítica, 1997), p. 45.

The uprising set for 15 December also failed, in spite of the fact that General Gonzalo Queipo de Llano and Major Ramón Franco managed to capture the Cuatro Vientos aerodrome for a few hours, from whence they fled to Portugal when they discovered that troops loyal to Berenguer's government were approaching, and that no one had gone on strike in Madrid. Meanwhile, most of the members of the revolutionary committee had been arrested. In the end, it was not insurrection that would bring about a republic.

Nor did the return to constitutional normality proposed by General Dámaso Berenguer's government produce concrete results. Berenguer stood alone, abandoned even by members of his cabinet with strong loyalty to the king, such as the Count of Romanones, and the general resigned on 13 February 1931. After various vain efforts to approach the liberal sectors, the king appointed Admiral Juan Bautista Aznar, who formed another government loyal to the monarchy. He only had time to call municipal elections for 12 April because two months later neither this government nor the monarchy existed.

The calling of elections caught the traditional parties of the conservative and liberal right in complete disarray, as well as the extreme right, those faithful to the deposed dictator, in the process of rearming and powerless to mobilise their counter-revolutionary forces, although they did try to do so with the formation in July 1930 of the Unión Monárquica Nacional, a pale imitation of the dictatorship's Unión Patriótica; among the members of this party were former ministers, such as José Calvo Sotelo, the intellectual, Ramiro de Maeztu, and the ex-dictator's son, José Antonio Primo de Rivera. The old politics were in their death throes, and the new authoritarianism had yet to find a niche.

The republicans' time had finally come: old, new and brand new republicans. The moment had also come for street politics, propaganda, meetings and calls for action to support the Republic. On 20 March 1931, at the height of the election campaign, the imprisoned revolutionary committee faced a court martial, an event that was transformed into a major manifestation of republican avowal. Having recovered their freedom, the members of this committee, future members of the republican provisional government, concentrated all their efforts on transforming this election day, 12 April, into a plebiscite between monarchy and republic.

And so it was. Up to the very end the monarchists thought that they were going to win, confident of their ability to manipulate the mechanism of government. And this is why they showed their 'consternation' and 'surprise' when they learned very soon of the republicans' victory in forty-one of the fifty provincial capitals. Only Juan de la Cierva proposed resorting to arms to prevent the rout of the monarchy. But the other ministers, headed by Romanones, acknowledged defeat. Aznar resigned on the night of 13 April. The following day, many municipalities proclaimed the Republic. Alcalá Zamora, president of the revolutionary committee, called on the king to leave the country.

The Republic was welcomed with celebrations in the streets, amid a holiday atmosphere that combined revolutionary hopes with a desire for reform. The crowds took to the streets, as may be seen in contemporary press reports, in photographs and in the numerous testimonies of those who wanted to put on record this great change that had a touch of magic, that arrived peacefully, without bloodshed. The middle class 'opted for the Republic' because of the 'disorientation of conservative elements', wrote José María Gil Robles a few years later.[6]

The revolutionary committee did not wait for the transfer of power, and, following the outcome of the election and in response to public pressure, its members formed the provisional government of the Republic. It was the evening of 14 April, a few hours after the Republic had been proclaimed in other locations, the first to do so having been the city council in Eibar, and Francesc Macià had proclaimed in Barcelona the Catalan Republic within the federal Spanish state. Niceto Alcalá Zamora went out on to the balcony of the Interior Ministry, and in a message broadcast by radio, officially proclaimed the Republic. At a meeting the same night, the provisional government drew up its own Legal Statute that would define its situation until the Cortes Constituyentes was called.

The government was headed by Alcalá Zamora, an ex-monarchist, a Catholic and a man of order, who was a key piece in ensuring the necessary support of the more moderate republicans for the new regime. As well as the prime minister, there were eleven ministers, including Alejandro Lerroux, the old *'Emperador del Paralelo'*, leader of the main republican party, the Partido Radical, and Manuel Azaña, who headed the representation of the leftist republicans, and who became minister of war. For the first time in Spain's history, socialists also took part in the government of the nation, with three ministers: Fernando de los Ríos, as minister of justice; Indalecio Prieto in finance; and Francisco Largo Caballero, as minister of labour.

They represented the professional middle classes, the petite bourgeoisie and the militant working class or socialist sympathisers. None of them, except Alcalá Zamora, had held a high political post under the monarchy, although they were by no means young untried amateurs: most of them were in their fifties and had spent a long time in the political struggle. Nor,

---

[6] José María Gil Robles, *No fue posible la paz* (Barcelona: Ariel, 1968), p. 32.

despite what has often been said, was it a government of intellectuals. Except for Azaña, in the government as leader of a republican party, none of the intellectuals who had done so much to goad the monarchy with their speeches and writings in 1930 was given a ministry: not Miguel Unamuno, or José Ortega y Gasset, Ramón Pérez de Ayala or Gregorio Marañón. The latter three, who on 10 February 1931, had founded the Agrupación al Servicio de la Republica, also soon vanished from public life or else ended up distancing themselves from the republican regime.

What this government did in the early weeks, with popular jubilation still in the air, was to legislate by decree. In fact, it is hard to imagine a government with more plans for political and social reform. Before the inauguration of the Cortes Constituyentes, the provisional government implemented a Military Reform Act, drawn up by Manuel Azaña, and a series of basic decrees issued by Francisco Largo Caballero, the minister of labour, whose aim was to radically modify labour relations. Such a reformist programme embodied the government's faith in progress and a political and social transformation that would sweep away the *cacique* system and the power of the military and ecclesiastical institutions. The Republic was taking its first steps.

The Parliament

The route that this government had mapped out included a general election and providing the Republic with a constitution. Elections with universal suffrage, both male and female, representative governments that answered to Parliament, and compliance with the law and the Constitution were the distinguishing features of the democratic systems that were emerging or being consolidated at that time in the main countries of western and central Europe. And this is what the republicans and socialists who governed Spain tried to introduce during the early years of the Second Republic, to a large extent successfully.

The general election to the Cortes Constituyentes was held on 28 June. According to the election writ, which modified the 1907 Electoral Act, there would be a single chamber, instead of the two that made up the monarchist Parliament. The voting age was lowered from 25 to 23, and suffrage was restricted to males, although females could now stand for election, with the decision on female suffrage to be taken during the future legislature. To thwart any of the traditional fraudulent *cacique*-type practices, the first-past-the-post system was to be replaced by open lists, with constituencies by province. By doing away with small districts, the system implemented by the Republic attacked the roots of *caciquismo* and introduced free, legitimate elections for the first time in Spain's history.

The electoral campaign found the right still in disarray and lacking a firm policy, with some of its leaders having fled to other countries in case they were brought to trial for their actions during the dictatorship. Ángel Herrera, the editor of the Catholic daily, *El Debate*, and other members of the Asociación Católica Nacional de Propagandistas who had accepted the Republic as 'the only scenario possible', created Acción Nacional on 29 April, with a primary objective of promoting a firm grass-roots policy, acting within the bounds of the Republic following the creed of 'the accidentality of forms of government', and defending the interests of order and the Church in the Cortes. Given the papal blessing and supported by a large number of bishops, this was the beginning of the Catholic grass-roots movement that burst with unexpected vigour on to the political stage of the Republic two years later. But in June 1931, still in its embryonic phase, Acción Nacional could only field thirty-nine candidates in sixteen constituencies.

The victory of the republican–socialist coalition was overwhelming. The Republic's first general election produced a Cortes of 470 deputies, made up of nineteen parties or groups, six of which won four seats or fewer. The principal novelty on the electoral map was the fact that the Partido Socialista, which had never had more than 7 deputies under the monarchy, now had 115, and it became the majority political force, with its votes coming mainly from the areas of the south with mainly large estates. The second biggest group was Alejandro Lerroux's radicals, with ninety-four deputies, a very important result which enabled the Partido Radical to occupy the republican centre, especially because the conservatives, led by Alcalá Zamora and Miguel Maura, obtained only twenty-two seats. The fifty-nine Partido Radical Socialista and thirty Acción Republicana deputies also showed the notable strength of the republican left, reinforced by the primacy of the ERC in Catalonia, which obtained thirty-five of the forty-nine seats contested there, and the sixteen deputies provided by the Federación Republicana Gallega.

The non-republican right-wing organisations obtained barely fifty seats and their results were favourable only in the Basque Country and Navarre, where sixteen of the twenty-four seats were won by the alliance of Carlists, Basque nationalists and independent Catholics. Even so, although they were few in number, there were some distinguished names among the right-wing deputies, with members of rich land-owning and industrial families, such as José Luis de Oriol, Julio de Urquijo, the Count of Romanones, the Count of Rodezno and Juan March. The common interests between landowners, order and religion were perfectly embodied by the rural deputies of Acción Nacional and by the Carlists and fundamentalists.

Figure 4 The Republic was welcomed with celebrations as the crowds took to the streets, amid a holiday atmosphere that combined revolutionary hopes with a desire for reform. © Agencia EFE

All but twenty-eight deputies were entering the Cortes for the first time. There were many intellectuals, journalists, teachers and lawyers, as well as members of the working class. And for the first time in history, there were three women: the republicans Clara Campoamor and Victoria Kent, and the socialist Margarita Nelken. At the opening session of the Cortes Constituyentes on 14 July 1931, Alcalá Zamora declared that 'today marks a high spot, a summit, a pinnacle in the history of Spain'. A few days later, the Cortes, with the socialist Julián Besteiro as Speaker, gave a vote of confidence to the provisional government, thereby making it the first official government of the Republic.

There was no sign in that Parliament of any radicalisation or polarisation of Spanish political life. There was no solid extreme right yet, let alone a fascist party, while the Communist Party, at the time vehemently opposed to the 'bourgeois Republic', had obtained very poor results and no seats. Two essential ingredients of the process of radicalisation on the European stage, fascism and communism, were missing in Spain, although there was a powerful anarcho-syndicalist movement outside the Cortes Constituyentes, an institution which was viewed by its most extreme sector as 'a bourgeois mechanism whose purpose is to consolidate the regime of constant exploitation'.[7] It was the only established force that stood clearly on the fringes of the system at the time, because the main party of the left, the PSOE, was part of the government.

The big difference with this Parliament, compared to those of other republics that emerged from the break-up of empires following the First World War, was that most of the deputies belonged to the coalition of parties that formed the government. Only around fifty seemed willing to defend the interests of traditional order and the Catholic Church. And this did not reflect the views of large sectors of Spanish society who had strong economic, social and cultural power, but they were not in the Cortes and thus would be unable to have any influence on the drafting of the Constitution. This was because the Republic arrived not as the result of the success of a republican movement with deep social roots, but because of a popular mobilisation against the monarchy, which reaped its rewards just when the king was losing his social and institutional support.

But this did not necessarily mean that the foundations of the Republic and democracy were shaky from the start. The results of the June 1931 elections showed that a large proportion of the Spanish people had placed their hopes in the new regime. And they showed it via the exercise of popular sovereignty, in elections in which only 70% of the male

---

[7] *Memoria del Congreso Extraordinario de la CNT celebrado en Madrid del 11 al 16 de junio de 1933* (Barcelona: Cosmos, 1931), pp. 188–9.

population went to the polls, in a vote of confidence for Cortes Constituyentes and a parliamentary government. Everything that happened later, the strengths and weaknesses of the system, its successes and failures, up until the *coup d'état* of July 1936, has its historical explanations, and no predestined fatal outcome was to be found in the origins of this democratic Republic.

One of the main tasks of these Cortes Constituyentes was to draw up and pass the first republican constitution in Spain's history, and this is what they devoted their energies to during the first few months. Between 28 August and 1 December 1931, the Cortes debated the project presented by a parliamentary commission presided over by the socialist Luis Jiménez de Asúa. The most serious hurdle to be overcome in the debate on the Constitution was the 'matter of religion', which left in its wake disturbances, quarrels, insults and angry declarations by the fundamentalists and the most incendiary and anti-clerical elements of the left alike. In the end Azaña's proposal was approved following his famous speech of 13 October, which moderated the original plan by restricting the constitutional precept of the dissolution of religious orders to the Jesuits only, and ratified the ban on teaching activities for those in holy orders.

The agrarian and Basque–Navarran deputies walked out of the Cortes after Article 26 of the Constitution (the 'matter of religion') was passed and published a manifesto declaring that 'the Constitution that is going to be passed cannot be ours' and that they would employ all their efforts in 'mobilising public opinion against it'. Article 26 called for declaring Church property as belonging to the state, and barring religious orders from taking part in industrial and trading activities, or in teaching. Alcalá Zamora and Miguel Maura, who had announced that they would vote against the article, resigned, and Manuel Azaña was nominated as the new prime minister, a post which he took up on 15 October.

The Constitution resulting from this long debate defined Spain, in Article 1, as 'a democratic Republic of workers of all types, structured around freedom and justice. All its authority comes from the people. The Republic constitutes an integrated state, compatible with the autonomy of its Municipalities and Regions.' This Constitution also declared the non-confessional nature of the state and the ending of state financing of the clergy, introduced civil marriage and divorce, and banned teaching activities for those in holy orders. Article 36, following heated debates, granted the vote to women, something that was being done in the democratic parliaments of the most enlightened countries during the inter-war years. It was a proposal defended by the Partido Radical deputy, Clara Campoamor, in spite of the fact that a good many leftist republicans, including the socialist-radical Victoria Kent, feared that women would be influenced by the clergy to give their vote to right-wing organisations. With socialist support, despite the misgivings of Indalecio Prieto, the article was passed by 160 votes to 121.

After this democratic and secular constitution, which confirmed the supremacy of the legislative power, was passed, it was time to elect the president of the Republic. He was to be elected not by direct universal suffrage as had been envisaged at first, following the pattern in other European republics, but by the Cortes. The government had agreed that the man for the job was Niceto Alcalá Zamora, in an attempt to bring back into the fold the conservative sector that had expressed its opposition to the articles regarding religion.

Alcalá Zamora called on Manuel Azaña to form a government. Azaña's intention was that all the political forces that had been in the government since the proclamation of the Republic should continue to be represented, in a similar proportion. Lerroux refused to carry on in the government with the socialists. Azaña would have to make a choice: either the socialists or the Partido Radical. He opted for the socialists: 'sending the socialists into opposition would turn the Cortes into a madhouse', he wrote in his diary on 13 December, convinced that introducing representatives of the working classes into the government of the nation was an indispensable condition for stabilising the Republic and democracy.[8]

The broad republican–socialist coalition that had governed in the early months of the Republic broke up in December 1931. Nevertheless, the alliance between leftist republicans, some 150 deputies, and the socialists, with 115, ensured the existence of a government, bearing in mind that the 94 deputies who went over to the opposition belonged to a historical republican party, Lerroux's Partido Radical, and the monarchist or Catholic opposition was very weak at that time. This government, with Azaña as prime minister and minister of war, was in power for almost two years, quite a feat in view of the previous history of the Republic. From the arrival of the Republic in April 1931 until the removal of Azaña in September 1933, the coalition governments of republicans and socialists undertook the reorganisation of the army, the separation of Church and State, and took radical and far-reaching measures concerning the distribution of agricultural land, the wages of the working classes, employment protection and public education. Never before had Spain experienced such an intense period of change and conflict, democratic advances or social triumphs.

---

[8] Manuel Azaña, *Memorias políticas y de guerra*, 2 vols. (Barcelona: Crítica, 1981), vol. I, p. 335.

Of all these reforms, those in agriculture were the most eagerly awaited and also the most difficult. There was no easy solution for what was known as the land problem in Spain for various reasons. Firstly, the complexity of the ownership structure: extremes predominated, with very few mid-size properties, and regional differences were marked, with a great many small-holdings in the north and mainly large estates in the south. The second reason was that although reformist politicians had been advocating some sort of agrarian reform since the end of the eighteenth century, barely anything had been done by the beginning of the Republic. Repression, rather than negotiation, had always been the weapon used by the state against peasant protests. And, finally, it was practically impossible to distribute land without arousing strong opposition. The largest properties were not in the hands of the Church, foreign owners or the aristocracy, which would have facilitated matters as it had done in other countries that undertook agrarian reform in the contemporary era. In Spain, as Edward Malefakis wrote more than forty years ago, land had to be taken from middle-class owners who, broadly speaking, were fully integrated into the structure of the nation, and who could not take any further pressure without the risk of calling into question many of the basic principles of this political structure. This was why any agrarian reform, however moderate, would have been seen by the owners as a revolution of compulsory seizures. And this was also why land became one of the fundamental pivots of conflict during the Republic and ended up being a substantial component of political violence on the two sides that fought the Civil War.[9]

The scope of the law was limited because republican governments were always wary of resistance from the owners and the effects of a real social transformation on the rural world. Most of these reformist laws coming from the republican–socialist coalition governments were moderate in practice but threatening in principle. Those who felt threatened very soon organised themselves to fight them. The old ruling classes, property-owners and people of order, displaced from power by the republican regime, reacted energetically and resoundingly to the reforms. The labouring classes, with their organisations, protests and mobilisations, appeared on the public scene, in the streets, factories and the fields, as powerful contenders who could no longer be excluded from the political system, demanding the speeding up of reforms or revolution.

[9] Edward Malefakis, *Agrarian Reform and Peasant Revolution in Spain* (New Haven, CT: Yale University Press, 1970).

Conflicts

With the coming of the Republic, those who hitherto had had no power
found new opportunities to become involved in politics, to influence the
authorities, thanks to the change of regime and the weakened state in
which those who had up to then occupied positions of power now found
themselves. With the loss of control in the city councils and the increase of
socialist influence, capitalising on the legal framework set up by the
Ministry of Labour to run labour relations, the owners' resistance to
republican legislation greatly intensified. This hostility was particularly
acrimonious in areas with large estates and a rural proletariat, where
social struggles seemed to be most intense. Employers' failure to comply
with the regulatory principles of agricultural labour and, in general,
republican social legislation, unleashed workers' protests. What they
were asking for in these conflicts was not social revolution, confiscations
from the rich or land collectivisation, claims which could be found in the
most radical pamphlets, but better salaries, employment rights and access
to land.

The Republic arrived in Spain in the midst of an unprecedented
international economic crisis and although, as experts have pointed
out, economic factors played no part in its tragic denouement, they did
hamper the management and implementation of reforms. Initial expectations started to founder when it became clear that agricultural reform
was going to be a slow process, unemployment rose, crops failed and
some of the most radical protests ended with harsh reprisals by the
armed forces. In those early years there were serious public order problems, a good many protests, revolutionary skirmishes and anarchist
insurrections.

Faced with these protests, the republican governments employed the
same mechanisms of repression that had been used by the monarchist
governments. In fact, public order was beginning to become an obsession
with the republican authorities: a well-founded obsession because there
was constant defiance of public order, but the substantial bloodshed
caused by these conflicts very soon undermined the prestige of the republican regime. The fledgling regime provided itself with a 'Legal Statute'
which gave the provisional government 'full powers', a situation that was
maintained until the Defence of the Republic Act of 21 October 1931, and
extended by means of the Public Order Act of July 1933. In addition, the
provisional government set up a new armed police force for the cities, the
Assault Guard, organised by Lieutenant Colonel Agustín Muñoz Grandes
who, according to Miguel Maura, then the interior minister, 'built from
nothing a perfect body of trained, uniformed, select and impeccably

disciplined troops'.[10] They wore dark blue uniforms and were armed with pistols and truncheons instead of the Mauser rifles that were carried by the Civil Guard.

The Civil Guard, as events proved time and again during those years, was incapable of maintaining order without opening fire. The landowners, wrote Azaña, adored this corps 'as the only upholder of social order', but the workers, particularly agricultural workers, hated it.[11] It was a hate that was shown clearly in Castilblanco, Extremadura, on 31 December 1931, after the Civil Guard shot and killed a striker. The peasants rushed against the four guards who were putting down the protest and killed them with stakes, stones and knives.

Enraged, undisciplined and faced with the passive attitude of certain government authorities, the Civil Guard worked off steam during the first few days of 1932 with deadly reprisals in various towns and villages in Spain. The most repressive events took place on 5 January in Arnedo, La Rioja, where the putting down of a peaceful demonstration left a trail of blood in the Plaza de la República: six men and five women dead; eleven women and nineteen men wounded. The lieutenant in command of the guards lined up in the square ordered them to open fire, without warning, in spite of the fact that his superiors, the civil governor and the lieutenant colonel of the local Civil Guard, who were at a meeting in the town hall at the time, had given no orders for the demonstration to be dispersed.

The 'outcry' that arose against the Civil Guard following these events was, as Manuel Azaña noted, 'deafening'. The prime minister telephoned General José Sanjurjo, the director general of the Civil Guard, to notify him of his dismissal. In the conversation that Azaña quotes in his diary, Sanjurjo blamed the Republic for allowing the entry of socialists in town and city councils, which were full of 'riff-raff', 'undesirables' who 'incite disorder, intimidate employers, cause damage to property and feel bound to clash with the Civil Guard'. Socialists, said the general to Azaña, should not be in the government 'because their presence encourages those who favour excess'.[12] Such was the atmosphere of disorder that he believed existed that a few months later he led the first military uprising against the republican regime. It failed because this way of overthrowing the Republic by force did not yet enjoy, one year after its proclamation, widespread

---

[10] Miguel Maura, *Así cayó Alfonso XIII*, p. 275.
[11] Azaña, *Memorias políticas y de guerra*, vol. I, p. 362.
[12] Annotation on 6 January 1932, *ibid.*, vol. I, p. 365. Extensive information and analysis of these conflicts can be found in Julián Casanova, *Anarchism, the Republic and Civil War in Spain* (London: Routledge, 2004), pp. 24–6.

support, except from certain sectors of the military, the aristocracy and the extreme right.

The socialists were in the government and the town and city halls, while anarchism, the other ideology that was followed by a large sector of workers in Spain, remained on the fringes of the institutions. Although they declared themselves to be anti-parliamentarian, the leaders of the CNT, the anarcho-syndicalist organisation that had begun to take hold in the final years of the Restoration, were constantly arguing over whether to take up the fight from the beginning of the republican regime or not. Many of them thought that the freedoms that the Republic had brought in, after the years of silence imposed by Primo de Rivera's dictatorship, would enable them once more to occupy the public domain, organise the workers and mobilise them against the employers and bourgeois order. Others preferred not to wait and opted for confrontation with the Republic, a symbol for them of repressive forces and its socialist 'traitors'.

The struggle for the distribution of trade union recognition and control of the labour market, a scarce resource in these times of crisis, very soon became the main cause of harsh confrontations between the two trade union organisations. On the government's side the UGT, under Largo Caballero, legislating and using the apparatus of the state, gained more and more ground in the field of labour relations, thereby reinforcing its positions in negotiations and control of employment contracts. The CNT denounced this favouritism and, instead of taking part in the joint arbitration committees set up by the Ministry of Labour, launched an all-out attempt to embrace other means of achieving the monopoly of labour negotiation, via direct action, without state intermediaries. This direct action, which at first merely envisaged warnings and threats, later expressed itself, with the rise in unemployment and conflicts, in coercion and violence.

The hard core of the anarchist movement used government repression as an excuse and motivation for mobilisation against the Republic and the leaders of the CNT at that time. The internal struggle led to a schism with thousands of militants in the most industrialised areas, where the organisation was most firmly entrenched, leaving the CNT, including some of its most outstanding leaders such as Juan Peiró and Ángel Pestaña. Meanwhile, those who backed the organisation, activists and members of the FAI, began to preach revolution through disturbances and revolt.

There were three attempts at armed insurrection in two years, incited by anarchist militants, supported to some degree by workers and peasants. The first two, in January 1932 and 1933, were directed against the republican–socialist coalition government. The third, the one with the most casualties, occurred in December 1933, a few days after Lerroux's radicals and the right won the elections. It was the tragic events at Casas Viejas, however, that had the most repercussions on republican policy.

There was nothing particular about this town in Cádiz, with barely 2,000 inhabitants, to distinguish it from dozens of towns in Andalucía, Extremadura or La Mancha: hunger, harsh working conditions, unequal distribution of wealth and exploitation. It all began in the early hours of 11 January 1933, when groups of peasants affiliated to the CNT, following the preparatory instructions issued by anarchists in the district of Jerez, took up positions in the town and surrounded the Civil Guard barracks armed with a few pistols and shotguns. Inside were three guards and a sergeant. After an exchange of fire, the sergeant and one of the guards were fatally wounded.

That same afternoon, several Civil and Assault Guards arrived in Casas Viejas, liberated the two guards left in the barracks and secured the town. With the help of the two guards who knew the inhabitants, they began to search for the rebels. They brought in two of the inhabitants and beat them until they gave the name of the family of Francisco Cruz Gutiérrez, 'Seisdedos' (six-toes), a 62-year-old anarchist who had not taken part in the insurrection. But two of his sons and his son-in-law had, and following the siege of the barracks, they had taken refuge in Seisdedos's house, a flimsy shack of mud and stones.

The captain of the Assault Guard, Manuel Rojas, who had been told by Arturo Menéndez, the director of security, to go to Casas Viejas to put down the insurrection, ordered the house to be burnt down. Eight dead was the final toll. But Rojas sent three patrols to search the houses in the town: they killed a 75-year-old man at the very beginning and arrested twelve more, whom they dragged to Seisdedos's house, and shot there and then. The massacre concluded with nineteen men, two women and a child dead. Three guards suffered the same fate. The truth about the incident took time to be made public, because the early versions had all of the peasants killed in the attack on Seisdedos's shack, but the Second Republic now had its tragedy.[13]

Dozens of peasants were arrested and tortured. The government, in an attempt to ride out the attacks against it from left and right over the excessive cruelty it had used to put down the uprising, washed its hands of all responsibility. 'There is no evidence of any government blame here', claimed Azaña in a speech to the Cortes on 2 February of that year. 'In Casas Viejas, as far as we know, nothing untoward happened ... A dozen men hoisted the libertarian communist banner, armed themselves and

[13] The account is based on the excellent description of this insurrection by Jerome R. Mintz, *The Anarchists of Casas Viejas* (University of Chicago Press, 1982), pp. 189–255.

attacked the Civil Guard, causing several deaths. What was the government supposed to do?'[14] The CNT, whose only benefit from all this was the acquisition of more martyrs for the cause, demonstrated with these insurrectional actions that it did not accept the system of representative institutions and republican democracy, and that it believed in force as the only way of eliminating class privilege and its corresponding abuse of power. CNT opposition deprived the Republic of a fundamental social cornerstone. But although anarchist radicalism helped to spread the culture of confrontation, it was not the only, nor even the most powerful, movement to frustrate the consolidation of the Republic and its reformist project. The dominant groups who had been removed from political institutions with the arrival of the Republic were not slow to react. In less than two years, Catholicism took root as a mass political movement, with the support of hundreds of thousands of small and medium-sized rural landowners, and launched a destabilising offensive that concluded only when it had met its objective of overthrowing the reforms and removing the threat of revolution.

Until the bursting on to the scene of Catholicism as a political movement, Lerroux's radicals, who had left the government in December 1931, after the passing of the Constitution, had become the surest guarantee of order for the employers against Azaña and the socialists, and in many places it had also become a haven for *caciques* and hardened monarchists. With this mixture of classes, the party's propaganda was directed 'towards all Spaniards' and aimed to exploit, using any means, in rallies and meetings with employers and businessmen, any sign of unrest against all socialists.

The proclamation of the Republic had not sat well with the business world, which saw the socialists' participation in government, particularly with Largo Caballero in the Ministry of Labour, as a threat to its interests and to the nation's wealth. 'Socialists out!' became the unanimous war-cry of businessmen and employers in the spring and summer of 1933, when the economic crisis and unemployment were at their height, and the CNT was concentrating its strikes and mobilisations against the joint arbitration committees.

Opposition from the radicals, businessmen, landowners and the appearance of the Confederación Española de Derechas Autónomas (CEDA – the Spanish Confederation of the Autonomous Right) as a mass political movement in February 1933 generated a great deal of tension between a Parliament dominated by the left and broad sectors of society, including

[14] Manuel Azaña, *Obras completas*, 7 vols. (Mexico City: Oasis, 1966–8), vol. II, pp. 334–6.

the CNT trade unions, who severely criticised the government's legislation. During the first few months of 1933, there were clear signs that the governing coalition was losing support. At the time the Cortes were debating the Religious Confessions and Congregations Bill, which gave rise to strong Catholic mobilisation and, although it was passed on 17 May, the president of the Republic, Alcalá Zamora, a Catholic, did not sign it until 2 June, leaving no doubts as to his discontent with the government.

Despite the pressure he was under to break with the socialists, Azaña still held the conviction, originating from his first constitutional government in December 1931, when Lerroux's radicals withdrew, that in order to build a democratic parliamentary system what was needed was the collaboration of the socialists and control of their trade union force. And the socialists had also made it quite clear on various occasions that their commitment to participation in the government depended on Azaña's continuing as prime minister. And they wanted it to stay that way until Alcalá Zamora, who from then on would play a major role in resolving all political crises, prevented it.

The big opportunity to break this alliance was presented to Alcalá Zamora at the beginning of September 1933, following the elections to the Constitutional Safeguards Tribunal, an institution whose remit included hearing appeals against laws for their non-constitutionality or conflicts over powers to act between the state and the Autonomous Communities. The opposition turned this election of fifteen members by the city councils into a plebiscite on Azaña's government. The vote took place on 3 September. The right gained ground and the Partido Radical obtained more votes than any other republican party, including the PSOE. Lerroux made it quite clear what he wanted: a republican-only government led by himself.

Azaña asked for a vote of confidence in the Cortes. He won, but on the next day, 7 September, Alcalá Zamora withdrew his confidence, which was tantamount to a sacking. Manuel Azaña was defeated not by the Cortes but by a decision of the president of the Republic, who asked Alejandro Lerroux to form a government that would re-establish 'brotherly understanding between all republican factions'. There would be no socialists in this government, something which all the parties of the right and almost all the republicans had been wanting for a long time. Nor did the socialists want to form a part of it under these conditions, with a government presided over by Lerroux; on 11 September, its executive committee unanimously passed a motion proposed by Largo Caballero that declared 'broken all the commitments agreed upon' with the republicans and that each party 'fully regained their independence to follow the path that they deemed pertinent to the defence of their interests'. The 1930 commitment, the one that had helped to give birth to the new regime, was breaking up and this rupture was to have major repercussions for the socialists and the Republic.

The left-wing republicans and the socialists refused to back Lerroux's government in the Cortes and Alcalá Zamora asked Diego Martínez Barrio, vice-president of the Partido Radical to form a new government. The day after the new government was formed, 9 October, the decree dissolving the Cortes was issued. A government led by the radicals would organise the general election, called for 19 November. The big novelty was to be the women's vote in a general election for the first time in Spain's history, which was to incorporate more than 6,800,000 new voters, over half the electorate.

The result of the second election to be held in the Republic was a resounding victory for the Partido Radical and the CEDA. There are various ways of explaining this victory and the defeat of the left. Electoral legislation benefited broad coalitions, and the socialists, who stood alone, and the republicans, who were disunited, lost ground. The more conservative forces, directionless and disorganised in 1931, had reorganised and united around the defence of order and religion. The radicals had also moved to the right, while anarchist propaganda in favour of abstention and confrontation between the two trade union organisations, the CNT and the UGT, took votes away from the republicans and socialists.

There is no doubt that there were many Catholic women in Spain who had voted for the right in 1933. But to say that women were responsible for the victory of the right, including under this label the CEDA and the Partido Radical, as particularly the republicans and some socialists who had spoken against women's suffrage in the debates of 1931 had done, seems to be unfounded. The electorate's shift to the right in 1933 was a general phenomenon, not just the result of the female vote. Women also voted in 1936, many of them for the CEDA, and yet it was the parties of the left, who had grouped themselves into the Popular Front coalition, that won those elections.

Alcalá Zamora's decision to withdraw his confidence from a government with a parliamentary majority, and to declare the job of the Cortes Constituyentes concluded, opened a period of political instability that hitherto had not been seen. It is often said that the governments of the Republic were weak and that they lasted for an average of 101 days. But this assessment does not hold true for the situation in the first two years. Azaña was prime minister for almost two years, with no crises. The governments under the Partido Radical after the 1933 elections never lasted more than an average of three months, and between September 1933 and December 1935 there were twelve governments, with five different prime ministers and fifty-eight different ministers.

The reformist projects of the republican–socialist coalition government, the implementation of secularising measures and control of the Church, the granting of Catalonia's statute of autonomy and, in general, the legislation of the Cortes Constituyentes had provoked the appearance of strong reactions and tensions in Spanish society. New paths were opening up for the Republic, without the socialists and leftist republicans. Lerroux's radicals promised to review the most 'socialising' aspects of the policy of the first biennium. Gil Robles and the CEDA wanted 'total rectification'. Coming to an agreement would not be easy.

6   A republic beleaguered

After the CEDA's and Partido Radical's victory in the November 1933 elections, Niceto Alcalá Zamora asked Alejandro Lerroux to form a 'purely republican' government of the centre, which would not include leftist republicans or the CEDA, which had failed to declare publicly its adherence to the Republic. The veteran leader of the Partido Radical thought that a parliamentary alliance with the CEDA would ensure a majority, and therefore governability, and would enable this 'accidentalist' right to be incorporated into the Republic, isolating the monarchist extreme right. However, the CEDA's strategy included forming a government, presiding over it and revising the Constitution.

The CEDA threatened violence unless they were allowed to govern, and the socialists proclaimed their intention of unleashing a revolution if the CEDA entered the government. After the revolution of October 1934, the potential centrist solutions proposed by Lerroux and his supporters were blocked by the CEDA's strategy of winning power. The employers went into action and recovered the ground they had lost with the arrival of the Republic. Agrarian reform became a thing of the past and Gil Robles, minister of war from May to December 1935 reinforced, with his appointments policy, the power of the anti-Azaña officers and introduced a rightist element into the army.

Just when it seemed that this rectification of the reformist Republic was firmly in motion, a series of political scandals discredited the Partido Radical, and Alcalá Zamora prevented Gil Robles from taking on the post of prime minister. Faced with the possibility of governing from the centre and non-republican right, the president of the Republic signed the decree of the dissolution of the Cortes. Behind lay two years of destruction of reformist policies. Fresh elections would decide the course of the Republic.

Order and religion

The reformist legislation of the first republican biennium reinforced the traditional identification between order and religion. The gulf between two cultural worlds at loggerheads, practising Catholics and hardline anti-clericals, which had opened up in the nineteenth century, widened with the proclamation of the Republic and drew in a large number of Spaniards who had hitherto shown indifference to this struggle. The religious problem, said Gil Robles, became the 'seed of discord'.[1] This discord was to be seen in Parliament, with the discussion over Article 26 of the Constitution, as well as in the streets, with the mobilisation of Catholics against the Republic.

This battle was over fundamental issues affecting the Church, such as the non-confessional nature of the state, the ending of state financing of the clergy and the ban on teaching activities for those in holy orders, although we should not forget other issues that fuelled the day-to-day conflict between the pro- and anti-clericals, such as the divorce and civil marriage laws passed in March and June 1932. Many priests and Catholics also came into conflict with the local authorities elected in April 1931 over religious rites and symbols of marked significance for the Catholic faith: bell-ringing, processions, baptisms, weddings and funerals. The abolition of processions caused innumerable conflicts in many towns, as borne out by the large number of telegrams sent by mayors and civil governors to the interior minister. And the burning of churches, religious schools and convents on 11 May 1931, the day after two people were killed in Madrid following an incident with young monarchists and confrontations with the Civil Guard, remained etched in the memory of many Catholics as being the first attack on the Church by a secular and anti-clerical Republic.

This campaign of mobilisation and accusations against the Constitution and the 'socialising' policy of the government was stepped up with the founding of the CEDA at a congress held in Madrid at the end of 1933, attended by 400 delegates who claimed to represent 735,058 members. The CEDA channelled widely diverse interests, from the small landowners to those in the agrarian and financial oligarchy, which is why its propaganda was often able to say that it was not a class-based organisation. It is true that its social composition was very broad, with many women in the main cities, but its identity and intentions seemed to be reasonably clear from the outset. Dominated and led by large landowners, urban professionals, this first mass party in the history of the Spanish right set itself up to defend 'Christian civilisation', combat the 'sectarian' legislation of the Republic and 'revise' the Constitution.[2]

---

[1] Gil Robles, *No fue posible la paz*, p. 31.
[2] The origins and consolidation of this popular Catholic movement have previously been described in José R. Montero, *La CEDA: el catolicismo social y político en la II República* (Madrid: Ediciones de la Revista de Trabajo, 1972).

Some of the merit for turning Catholicism into a mass political move-ment must go to José María Gil Robles, a young and hitherto little-known lawyer from Salamanca, from a Carlist family and a protégé of Ángel Herrera, who very soon made a name for himself as a parliamentarian for his questions to the government over religious matters. He was 34 years old. His strategy consisted of hoisting the 'banner to unite Catholics and attract a large mass of the detached', mobilising them and uniting them politically. This meant involving the Church hierarchy and obtaining funding from landowners and industrialists. Also clear in Gil Robles' mind was how to organise this mass Catholic response: providing the right, 'via mass rallies, with its lost self-awareness'; 'getting it used to confronting left-wing vio-lence and fighting back, when necessary, in the streets'; and 'disseminating an ideology and proselytising, by presenting the doctrine'.[3]

The mobilisation of Catholics against the articles of the Constitution that were detrimental to the Church's interests was embodied in an open attack on Manuel Azaña and his republican–socialist coalition government. Azaña was adamant that the Religious Confessions and Congregations Act would be complied with 'from beginning to end, with complete adherence, with total stringency', because, as he stated on various occasions, this act was the expression of Article 26 and 'the constitutional mandate' had to be complied with 'in all its requirements'. The Catholics classed it as a despotic and authoritarian act that ignored the essential characteristics and traditions of the Spanish nation. They set into motion all the many mechanisms at their disposal to defeat it. Azaña and the republican govern-ment rejected the power of the Church and the Catholics and, yet, two years after the proclamation of the Republic, there they were mobilising in the streets, in the media and in the pulpit. The opponent was indeed powerful, a genuine national bureaucracy, with some 115,000 clergy dis-tributed throughout all the villages, towns and cities, exercising an ideo-logical control that was without comparison in western societies. It was also a Church that had no respect for secular authority, unless this authority submitted to its commandments.[4]

Hostility towards the Republic could also be found in 1933 with the setting up of certain extreme right and fascist organisations, inspired by news of the overthrow of the Weimar Republic in Germany by Hitler and the Nazis. Fascism appeared later in Spain than in other countries,

---

[3] Gil Robles, *No fue posible la paz*, p. 64.
[4] The attitude of the Catholics towards Manuel Azaña and the scant attention paid by Azaña to this emerging Catholic movement are analysed extensively in Santos Juliá, *Manuel Azaña, una biografía política: del Ateneo al Palacio Nacional* (Madrid: Alianza Editorial, 1990), pp. 243–56.

particularly in comparison to Italy and Germany, and was very low-key as a political movement until spring 1936. During the early years of the Republic, it was barely noticed on a stage occupied by the extreme monarchist right and the moving to the right of political Catholicism. Definitely not fascist – despite the fact that they later sympathised with many of their ideas – were the monarchist right groups, Alfonsine and Carlist, who from the outset preached the violent overthrow of the Republic, albeit with very limited resources.

None of these radical monarchist ideas had shown, up to that time, any particular interest in fascist ideology, the early manifestations of which were following different courses in Spain. They began with cultural and journalistic projects. The first initiative came from Ernesto Jiménez Caballero with his avant-garde journal *Gaceta Literaria*, launched in 1927, although the first organised fascist group grew up around Ramiro Ledesma Ramos, a young intellectual post office official, and his weekly journal *La Conquista del Estado*, founded in March 1931. A few months later, in October, Ledesma Ramos and Enésimo Redondo, an extreme Catholic lawyer from Valladolid, launched the Juntas de Ofensiva Nacional Sindicalista (Unions of the National Syndicalist Offensive – JONS). Ledesma tried to instil a fascist-style revolutionary nationalism in the JONS, using direct action, which could compete with the anarcho-syndicalists in the working classes, but he never attracted more than a few hundred sympathisers, all recruited in the heartlands of Old Castile.

Hitler's ascendancy in Germany attracted the interest of many extreme right-wingers who, while still knowing little about fascism, saw in the Nazis a good example to follow in their attempts to overthrow the Republic. In Spain, however, any fascist project that wanted to flourish had to count on the monarchists to obtain funds, and this was the road that led to the founding of the Falange Española (FE) that year. José Antonio Primo de Rivera, the son of the late dictator, was the link between monarchist authoritarianism and the Italian-flavoured fascist ideas. Together with Rafael Sánchez Mazas and Julio Ruiz de Alda, he founded a splinter group, the Movimiento Español Sindicalista, which managed to obtain an undertaking from the Alfonsines of Renovación Española to finance the new party, in exchange for a brief mention in their political programme of the authoritarian concept of order advocated by traditional Catholicism.

This gave José Antonio Primo de Rivera better financial backing than the JONS had, and even enabled him to be elected to the Cortes as the right-wing candidate for Cádiz. In that electoral campaign, Primo de Rivera and Ruiz de Alda held an 'act of rightist affirmation' in the Comedy Theatre in Madrid on 29 October 1933, an event that was considered to be the origin and founding of Falange Española. Also present was Alfonso García

Valdecasas, an intellectual and pupil of Ortega y Gasset, a former member of the Agrupación al Servicio de la República (Group in the Service of the Republic), who a few months previously, during a period in which there was a mushrooming of pro-fascist splinter groups, had founded the Frente Español. At the beginning of 1934, the Falangists merged with the JONS to form the Falange Española de las JONS, remaining until the spring of 1936 a minuscule organisation with just a few thousand affiliates, which tried to obtain funding from monarchists and from Italy with limited success.

The CEDA was the party that obtained the most votes in the 1933 elections, in which José Antonio Primo de Rivera won a seat. It obtained 115 seats in the new Cortes. The radicals won 104 seats but, after two years in opposition, the party had won only ten seats more than in the elections for the Cortes Constituyentes. Manuel Azaña's Acción Republicana lost 23 of the 28 seats it had obtained in 1931 and the socialists went down from 115 to 58 seats. In all, the non-republican right went from 40 seats in 1931 to 200 in 1933, and the left from 250 to around 100. It was a highly fragmented parliament, with twenty-one groups represented and a good many new deputies: more than 60% of the radicals were in this category and only ten CEDA deputies had had previous parliamentary experience. With these results, it was going to be hard to establish a stable coalition.

The Cortes held their opening session on 8 December, and on 19 December Lerroux presented his government, made up of seven radicals, two independent republicans, one liberal democrat and the landowner and monarchist, José María Cid. Thus began what Lerroux called 'a Republic for all Spaniards'. After almost half a century of toiling away in politics, always for the republican cause, Lerroux was now prime minister of the Republic. He had been born in La Rambla, in the province of Córdoba, on 4 March 1864. By the time he had achieved his life's wish, he was 69.

Lerroux formed his government while the bodies were still being buried of those who had been killed in the third and last anarchist insurrection, promised by the CNT before the elections if the 'fascist tendencies' won. The confrontations between the authorities and the insurgents lasted from 8 to 15 December, particularly in Aragón and La Rioja, leaving behind a heavy toll: 75 dead and 101 wounded among the insurgents; 11 Civil Guards dead and 45 wounded; 3 Assault Guards dead and 18 wounded. The gaols filled up with anarchists and there were a great many allegations of torture. The CNT was broken, in disarray, with no mouthpiece. In short, it was just a remnant of what, two years earlier, promised to be a devastating force.

Just when the anarchists were exhausting their insurrectional options, and criticisms were being voiced from within the movement of the futility of these actions by 'rash minorities', the socialists were announcing revolution. After their exit from government in September 1933 – 'expulsion' some of their representatives would say – the legal struggle and reformism within the parliamentary Republic gave way to preaching revolution. In fact, they were beginning to tread paths that had previously been trodden by the anarchists: accusations of persecution and repression, general strikes and frustrated uprisings that were independent of daily working-class struggles.

As proposed from the outset, the socialist notice of revolution that followed their exit from the government and their break with the republicans was a defensive strategy to stop the CEDA, the non-republican right, from coming to power in a Republic that they, as its founders along with the republican left, considered to be theirs. The revolutionary uprising depended on a third-party decision – that Alcalá Zamora, the president of the Republic, would agree to admit the CEDA into the government; but the socialists spent several months preparing the way, in case that occurred.

And so began the government of a centrist republican coalition under Lerroux: with one recent anarchist uprising steeped in blood and the announcement of another socialist uprising to come. Lerroux wanted to revise the policies of the first biennium without the need to repeal some of its reforms. As some Partido Radical leaders said, he wanted to shift the Republic to the centre. But from the outset the non-republican right, upon whom he depended in order to govern, put pressure on him for a thorough revision which would act on the essential points of the reforms implemented by the republican–socialist coalition in the two previous years. Gil Robles warned him time and again in his speeches: either the government implemented a 'complete rectification' or the CEDA would be forced to bid for power.

One of the non-republican right's first objectives was to prevent the implementation of the Religious Confessions and Congregations Act which had been passed in June 1933. And they got their way. Catholic schools continued operating normally, and a law passed on 4 April 1934 partially reintroduced the payment of clergy salaries by the state. The effects of this highly anti-clerical law had been frozen, and religious displays, particularly rosaries and processions, were once again to be seen in many locations in Spain.

The Partido Radical had never liked the socialist-type labour legislation and the main employers' associations, happy with the centre–right election victory, called for 'proper rectifications'. Although they did not disappear, the joint arbitration committees changed the procedure for electing their presidents; they were now to be elected from among professionals, not appointed by the Ministry of Labour, and the power of these committees was transferred from the unions to the employers. The Municipal Districts Act was modified and, in practical terms, repealed. The landowners discriminated against the most contentious of the socialist militants and anarchists, lowered wages and recovered a large part of the power they had lost in the early days of the Republic. The socialists denounced the situation in their media, and in the Cortes the more moderate radicals acknowledged that *caciquismo* had come back to many towns and villages. The Partido Radical, which many people had long considered to be the epitome of nepotism and influence-peddling, now attracted *caciques* and monarchists, and its leaders received hundreds of letters seeking favours. 'They all want jobs, they are all asking for posts', wrote the Galician deputy, Gerardo Abad Conde, in a letter to Lerroux.[5]

However, the Partido Radical's pact with the CEDA was soon to cause major tension within the leadership, which eventually led to a split between the parties. Diego Martínez Barrio, the party's vice-president, complained on several occasions of the shift to the right and criticised its collaboration with the CEDA while it was unwilling to declare itself republican. Gil Robles threatened to 'withdraw its support from the government' and Martínez Barrio, increasingly isolated, resigned his portfolio as minister of war at the end of February 1934. This was the first of the various crises that the CEDA would provoke in the radical governments.

The crisis that was to come shortly afterwards had worse consequences for the Partido Radical. The government brought before the Cortes a proposal for amnesty for those involved in the military uprising of August 1932, particularly for General Sanjurjo, its leader in Seville: an amnesty that was part of the election programme for both the CEDA and the Partido Radical, and which revealed the possible debt that Lerroux owed to the insurgents. After angry exchanges in Parliament, the law was passed on 20 April and included, finally, those involved in the *sanjurjada* and those imprisoned for the anarchist insurrection of December 1933.

Alcalá Zamora refused to sign it, as he had warned he would, because in his opinion the law weakened the Republic by releasing its enemies. He wanted to send it back to the Cortes for their reconsideration, but not one government minister backed him, a prerequisite for these cases under Article 84 of the Constitution. So Alcalá Zamora signed the new law but attached a 34-page memorandum listing all his personal objections. Gil Robles tried to take advantage of the situation to force the president's

[5] Quoted in Nigel Townson, *La República que no pudo ser: la política de centro en España (1931–1936)* (Madrid: Taurus, 2002), p. 247 (English version: *The Crisis of Democracy in Spain: Centrist Politics under the Second Republic 1931–1936* (Brighton: Sussex Academic Press, 2000)).

resignation, but Lerroux refused to co-operate and was forced to present his resignation as a matter of protocol. This happened on 25 April, and the following day Alcalá Zamora invited the minister of labour, Ricardo Samper, a jurist and veteran republican from Valencia, to form a government, something that Lerroux accepted so as not to provoke a greater crisis. It was the third radical government in four months and the crisis also showed that, by his excessive meddling, Alcalá Zamora would not let the parliamentary system operate normally. However, Samper was not the leader of the radicals, and soon after taking office, the party split, leaving his position even weaker.

The split came from the left wing of the Partido Radical and was led by Martínez Barrio just over two months after he had left the government. The dissidents, who some months later were to form Unión Republicana, were leaving the party, as they explained in a manifesto published on 19 May, because it had moved away from the 'old radical ideology'. A few days later, Martínez Barrio declared that Lerroux had changed the centrist policy of the radicals for one of 'sectarian' right which rejected the 'liberal, democratic theories' of the Republic. Nineteen deputies left the Partido Radical, and the split also affected a large number of provincial leadership structures. Townson remarked that the schism not only shifted the party *to* the right, but also made it more dependent *on* the right.[6]

Ricardo Samper governed from 28 April 1934 to the beginning of October that same year and during that time he had to deal with growing trade union mobilisation, major social conflicts in Madrid, Barcelona and Zaragoza and a general land-workers' strike. Beleaguered by these conflicts, and harshly criticised by the employers, who accused it of weakness and of failing to support their interests against the unions, Samper's government was at the mercy of the CEDA and the strategy of Gil Robles, who was now thinking of the second phase of his plan: entering government. After the 1934 parliamentary summer recess, but before the first session of the Cortes on 1 October, Gil Robles decided to tighten the thumbscrew: he officially withdrew the CEDA's support from Samper's government, asked for a reshuffle and announced that the CEDA should enter the new government.[7]

The radicals, with Lerroux at their head, knew that they could not continue in government without the CEDA. Samper tried to defend his record in the opening session of the Cortes, but Gil Robles publicly repeated his proposal: a government that reflected the parliamentary majority.

[6] *Ibid.*, p. 277.
[7] The obstacles placed by the CEDA against Samper's government are summarised *ibid.*, pp. 303–10.

Samper resigned. Alcalá Zamora did not want to dissolve the Cortes, because the Constitution allowed him to do so only twice, and so he gave in to the non-republican right's proposal and asked Lerroux to form a new government; it was announced on 4 October and included three CEDA ministers: Manuel Giménez Fernández in agriculture, Rafael Aizpún in justice and José Oriol Anguera de Sojo in labour.

The non-republican right began to govern the Republic with the most traditional republican parties. The republican left warned of the 'betrayal' involved in 'the monstrous act of handing over the government of the Republic to its enemies'.[8] Martínez Barrio, Lerroux's former lieutenant who was no longer in the party, asked Alcalá Zamora to give power to the left to save the Republic. The socialists declared their revolution. Nothing would be the same after October 1934.

General strike and revolution

The revolution, according to the socialist revolutionary committee, was to start with a general strike in the main cities and industrial centres, supported by sympathetic sectors of the armed forces. There were major strikes in Madrid, Seville, Córdoba, Valencia, Barcelona and Zaragoza, with brief outbreaks of armed uprising in certain locations in the latter province. In the mining area to the west of Bilbao, the army and the Civil Guard fought the insurgents for a few hours, and in Eibar and Mondragón the violent actions of the revolutionaries killed certain well-known rightists, such as the Carlist deputy, Marcelino Oreja. Nowhere, however, did the soldiers leave their barracks to support the revolution, and the armed uprising was limited to Asturias, although the rebellion of the Generalitat – the institution under which the autonomous community of Catalonia is politically organised – against central power also had a strong political impact.

The general strike began in Catalonia on 5 October without the official support of the CNT. At 8 p.m. the following day, President Lluís Companys announced that the government of the Generalitat was breaking all links with 'spurious institutions' – as all the republican left parties had already done when the CEDA entered the government – and proclaimed 'the Catalan State within the Spanish Federal Republic' as a measure against the 'monarchist and Fascist forces . . . who had seized power'.[9]

[8] The 'betrayal' of the Republic and the socialists' condemnation of this 'betrayal' may be found in Santos Juliá, 'Los socialistas y el escenario de la futura revoluciòn', in Gabriel Jackson et al., Octubre 1934: cincuenta años para la reflexión (Madrid: Siglo XXI Editores, 1985), pp. 126–7.

[9] Enric Ucelay da Cal, La Catalunya populista: imatge, cultura i politica en l'etapa republicana (1931–1936) (Barcelona: Ediciones de la Magrana, 1982), pp. 216–17.

Despite the preparations for rebellion carried out by Josep Dencás, the *conseller de Governació*, General Domingo Batet, the head of the military garrison in Barcelona, ignored the orders given by Companys as the highest authority in Catalonia, and took over the city. In the early hours of the following day, he placed his troops outside the Generalitat building, and after limited resistance and artillery fire, the Catalan government surrendered. The unsuccessful rebellion left a death toll of forty-six people: eight soldiers and thirty-eight civilians.

This failure occurred at the same time as the failure of most of the strikes and attempted uprisings that had observed the order of the revolutionary committee. The aim had been to stop the CEDA entering the government, but to no avail. Quite a different story was to be found in Asturias, with revolutionary violence and subsequent brutal repression hitherto unseen in Spain. It was a genuine attempt at social revolution: October 1934, 'red' October.

In Asturias, preparations for the uprising involved stealing rifles, machine guns and sticks of dynamite. These arms were not enough to defeat the security forces and the army, but they were enough to launch thousands of militants in a struggle against the Civil Guard in their barracks. The presence of these arms explains why it was in Asturias, and only in Asturias, that the revolutionaries were able to occupy and control various towns and cities for several days.[10]

The uprising began on the night of 5 to 6 October when several thousand trade union militants seized the Civil Guard posts in the mining areas, took control of Aviles and Gijón, took over the ordnance works in Trubia and occupied the centre of Oviedo. Fierce fighting ensued there between the forces of order and the revolutionaries in the area of the Civil Government building, the Telefónica building and the cathedral. The regional committee of the Alianza Obrera, led by the socialist, Ramón González Peña, co-ordinated the large number of local committees which sprang up in the various towns, and tried to guide the 'revolutionary order'. Swift control was established of the public and transport services and supplies for besieged locations; in some places the official coinage was suppressed and the first examples of violence against employers, people of order and the clergy appeared.

Thirty-four priests, seminarists and brothers from the *Escuelas Cristianas* in Turón were killed, with the legislative persecution of the first biennium giving way to the physical destruction of members of the Church, something which had not occurred in the history of Spain since the

[10] Paco Ignacio Taibo, 'La diferencia asturiana', in Jackson *et al.*, *Octubre 1934*, pp. 231–41.

massacres of 1834–5 in Madrid and Barcelona. Furthermore, the purifying fire appeared once more in Asturias: fifty-eight churches, the bishop's palace, the seminary with its magnificent library and the *Cámara Santa* in the cathedral were burnt or blown up.

To co-ordinate the military operations and repression for this insurrection, Diego Hidalgo, the minister of war, passed over the chief of the General Staff, General Carlos Masquelet, and instead appointed General Francisco Franco, with whom he had recently attended military manoeuvres in León. For a few days Franco was effectively the minister of war, with total command over public order and, for the first time in his life, was able, in the words of Paul Preston, to experience 'an intoxicating taste of unprecedented politico-military power'.[11] Furthermore, to put down the workers' rebellion, he used the Legion and the *Regulares* of Morocco, under the command of Lieutenant Colonel Juan Yagüe, and deployed for the first time some of the methods of repression that he would later use in the Civil War. On 18 October, the last insurgents surrendered.

To confront the revolutionary violence, there were summary executions under martial law. The best estimate of victims suggests 1,100 deaths among those who supported the rebellion, some 2,000 wounded, and some 300 deaths among the security forces and the army. In the first phase of repression, hundreds of prisoners were beaten and tortured, a measure in which the Civil Guard major Lisardo Doval, a long-standing colleague of Franco's, played a leading role by imposing genuine police brutality, until he was dismissed in December. Luis de Sirval, a journalist who had investigated and denounced the excesses of Yagüe's mercenaries, was murdered by a foreign officer of the Legion, Lieutenant Dimitri I. Ivanov. A large number of leading republican and socialist politicians, including Largo Caballero and Azaña, were arrested. The gaols filled up with prisoners, revolutionaries and leftist militants, and repression became a recurrent theme in political debate over the following months.

Although this uprising was better organised and had more backing and weaponry than the anarchists had had in 1932 and 1933, its failure is easily explainable. The forces of public order and the army were loyal to the government, and there was no chance of their joining the revolutionaries or refusing to repress them. Against a state that keeps its armed forces intact and united, a revolutionary strategy based on scattered support can never spark widespread disruption and ends up being easily repressed. The military preparation for the uprising was left in the hands of groups of young people who were able to erect barricades in certain *barrios* in the

---

[11] Paul Preston, *Franco: A Biography* (London: Harper Collins, 1993), p. 103.

cities, or to fight with more arms in the mining areas, but not to oppose a united army. Following the Russian precedent in 1917, where the army was demoralised after heavy defeats and hundreds of thousands of casualties in the First World War, no worker or peasant uprising succeeded in Europe, with the exception of Bela Kun's regime for a few months in Hungary in 1919. For armed revolutions to succeed, they need to have some of the army on their side. And the revolutionary process requires, as the military coup in July 1936 proved, the collapse and division of the mechanisms of coercion and defence of the state. None of this happened in October 1934.

With this rebellion, the socialists showed the same condemnation of parliamentary democracy as the anarchists had done in previous years. The same preaching of revolution, determined by the CEDA's entry into the government, was a means of coercion against the established legitimate political authority. Leaving aside the alleged circumstances of their radicalisation, the socialists broke with the democratic process and the parliamentary system as a means to press for a re-orientation of politics. The movement's leaders, at the instigation of the younger members, who formed militias and developed a taste for a military framework, tried to copy the Bolshevik model in Spain.

The militants in the Juventudes Socialistas were the first to applaud the socialists' exit from the government in 1933 and the tearing up of all their agreements with the republicans; it was this that closed the 'bourgeois democracy' phase and saw the start of their headlong rush to social revolution.[12] The increase in calls for violent action matched the loss of confidence in the legality of the republic. The appearance of Falange Española, Hitler's rise to power, the crushing of the Austrian socialist movement by Chancellor Engelbert Dollfuss in February 1934, the verbal aggression of Gil Robles, with his constant rants against democracy in favour of the 'totalitarian concept of the state', and the obvious fascist leanings of the youth wing of Acción Popular (JAP), mobilised young people, both students and workers; in the first few months of 1934 they launched violent political confrontations such as had not been seen during the early years of the Republic.

Yet to suggest that the October uprising marked the end of any possibility of constitutional coexistence in Spain, the 'prelude' or 'opening battle' of the Civil War, is to place a workers' uprising, defeated and repressed by republican order, on the same plane as a military rebellion carried out by the armed forces of the state. The Republic always repressed uprisings and

---

[12] Sandra Souto Kustrín, 'Y ¿Madrid? ¿Qué hace Madrid?' Movimiento revolucionario y acción colectiva (1923–1936) (Madrid: Siglo XXI Editores, 2004).

imposed order. After October 1934, socialists and anarchists alike aban-doned rebellion as a stratagem and the possibilities of trying it again in 1936 were practically nil, now that their ranks were split and considerably weakened. For the non-republican right, however, October 1934 marked the way. They always had the army, the 'backbone of the Fatherland', as José Calvo Sotelo would often refer to it then.

After October 1934, the left tried to re-establish its democratic political activity, win at the polls and surmount its insurrectional failures. The CEDA grew, defended repression to the hilt, and shed any possibility of stabilising the Republic with its coalition partner, the Partido Radical. Any potential centrist solutions proposed by Lerroux and his team ended up swamped by the CEDA's conquest of power strategy, and by the scandals that, barely a year after that October, engulfed them until they were eliminated from the political scene.

The brunt of the blame for the rebellion was placed, at the instigation of the CEDA and one sector of the Partido Radical, on Manuel Azaña, the socialists and the Statute of Catalonia as a symbol of the 'disunity of the Fatherland'. Azaña had gone to Barcelona on 28 September to attend the funeral of Jaume Carner, his former finance minister. After the funeral, Azaña remained in Barcelona and, although he took no part in what was called the rebellion of the Catalans, beginning on the evening of 6 October, he was arrested and held in a prison ship, accused by the Republic's public prosecutor of the crime of rebellion, until he was released by order of the High Court on 28 December 1934.

The next step in the search for scapegoats was to try and discredit the Statute of Catalonia and have it abolished. Following a debate between the government coalition partners, in which some wanted it modified and others abolished, a law was passed on 14 December suspending Catalonia's autonomy indefinitely, and the central administration took back the powers transferred in the two previous years. The whole of Catalonia was being punished for the rebellion by certain members of its governing party. A few days later, Lerroux's government appointed as governor general a veteran politician of the monarchist Partido Liberal, Manuel Portela Valladares, and he handed the Barcelona city council over to the radicals.

More than 3,000 people were arrested in Catalonia, and the first death sentences were handed down for the October rebellion by the military courts on to Major Enrique Pérez Farrás and Captains Federic Escofet and Joan Ricart, who had been involved in the uprising as heads of the autonomous police force, the *mossos d'esquadra*, and the *somatén*. On 17 October the government voted for the executions, although the president of the Republic, Alcalá Zamora, reminded them that they had pardoned those responsible for the military uprising of 10 August 1932 and, despite the vehement opposition of the CEDA and others who advocated a firm hand, he managed to persuade Lerroux to commute the death sentences on 31 October. However, the trials continued, and this time it was Companys and his *consellers* who, on 6 June 1935, were sentenced to thirty years' imprisonment for 'military rebellion'.

Meanwhile in Asturias, the beatings in the gaols went on, and the repression aggravated the division in the governing coalition. The prisoners signed letters denouncing the use of torture, and British and French socialist politicians visited the region and pleaded for amnesty for the accused. Only two death sentences were carried out in February 1935, a sergeant who had deserted the army to fight on the side of the revolutionaries, and a worker accused of several murders. The rest of the death sentences were commuted although, when the cabinet met on 29 March to discuss the cases of Ramón González Peña, the most prominent leader of the insurrection, and Teodomiro Menéndez, the government was split, with Lerroux and six other radicals voting in favour of a reprieve, and the three CEDA ministers, the Agrarian and the Liberal Democrat against.

Protests about the arbitrary and, as time went on, unnecessary repression left the radical ministers 'consumed within', as César Jalón, the radical minister of communications in the government that Lerroux formed on 4 October 1934, later wrote: 'Asturias, it's always Asturias ... The nightmare of revolution and the nightmare of Spain would always be the spectre that followed us until it overthrew us.'[13]

'Full power for the chief'

Indeed, the CEDA and the non-republican right wanted to take revenge to its ultimate consequences, and they provoked the government crises that were needed to achieve their aim of seeing Gil Robles as prime minister, the final phase of their strategy. Taking the reprieve of Pérez Farrás as his excuse, Gil Robles sounded out the possibility of the army imposing a 'solution of force' to restore the 'legitimacy violated by the president'.[14] Generals Joaquín Fanjul and Manuel Poded, leading figures in all the conspiracies against the Republic from 1932 until it was overthrown in 1936, advised the CEDA leader to maintain the party's collaboration in government, as the army could not yet guarantee a united position of strength to squash the left.

---

[13] Quoted in Townson, *La República que no pudo ser*, p. 323.
[14] Gil Robles, *No fue posible la paz*, pp. 145–8.

After provoking several crises in which the CEDA succeeded in turning out various ministers, Gil Robles prepared his incorporation into the government. On 3 April, the three CEDA ministers resigned over the reprieve of twenty prisoners condemned to death by the military courts for the Asturias insurrection, including Rafael González Peña and Teodomiro Menéndez. In new consultations set up by Alcalá Zamora as a result of the crisis, the CEDA and José Martínez de Velasco's Agrarians requested more posts in the government. After Alcalá Zamora, who was unwilling to give more power to the CEDA, refused this request, Gil Robles threatened to dissolve the Cortes, and the JAP asked for 'full power for the chief' at a rally with fascist paraphernalia held in Madrid on 23 April.

Lerroux agreed to form a new government to include the CEDA once more. But this time it was with a non-republican right majority, the first time this had occurred during the Republic. There were only three radical ministers, two Agrarians and five from the CEDA. José María Gil Robles entered the government as minister of war. It was 6 May 1935. Since Azaña's departure in September 1933, the radicals had formed seven governments in barely twenty months.

This was when the real 'rectification' of the Republic began, with the radicals, who had broken any possible links with the leftist republicans and socialists, subject to the will of the CEDA and the demands for revenge from employers and landowners. Hundreds of joint arbitration committees were disabled or suppressed, with an express amendment of the labour reforms passed in the first two years by Francisco Largo Caballero. Thousands of workers were dismissed for belonging to the UGT or CNT unions or on the pretext of having taken part in the October uprising and strikes. The employers, who at the beginning were confident that the radicals would look after their interests and summarily dispense with the socialist reforms, went into action and recovered the status they had lost with the coming of the Republic.

This offensive was most noticeable in the rural environment and in the conditions of the land-workers, a collective that had already more than paid the price for their insubordination with their strike in 1934. In October 1934 the agriculture portfolio was in the hands of Manuel Giménez Fernández, a law lecturer from Seville who defended social Catholicism in a CEDA dominated by reactionary and authoritarian postures. His bill, which materialised as the Ley de Arrendamientos Rústicos (Law of Rural Lettings), passed on 15 March, proposed that tenants could take possession of any land that they had worked for at least twelve years. The extreme right called it 'Marxism in disguise', his own party colleagues dubbed it 'white Bolshevism', and on 6 May 1935 he resigned as minister of agriculture, the same day that the CEDA increased its presence in the government.

Giménez Fernández's defeat, as Malefakis points out, meant that any hope of serious social reform vanished.[15] Following the new conditions established after October 1934, a coalition of extreme right and CEDA deputies finally saw their ambition to quash the September 1932 Ley de Reforma Agraria accomplished. These included figures such as José Antonio Lamamié de Clairac, the traditionalist who had so strongly opposed the act in the Cortes Constituyentes, and representatives of the landowners and the reactionary wing of the CEDA, such as Cándido Casanueva and Mateo Azpeitia.

Giménez Fernández was replaced by Nicasio Velayos y Velayos, a rich, ultra-conservative Valladolid landowner, of the Partido Agrario. On 3 July, Nicasio Velayos presented his 'Reforma de la Reforma Agraria' bill. It needed just five days of debate in the Cortes to be passed, while discussions over the 1932 Ley de Reforma Agraria had taken five months. In practice, this act marked the end of agrarian reform. The rightist majority in the Cortes wanted no land reform at all, either radical or conservative. Furthermore, this was all made possible because the government decided that more than 2,000 socialist and leftist republican town councils, 20% of Spain's total, were to be replaced by management committees of the Partido Radical and the CEDA from October 1934.

Nobody believed in the Partido Radical's promise of a 'Republic for all Spaniards' any longer, at a time when the government, controlled by the most reactionary sector of the CEDA, only looked after the interests of the big landowners and the employers. Some radicals protested, although Lerroux had decided that in order to hold on to the prime ministership, he needed to avoid public confrontation with the CEDA. Clara Campoamor, the only female Partido Radical deputy, who had fought so hard for women's suffrage, left the party, and was also unable to do anything as director general of Beneficencia (Charity), a post attached to the Ministry of Labour, in the hands of the CEDA since October 1934.

Gil Robles, the minister of war from May to December 1935, did not have time to undo all the reforms of earlier years in military matters, but with his appointments policy he did reinforce the power of the anti-Azaña officers and introduced a rightist element into the army. He appointed General Joaquín Fanjul, a former extreme right Agrarian deputy, under-secretary in the ministry. General Emilio Mola became head of the army in Morocco and Manuel Goded director general of aviation, and Gil Robles appointed Colonel José Monasterio his aide-de-camp. When Gil Robles moved in cabinet for the appointment of General Franco as chief

---

[15] Malefakis, *Agrarian Reform and Peasant Revolution in Spain*, pp. 350–1.

of the General Staff, a motion which was carried on 17 May 1935, Lerroux voted in favour and Alcalá Zamora against, with the latter, according to Gil Robles, repeating several times in the meeting: 'Young generals tend to be would-be coup warlords.'[16]

The president of the Republic was right. Without exception, all these officers played leading roles in the uprising against the Republic in July 1936. On the other hand, many officers with a republican background were dismissed from their posts and suffered professional reprisals. And it is highly likely that some officers appointed by Gil Robles, such as General Fanjul, encouraged and protected the Unión Militar Española (UME), the semi-clandestine association organised and led since the end of 1933 by Captain Bartolomé Barba Hernández and Lieutenant Colonel Valentín Galarza, both of the General Staff.

The final project was the reform of the Constitution, one of the pet objectives of Gil Robles and the CEDA which, had it come to fruition, would have disposed of the 1931 Constitution. But the CEDA was in no hurry, because under the terms of Article 125b of the Constitution, any reform adopted before 9 December 1935, in other words, 'during the first four years of the life of the Constitution', needed the agreement of two-thirds of the Cortes, but after that date an absolute majority was enough. Furthermore, if the reform was passed, the law stipulated the dissolution of the Cortes, and fresh elections, and what Gil Robles wanted was to be prime minister before undertaking this constitutional reform. On 1 September, at a JAP rally in Santiago de Compostela, with clearly fascist trappings, Gil Robles announced that he sought a 'complete revision' of the Constitution. And if the Cortes failed to pass this revision, he added, 'the Cortes are dead and must disappear'.[17]

As the Partido Radical also sought a reform of the Constitution, albeit less far-reaching, Lerroux's government presented a bill before the Cortes on 5 July, to reform forty-one articles dealing with religion, the family, property and regional autonomy. A parliamentary commission was set up, chaired by Ricardo Samper, but because of the divergence between the Partido Radical and the CEDA over the scope of the revision, it did not start work until October. By then, however, Lerroux was no longer prime minister. Yet another crisis was to remove him from this post, a post that he would never hold again.

The crisis began unexpectedly with the resignation on 19 September of the minister for the navy, Antonio Royo Villanova, a fierce opponent of

---

[16] Gil Robles, *No fue posible la paz*, p. 235.
[17] Stanley G. Payne, *Spain's First Democracy: The Second Republic, 1931–1936* (Madison: University of Wisconsin Press, 1993).

Catalan nationalism from Zaragoza and a member of the Partido Agrario, in protest over the delegation of powers regarding certain state highways to the restored Generalitat of Catalonia. He was backed by another Partido Agrario member in the government, Minister of Agriculture Nicasio Velayos. Lerroux resigned to reorganise the coalition, this time without Agrarian support, but Alcalá Zamora asked the Speaker of the Cortes, Santiago Alba, a former monarchist now in the Partido Radical, to form a government. After seeing the problems involved, Alba refused, and on 25 September the task was finally handed over to Joaquín Chapaprieta, a liberal financier, friend of Alcalá Zamora, who had been finance minister in the outgoing government.

However, this government was extremely short-lived. Even as it was formed, Alcalá Zamora already knew that 'relatives and friends' of Lerroux's were involved in a corruption scandal with bribes included. Daniel Strauss, a shady businessman who passed himself off as Dutch, but who in fact was of German origin and held Mexican nationality, tried to introduce into Spain a roulette-type game, and to obtain a permit he gave various sums of money and gold watches to certain members of the Partido Radical, including Joan Pich i Pon, since April 1935 the president of the restored Generalitat, and Aurelio Lerroux, the adopted son of the radical leader. In spite of the sums of money paid out, the permit was not forthcoming, and the inventors and promoters of the game, Strauss and Perle, sought compensation and wanted the scandal to be brought to light.

At the beginning of September 1935, Strauss sent Alcalá Zamora a comprehensive dossier detailing all the interviews, promises and pay-offs, with the names of all those involved. The president of the Republic presented it to Lerroux just before the September crisis, but the old radical leader was unconcerned and replied that it would be very hard to prove his contacts with Strauss. At the beginning of October, Alcalá Zamora revealed the details to Chapaprieta, the matter was raised in the Cortes and a judicial inquiry was opened. The radical ministers were forced to resign on 29 October. Chapaprieta formed a government without the radicals. This marked the breaking of the *straperlo* scandal, a neologism that combined the surnames of the game's two promoters, and which became, particularly after the Civil War, the most common term used to denote the black market.

Everyone, left and right, including Alcalá Zamora, who was keen to occupy the centreground Lerroux had left, exploited the scandal. It had immediate and devastating consequences for many of the leading figures in the party. Soon afterwards, moreover, when Lerroux was announcing a reform, 'a new era of bountiful life' for the organisation, another scandal involving the radicals came to light over irregularities in the illegal payment of public funds to a businessman. Chapaprieta, isolated, without a party, and with his economic reforms blocked by the CEDA, tendered his resignation on 9 December. This was Gil Robles' opportunity to govern and undertake the revision of the Constitution.[18]

But Alcalá Zamora blocked Gil Robles' appointment as prime minister because, as he wrote later in his memoirs, the CEDA leader had never made an 'explicit declaration of his total adherence to the regime'.[19] Gil Robles, on the other hand, thought that this refusal to hand power over to him was what led many 'conservatives' to see violence as the only solution. There were rumours of a *coup d'état*. General Fanjul, the under-secretary in the Ministry of War, told Gil Robles that if he were so ordered, he would mobilise the troops and, according to Gil Robles himself, it was Francisco Franco, the chief of the General Staff, who convinced Generals Fanjul, José Enrique Varela and Goded 'that at this time, the army cannot and should not be counted on to stage a *coup d'état*'.[20]

On 14 December, with the Partido Radical discredited by the scandals, and the CEDA vetoed by the president of the Republic, Manuel Portela Valladares formed a government with independents and liberal democrats. Three weeks later, on 7 January 1936, faced with the impossibility of governing without the support of either of the two major parties, Alcalá Zamora signed the decree to dissolve the Cortes and gave Portela the job of organising new elections. Short-lived governments were now to become a thing of the past. Fresh elections would once again decide the course of the Republic.

In the months leading up to this, Manuel Azaña and Indalecio Prieto had corresponded about the need to build a coalition similar to the one that had governed in the first two years of the Republic. After their drubbing in the November 1933 elections, the leftist republicans were gradually recovering and reorganising. In April 1934, Acción Republicana, Casares Quiroga's Partido Republicano Gallego, and Marcelino Domingo's independent socialist radicals joined forces in a new party called Izquierda Republicana, with Manuel Azaña as the leader. And in September of that same year, Partido Radical dissidents, led by Martínez Barrio, and a splinter group from the Partido Radical Socialista, under Félix Gordón Ordás, formed Unión Republicana. With this policy of grouping together, the leftist republicans put a brake on the marked tendency towards dispersal that had begun in 1933 and could think of a return to their origins, a large electoral coalition with the socialists.

---

[18] The best information on these scandals is to be found in Townson, *La República que no pudo ser*, pp. 368–80.

[19] Niceto Alcalá Zamora, *Memorias* (Barcelona: Planeta, 1977), pp. 341–4.

[20] Gil Robles, *No fue posible la paz*, pp. 365–6.

Largo Caballero, the leader of the UGT, opposed this agreement, although with the calling of elections he agreed to join in on condition that after the elections, if the coalition won, only republicans would govern. Furthermore, he demanded that the Partido Comunista de España (PCE), which was beginning to emerge from the isolation it had been in since the early days of the Republic, should be part of this electoral coalition. And it was precisely the communists who named this coalition Frente Popular, a name that Manuel Azaña never accepted.

The pact was officially announced on 15 January, signed by the leaders of the leftist republican parties, Azaña of IR and Martínez Barrio of UR; the socialist movement, including the PSOE, the UGT and the Juventudes Socialistas; the PCE; the Partido Obrero de Unificación Marxista (POUM), a new organisation set up in September 1935 resulting from a merger of Joaquín Maurín's Bloc Obrer y Camperol and Andreu Nin's Izquierda Comunista; and finally the Partido Sindicalista, founded by Ángel Pestaña after his expulsion from the CNT.

This time the right was not so united, and the CEDA, which was stronger in the provinces, set up electoral pacts with conservative republicans, radicals, or monarchist and fascist movements. In Catalonia, the CEDA, the Lliga, radicals and traditionalists formed an all-embracing Front Català de l'Ordre. The radicals, discredited and in disarray, were forced to field their candidates separately from the two main alliances.

The left published a manifesto calling for 'full amnesty' and reinstatement of those dismissed from their jobs as common themes. The nucleus of the CEDA's campaign, 'Against the revolution and its collaborators!', presented a catastrophist view of what the Republic had represented up to then. For the left, two years of destruction of republican reforms, the 'black biennium', were over. The CEDA, which had been unable to fulfil its aim of totally reversing the course of reform, promised a complete revision of the Constitution. The extreme right, under Calvo Sotelo, considered the Republic was now finished, and promised an unequivocal authoritarian and corporate state. The date for the elections to decide all this, resulting in either a new course for the Republic or its conclusive end, was set for Sunday, 16 February 1936.

7   1936: the destruction of democracy

The Frente Popular coalition's victory in the February 1936 elections was wildly celebrated in many cities, while at the same time various generals were planning a military coup. Manuel Azaña and the leftist republicans returned to power, in what appeared to be the second act of a work begun in April 1931 and interrupted in the summer of 1933. There were urgent jobs to do and many promises to be met. Azaña asked for union under the same banner that would include 'republicans and non-republicans, and all those who love the fatherland, discipline and respect for established authority'.[1]

The leading players may have returned, and expectations may have been high, but the atmosphere after the left's victory bore little relation to the one that reigned in that spring of 1931 which had seen the birth of the Republic five years earlier. The Partido Radical, the oldest of the republican parties, the founder of the Republic, and the governing party between September 1933 and December 1935, sank without trace in the elections. People of order felt threatened by the advance of the left in Parliament and local authorities and by the new upsurge in trade union organisations and the protests they generated. Now the defeated non-republican right thought only of force as a resource against the government and the Republic. A significant sector of the army plotted against them and did not stop until they were defeated. February 1936 saw free democratic elections; July 1936, a *coup d'état*. This Republic had experienced more than five years of peace, until a military uprising and a war destroyed it by force of arms.

The Frente Popular

Nearly three-quarters, 72%, of the adult Spanish population, men and women, voted in February 1936, the highest turnout of the three general elections held during the Second Republic. As Javier Tusell showed years

---

[1] Azaña, *Memorias políticas y de guerra*, vol. II, pp. 19–20.

ago, it was also a clean election, in a country with democratic institutions and with many sectors of the population believing that this election would be decisive for the country's future.[2] This is why the election campaign was so intense, so feverish. The Frente Popular presented a moderate programme, with a political amnesty, a reinstatement of reforms and political solutions as its basic points. The non-republican right spent vast sums of money on printed material to remind people of the horrors of the revolution in Asturias, and never tired of saying that it was a battle 'for God and for Spain', between 'Catholic Spain ... and appalling, barbaric, horrendous revolution'. The extreme right – monarchists and fascists – were already advocating armed struggle, with dictatorship as the solution.

Other than this verbal aggression, there were very few incidents during the election campaign. The winner, by a very few votes, was the Frente Popular, although the majority system established by the electoral regulations gave it a comfortable majority in the Cortes: the Frente Popular won 263 seats, the right 156 and the various parties of the centre 54. The electorate voted mainly for the socialists, the republican left and the Catholics. In the Frente Popular, the leading positions on the lists were almost always taken by the republicans of Azaña's party, and on the right by the CEDA, which did not, contrary to what others have said at times, mean it was a victory for the extremists. The Communist candidates were always the last to figure on the Frente Popular lists and the sixteen seats they obtained, having received only one in 1933, were the result of having managed to join this coalition, not a reflection of their real strength. The Falange managed just 46,466 votes, 0.5% of all the votes cast. Thirty-three parties were represented in the Cortes, of which only eleven won more than ten seats. It was a highly fragmented, rather than polarised, Parliament in which the political force that had governed during the two previous years, the Partido Radical, won just four seats, ninety-nine fewer than in 1933, becoming a mere spectator of what was about to happen. Alejandro Lerroux was not even elected.

As soon as the early results came in, Gil Robles tried to persuade Portela Valladares, the prime minister, not to resign and to declare a state of emergency. General Franco, the chief of the General Staff, telephoned General Sebastián Pozas, the director general of the Civil Guard, asking him to join in a military action and occupy the streets to prevent unrest and revolution. Pozas, an old *Africanista* loyal to the Republic, refused and Franco then put pressure on General Nicolás Molero, the minister of war.

---

[2] Javier Tusell, *Las elecciones del Frente Popular en España* (Madrid: Edicusa, 1972).

General Goded wanted to mobilise the Montaña barracks in Madrid, and two other generals who had taken part in all the plots against the Republic, Joaquín Fanjul and Ángel Rodríguez del Barrio, sounded out other garrisons in the capital. Franco felt that the time was not ripe, and he backed off, although from 17 to 19 February he was, says Paul Preston, 'nearer to engaging in a military coup than ever before'.[3] Such an action was avoided by the firm attitude of Pozas and General Miguel Núñez de Prado, the police chief.

Pressured on all sides to declare a state of emergency and annul the election results, and concerned by rumours of a military coup and agitation in various cities to release political prisoners, Portela resigned on 19 February. Niceto Alcalá Zamora, the president of the Republic, called on Manuel Azaña to form a government. The republican leader and one-time prime minister was not happy with this way of receiving power, before the constitution of the new Cortes: 'I have always been afraid that we would come back to govern in adverse conditions', he wrote in his diary on 19 February. 'They could not be worse now. Once more, the corn must be harvested before it is ripe.'[4]

The government consisted of republicans only, as Azaña had agreed with the socialists before the elections, particularly because the socialists rejected the possibility of again forming a coalition government with the republicans. Nine ministers were from Izquierda Republicana, three from UR, and there was also one independent, General Carlos Masquelet, a former adviser to Azaña in the early years of the Republic, who was now appointed minister of war. It was a moderate government (to call it a Frente Popular government would be a misnomer), mostly made up of university professors and lawyers, some of whom, including José Giral, Santiago Casares and Marcelino Domingo, had been close allies of Azaña in 1931–3. But the two parties represented in this government occupied less than a quarter of the seats in the Cortes, and this potentially threatened its stability.

Although it is often claimed that Spain saw in the beginning of spring 1936 with an unprecedented wave of strikes or, in the words of Stanley G. Payne, a time of extreme 'civil disorder',[5] the evidence and research available show that there were fewer and less serious conflicts than in the period 1931–3. But after the experience of October 1934, the defeat of the right in the elections and the return of the republican left and socialists to local and provincial political institutions, public awareness of the threat to

---

[3] Preston, *Franco*, p. 119.   [4] Azaña, *Memorias políticas y de guerra*, vol. II, p. 11.
[5] Stanley G. Payne, 'Political Violence During the Spanish Second Republic', *Journal of Contemporary History*, 25, 2–3 (1990), p. 279.

social order and the breaking down of class relationships became more heightened in 1936 than in the early years of the Republic.

The political stability of the regime was also under greater threat. The class struggle, with its talk about social divisions and its incitements to malign the adversary, had gradually permeated the atmosphere in Spain since the reformist plans of the early republican governments began to meet insurmountable obstacles. Violence, too, was present, with assassination attempts against prominent people, and armed clashes between left and right political groups, occasionally with bloodshed, served to give practical expression to the verbal excesses and aggression of certain leaders. And, as if that were not enough, neither of the two leading parties in the Cortes, the PSOE and the CEDA, contributed during those months to the political stability of the democracy and the Republic. Spanish politics and society displayed unequivocal signs of crisis, although this did not necessarily mean that the only solution was a civil war.

On 12 March, in Madrid, several Falangist gunmen fired on Luis Jiménez de Asúa, a prominent socialist leader and a professor of law, one of the main drafters of the 1931 republican Constitution. He was unharmed, but his police escort, Jesús Gisbert, was killed. The funeral of the police officer gave rise to displays of condemnation and serious incidents, including the burning of churches and of the premises of the right-wing newspaper *La Nación*. The police arrested various Falangists, although the perpetrators of the shooting managed to escape to France in a light aircraft piloted by the military aviator, Juan Antonio Ansaldo. The Directorate General of Security, on government instructions, ordered the arrest of the Falange's political board and national leadership. On 14 March, José Antonio Primo de Rivera was arrested in his home, as were other leaders, such as Julio Ruiz de Alda, Raimundo Fernández Cuesta, Rafael Sánchez Mazas and David Jato. The instructing judge said that the Falange programme that they defended was unconstitutional, and ordered them to be held on remand before trial for unlawful assembly. They were sent to the political prisoners' wing in the Modelo gaol.

A month later, on 13 April, Manuel Pedregal, the magistrate who had just sentenced some of those involved in the assassination attempt against Jiménez de Asúa, was also murdered. Right- and left-wingers clashed in various parts of Madrid over the next few days, producing a toll of seven dead and forty wounded. Most of these incidents, in which right- and left-wing groups showed very little concern for human life, occurred in Madrid, which magnified their impact, while for Barcelona, which had from 1931 to 1934 experienced a large number of violent conflicts and uprisings, it was a quiet spring, with considerably fewer strikes and less political violence than in the Republic's capital.

Meanwhile, the Cortes, which had been inaugurated on 15 March with Diego Martínez Barrio as Speaker, were somewhat paralysed by debate over the official election results and, above all, by the process of replacing the president of the Republic. It was a crisis, all the experts agree, that weakened the leftist republican government and smoothed the path for a military plot.

Nobody wanted Alcalá Zamora to stay on as president of the Republic. The CEDA, under Gil Robles, believed he had robbed them of the chance to hold total power in December 1935. The left, and Azaña in particular, never forgave him for having withdrawn his confidence in September 1933, leading to the fall of Azaña's government and the breaking-up of the coalition between socialists and republicans that had governed in the two previous years. Furthermore, Alcalá Zamora had tried to assemble a centrist party for the February 1936 elections, using the mechanisms of presidential power, and the ballot boxes were testimony of his failure. He was not the president that the republican left wanted on its return to power, and the right was not going to lift a finger to impede his removal either.

Article 81 of the Constitution allowed for the removal of the president of the Republic in the event of his dissolving the Cortes twice, and the new Parliament considered that the latest dissolution, on 7 January 1936, was inadmissible. The debate was held on 7 April: 238 deputies voted in favour of his dismissal and only 5 of Portela's deputies voted against. The right, which had supported the measure, abstained. Alcalá Zamora was thus dismissed by the Cortes. A new president of the Republic was to be elected.

The Speaker, Diego Martínez Barrio, took over as interim head of state and his party, Unión Republicana, put forward as its candidate Manuel Azaña, who had widespread support, although Largo Caballero and the socialist left preferred Álvaro de Albornoz. If we accept the view of Santos Juliá, one of his foremost biographers, Azaña too wanted this post, because his idea was once more to form a republican and socialist coalition government, under Indalecio Prieto. The two offices, that of president of the Republic and that of prime minister, would thus be held by two people with authority and the backing of the main parties that had won the February elections.[6]

The president of the Republic, according to the Constitution, was to be elected by indirect suffrage. In the voting for representatives for the electoral college, held on 26 April, most of the right abstained. The Frente Popular obtained 358 representatives, and the opposition 63. Two weeks

[6] Juliá, *Manuel Azaña, una biografía política*, pp. 483–7.

later, on 10 May, in the Palacio de Cristal in the Retiro, Manuel Azaña was elected president of the Republic by an overwhelming majority and the blank votes of the CEDA.

However, things did not turn out as Azaña had planned. Azaña's invitation to Prieto to form a government was opposed by the UGT and the socialist left, who threatened to break the pact with the Frente Popular if Prieto became prime minister. The socialist parliamentary group, under Largo Caballero, discussed this matter, and the motion that the socialists should form part of the government again was defeated by a comfortable majority of 49 votes against and 19 in favour. Now that a coalition government presided over by the socialists was not an option, Azaña turned to one of his most loyal collaborators, Santiago Casares Quiroga, who became prime minister of the new government and also took on the war portfolio. Made up of leftist republicans only, including the ERC, it has passed into history as the weak government that permitted conflicts and political violence, instead of repressing them, and which was unable to stop the military coup, the blame for which has tended to be placed on Casares Quiroga's shoulders. Yet, in this case, history is somewhat more complex.

The schism that had existed in socialism since December 1935, with two independent leaders in confrontation with each other, the PSOE in the hands of Indalecio Prieto's 'centrist' faction and the UGT in the power of Francisco Largo Caballero's 'leftist' wing, impeded any opportunity of reinforcing the republican government. Indalecio Prieto, who had already committed the grave error of condoning and collaborating in the preparation of the October 1934 revolutionary movement, embarked on the process of replacing Alcalá Zamora without having assured his alternative policy of leading the government and, with Azaña, strengthening the republican state.

Meanwhile, Largo Caballero was unable to offer any solution other than waiting for the revolution, which would come as a response to any coup by the right or the military, and radicalising his ideas. He was supported in this endeavour by the Juventudes Socialistas, ever more intent on creating militias, a paramilitary framework and armed confrontations with groups of young fascists. In June, under the leadership of Santiago Carrillo, they merged with the Young Communists, thereby creating the Juventudes Socialistas Unificadas, a prelude to the Communist dream of uniting the two Marxist workers' parties. During these months, the PCE set out its moderate policy of fighting fascism, putting a brake on strikes and focusing its political struggle in Parliament, but at the same time it benefited from the split in socialism, the Bolshevisation of its youth, to grow and make inroads into the UGT unions.

At the opposite extreme of parliamentary politics, the CEDA began a decisive shift to authoritarian ideas, something which had been extremely obvious for months in its youth movement, with the language they used and their fascist salutes and the uniforms they wore. The February 1936 elections marked the end of 'accidentalism' in the Catholic movement. When it became obvious that the corporate-based 'revision' of the Republic could not be achieved via the acquisition of power in Parliament, an objective that was shared by Gil Robles and the Church hierarchy, they began to think of more effective methods. Following the electoral defeat of February 1936, everyone got the message: they needed to abandon the ballot box and take up arms. The fundamentalist idea of the 'right to rebellion' advocated in a book published in 1934 by Aniceto Castro Albarrán, the canon preacher of Salamanca, of a rebellion in the shape of a patriotic and religious crusade against the atheistic Republic, started gathering followers.[7] The Juventudes de Acción Popular were swelling the ranks of the Falange, with more than 15,000 affiliates transferring from one organisation to the other, and in the Cortes Gil Robles endorsed the anti-system rants of José Calvo Sotelo.

The conquest of power

The Catholic and extreme right-wing press incited their readers to rebellion against the disorder that they attributed to the 'tyrannical Frente Popular government', 'the enemy of God and the Church'. The clash between the Church and the Republic, between clericalism and anticlericalism, once more dominated the scene after the February 1936 elections. Once more, there were disputes over symbolic matters, with local authorities banning processions, bell-ringing and open-air religious activities. Back came the proposal to replace confessional education, as envisaged in the 1933 Religious Confessions and Congregations Bill, paralysed by the victory of the radicals and the CEDA in that year's elections.

First Azaña's and then Casares Quiroga's government reopened some of the issues that had already divided Catholics and republicans during the early years: the closing of Church schools, co-education and the consolidation of public education at the expense of religious tuition. But of the more than 250 deaths that are said to have occurred between February and July as a result of 'political violence', not one cleric was killed, which contradicts the memory that is often still conveyed about that spring of

---

[7] Aniceto de Castro Albarrán, *El derecho a la rebeldía* (Madrid: Gráfica Universal, 1934).

1936, echoing all that was written then to justify the Church's support of the military coup: that the 'extermination of the Catholic clergy' had begun before July 1936.

The catastrophist viewpoint swallowed up what little was left of social Catholicism, which was well represented in the Basque Country with politicians such as Manuel Irujo and José Antonio Aguirre and in Catalonia with the ecclesiastical renewal sectors led by Cardinal Franscesc Vidal i Barraquer. As early as 20 February *El Pensamiento Alavés* was saying that 'it will not be in Parliament that the final battle is fought, but on the battleground of armed struggle'. It was no coincidence that it was Navarre and Álava which during those months saw the consolidation of the *Requeté*, the 'red berets', a military organisation which had numerous locations for manoeuvres and military training which were attended by priests and the people of order of the region. In fact, military training and instruction had, for some time, carried more weight in Carlist circles than traditionalist political theory. When the time came, the *Requeté*, with its strict hierarchy and intensive training, was the civil militia that the military rebels would most rely on.[8]

But none of this offensive launched by the extreme right and the Catholics of the CEDA would have achieved the desired result – overthrowing the Republic and eradicating the threat of socialism and libertarianism – had they not been able to rely on the weaponry of a large sector of the army. In the first few weeks after the February elections until the middle of March, Azaña's recently elected government acted on a proposal by General Carlos Masquelet, the minister of war, and ordered major changes and transfers affecting high-ranking officers who were suspected of having taken part in plots or who had stated the need for military intervention. Franco was replaced as chief of the General Staff and was sent out to the Canary Islands. Fanjul, the under-secretary at the Ministry of War who had been appointed by Gil Robles, was left without a posting, as were other significant anti-Azaña and anti-republican officers such as Luis Orgaz, Rafael Villegas and Andrés Saliquet. General Goded, the director general of aviation, was posted to the Balearic Islands and Mola was transferred from Morocco to the 12th Brigade stationed in Pamplona. They were replaced by officers who were republicans or supposedly loyal to the established rule, although events were soon to prove that this transfer policy failed to put a brake on the plotting and the coup. In addition, some of the transferred officers felt insulted. Franco, for

[8] Martin Blinkhorn, *Carlism and Crisis in Spain 1931–1939* (Cambridge University Press, 1975); Javier Ugarte, *La nueva Covadonga insurgente: orígenes sociales y culturales de la sublevación de 1936 en Navarra y el País Vasco* (Madrid: Biblioteca Nueva, 1998).

example, says Paul Preston, 'perceived it as a demotion and another slight at the hands of Azaña', a 'banishment'.[9]

In charge of the organisation of the plot were various extreme right-wing officers, including some from the UME, a semi-clandestine anti-leftist organisation consisting of several hundred officers. On 8 March, Francisco Franco, who was due to leave for the Canary Islands the next day, Generals Mola, Orgaz, Villegas, Fanjul, Rodríguez del Barrio, Miguel García de la Herrán, Varela, Manuel González Carrasco, Miguel Ponte, Saliquet and Lieutenant Colonel Valentín Galarza met in Madrid, at the home of José Delgado, a stockbroker and friend of Gil Robles, 'to agree on a rising to re-establish internal order and the international prestige of Spain', according to surviving documents on 'the preparation and development of the National Rising'. They also agreed that General Sanjurjo, who was then living in Portugal, would head the uprising.[10]

In the end, however, the main player in the plot was General Mola, who talked to the leaders of the rebellion and issued, under the pseudonym of 'El Director', various reports, instructions and enclosures for the various division leaders' eyes only. He signed the first of the 'five confidential instructions' on 25 May, somewhat later than the date proposed for the coup at the meeting on 8 March, in which he explained the conditions required 'for the rebellion to be an outright success'. It was also in this first 'confidential instruction' that Mola proclaimed the need for violent repression: 'Bear in mind that the action will need to be uncommonly violent in order to bring down the enemy, who is strong and well organised, as soon as possible. Naturally, all leaders of political parties, companies or unions that are not sympathetic to the Movimiento will be imprisoned, and they will be dealt exemplary punishments to stifle any rebellious or strike movements.'

The officers were slow to respond to the call to take part in the coup, but by the time Mola drafted this first 'confidential instruction', he already knew that the garrisons in Morocco were prepared to revolt. Also important were Mola's contacts with Gonzalo Queipo de Llano, the head of the Carabineros, and the discussions he had on 7 June with General Miguel Cabanellas, commander of the 5th Division, confirming Cabanellas' participation in the coup and establishing the resources he would need to

[9] Preston, *Franco*, p. 120.
[10] Copy of the documents provided by Lieutenant Colonel Emiliano Fernández Cordón, regarding the preparation and running of the National Rising (75 pp.), housed in the Servicio Histórico Militar, Madrid. The quotes that follow by General Mola also come from this document.

confront the opposition that in Zaragoza 'will almost certainly come from the union masses', as well as the organisation of the 'columns that will be needed to prevent the Catalans from invading Aragonese territory'. By the end of June everything was ready in the 5th Division for the rebellion, with Colonel Monasterio, who had been Gil Robles' military adviser and confidant in the Ministry of War, at the centre of the plot. Also by this time the military conspirators had assigned tasks to the various regions. On 4 July, the wealthy businessman Juan March agreed to provide the money for a plane to fly Franco from the Canary Islands to Morocco. The aircraft, a De Havilland Dragon Rapide, was chartered two days later in England for £2,000, paid for by Luís Bolín, the London correspondent of the daily newspaper *ABC*.

The assassination of José Calvo Sotelo convinced the plotters of the urgent need to intervene and brought into the fold many of the undecided, who were waiting for things to become clearer before agreeing to take part in the coup and risk their salaries and their lives. On the afternoon of Sunday, 12 July, in a street in central Madrid, several right-wing gunmen, traditionalists according to Ian Gibson's research, shot down José del Castillo, a lieutenant of the Assault Guard, whose socialist sympathies were widely known. In the early hours of the following day, some of his colleagues, led by a Civil Guard captain, Fernando Condés, who like Del Castillo had previously served as an army officer in Morocco, went to the home of Calvo Sotelo, at number 89 of the *calle* Velásquez, and while they were supposedly taking him to the central barracks of Pontejos, they murdered him and left his body in the morgue at the Almudena cemetery.[11]

Calvo Sotelo, the leader of the Bloque Nacional, had in previous months been involved in harsh confrontations with the left in the Cortes, and his murder by members of the Republic's police naturally caused indignation among his followers and politicians of the right. The monarchist leader Antonio Goicoechea, speaking at his funeral, uttered these words that were subsequently repeated many times: 'We swear a solemn oath to dedicate our lives to this threefold task: to imitate your example, avenge your death and save Spain.' During a session of the Permanent Delegation of the Cortes, held on 15 July, Gil Robles said to the leftist deputies that 'the blood of Señor Calvo Sotelo is on your hands'. The government was not involved in the murder, said the CEDA leader, but it was 'morally responsible' for 'sponsoring violence'.[12]

When General Franco received the news on the morning of 13 July, he said to the messenger, Colonel Teódulo González Peral, in words that

[11] Ian Gibson, *La noche que mataron a Calvo Sotelo* (Barcelona: Argos Vergara, 1982).
[12] Gil Robles, *No fue posible la paz*, pp. 749–65.

were later constantly quoted by apologists for the coup to show the connection between this murder and Franco's ultimate decision to intervene: 'The *Patria* has another martyr. We can wait no longer. This is the signal!'[13] The next day the Dragon Rapide arrived in the Canary Islands. On the evening of 17 July, the garrisons of Melilla, Tetuán and Ceuta rose in Morocco. In the early hours of 18 July, Franco declared a state of war and pronounced himself in opposition to the government of the Republic. On 19 July he arrived at Tetuán. Meanwhile, many other military garrisons in the peninsula joined the coup. Peace was over in the Republic.

The Republic had had problems in consolidating itself and had to face firm challenges from above and below. It went through two years of relative stability, followed by another two years of political uncertainty and a final few months of harassment and insurrection. The first firm challenges, which were the most visible as they usually ended up as clashes with the police, came from below, first as social protests and later as insurrections from anarchists and socialists. However, the *coup de grâce*, the challenge that finally overthrew the Republic with the force of arms, came from above and from within, that is to say, the military command and the powerful ruling classes that had never tolerated it.

Before that, the Republic had seen serious breaches of order, such as the military rebellion of General Sanjurjo in August 1932, the anarchist uprisings of 1932 and 1933, and particularly the revolutionary movement of October 1934. These armed rebellions hindered the survival of the Republic and the parliamentary system; they showed that violence was a resource commonly employed by certain sectors of the left, by the army and by the guardians of traditional order, but they were not the cause of the end of the Republic, let alone of the beginning of the Civil War. And this was because, when the army and the state security forces were united and loyal to the regime, insurrectional movements were easily put down, albeit at the cost of heavy bloodshed.

In February 1936 there were free elections, with no government rigging, in which the CEDA, like the rest of the parties, invested all its many resources into trying to win them. It lost, and its political space began to be occupied by extra-parliamentary, anti-system forces of the extreme right. At that time there was no mass fascist movement in Spain, as there had been in Italy in 1922 or Germany in 1933, because Spain was not involved in the First World War, and therefore did not have numerous ex-combatants that might have swelled the ranks of paramilitary organisations, an essential breeding ground for fascism as a political and social

---

[13] Quoted in Preston, *Franco*, p. 137.

movement. Neither did Spain suffer the consequences of the 1929 economic crisis as brutally as other countries did, while at the same time the
weakness of Spanish nationalism and the weight of traditional, reactionary
bureaucracies, such as the army and the Catholic Church, hindered the
advance of a movement – whose principles were identified with a modern,
radical nationalism – to mobilise the middle classes against the revolution,
but also against the political practices of the established ruling classes.

Yet barely three years after their appearance, Falange Española y de las
JONS, together with Renovación Española, Carlism and political
Catholicism, were at the forefront in the harassment and overthrow of
the Republic. They did their best, using all the social and economic means
at their disposal, to sabotage the republican reformist project, the consolidation of workers' rights and the representative power obtained by left-
wing organisations. As such, although a 'genuine' mass fascist party had
not taken root in Spanish society, what had germinated and gathered
strength was a counter-revolutionary politico-cultural tradition which,
like 'pre-fascism' in Italy and '*völkisch*' nationalism in Germany, could
be mobilised to play a similar role.[14]

In the first few months of 1936, Spanish society was highly fragmented,
with uneasiness between factions and, as was happening all over Europe,
with the possible exception of Britain, rejection of liberal democracy in
favour of authoritarianism was rife. None of this need have led to a civil
war. The war began because a military uprising weakened the state and
undermined its ability and that of the republican government to maintain
order. The division of the army and security forces thwarted the victory
of the military rebellion, as well as the achievement of their main objective:
the rapid seizure of power. But by undermining the government's power
to keep order, this *coup d'état* was transformed into the unprecedented
open violence employed by the groups that supported and those that
opposed it. It was then, not October 1934 or the spring of 1936, that the
Civil War began.

[14] Martin Blinkhorn, 'Conservatism, Traditionalism and Fascism in Spain, 1898–1937', in
Blinkhorn ed., *Fascists and Conservatives: The Radical Right and the Establishment in
Twentieth-Century Europe* (London: Unwin Hyman, 1990), pp. 118–37.

Part III

The Civil War

8   Spain split in two

The officers who planned the uprising were aware that they enjoyed substantial backing and expected a swift victory. But things did not turn out that way, and the result of this uprising was a long civil war lasting nearly three years.

There were several distinct conflicts during this war. Firstly, a military conflict was initiated when the *coup d'état* buried political solutions to replace them with arms. It was also a class war, between differing conceptions of social order; a war of religion, between Catholicism and anti-clericalism; a war revolving around the idea of *patria* and nation; and a war of ideas, beliefs that were at that time at loggerheads on the international stage. It was a war that was impossible to reduce to a conflict between communism and fascism, or between fascism and democracy. In short, the Spanish Civil War was a melting pot of universal battles between employers and workers, Church and State, obscurantism and modernisation, settled in an international context that had been thrown out of balance by crises of democracies and the onslaught of communism and fascism.

The Spanish Civil War has gone down in history, and in memory, for the way it dehumanised its adversaries and for the horrific violence that it generated. Symbolised by the '*sacas*', '*paseos*' and mass killings, it served the two sides in their struggle to eliminate their respective enemies, whether natural or unforeseen.[1] While carrying out this extermination, the rebels were also given the inestimable blessing of the Catholic Church from the very beginning. The clergy and sacred objects, however, were the prime target of popular rage, of those who took part in defeating the

---

[1] A *paseo* (a walk) was the euphemism used to describe the murder of thousands of people in the two zones that divided Spain following the military coup, particularly during 1936. *Dar el paseo* (to take a walk) meant to seize the victim, murder him and leave him in a ditch, well, mineshaft or common grave. The term *saca* was used in the Civil War to denote the operation of removing prisoners from gaol to murder them in the countryside, usually at night. There were *sacas* on both home fronts, but a great many of them occurred in November 1936 in the Madrid gaols, from where tens of thousands of officers and right-wingers were 'removed' and taken to Paracuellos del Jarama to be murdered.

military rebels and who played leading roles in the 'popular terror' that took place in the summer of 1936.

Spain was split into two. This Republic at war went through three different stages, with three prime ministers. Revolution and the trade unions dominated the first year, before the socialist Juan Negrín became its leader. The rebels had less trouble in finding a single military and political head: from 1 October 1936 General Francisco Franco was their undisputed leader.

Rebellion and the breakdown of order

The uprising met with success in almost the whole of northern and north-west Spain: Galicia, León, Old Castile, Oviedo, Álava, Navarre and the three capitals of Aragón; the Canary and Balearic Islands, except for Menorca; and large areas of Extremadura and Andalucía, including the cities of Cáceres, Cádiz, Seville, Córdoba, Granada and, from 29 July, Huelva. However, the military rebels were defeated in most of the big cities, including Madrid, Barcelona and Valencia, where they came up against the united resistance of other armed forces loyal to the Republic and political and trade union militants. The division of the army and police forces thwarted the military rebellion, as well as the achievement of their main objective: the rapid seizure of power. But by decisively undermining the republican government's ability to maintain order, this *coup d'état* gave way to the Civil War and the violence of opposing armed groups.

Thus it was not the army 'en masse' that rose up against the Republic, nor could it be called 'the rebellion of the generals', although this term is still being used. Of the eighteen divisional generals, including those in the Civil Guard and the Carabineros – in other words, those who commanded the most important units of intervention – just four took part in the uprising: Cabanellas, Queipo, Goded and Franco, and only one of them, Cabanellas, commanded troops in the peninsula. There were two further divisional generals, at that time without a posting, who took part in the uprising, Fanjul and Saliquet, while Generals José Riquelme and Masquelet, who were in special postings, remained loyal to the republican government. Nor were the brigade generals unanimous in their support for the uprising: fourteen of the fifty-six who were serving on 18 July rebelled against the government.[2]

The most active role in the uprising was played by the corps of field officers, whose action drew in several senior officers who were not involved at the beginning, and who were not averse to using violence against the

---

[2] Gabriel Cardona, *Historia militar de una guerra civil: estrategias y tácticas de la guerra de España* (Barcelona: Flor del Viento, 2006).

undecided or those who opposed their plans. Of the 15,301 officers in all branches, corps and services serving in July 1936, just over half clearly supported the rebellion. The rebels initially had some 120,000 armed men, of the 254,000 in the peninsula, the islands and Africa at that time, including the forces of public order. However, various factors came together to give superiority to the rebels and lessen the effectiveness of those who remained loyal to the Republic. Firstly, the order from the republican government to demobilise the troops, with the idea of under-mining the military rebels, achieved the opposite result, because many of these soldiers, in areas where the uprising failed, subsequently refused to go back to their units and, in response to the popular and revolutionary call, joined the militias. Secondly, the anarchists and socialists, the first to organise militias, were traditionally anti-militarist, leading them to dis-trust many of these officers who at least had not risen up against the Republic. A substantial part of what could have been the republican army from the beginning was fragmented, in scattered units and with no possibility of imposing its discipline on the militias – 'the people in arms' – that were emerging everywhere.

Among the rebels, however, things were very different because, despite the fact that the peninsular army was also under-prepared for war, they did have disciplined and organised troops, and above all they had the Africa Army from the outset, with almost all its 1,600 officers and 40,000 men under their command. Its best-known and best-trained troops were the *Tercio de Extranjeros*, the Legion, founded by José Millán Astray and Franco in 1920, and made up of deserters, criminals, outcasts and fugi-tives, who were trained to venerate virility and violence. At the time it had two regiments – legions – one in Melilla and the other in Ceuta, the latter under the command of Lieutenant Colonel Yagüe, Franco's right-hand man in the repression in Asturias in October 1934 and Mola's represen-tative for the plot in Morocco. Alongside the Legion were the Fuerzas Regulares Indígenas, made up of Moroccan mercenaries and some Spaniards.

By 19 July Franco was in Tetuán in command of this powerful Morocco garrison, and it was this post that gave rise to what Paul Preston calls 'the making of a *Generalísimo*'.[3] The problem now was to transport these troops to the mainland, as the Strait of Gibraltar was under the control of the crew of the republican fleet that had mutinied against their rebel officers, and only a small contingent of African troops had managed to reach Andalucía in the early hours of the rising.

---

[3] Preston, *Franco*, pp. 144–70.

So Franco turned to Hitler and Mussolini for help. He used two German businessmen resident in Spanish Morocco and local representatives of the Nazi Ausland-Organization (Foreign Organisation), Adolf Langenheim and Johannes Bernhardt, to meet Hitler, via a series of elaborate contacts. On 23 July, Bernhardt, who in fact had offered his services to Franco, flew to Berlin with a message from Franco to the Führer asking for fighter and transport aircraft. He first met Rudolf Hess, Hitler's right-hand man and, two days later, the Führer himself. Hitler was hesitant at first but, after being convinced by Bernhardt that what Franco wanted was to save Spain from an imminent Bolshevik revolution, he decided to send aid. On 29 July, some twenty Junker 52 transport aircraft and six Heinkel fighters set out for Tetuán.

According to Enrique Moradiellos, Hitler initially decided to support the military rebels and then later intervene in the war 'for political and strategic reasons': if the military coup in Spain were successful, it would deprive France of a definite ally on its south flank, while a government victory would 'reinforce Spain's link to France and the USSR, the two powers that surrounded Germany from the east and west, and which opposed the Nazis' expansionist plans'.[4]

Mussolini, who received repeated calls for help from Franco via the Italian consul in Tangier and his military attaché, also decided to help the rebels for geo-strategic reasons: he would gain an ally in the western Mediterranean and thereby weaken France's military position. On 28 July he sent a squadron of twelve Savoia-Marchetti SM.81 bombers and two merchant ships with Fiat CR.32 fighters. Thus, in the words of Preston, 'Mussolini and Hitler turned a *coup d'état* going wrong into a bloody and prolonged civil war.'[5] All these aircraft, with their crews and technicians, enabled Franco to evade the republican navy blockade, transport his troops to Andalucía and thus begin his advance on Madrid. On 7 August, one day after a convoy of African troops had crossed the Strait, Franco installed himself in Seville.

Franco had at his disposal the military forces of the Moroccan protectorate, and in Navarre General Emilio Mola had the unanimous support of the *Requeté*, the 'red berets', a disciplined military organisation that had instructed and prepared hundreds of local militants, young people, students, priests and people of order for rebellion against the Republic. The network set up by the plotters in Navarre was the most valuable structure

[4] Enrique Moradiellos, *El reñidero de Europa: las dimensiones internacionales de la guerra civil española* (Barcelona: Península, 2001), pp. 88–9.
[5] Paul Preston, *A Concise History of the Spanish Civil War* (London: Fontana Press, 1996), p. 87.

on the mainland. General Mola, five years older than Franco, had spent a large part of his career in the army of Morocco. He was tried by the Republic for his performance as director general of security under Berenguer throughout 1930 and until April 1931, pardoned in 1934, and rehabilitated when Gil Robles was minister of war and Franco chief of the General Staff. After the Frente Popular's election victory in February 1936, he was transferred from the command of the military forces in Morocco, an appointment made by Gil Robles in 1935, to the 12th Infantry Brigade, a post which included the Military Command in Pamplona. It was there, from 14 March 1936 onwards, that he issued the various 'confidential instructions' as 'director' of the conspiracy and organised the deployment of the various generals and officers who were to command the rebel forces.

According to these plans, the officer leading the uprising was supposed to be General José Sanjurjo, but this was not possible because the aircraft that was carrying him to Spain from his exile in Portugal on 20 July crashed on take-off and burst into flames near the aerodrome at Cascais. Sanjurjo was killed, while the pilot, the Falangist Juan Antonio Ansaldo, escaped unharmed from the crash.

Sanjurjo's death, and Fanjul's and Poded's unsuccessful uprisings in Madrid and Barcelona, meant that the military rebels were forced to change their plans. On 21 July Mola flew to Zaragoza to talk to General Miguel Cabanellas, whose uprising there had been successful, and he invited the latter to preside over the Junta de Defensa Nacional, the senior board for military co-ordination in the rebel zone, which was set up in Burgos three days later.

The coup did not overthrow the Republic but, by opening a wide breach in the army and the security forces, it did destroy its cohesion and caused unrest. The prime minister, the republican Santiago Casares Quiroga, fearful of revolution and the popular unrest that might break out, ordered the civil governors not to distribute arms to the workers' organisations. There was little else he could do, because events very soon overtook him. He resigned on the night of 18 July. The person who might have succeeded him, the experienced Diego Martínez Barrio, spent the whole night trying to reach an impossible compromise with Mola by offering him, if various sources are to be believed, a post in government. The task was finally accepted on the morning of 19 July by José Giral, a friend and confidant of Manuel Azaña. This government consisted of leftist republicans only, practically the same faces as had previously served under Casares Quiroga. It was Giral who decided to arm the most politically committed militant workers and republicans, and they took to the streets to fight the rebels wherever the loyalty of certain military commanders, or the indecision of others, permitted.

Thus, there is no need to continue feeding the myth. It was not the people, 'the people in arms', who, alone, defeated the rebels in the streets of the major cities of Spain. The republican state, however, by surrendering its monopoly on arms, was not capable of preventing the beginning of a sudden and violent revolutionary process, aimed at destroying the positions of the privileged classes, wherever the insurgents were defeated. The streets were taken over by new players, armed men and women, anarchists and outcast people, many of whom had become known for their vehement opposition to the existence of this selfsame state. They were there not exactly to defend the Republic, which had had its chance, but to take part in a revolution. Wherever the Republic had not gone far enough with its reforms, they would with their revolution. Political measures gave way to armed action.

A counter-revolutionary *coup d'état*, with the intention of halting a revolution, ended up by unleashing one. The was not the first time, nor would it be the last, that this had happened in history. It is very likely that but for the coup, and the collapse of the state's coercion mechanisms, this revolutionary process would never have got off the ground. Naturally, if support for the rising among the armed forces had been unanimous, any resistance would have easily been put down. The trade union militias, even with arms, would not have been able to do anything against a united army. The revolutionary organisations had the ability to undermine and destabilise the Republic, but not to overthrow and replace it. In the Spanish army in July 1936 there was hardly any sympathy for revolutionary ideas, while a large number of officers were clearly in favour of the authoritarian and counter-revolutionary cause.

José Giral and his government soon became aware of the problems the Republic was going to face to obtain international aid. On 19 July, according to the socialist Léon Blum, the prime minister of France, the recently appointed Spanish prime minister, José Giral, sent him a telegram: 'We have been caught unawares by a dangerous military coup. Please contact us immediately to supply us with arms and aircraft.'[6]

The initial reaction of the French Popular Front government, made up of socialists and radicals, was to 'implement an aid plan ... to provide materiel to the Spanish Republic'. This seems to have been motivated by political and military reasons: both countries were democratic republics, and it was in France's interest to have a friendly regime on the Pyrenean

---

[6] *Rapport fait au nom de la Comission chargée d'enquêter sur les événements survenus en France du 1933 à 1945* (Imprimerie de l'Assemblée National, 1951), reproduced in Moradiellos, *El reñidero de Europa*, pp. 268–71. Subsequent quotes on this matter come directly from Blum's *Rapport*.

border which, in the case of a European war, would guarantee safe passage between its African colonies, where a third of its army currently was, and France itself.

However, this aid plan could not be put into practice. French public opinion was divided. While the left in general expressed its sympathy for the republican cause, the political right – Catholics and broad sectors of the administration and the army – rejected 'the aid plan'. By the end of July, the right-wing press had already made it quite clear that an intervention in Spain would mean 'the beginning of the conflagration in Europe that Moscow is hoping for'. The leaders of the Radical Party had also advised their colleague, Yvon Delbos, the minister of foreign affairs, of their 'apprehension over the initiative'. Delbos and Édouard Daladier, the radical minister of national defence, paid heed to this pressure and began to express their opposition.

As if this internal opposition were not enough, the attitude of the United Kingdom government, France's main ally in Europe, ended up by tipping the scale against the initial decision to send aid. The British Conservatives, in power since 1931, were afraid that any intervention in the Spanish conflict would hamper their policy of appeasement of Germany. Meanwhile British commercial groups, with substantial interests in Spain at the time, reacted adversely to the revolution unleashed in the major Spanish cities as a consequence of the coup. 'I urge you to be cautious', said Anthony Eden, the British foreign minister, to Blum on 24 July. Albert Lebrun, the president of the French Republic, also warned Blum that 'handing over arms to Spain might mean war in Europe or revolution in France'. On 25 July 1936, after the first of three French government cabinet meetings held to discuss the events in Spain, the decision was announced 'not to intervene in any way in Spain's domestic conflict'.[7]

This marked the basis of the non-intervention policy that would be implemented from the summer of 1936. The French Popular Front authorities, with Blum at the head, believed that this was the best way of bringing calm to the internal situation, maintaining the vital alliance with Britain, and avoiding the internationalisation of the Spanish Civil War. Things did not turn out that way, because Franco's requests for aid from Hitler and Mussolini had more success, and furthermore Nazi Germany and fascist Italy never observed this non-intervention policy. Consequently, the Republic, a legitimate regime, was left initially without aid, and the military rebels, lacking all legitimacy, received, almost from the opening shot, the aid that was vital to wage a war that they themselves had started.

---

[7] Moradiellos, *El reñidero de Europa*, pp. 87 and 81 for Baldwin's directive to Eden.

The rebels were already starting with a clear advantage. The *coup d'état*, which had not achieved its principal aim, the seizure of power, evolved into a civil war because Italo-German aid enabled the rebels to transfer the army from Africa to the mainland. The transfer of more than 10,000 troops during the summer was essential for the domination of Andalucía and the advance through Extremadura towards Madrid.

The faces of terror

The Spanish Civil War has gone down in history, and in memory, for the way it dehumanised its adversaries and for the horrific violence that it generated. If we go by the meticulous research carried out in the past few years, there were at least 150,000 fatalities of this violence during the war: almost 100,000 in the zone controlled by the military rebels, and just under 60,000 in the republican zone. And, even without these figures, we have a wealth of information about this terror at our disposal.[8]

From the very first moment of the coup, destruction of the adversary became the absolute priority. The military rebels gave a taste of their sword to tens of thousands of citizens. Nobody knew better than they did how useful terror could be to paralyse any potential resistance and eliminate their opponents. Many of them had cut their teeth in the colonial wars, ideal settings for learning to reject human values and civic virtues, to become educated in the veneration of violence. The violence that was envisaged before the coup, during the plotting stage, was nothing compared to what was to begin in July 1936. They started by spreading terror from the very first day, intimidating, killing, crushing any resistance. With the declaration of martial law, anyone defending the Republic was deemed a 'rebel'.

The course of events was very similar in all the cities where the rising was successful. The army left their barracks, swarmed the streets and proclaimed martial law, thus banning meetings, strikes and the possession of arms. Military squads with their machine guns installed outside the main public buildings showed that they meant business. Civil governors were replaced by officers. From their new post they dismissed the political authorities, beginning with the mayors and regional council leaders, and

---

[8] Dozens of studies on the political violence in the rears of the two sides in the struggle have appeared in recent years. The first synthesis that presented such violence in a global perspective was Santos Juliá (ed.), Julián Casanova, Josep María Solé i Sabaté, Joan Villarroya and Francisco Moreno, *Víctimas de la guerra civil* (Madrid: Temas de Hoy, 1999). The latest, and most comprehensive, is Paul Preston, *The Spanish Holocaust: Inquisition and Extermination in Twentieth-Century Spain* (London: Harper Collins, 2011).

ordered the Civil Guard in the various towns and villages to join the uprising.

Thus began mass jailings, selective repression to eliminate resistance, systematic torture and 'hot-blooded' terror, the type of terror that abandoned people wherever they had been shot, in roadside ditches, against cemetery walls, in rivers or in disused wells and mines. Mayors, civil governors, local councillors, trade union and Frente Popular leaders were the first to suffer the terror of the *paseos*. The fury of the army and Falangists was particularly aimed at the Frente Popular coalition deputies elected in February 1936. A report drawn up by the secretariat of the Congreso de los Diputados, published on 22 August 1938, stated that forty had been murdered and twelve were either prisoners or 'missing' in 'rebel territory'. This was no mean figure, considering that most of the 263 deputies in this coalition were elected in provinces and cities in which the rebellion had been put down.

Some of these politicians, intellectuals and professionals were also Masons, and many others were falsely accused of being members of Freemasonry. In fact, as José Antonio Ferrer Benimelli has shown, the fervent zeal of the fascists in the summer of 1936 decreed that being a Mason was considered to be a 'crime against the Fatherland'. And a genuine process of extermination was what the military rebels and the Falangists set in motion against Freemasonry, with lodges being demolished and all their members murdered, as was the case in several cities in Galicia, and in Zamora, Cádiz, Granada, Huelva, Las Palmas and Zaragoza. Nearly 100 people were shot in Huesca accused of Masonry, although there were barely a dozen Masons there.[9]

As well as political authorities, intellectuals and schoolteachers, this selective repression also took in a considerable number of workers' organisations' leaders and militants. Socialists and anarchists, communists, UGT and CNT union members fell like flies. Officers, Falangists, bosses, owners and people of order settled old scores, fed up with workers' disputes, their revolutionary threats, their social aspirations and their agrarian reform. In general terms, the repression was a great deal more systematic and there was more of it in places where social conflicts had been most intensive – areas where socialist trade unionism or anarcho-syndicalism had been consolidated and those places where the Frente Popular had been successful in the February 1936 elections.

This wave of extermination also caught up thousands of people who had never been conspicuous for their public actions, or so they

---

[9] José Antonio Ferrer Benimelli, *La masonería española* (Madrid: Itsmo, 1995), pp. 144–5.

thought. Under this lawless new order, someone only had to state that such-and-such a person never attended mass, used to frequent the local party headquarters or the *ateneo libertario*, had celebrated republican election victories or was simply 'known to be against the Movimiento Nacional'. It was a reflection of opposition and confrontation between two worlds, of the socio-economic and cultural imbalance between the 'haves' and the 'have-nots', between those who had had the chance to acquire culture and the illiterate. In short, it was a reflection of class repression, from the top down, accompanied and reinforced by political persecution, although personal and family quarrels, or religious, nationalist and linguistic divisions, meant that the more conventional images regarding class conflict propagated by militant literature should be rejected.

This 'hot-blooded' terror needed no procedures or safeguards. Three-quarters of the 1,830 killed in Cáceres were 'taken for a walk', almost all of them in the first few months, while only 32 of the 2,578 victims of repression in the city of Zaragoza during 1936 faced a court martial. Thousands of deaths were never registered, while many others appeared as 'an unidentified man or woman'. There was no longer any room for the dead in the cemeteries, and so large mass graves were dug, as in the case of Lardero, a small village near Logroño where close to 400 people were shot and buried, or in Víznar, a few kilometres from Granada, where Federico García Lorca met his death.

The highest number of killings in almost all the regions that had been under the control of the rebels from the beginning took place during the final days of July and the months of August and September 1936. More than 90% of the close to 3,000 killings in Navarre, and 37% of the 7,000 in Zaragoza, occurred in 1936. But the percentages were very similar in Córdoba, Granada, Seville, Badajoz and Huelva, the provinces in which, together with Navarre and Zaragoza, the stench of death was at its strongest in that wave of summer terror. In none of these provinces was the death toll below 2,000 victims, in barely 70 days.

The purge was massive and dramatic in the rural environment, where close personal relationships favoured the flourishing of old disputes and passionate family quarrels, mixed with political and class hatred, and the thirst for vengeance from landowners who felt threatened by the rise of popular movements. For long years afterwards, many of them were yet to discover where their dead were, scattered as they were in the most unlikely places, until they found them in registry office and cemetery lists published in various studies. Others have been less lucky and have been deprived of this sentimental and symbolic satisfaction, because their dead were never registered.

They were also dark days for many women, countless numbers of whom were killed, although in no province did the number of executions of women reach 10% of the total; but above all they suffered humiliations ranging from having their hair shorn to sexual harassment, as well as being given castor oil laxatives or being forbidden to show their grief through mourning. There were women who had to open their doors to Falangists at night and tell the murderers where they could find their absent husbands and sons. Thousands of widows and orphans had lost their parents and husbands in the prime of life – most of the murdered were between 19 and 40 years old, according to the most comprehensive studies – with their own lives shattered and in ruins, and with the stigma of being related to dead reds.

Falangists, *Requetés*, citizen militias and volunteers were the most visible manifestation of this rightist mobilisation which had been facilitated by the military uprising. All these reactionary sectors accompanied the army in carrying out the terror; and while it often left the cleansing work to these paramilitary groups, it was the army that was in charge of the violence by declaring martial law, taking on all powers related to public order, and submitting ordinary justice to the military. During these early months, its commanders and officers never put a brake on a repression that they controlled at all times, in spite of the appearance of 'unrestraint' that encompassed many *sacas* and *paseos*.

In the republican zone, in places where the uprising was unsuccessful and the breakdown of order gave way to revolution, it was the army and particularly the clergy that were main targets for violence. In addition, during these first few weeks, conservative politicians, landowners, smallholders, farmers, the middle classes, shopkeepers, workers who were known in the factories for their moderate ideas, engineers and personnel managers in the various industries were killed, as well as Catholics – above all, Catholics. The principal perpetrators of these crimes were the revolutionary committees that emerged from the overthrow of republican power, the militias and the various 'investigation and vigilante groups' that were set up by the political and trade union organisations in the major cities.

Most of the almost 60,000 murders in the republican zone were committed in the first few months of the war, at a time when the power of the committees and militias was at its height. Afterwards, from the autumn of 1936 onwards, thousands of prisoners' lives were saved by the order and discipline in the rear imposed by the political organisations represented in the governments of Francisco Largo Caballero and Juan Negrín.

This violence against people of order and the clergy did immense damage to the republican cause abroad. The image of burning convents, the persecution of the clergy and the massacre at Paracuellos de Jarama, in November 1936, went all round the world, while the mass killings perpetrated by the military rebels in the summer of 1936, in Seville, Zaragoza and the bull ring in Badajoz, had no repercussion in the political, diplomatic and financial circles of London or Paris. Furthermore, the 'red terror' damaged the efforts of the Republic to obtain international support, although it was not the principal reason why the democratic powers decided to leave the Republic abandoned and almost on its own against the Nazi and fascist threat.

A special place in the account of these thousands of killings in the republican zone was reserved for José Antonio Primo de Rivera. At the time of the military rising, the Falangist leader was in prison in Alicante, where he had been taken on 5 June from the Modelo prison in Madrid. The uprising was unsuccessful in the region of Valencia, and from that moment Primo de Rivera spent several months in which, while his allies were planning his escape or an exchange of prisoners – something which other leading right-wingers such as Ramón Serrano Súñer and Raimundo Fernández Cuesta managed to secure – the Committee of Public Order in Alicante was thinking of 'taking him for a walk' on the pretext of a transfer to the gaol in Cartagena.

On 16 November, along with his brother Miguel, he faced a Popular Tribunal, made up of three magistrates and a fourteen-man jury, and answered questions about his connections with the conspirators and the preparation of the military uprising. José Antonio denied both his participation in the plot and the Falange's responsibility for acts of violence. On 18 November, the magistrates accepted the prosecutor's request for the death penalty, while the sentence for his brother Miguel was life imprisonment. José Antonio was shot at dawn on 20 November 1936, at the age of 33.

This marked the beginning of the legend of the '*ausente*', cleverly cultivated by Franco. Dozens of edifices were built in his honour after the war, and hundreds of streets, squares and schools were named after him; inscriptions on the walls of churches read '*José Antonio Primo de Rivera, ¡Presente!*' In fact, before his death, he had made little impact on the political scene, as may be seen from the fact that he failed to win a seat in the February 1936 elections.

The obvious conclusion to be drawn from so much killing was that violence was inseparably linked to the *coup d'état* and the development of the Civil War. Symbolised by the *sacas*, *paseos* and mass killings, it was used by the two sides in their struggle to eliminate their respective enemies, whether natural or unforeseen. It was an essential part of the 'glorious National Movement', its onslaught against the Republic and the gradual conquest of power, skirmish by skirmish, massacre by massacre, battle by battle. It also became a basic ingredient of the diversified chaotic response provided by left-wing political and trade union organisations to the military coup. Contrary to appearances, this violence was not so much a consequence of the war as the direct result of a military uprising which from the outset went hand in hand with unpunished murder and the *coup de grâce*. It was a strategically designed plan which, in the places where it failed, was met by a sudden armed response against the main players in the uprising and those considered to be their material and spiritual brothers-in-arms.

While carrying out this extermination, the rebels were also given the inestimable blessing of the Catholic Church from the very beginning. The clergy and sacred objects, however, were the prime target of popular rage, of those who took part in defeat of the military rebels and who led the 'cleansing' undertaken in the summer of 1936.[10]

From the very beginning, the principal representatives of the Catholic Church offered their support and blessing to the rebels. The Fatherland, order and religion, three things that for them were basically the same, had to be saved. And they lent their full weight to this cause from the pulpit, with sermons, exhortations and episcopal declarations, although there was no shortage of clergy with red berets and pistols, dressed up as soldiers, Falangists or *Requetés*.

The first bishops to speak out were those who felt safer alongside the military rebels, basically because the coup had been a resounding success in the zone that contained their dioceses. These were the dioceses of almost the whole of northern Spain, from Pamplona and Zaragoza to Galicia, with Burgos, Valladolid, Salamanca and Zamora in between; thirty-two sees of the sixty-one dioceses in Spain were, by the second half of August, in the rebel zone. According to data furnished by Alfonso Álvarez Bolado from *Ecclesiastical Gazettes*, 'in no fewer than 11 dioceses ... through 18 interventions, the bishops had made their position absolutely clear' before the first official declaration by Pope Pius XI on 14 September 1936. Furthermore, three of them, the bishop of Pamplona and the archbishops of Zaragoza and Santiago de Compostela, had already labelled the Civil War a 'religious crusade' before the end of August.

Almost all of these declarations followed a substantially similar line: they unblushingly sided with the military coup, which they celebrated with the Catholic masses as a liberation; they urged people to join the struggle against 'the lay-Jewish-Masonic-Soviet elements', an expression coined

---

[10] For a comprehensive account of the ideology and practices of clericalism and anti-clericalism, and the violence they brought about, see Julián Casanova, *La Iglesia de Franco* (Barcelona: Crítica, 2005).

by the Bishop of León, José Alvarez Miranda; and they saw no outcome to the conflict other than the resounding victory of 'our glorious army' over 'the enemies of God and of Spain'.[11]

The Church has always tried to justify its postures and attitudes by citing the vicious anti-clericalism that was unleashed in areas where the rising was defeated, a message with a clear impact, although the enthusiastic support by many ecclesiastical personnel for the coup came before, and in many cases ran parallel with, the clergy killings. It was not the 'Satanic hatred' of the 'Communist hordes' that caused the Church and Catholics to take sides with the military rebels. It is true that it did reinforce their posture. But it was not the cause.

Furthermore, the clergy's complicity with the terror unleashed by the army was absolute and did not need anti-clericalism to manifest itself. From Cardinal Isidro Gomá to the humble priest who lived in Zaragoza, Salamanca or Granada, all were aware of the killings, heard the shots, saw how the people were taken away, how relatives of the prisoners or the missing would come to them and desperately beg for help and mercy. And except on rare occasions, the most common attitude was silence, either voluntary or imposed by their superiors, or else accusation and denunciation. The violence of the military insurgents was legitimate because it was used 'not to promote anarchy, but legally, to the benefit of order, the Fatherland and Religion', declared the archbishop of Zaragoza, Rigoberto Doménech, on 11 August.[12]

While this was going on, the other half of the Church, in the areas where the rebellion had failed, was undergoing what Gomá called 'Satanic rage', a devastating retribution of vast dimensions. More than 6,800 ecclesiastics, both lay and regular, were killed; a large number of churches, hermitages and sanctuaries were burnt or suffered looting and desecration, with their works of art and items of worship totally or partially destroyed. Nor did cemeteries or graveyards fare any better, with a great number of priests' graves desecrated and the remains of monks and nuns exhumed.

Burning a church or killing a priest was the first thing that was done in many villages and towns where the military uprising was unsuccessful. 'Direct action', nothing less: that was what the clergy deserved. Andreu Nin, one of the big names in POUM, publicly stated as much at the beginning of August 1936. Nin, who a few months later was to be kidnapped and murdered by the Communist secret services, thought and said the same as many other revolutionaries, leftist republicans and union leaders:

---

[11] Alfonso Álvarez Bolado, *Para ganar la guerra, para ganar la paz: iglesia y Guerra Civil: 1936–1939* (Madrid: Universidad Pontificia de Comillas, 1995), pp. 50–3.
[12] *Heraldo de Aragón*, Zaragoza, 11 Aug. 1936.

that the 'bourgeois' Republic's anti-clerical legislation had done nothing to solve the 'problem' of the Church. It had had to be solved by the working class in the revolutionary flare-up initiated by the military coup. And it had been solved by the workers and revolutionaries in the way that they knew how, by 'attacking the roots', leaving no church standing, suppressing 'the priests, churches and worship'.[13]

Spain in 1936 had some 115,000 clergy, in a population of 24 million. Of these, nearly 60,000 were nuns, 35,000 priests and 15,000 monks. According to the study published by Antonio Montero Moreno in 1961, 4,184 diocesan priests, 2,365 monks and 283 nuns were murdered. Thirteen bishops and the apostolic administrator of Orihuela met the same fate. Of the 6,832 victims of the anti-clerical violence, 839 were killed in July following the coup and 2,055 in August. In other words, 42.35% of the total number of victims met their death in the first forty-four days and ten of the thirteen bishops were killed before 31 August, irrefutable proof of the swiftness and immediacy of the torment experienced by the clergy. In fact, with the exception of the Basque Country, where only fifty-four clergy were murdered, wearing a cassock became a symbol of relentless persecution in the whole of the republican zone, albeit to a lesser degree in Murcia, Albacete, Badajoz and Santander.

Catholicism and anti-clericalism were passionately involved in the battle over basic themes related to the organisation of society and the state that was being unleashed in Spanish territory. Religion was extremely useful from the outset because, as Bruce Lincoln maintains, it proved to be the only element that systematically generated a current of international sympathy for General Franco's nationalist cause.[14] On the other hand, the violent anti-clericalism that broke out with the military rising brought no benefit at all to the republican cause. The fact that the violence of the military rebels was meted out in the name of values as elevated as the Fatherland and Religion made things much easier, in comparison with the other side's violence 'in the service of anarchy'. This was how it was perceived in Spain and beyond its frontiers. It was yet another battle that the Republic lost in the eyes of the rest of the world.

An international war

The international situation at the end of the 1930s was hardly conducive to peace, and this played a decisive role in the duration, progress and final

---

[13] *La Vanguardia*, Barcelona, 2 Aug. 1936.
[14] Bruce Lincoln, 'Revolutionary Exhumations in Spain, July 1936', *Comparative Studies in Society and History*, 27, 2 (1985), pp. 231–60.

result of the Spanish Civil War, a conflict that was clearly internal in its origin. The rearmament policies followed by the principal countries of Europe since the beginning of that decade created a climate of uncertainty and crisis which undermined international security. The Soviet Union began a large-scale programme of military and industrial modernisation that was to place it as the leading military power over the next few decades. At the same time, the Nazis, under Hitler, committed themselves to overturning the Versailles agreements and restoring Germany's dominance. Mussolini's Italy followed the same path and its economy was increasingly devoted to preparing for war. France and Great Britain began rearming in 1934 and this process escalated after 1936. The world arms trade doubled between 1932 and 1937.[15]

Under these circumstances, none of these countries showed any interest in stopping the Spanish Civil War. International support for both sides was vital for fighting and continuing the war during the early months. Italian and German aid enabled the military rebels to move the Africa Army to the peninsula at the end of July 1936, and Soviet aid made a decisive contribution to the republican defence of Madrid in November 1936. The USSR's military support for the Republic served as a pretext for the Axis powers to increase their military and financial support to Franco's side. These manifestations of support were maintained almost unchanged until the end of the war, while the rest of Europe, with Britain at its head, appeared to observe the Non-Intervention Agreement.[16]

Barely two weeks after the military rising, the governments of the principal European powers had already shaped their policies with regard to this fledgling conflict in Spain. The British Foreign Office declared 'strict neutrality' and asked the French to do the same. In Paris, Léon Blum went back on his original decision to help the government of the Republic and opted for non-intervention. Germany and Italy were willing to help the military rebels. And, although the USSR would very soon change its posture, it initially kept a guarded distance. Outside Europe, the United States followed Britain's neutral line. Many other small countries in Europe and South America showed no outward signs of concern, although there was unspoken support for the military rebels. The only country to express clear support for the Republic was Mexico.

[15] Richard Overy, 'Warfare in Europe Since 1918', in T. C. W. Blanning (ed.), *The Oxford History of Modern Europe* (Oxford University Press, 2000), pp. 219–20.
[16] The basic ingredients of this international dimension have been made well known through studies by historians such as Enrique Moradiellos and Ángel Viñas. See, for example, Moradiellos, *El reñidero de Europa*; and Viñas, *Franco, Hitler y el estallido de la guerra civil* (Madrid: Alianza Editorial, 2001).

The non-intervention policy was an initiative of the French Popular Front government. After discovering on 30 July that the Nazis and Italian fascists had started to help the military rebels, because two planes sent by Mussolini landed in Algeria by mistake, the French proposed that the principal countries of Europe sign a Non-Intervention in Spain Agreement. In the words of Léon Blum's secretary, it was 'in order to stop others doing what we were unable to do'.[17] Since it could not help the Republic, because that would have created an internal conflict with unforeseen consequences in French society, it would at least force Germany and Italy to withdraw their support for the rebel side. The non-intervention attitude of the minister of foreign affairs, the radical Yvon Delbos, was strictly enforced from the first week of August. The French High Command also wanted to avoid an intervention that would turn Italy against France and endanger peace in the Mediterranean. France's proposal also included a ban on the export and sale of arms to the republicans and rebels. On 13 August, the government closed the Pyrenean border.

In Britain, the aristocratic diplomatic circles, the middle class and the Anglican Church authorities, with the exception of the Bishop of Cork in Ireland, supported the military rebels, while the Labour Party, the trade unions and many intellectuals were behind the republican cause. As K. W. Watkins' study showed some time ago, British society suffered a 'deep' schism. And Paul Preston stressed the idea of a 'divided' Great Britain: while public opinion was 'overwhelmingly' behind the Republic, the inner circle that took the really 'crucial decisions' declared themselves to be in favour of the military rebels. For these conservatives, the Spanish Civil War was also a class conflict, and they knew perfectly well whose side they were on.[18]

London and Washington, which had not shown any sympathy for the Republic during its five years of peace, very soon took a position of what Douglas Little called 'malevolent neutrality'.[19] The non-intervention policy would serve, following the diplomatic objectives set by the Foreign Office, to confine the struggle within Spanish borders and avoid confrontation with Italy and Germany. This policy put a legal government and a group of military rebels on the same footing.

At the end of August 1936, the twenty-seven European states – all except Switzerland, whose constitution decreed its neutrality – had

---

[17] Quoted in Moradiellos, *El reñidero de Europa*, p. 95.
[18] Paul Preston, *The Spanish Civil War* (London: Harper Perennial, 2006), pp. 137–8; and K. W. Watkins, *Britain Divided: The Effects of the Spanish Civil War on British Political Opinion* (London: Thomas Nelson & Sons, 1963), p. 70.
[19] Douglas Little, *Malevolent Neutrality: The United States, Great Britain and the Origins of the Spanish Civil War* (Ithaca, NY: Cornell University Press, 1985).

officially subscribed to the Non-Intervention in Spain Agreement, whereby they deplored 'the tragic events being enacted in Spain', decided 'to strictly abstain from all interference, either direct or indirect, in the internal affairs of this country' and banned 'the exporting . . . re-exporting and delivery to Spain, Spanish possessions or the Spanish zone in Morocco, of all types of arms, munitions and war materiel'.[20] The monitoring of this agreement was conducted by a Non-Intervention Committee, set up in London on 9 September under the chairmanship of the Conservative Lord Plymouth, the parliamentary under-secretary to the Foreign Office, and a Non-Intervention Subcommittee made up of representatives from the states bordering Spain and the major arms producers, including Germany, France, Britain and the Soviet Union.

In practice, non-intervention was a complete 'farce', as it was termed by people at the time who saw that it put the Republic at a disadvantage in comparison to the military rebels. The Soviet Union, which had little faith in the agreement, decided in principle to observe it in order to keep on good terms with France and Great Britain. But Germany, Italy and Portugal systematically flouted the commitment and continued sending arms and munitions. For Germany and Italy, intervention in the Civil War marked the consolidation of a new diplomatic alliance which, via the official setting up of the 'Rome–Berlin Axis' in October 1936, was to have major repercussions on international politics in the future. It was made clear that Germany and Italy were not going to observe the agreement they had signed when, on 28 August 1936, Admiral Wilhelm Canaris and General Mario Roatta, the heads of their respective countries' military intelligence, met in Rome and decided to 'continue (in spite of the arms embargo) supplying war materiel and munitions deliveries, in response to the requests of General Franco'.[21]

Nazi and fascist military aid was considerable and decisive for Franco's victory. Between the end of July and the middle of October twenty German Junkers 52s and six Heinkel 51 fighters transported more than 13,000 men of the Africa Army and 270 tonnes of materiel. Later, with the Condor Legion, which from November 1936 took part in all the major battles of the war, Nazi Germany sent 600 further aircraft that dropped a total of approximately 21 million tonnes of bombs. For their part, the Italians began by sending 12 Savoia 81 bombers to transport the Moroccan troops to the mainland and, during the course of the war, according to John F. Coverdale, their military aid consisted of materiel worth over 6 billion lira, 64 million pounds sterling at 1939 exchange rates, including

[20] The document is reproduced in Moradiellos, *El reñidero de Europa*, p. 99.
[21] *Ibid.*, p. 101.

nearly 1,000 aircraft, 200 field guns, 1,000 armoured vehicles and several thousand machine guns and automatic weapons.[22]

International diplomacy was making its move just when the Second Republic's diplomatic corps had been left divided and fragmented as a consequence of the *coup d'état*. Most of the embassy and consular staff in the main countries of Europe abandoned the Republic, and those who had not done so were actually serving the military rebels' cause. The ambassadors in Rome, Berlin, Paris and Washington resigned in the first few weeks, after doing all they could to hamper republican attempts to redefine its foreign policy. The socialist Julio Álvarez del Vayo, the new foreign minister in Largo Caballero's first government, formed on 4 September 1936, calculated that 90% of the diplomatic and consular corps had deserted.

Thus, in an international context, all this seemed to favour the military rebels. The Italians and Germans had managed to strengthen the system of military aid to the rebels, while Britain and France were strictly observing the Non-Intervention Agreement. Things changed, however, when Stalin decided to intervene in the conflict, two months after its outbreak.

At first the Spanish Civil War provided no advantage to the interests of the Soviet Union, and on 22 August Maxim Litvinov, the foreign affairs commissar, signed the Non-Intervention Agreement. But the evidence that Hitler and Mussolini were aiding the rebels, in spite of the Non-Intervention Agreement, alarmed Stalin. If the Republic were defeated quickly, France's strategic position with regard to Germany would be radically weakened, and the increase of Nazi and fascist power would also have negative repercussions for the Soviet Union. Stalin prepared the way. He notified the Non-Intervention Committee that he would be forced to breach the agreement if Germany and Italy continued doing so, and he calculated the potential costs of the aid so that the British government did not see it as support for a revolution that was spreading throughout the republican zone, and the Nazis did not take it as open intervention.

In October the first shipments of arms arrived in Spain. The Soviet Union began to do what Italy, Germany and Portugal were already doing: breaching the non-intervention accords without officially abandoning this policy. From that moment on, Soviet military aid to the Republic, paid for with the Bank of Spain's gold reserves, was continuous up to the end of the war and was vital for sustaining the Republic's cause against Franco's army and the support of Hitler and Mussolini. As well as war materiel, a

---

[22] John F. Coverdale, *Italian Intervention in the Spanish Civil War* (Princeton University Press, 1977).

substantial quantity of aircraft and armoured vehicles, numbering some 700 and 400 units respectively, the USSR also sent food, fuel, clothes and a considerable number, around 2,000 in total, of pilots, engineers, advisers and members of the secret police, the NKVD, under the command of Alexander Orlov. The Soviet people contributed millions of rubles to buy clothes and food, generating the biggest mobilisation of foreign humanitarian aid in history.[23]

At the same time as the first arms shipments, the first foreign volunteers for the International Brigades began to arrive, recruited and organised by the Communist International, which was well aware of the impact of the Spanish Civil War on the world, and of the desire of many anti-fascists to take part in this struggle. With the Soviet intervention and the International Brigades, the Nazis and fascists increased their material aid to Franco's army and also sent thousands of professional servicemen and volunteer fighters. The war was not a Spanish domestic matter. It became internationalised, thereby increasing its brutality and destruction. Spanish territory became a testing ground for new weaponry that was being developed during those rearmament years prior to a great war that was on the horizon.

The number of brigadists varies according to sources, from the 100,000 quoted by the Nationalists to exaggerate their influence and the significance of international communism, to the 40,000 referred to by Hugh Thomas in his classic study on the Civil War. One of the latest and most exhaustive studies on the International Brigades, by Michel Lefebvre and Rémi Skoutelsky, provides a figure of nearly 35,000, accepted today by quite a few historians, although there were never more than 20,000 combatants at a time, and in 1938 the number had reduced considerably.[24] Some 10,000 volunteers died in combat; they came from more than fifty countries. France provided almost 9,000 while barely 150 came from Portugal. The military reports logging their presence in the training base in Albacete tell us that the two greatest concentrations of volunteers there coincided with the first few months of their intervention, from October 1936 to March 1937, and with the battles of Teruel and Aragón, from December 1937 to April 1938.

There were also many foreigners fighting with Franco's troops. They – like the International Brigades – came from a wide range of countries. Not many of them were volunteers, because the majority of those who fought,

[23] Daniel Kowalsky, *Stalin and the Spanish Civil War* (New York: Columbia University Press, 2004).
[24] Michel Lefebvre and Rémi Skoutelsky, *Brigadas Internacionales: imágenes recuperadas* (Barcelona: Lunwerg Editores, 2003).

particularly Germans and Italians, were regular soldiers, well prepared, who were paid in their countries of origin. Chief among the genuine volunteers, between 1,000 and 1,500, were Irish Catholics, under the command of General Eoin O'Duffy, who subscribed to the idea of a crusade as held by the Spanish Catholic Church and Pope Pius XI in the Vatican. They bore various religious emblems, rosaries, images of the *Agnus Dei* and the Sacred Heart, as did the Carlists, and they left Ireland, according to O'Duffy himself, to fight Christianity's battle against communism. They only fought in the Battle of the Jarama, in February 1937, where, in view of their lack of military experience, they failed to acquit themselves well, and a few months later they returned home.

In answer to the International Brigades, Germany and Italy sent tens of thousands of soldiers to fight alongside the military rebels. So that there would be no doubt as to the purpose of this intervention, on 18 November 1936, the month of the major Francoist offensive on Madrid, the governments of the two Axis powers officially recognised Franco and his Junta Técnica del Estado, set up on 2 October to replace the Junta de Defensa Nacional, and soon afterwards the first two ambassadors arrived in Burgos: General Wilhelm von Faupel and the fascist journalist Roberto Cantalupo.

At around this time Hitler decided to send an airborne unit that would fight as an independent corps, with its own officers, in the Francoist ranks. Called the Condor Legion, it arrived in Spain by sea in the middle of November under the command of General Hugo von Sperle and later of Colonel Baron Wolfram von Richthofen, both Luftwaffe officers. It consisted of some 140 aircraft divided into 4 fighter squadrons with Heinkel 51 biplanes plus another 4 squadrons of Junkers 52s, backed up by one battalion of 48 tanks and another of 60 anti-aircraft guns. Thus the Spanish Civil War became the Luftwaffe's testing ground, a rehearsal for the fighters and bombers that would, shortly afterwards, be used in the Second World War.

Research by Raymond L. Proctor reveals that the total number of Condor Legion combatants during the course of the war amounted to 19,000 men, including pilots, tank crews and artillerymen, although there were never more than 5,500 at a time, as they were frequently relieved so that as many soldiers as possible could gain experience. The Condor Legion took part in nearly all the military operations conducted during the Civil War, and 371 of its members lost their lives in action.[25]

---

[25] Raymond L. Proctor, *Hitler's Luftwaffe in the Spanish Civil War* (Westport, CT: Greenwood Press, 1983).

A much larger contribution was made by the Italians, who began to arrive in Spain in December 1936 and January 1937, after the secret pact of friendship signed by Franco and Mussolini on 28 November. Up to that time, the Italians piloting the Savoia 81s and Fiat fighters had been fighting in the Foreign Legion. After the signing of this pact, Mussolini organised the Corpo di Truppe Volontarie (CTV), commanded by General Mario Roatta until the disaster at Guadalajara in March 1937, and then by Generals Ettore Bastico, Mario Berti and Gastone Gambara. The CTV had a permanent force of 40,000 soldiers and its total number, according to figures published by Coverdale, rose to 72,775 men: 43,129 from the army and 29,646 from the fascist militia. They were joined by 5,699 men from the Aviazione Legionaria, thus bringing the total number of Italian combatants to 78,474, much higher than the German or International Brigades figures.[26]

Thus, tens of thousands of foreigners fought in the Spanish Civil War. It was really a European civil war, with the tacit approval of the British and French governments. A little over 100,000 fought on Franco's side: 78,000 Italians, 19,000 Germans and 10,000 Portuguese, plus more than a thousand volunteers from other countries, not counting the 70,000 Moroccans who made up the native *Regulares*. On the republican side, the figures given by Rémi Skoutelsky show nearly 35,000 volunteers in the International Brigades and 2,000 Soviets, of whom 600 were non-combatant advisers. Contrary to the myth of the communist and revolutionary threat, what in fact hit Spain through an open military intervention was fascism.

---

[26] Coverdale, *Italian Intervention in the Spanish Civil War*.

9   Politics and arms

'We are waging war because it is being waged on us', said President Manuel Azaña in a speech in the Valencia City Hall on 21 January 1937.[1] It was a terrible war which in barely half a year saw the cruel terror of the rebel army and Falangists accompanied by a violent upheaval of social order. And the Republic was indeed forced to fight in a war that it did not start, and the political organisations of the left had to adapt to a military activity that they knew practically nothing about. The varying ideas on how to organise the state and society held by the parties, movements and people who fought on the republican side ostensibly played a major part in frustrating a united policy against the military rebels. And there was nothing new in this situation, as it had been going on for years and had complicated the life of the Republic in peacetime as well.

Policy and military strategy did not always coincide in the republican camp. And there was more conflict and disunity than in the Nationalist camp. Aid from the fascist powers to the military rebels was much more direct than that from the Soviet Union or the democratic powers to the republican side, and the military authorities, under the sole command of Franco, controlled the home front with an iron fist. Those who shared their values were happily experiencing the renaissance of a new Spain because their army always won its battles and so loss of morale was out of the question. For those who did not support them, a savage violence awaited them, implemented from the very day of the uprising, a violence that did not cease until many years after the end of the war. The rebels won the war because they had the best trained troops in the Spanish army, economic power and the Catholic Church on their side, and the winds of international sympathy also blew their way.

The Republic at war

This Republic at war went through three different stages, with three prime ministers. The first stage, with José Giral as premier, was marked by the

---

[1] Manuel Azaña, *Los españoles en guerra* (Barcelona: Crítica, 1982), p. 19.

resistance to the coup, the formation of militias, revolution and the elimination of the symbols of power and people of order. Giral (1879–1962), a left-wing republican, from the same party and generation as Manuel Azaña (1880–1949), had held the chair of inorganic chemistry at the Universities of Salamanca and Madrid, was rector of Madrid University in 1931 and had taken an active part in politics during the Republic: he had been the navy minister in Azaña's governments between 15 October 1931 and June 1933 and, after the Frente Popular coalition victory in February 1936, Azaña once more called on him to occupy the same post, and he stayed there in Santiago Casares Quiroga's government until the military uprising.

In the first few weeks of war, with José Giral in the government, the militias, particularly those organised by the anarchists, set up revolutionary committees in any town they passed through, settled scores with people of order, right-wingers and clergy, and preached a revolution of expropriation and collectivism. Committees sprang up everywhere. During that summer of 1936, republican Spain was a hotbed of armed and fragmented powers, difficult to keep in check. Catalonia had its Central Committee of Anti-Fascist Militias, in which the anarchists, led by Juan García Oliver, Aurelio Fernández and Diego Abad de Santillán, attempted to impose their will. Very soon afterwards, at the beginning of August, the Popular Executive Committee, with all political organisations represented, made its appearance in Valencia. In Málaga and Lérida there was a Committee of Public Health. And in Madrid, as well as National Committee of the Frente Popular, which organised militias and the life of the city, there was Giral's government which – made up of left-wing republicans only – could not represent this jumble of committees, militias and control patrols in which socialists and anarchists, UGT and CNT syndicalists, were running the revolution, a revolution of destruction and murder, a revolution which was attempting to coax something new out of the ashes.

Giral did what he could and what his duty as a loyal republican dictated. And considering that he was only a month and a half in office, what he did was fairly substantial. He asked France and the USSR for aid to defeat the military rebellion, started using the Bank of Spain's gold reserves to finance the war, dismissed any public servant suspected of siding with the rebels, and pronounced the first measures to check indiscriminate violence in the rear. This was on 23 and 25 August 1936, immediately after the murder of leading right-wingers and politicians in the Modelo prison in Madrid. Special tribunals were set up 'to try crimes of rebellion and sedition, and those committed to harming the security of the state'. This 'emergency justice' of the Republic incorporated 'summary judgement' and several elements of military procedure without the need to resort to 'martial law', something the republican government did not declare throughout its territory until 9 January 1939.[2]

But Giral's government did not represent this new open social and political mobilisation against the military rebellion, which was also directed against what was left of the republican state itself, nor the various revolutionary and trade union powers that were emerging, the only powers that exercised any authority in the chaos of the summer of 1936. Furthermore, the Africa Army was advancing relentlessly on Madrid, after overrunning Extremadura and large areas of Castile-La Mancha. On 3 September, Yagüe's columns arrived at Talavera. That same day, in the north, where General Mola had launched an attack on Guipúzcoa, Irún fell. 'The government of the Republic is dead. It has no authority or competence, no plan for waging all-out war and finishing it with an absolute victory for the revolution', wrote Luís Araquistáin, the left-wing socialist ideologist, to Largo Caballero on 24 August.[3]

Now that the military rebels were in Talavera, Giral really believed that he had no authority or backing, and he decided to 'present to H.E. the president of the Republic all the powers received from him, as well as the resignation of all the ministers', so that he could replace them with a government that would 'represent each and every one of the political parties and trade union or workers' organisations acknowledged as having influence among the Spanish people'. The hour had come for the trade unions and Largo Caballero, the undisputed leader of the UGT.

On 4 September 1936, Largo Caballero, who had opposed the idea of Indalecio Prieto forming a government of republicans and socialists in May 1936, and who had refused to do so after the *coup d'état* in July, finally agreed to lead 'a coalition government', on the advice of Araquistáin, in which he himself would also be the minister for war. It was a socialist government which also included five republicans, two Communists and a Basque nationalist. It was, in fact, the first and only government in Spain's history to be led by a workers' leader, and the first time that there were Communist ministers in a west European government.

Two months later, on 4 November, the CNT entered the government with four representatives, including a woman, Federica Montseny, as minister of health, the first woman to hold a post of this calibre in Spain's history. It was indeed a historic moment when anarchists formed part of a

[2] Glicerio Sánchez Recio, *Justicia y guerra en España: los Tribunales Populares (1936–1939)* (Alicante: Instituto de Cultura 'Juan Gil-Albert', 1991).
[3] Quoted in Santos Juliá, 'El Frente Popular y la política de la República en guerra', in Juliá (ed.), *Historia de España de Menéndez Pidal: república y guerra civil*, 42 vols. (Madrid: Espasa Calpe, 2004), vol. XL, p. 126. The subsequent quote from Giral's letter to Azaña comes from the same source.

national government, and it was hailed as such by the libertarian press. Very few noteworthy anarchists refused to support this new situation, because they believed that revolutionary change could be consolidated only from a position of power, and there was also very little resistance from the grassroots anarchists, trade union members who had hitherto displayed revolutionary opposition to the reformist leaders. They were to change their tune after the events of May 1937, following their expulsion from the government, and exile: for them, Largo Caballero's entry into the government had meant the absolute renunciation of every anti-political and revolutionary principle.[4]

However, their entry into the government did not come at the best of times. On the very same day, Franco's troops were at the gates of Madrid, the scene of what was to be the most decisive battle of the first phase of the war. General Franco, head of the military rebels since 1 October 1936, ordered the concentration of all his forces to take the capital, with the Africa Army in the vanguard, reinforced by squadrons of German and Italian aircraft.

The government was incapable of organising the defence of the capital effectively. On 6 November, during the first cabinet meeting attended by the CNT ministers, it was decided unanimously to transfer the government from Madrid to Valencia. This was an impetuous move, stealthily carried out, and no public explanation whatsoever was given. To the public, it looked as if the government was fleeing and the people were being left to their fate. Just before the transfer, Largo Caballero ordered the setting up of a Junta de Defensa under General José Miaja, which was to run things in a Madrid that was under siege from that day until 22 April 1937.

And before leaving Madrid, Largo Caballero also appointed Vicente Rojo, who had been promoted to lieutenant colonel a month earlier, as General Miaja's chief of staff. It looked as if the rebel army would take Madrid in a matter of days but, despite the confusion and disorder that reigned at that time in Madrid, apparent also in the *sacas* and killing of prisoners, Franco's army failed in its objective. Rojo and Miaja, with the help of various officers who had remained loyal to the Republic, such as Lieutenant Colonel Arnoldo Fernández Urbano and Major Manuel Matallana, organised the defence with all the forces at their disposal, which included, for the first time in the war, the International Brigades. Arriving just in time was the Soviet military aid, by then paid for by the shipment of the gold reserves. The whole city, stirred up by the constant

---

[4] The subject of this 'momentous' incorporation of anarchists into the government is analysed in detail in Julián Casanova, *Anarchism, the Republic and Civil War in Spain*, pp. 116–22.

air raids and bombardments from the rebel army, helped to stem the advance of the attackers. Many saw it as a decisive battle between international fascism on one side, and communism and democracy on the other. 'Madrid, the heart of Spain', wrote the poet, Rafael Alberti.

Women and children lay dead among the rubble, as may be seen from the wealth of documentary evidence testifying to those 'heroic feats'. Among the combatants who died was the anarchist leader Buenaventura Durruti, on 20 November, who had arrived with his column a few days previously. To die in a defenceless Madrid that his old comrades had abandoned: that was the final proof of his strength as against the weakness of those who had become involved in the game of politics. The hero was buried in Barcelona, two days later, in the biggest demonstration that the city had known during those tumultuous years of the Republic and war.

The Communist Party, with a decisive presence in the Junta de Defensa, grew markedly from then on. It had been a minor party in the elections of February 1936, although before the war it had managed to unite young socialists and communists to form the Juventudes Socialistas Unificadas (JSU), and soon after the defeat of the rising in Barcelona, various Catalan socialist and communist groups had set up the Partit Socialista Unificat de Catalunya (PSUC), an organisation that was quickly to come into open conflict with POUM and the anarchists for political control in the rear. However, its growth and reputation were linked to the presence of the International Brigades, Soviet aid and the order and discipline that its leaders managed to impose on the running of the war.

Between September 1936 and May 1937, Largo Caballero, with the collaboration of all the political and trade union forces fighting on the republican side, oversaw the reconstruction of the state, the militarisation of the militias, the contention of the anarchist revolution and the centralisation of power, all the while having to deal with challenges from the regions and nationalism, as Negrín would have to later. In Catalonia, the government of the Generalitat which had incorporated all the region's political forces on 26 September, thereby putting an end to the Central Committee of Anti-Fascist Militias, set up its own army, had full political and economic autonomy and, up to May 1936, exercised absolute control of the police and public order. In the Basque Country, after the Cortes had passed its Statute on 1 October 1936, José Antonio Aguirre's nationalist coalition government organised, during the eight months it lasted, until the fall of Bilbao on 19 June 1937, an almost autonomous state.

However, militarisation, control of the rear and the reconstruction of republican power were tackled amid heated debate between some of the political sectors that made up Largo Caballero's coalition government. Confrontation broke out in Barcelona, a city isolated from the front, a symbol of anarcho-syndicalist revolution, at the beginning of May 1937, with fighting that left dozens of dead and injured in the streets. It was the culmination of a struggle in which the Communists and Indalecio Prieto's socialists were firmly committed to getting rid of Largo Caballero's government and the trade union organisations, which they saw as being the main obstacles to joining forces in the political, socio-economic and military fields.

The government was in crisis. According to the republicans, communists and Prieto's socialists, Largo Caballero was not the right man to impose unity in the republican agricultural sector or order in the rear, or to win the war. The veteran trade union leader, whom everyone had backed a few months earlier, before Málaga fell to the Nationalist troops in February 1937 and the violent confrontations in Barcelona in May, now found himself ostracised, isolated and unable to count on the support of even his own trade union.

Azaña decided to ask Juan Negrín to form a new government. As well as prime minister, Negrín would continue as minister of finance, a post he had occupied under Largo Caballero since 4 September 1936. The eighteen ministries in Largo Caballero's government were reduced by half. It was a Frente Popular government, without the trade union organisations, which had been received, according to Azaña, 'with great satisfaction'.[5]

Negrín was to be the Republic's man until the end of the war. And he was nominated not by the Communists, as many have repeatedly claimed, in an attempt to show that Negrín, who sent the gold to Moscow, had sold out to communism and the International. He was nominated by Azaña who, as president of the Republic, was the person who had the power to do so, and he did it because Negrín, besides his 'unruffled energy', possessed other qualities. 'His effectiveness in the Finance Ministry of a country at war was no mean feat', writes Ricardo Miralles. Unlike Indalecio Prieto, he had no history of confrontations with the Communists and the CNT. But, according to Santos Juliá, the 'decisive reason' that Azaña chose Negrín was one of international politics. Almost from the beginning, Azaña believed that the Republic could not win the war and that the only possible exit strategy was international mediation. Negrín, not Largo Caballero, was the ideal man for brokering peace with outside help. He was an educated politician, who spoke several languages and had nothing of the revolutionary about him.

Such was the man chosen by Azaña: physiologist, socialist, polyglot and an acknowledged expert in financial affairs. Some months previously

---

[5] Manuel Azaña, 'El cuaderno de la Pobleta', annotation of 20 May, in *Memorias políticas y de guerra*, vol. II, p. 56.

he had organised the shipment of three-quarters of the Bank of Spain's gold reserves to the Soviet Union, and had reorganised the Cuerpo de Carabineros, the police force that looked after the frontier posts and was responsible for collecting customs duties. He was not nearly so well known as Prieto or other socialists, but Azaña had every confidence in this 'still young', 'intelligent', 'educated' man who seemed energetic, determined and courageous. 'Some people will think that the real prime minister will be Prieto. They are wrong . . . that is not in Negrín's nature.'[6]

And what Azaña expected of the new executive was 'a will to govern' and that it would put an end to the indiscipline and 'disarray' away from the front. The Republic's authority needed to be re-established in Catalonia, particularly with regard to public order. That prompted Negrín's first move. His government took over the enforcement of public order that up to then had been the Generalitat's responsibility, and on 11 August it dissolved the Council of Aragón, the governing body controlled by the anarchists and presided over by Ascaso, and appointed the republican, José Ignacio Mantecón, governor general of the territory. Several hundred CNT members, including Joaquín Ascaso, were imprisoned. The municipal councils controlled by libertarians were suppressed and replaced by 'executive committees' appointed 'by government order'. The new local power bodies, with the help of the security forces and the XI Army Division under the command of Enrique Lister destroyed the collective farms, confiscated all their assets and returned the land to its owners.

The other matter pending since May 1937, what to do with POUM, was resolved more swiftly and effectively. The Partido Comunista called for the immediate dissolution of POUM, 'Trotskyite *provocateurs*', 'an unconditional ally of the dissident *Junta* in Burgos'. There was no argument more categorical than to call someone a 'fascist' at precisely the time when an 'anti-fascist war' was being waged. What the Spanish Communists wanted, urged on by the Russian consul general in Barcelona, Vladimir Antonov-Ovsenko, was the destruction of this party of 'Trotskyite agents' and 'fascist spies' who were moreover openly criticising the execution of former Bolsheviks carried out by Stalin in the Moscow trials.

Some of POUM's militants were hunted down and tortured. On 16 June 1937, at the same time as POUM was being declared illegal, Andreu Nin, its political secretary, was arrested in Barcelona by the police, who transferred him to Madrid and thence to the prison at Alcalá de Henares. In spite of being guarded by members of the Special Brigade of the Directorate

[6] *Ibid.*, pp. 56–7.

General of Security, he was kidnapped on 21 June and murdered – no one knows when – by agents of the Soviet secret service in Spain, under the command of General Alexander Orlov. His body never appeared. Graffiti painted by his supporters with the question 'Where is Nin?' was answered by others with: 'In Burgos or Berlin'.

The scandal forced Negrín's government to do some juggling. Firstly, Julián Zugazagoitia, the interior minister, accused Soviet 'technicians' of the kidnap and the murder, and the Communist Colonel Antonio Ortega, director general of security, was dismissed, accused of connivance with the Soviet agents, in spite of the fact that the PCE ministers defended their comrade 'with extraordinary passion'. But Negrín never provided a convincing explanation of the affair in response to requests from Azaña, and investigations were called off after Ortega was replaced by the socialist Gabriel Morón on 14 July. Prieto said that it was Negrín who did not want the investigations to continue, possibly because it would have brought about a major government crisis, little more than a month after its formation, and because, as Gabriel Jackson states, he could not risk losing the delivery of Soviet arms over an internal affair that deep down he felt to be a minor matter.[7]

But minor it was not, because as well as Nin, other, mostly foreign, Trotskyites were kidnapped and went missing, including the journalists Kurt Landau and Mark Rein, as well as José Robles Pazos, a friend of the novelist John Dos Passos. The Nin affair caused friction between Negrín and Zugazagoitia and Irujo, the two ministers who were most anxious to clear up the matter, and it further deepened the distrust between the Communists and the rest of the political organisations fighting on the republican side, particularly the socialist left and the libertarian movement. The political violence in Catalonia and Aragón, which ended with the murders of various anarchists, Communists and POUM militants, plus the hundreds of deaths in the street violence in Barcelona in May 1937, were the clearest evidence yet that the Republic had a serious problem with its internal discord, a true stumbling block in any attempt to win the war.

Negrín wanted to win by fighting, with discipline in the rear and in the army, and organising a solid war industry, although the primary aim of his strategy was to bring about a radical change in the non-intervention policy, thereby obtaining the support of the western democratic powers.

---

[7] Information about Nin's disappearance and the subsequent information can be found in Gabriel Jackson, *Juan Negrín: médico, socialista y jefe del gobierno de la II República española* (Barcelona: Crítica, 2008), pp. 117–137; and Ricardo Miralles, *Juan Negrín: la República en guerra* (Madrid: Temas de Hoy, 2003), pp. 144–6.

The war would be long and it could be won. So thought Negrín when he took office, and in the two years of his premiership he experienced moments of optimism, but others that were disastrous, moments that seemed to herald the final defeat.

But the survival of the Republic depended not only on a good army and the resistance of the civilian population, but also on the abandonment of the non-intervention policy, something that was not to be despite the diplomatic efforts that Negrín dedicated to this vital end. If France and the United Kingdom were not going to change their minds, it was suggested that at least they could put pressure on the fascist powers to convince Franco to offer a negotiated settlement, an armistice that would prevent the 'reign of terror and bloody vengeance' that Negrín knew Franco would impose.

There was still hope in the summer of 1938, with the beginning of the Battle of the Ebro and the granting of a loan of $60 million from the Soviet Union, now that the gold reserves were about to run out. These hopes were frustrated, firstly on the international front, by the Munich Agreement at the end of September, whereby Britain and France handed Czechoslovakia over to Hitler; and secondly on the domestic front by the outcome of the Battle of the Ebro on 16 November, which ended with the Republic's army returning to the positions it had held on 24 July at the start of the battle, but with tens of thousands of casualties and a considerable loss of war materiel which it could no longer use to defend Catalonia against the decisive Nationalist offensive. With the signing of the Munich Agreement, which saw the end of Czechoslovakia, the only democracy left standing in central and eastern Europe, the western democracies also wiped out the Spanish Republic, wrote Helen Graham, because they showed their unshakeable commitment to appeasing the fascist powers and undermined Negrin's strategy of resistance and that of the Spaniards who believed in him.[8]

And it was when the Republic was risking everything, putting up a military resistance until a war broke out in Europe or, at worst, continuing the struggle in order to maintain a position of strength and negotiate a surrender without reprisals, that internal discord reappeared, one of the curses that plagued the Republic throughout the war. Many republican and socialist leaders became demoralised and began to criticise Negrín's resistance strategy and his dependence on the Soviet Union and the PCE. Food shortages also wore down resistance, but the end of the Republic was speeded up by the coup mounted by Colonel Segismundo Casado, head of the Army of the Centre, whose principal aim was to overthrow

[8] Helen Graham, *The Spanish Republic at War 1936–1939* (Cambridge University Press, 2002), p. 383.

Negrín's government and negotiate a surrender with Franco. He obtained support from various officers and politicians, including Cipriano Mera, an anarchist who was always in favour of insurrection, and now commander of the 4th Army Corps, and Julián Besteiro, who had already held conversations with agents of Franco and the underground Falange in Madrid. On 5 March, the rebels formed the National Defence Council. It was a military rebellion against the legitimate government, still in power, and as Azaña, surprised that Besteiro was involved, said, 'it repeated Franco's *coup d'état* and, what was worse, with the same pretext: the excessive preponderance or intolerable dominance of the Communists'.[9]

Fighting was intense in Madrid for a few days, until 10 March, leaving around 2,000 dead. It was not hard for the rebels to squash any Communist resistance, amid their fatigue and general malaise. They trusted Franco's promise of clemency, a promise that Negrín and many others knew he would not keep. The war waged by the July 1936 military rebels, with Franco at their head, was a war of extermination, and that meant destroying the roots of the enemy so that it would take decades for them to lift their heads again.

Rebel Spain

In the Nationalist zone, the construction of a new state was accompanied by the physical elimination of the opposition, the destruction of all the symbols and policies of the Republic, and the quest for an emphatic, unconditional victory with no possibility of any mediation. In this endeavour, Franco had the support and blessing of the Catholic Church. Bishops, priests and the rest of the Church began to look on Franco as someone sent by God to impose order in the 'earthly city', and Franco ended up believing that, indeed, he had a special relationship with divine providence.[10]

Francisco Franco was born in El Ferrol on 4 December 1892, and was 43 years old at the time of the rising against the Republic. Almost all his military service had been in Africa, and this provided him with rapid promotions for his exploits in battle, and a good number of decorations and distinctions. He entered the Military Academy in Toledo in 1907 and despite passing out 251st of the 312 officers in his year, by 1915 he was a captain; and in February 1926, at the age of 33, he had risen to brigadier. Between 1920 and 1925 he served in the Spanish Foreign Legion, or Tercio de Extranjeros, created in 1920 by José Millán Astray,

[9] Quoted in Cipriano Rivas Cheriff, *Retrato de un desconocido: vida de Manuel Azaña* (Barcelona: Grijalbo, 1979), p. 437.
[10] Julián Casanova, *La Iglesia de Franco*, pp. 87–9.

with Franco joining as second-in-command. He was appointed director of the Zaragoza Military Academy on 4 January 1928, where he served until it was closed down by the Second Republic, and then during the years of the Republic he was military commander of La Coruña in 1932, general commander of the Balearic Islands in 1933 and 1934, supreme commander of the Spanish forces in Morocco at the beginning of 1935, chief of the General Staff from 17 May 1935 until February 1936, and general commander of the Canary Islands from March until 18 July that year. He was promoted to major general at the end of March 1934, on the recommendation of the then minister of war, the radical Diego Hidalgo.

Franco was considered by his fellow officers to be a well-trained and competent commander, but his path to the highest command was smoothed by the disappearance from the scene of some of his more qualified rivals for the position. General José Sanjurjo, who had to fly from Portugal to Spain to head the rising, died on 20 July when his small aircraft, piloted by the Falangist Juan Antonio Ansaldo, crashed near Lisbon. Generals Joaquín Fanjul and Manuel Goded had failed in their attempt to take Madrid and Barcelona, and they were arrested and shot a few days later. José Calvo Sotelo, the far-right monarchist leader, who maintained close contact with the plotters, had been murdered on 13 July, and José Antonio Primo de Rivera, the head of the Falange, was in prison in Alicante, another city in which the uprising had failed.

Gonzalo Queipo de Llano, who led the rising in Seville, was, like Franco, a major general, although he had held this rank longer. The problem was that he had been a republican and plotted against monarchist governments, and thus not all the rebel officers considered him a reliable leader. That left Emilio Mola, who had prepared the plot and the rebellion as its director, although he was a lieutenant general, a lower rank than Franco. Potentially, however, he was a rival. His was the idea to set up the Junta de Defensa Nacional de Burgos, the first body to co-ordinate the military tactics of the rebels, and he had, with considerable help from the *Requeté*, been winning control of a large part of the northern zone of Spain, including almost the entire province of Guipúzcoa, since the beginning of September.

Franco played his cards with skill and ambition. He presented himself to the media and diplomats as the principal general of the rebels, and this is what he also told the Germans and Italians, so that a few days after the *coup d'état*, some European foreign ministries were already referring to the rebels as 'Francoists'. He also commanded the best-trained troops of the Spanish army, the 47,000 soldiers of the Foreign Legion and the *Regulares Indígenas*, which he managed to transfer to the peninsula thanks to the transport planes and bombers sent by Hitler and Mussolini. This, say the experts, was the decisive factor in placing Franco as the best candidate in the struggle for power: the control of the Army of Africa and his swift transfer of these troops to the peninsula, thereby ensuring that any aid from the fascist powers would pass through his hands alone.[11]

The first task was to create a single military command and a centralised political apparatus. The Third Reich authorities who were negotiating the loan of war materiel with Franco had been pressing him since the end of August to take up the reins. Meanwhile, certain generals fiercely loyal to Franco, including Alfredo Kindelán, Orgaz and Millán Astray, as well as his own brother Nicolás, formed, as Preston put it, 'a kind of political campaign staff committed to ensuring that Franco became first Commander-in-Chief and then Chief of State'.[12] Kindelán, the former head of aviation under the monarchy, who had asked to be released from the army with the advent of the Republic, suggested that a meeting be held of the Junta de Defensa Nacional and other generals to choose a supreme chief.

On 1 October Francisco Franco was named 'Head of the Government of the Spanish State', in the words of the decree drawn up by the monarchist, José Yanguas Messía, a professor of international law. In the investiture ceremony, General Miguel Cabanellas, in the presence of diplomats from Italy, Germany and Portugal, handed over power on behalf of the Junta de Defensa, over which he had presided since 24 July, and which was dissolved to be replaced by a Junta Técnica del Estado headed by General Fidel Dávila. Franco adopted the title of Caudillo, in an allusion to the medieval warrior lords.

By the end of 1936, all the political forces that backed the military uprising, once they had accepted the supreme command of Franco, were in favour of some kind of unification, although the problem lay in figuring out which force would predominate. The various political factions were concerned that it would be the Falange, which had experienced spectacular growth in the early months of the Civil War, when a good many of its leaders – some of them released from gaol by the military rising – channelled their energies into recruiting new members who were flooding into the fascist camp. It had been a small organisation before the elections of February 1936, although the defeat of the CEDA and the fascistisation of the right in subsequent months had swelled its membership by the eve of the *coup d'état*. Its radical thinking and paramilitary structure, as well as the loss of credibility of organisations such as the CEDA that had decided to accept the legitimacy of the Republic, made it a pole of attraction when arms replaced politics. By October 1936 there

[11] Preston, *Franco*, pp. 158–63.   [12] *Ibid.*, p. 177.

were in excess of 36,000 Falangists on the fronts, together with over 22,000 Carlists and more than 6,000 members of other tendencies, such as the Alfonsines or the CEDA.

Although it now had thousands of members, it still lacked the solid direction of undisputed or charismatic leaders. José Antonio Primo de Rivera, the national leader, was in prison in Alicante with his brother Miguel. Onésimo Redondo had died on 24 July in Labajos, Segovia, in a gun battle with republican militias. Julio Ruiz de Alda and Fernando Primo de Rivera, José Antonio's younger brother, were murdered in August in the Modelo prison in Madrid. Two months later, after a *saca* from the Las Ventas prison, it was the turn of Ramiro Ledesma Ramos. Also in prison were Raimundo Fernández-Cuesta, who was exchanged in October 1937, and Rafael Sánchez Mazas, who managed to escape a mass firing squad a little before the end of the war. As one of the backroom Falangist leaders, José Luna, the provincial head in Cáceres and an infantry captain, said: the Falange had gone from having 'a tiny body with a big head to a monstrous body with no head at all'.[13]

Franco was thinking of a party which would help him to gain even more power for himself. He was also being pressured in this direction by the Italian fascists. In February 1937, an envoy sent by Mussolini, Roberto Farinacci – who had used the highly radical and violent influence of the *Squadristi* to get himself appointed secretary of the Fascist party – urged Franco to create, 'with the political forces that have contributed combatants', a Spanish National Party with a genuine fascist and corporatist programme.[14]

Around the same time, Ramón Serrano Súñer arrived in Salamanca after managing to escape from republican Madrid with the help of Dr Gregorio Marañón. Serrano Súñer had been a CEDA deputy in 1933 and 1936 for Zaragoza, the city where he practised law. He was married to Carmen Polo's younger sister, Ramona or 'Zita' Polo, and had been a close friend of José Antonio since his time as a student at the Universidad Central in Madrid. He arrived in Salamanca with his wife and children, traumatised by his captivity and by having seen his brothers José and Fernando killed for organising his escape. According to Joan Maria Thomàs, Serrano Súñer, an expert in administrative law, was the ideal person 'to lay the legal foundations of the New State', a task for which neither Nicolás Franco nor the rest of the Generalísimo's collaborators

---

[13] Quoted in Javier Tusell, *Franco en la guerra civil: una biografía política* (Barcelona: Tusquets, 1992), pp. 91–2.
[14] *Ibid.*, p. 112.

were suited. 'It was Serrano Súñer who was finally to give specific shape to Franco's ideas for setting up a single-party regime.'[15]

Serrano Súñer explained to Franco that what he was running was a 'camp state', which was largely ineffective, with a barrack-room mentality, and which needed to be replaced by a permanent political mechanism, a new state similar to those run by fascist regimes. Serrano Súñer's plan consisted of creating a mass political movement based on the union of the Falange and the Traditionalist Carlist Communion, a venture in which Franco's brother, Nicolás, his right-hand man until Serrano Súñer's arrival, had had no success.

Franco first called Rodezno and other Navarran traditionalist leaders to tell them his decision: there would be no negotiations between the two groups, as this would smack of democratic party politics, and that he would be the one to decree unification. He was more worried about the Falange, because it was a bigger party, with totalitarian aims, but since the death of José Antonio its leaders had been locked in a power struggle: on the one hand there was Hedilla, closely supported by two fellow Cantabrians, the journalist Víctor de la Serna, son of the novelist Concha Espina, and Maximiano García Venero; and on the other, the militia chiefs Agustín Aznar and Sancho Dávila.

This power struggle developed into a bloody brawl between the two rival groups, a situation that was exploited by Serrano Súñer to silence any focus of resistance to unification. On 19 April 1937 the unification decree was issued, with a long preamble and three points, drawn up by Serrano Súñer. Falange Española and the *Requeté* would combine under the leadership of Franco in a 'single national political unit', Falange Española Tradicionalista y de las JONS, 'a link between the state and society', in which the 'Catholic spirituality' of the *Requeté*, 'the traditional force', would be integrated into 'the new force', as had happened 'in other countries with a totalitarian regime'. All the other groups that had supported the rebel war effort, including the Alfonsines and the CEDA, were excluded.[16]

In practice, this meant that the hierarchical structures of the Falangists and *Requeté* would disappear because, from that moment, the supreme chief was Franco. Hedilla would be reduced to a mere member of the Political Council, and not only did he not accept this, pressurised as he was by the 'old guard' and the *legitimistas* close to Pilar Primo de Rivera, José Antonio's sister, who accused him of 'betraying' José Antonio's Falange, but he also told his provincial bosses to obey his orders alone.

---

[15] Joan Maria Thomàs, *Lo que fue la Falange* (Barcelona: Plaza & Janés, 1999), p. 145.

[16] The process of unification is efficiently described *ibid.*, pp. 146–221, and in Tusell, *Franco en la guerra civil*, pp. 79–137.

On 25 April, Hedilla was arrested along with other dissident Falangists. Apparently, no less a personage than the German ambassador, von Faupel, had advised him to accept the post and even offered him an aircraft to take him to Germany.

Two months later, Hedilla appeared before two summary courts martial. The prosecution had been prepared by the military legal adviser in Franco's headquarters, Lorenzo Martínez Fuste, and by the Civil Guard major Lisardo Doval, the public order delegate for Salamanca and chief of the headquarters' police service, a crony of Franco's who had made a name for himself for his brutality in putting down the revolution in Asturias in October 1934. Hedilla was accused of 'supporting rebellion' and refusal to comply with the unification decree, and he was sentenced to death. In a letter that his mother delivered to Franco, Hedilla asked for 'mercy and magnanimity'. Pilar Primo de Rivera and Serrano Súñer also intervened for a reprieve, while von Faupel advised that 'in the current climate it is very dangerous to create martyrs'. Franco reprieved him, but he spent four years in gaol and, says Javier Tusell, 'Hedilla was to live the rest of his life in a situation of official ostracism, thinking about an independent Falange that would always remain an impossibility.'[17]

In view of the hold that Franco had on the situation, there was little chance of resistance, however angry the Carlists or the hardline sector of the Falange grouped around the founder's sister were about the way unification had come about. From the outset it was a party dominated by Franco, thus leaving him without any political rivals. Antonio Goicoechea dissolved Renovación Española, and Gil Robles, who enthusiastically accepted unification and gave instructions for Acción Popular to comply with the decree, saw no improvement in his situation. The Falangists never forgave Gil Robles for his spell in the government of the Republic and Franco had no intention of incorporating a representative of the old regime, especially as he had been his superior as minister of war.

And if anyone still had any doubts as to Franco's position, barely a month and a half after unification the only rival with any chance left was also eliminated. On 3 June 1937, the aircraft taking General Emilio Mola to inspect the front, at the height of the campaign to control the north, crashed near Alcocero, a small village in the province of Burgos. According to the official version, the plane crashed into a hill because of the fog, although there were rumours of sabotage and also that the aircraft, an Airspeed AS.6 Envoy manufactured in Britain, was shot down by friendly aircraft by mistake. The German ambassador, von Faupel, wrote shortly

[17] Tusell, *Franco en la guerra civil*, pp. 130–1, 301.

afterwards: 'There is no doubt that Franco feels relieved at General Mola's death.'[18]

Although Franco was the undisputed head of the Falange, and the unification attempted to satisfy the various groups in the rebel camp, the Falange, according to Javier Tusell, came out of it well at the beginning, and its leaders held the most important posts in the administration and the party. Proof may be found in the appointment of the fifty members of the National Council of FET y de las JONS in October 1937. Half of them were Falangists, while the traditionalists accounted for a quarter of the total, five were monarchists and there were also eight officers, all of them close to Franco or, as was the case with Queipo de Llano, who were difficult to dispense with at the time. The four councillors at the top of the list were Pilar Primo de Rivera, the Count of Rodezno, General Queipo de Llano and José María Pemán. At the beginning of December Franco appointed the first secretary of the FET y de las JONS, a post which was given to Raimundo Fernández Cuesta, the most prominent of the old guard remaining, who had just arrived in the rebel zone after being exchanged for the republican Justino de Azcárate.

The principal national delegations of the new party also went to ex-Falangists from the time of José Antonio: the Sección Femenina to Pilar Primo de Rivera; Press and Propaganda to the Navarran priest Fermín Yzurdiaga; and Auxilio Social, the former Auxilio de Invierno, to Mercedes Sanz Bachiller. And other leaders who had been imprisoned for the events of April 1937, such as Agustín Aznar and Sancho Dávila, were rehabilitated and promoted to important posts. No former leading figure of the Falange, with the exception of the odd Hedilla supporter, was left without a share of the cake. These figures included Dionisio Ridruejo, Alfonso García Valdecasas, José Antonio Giménez Arnau, Pedro Gamero del Castillo, Antonio Tovar and Julián Pemartín.

It took somewhat longer for this pet project of Serrano Súñer's, the creation of the new state, to take shape, although major progress was already being made during the war. The 'field state' gradually gave way to a bureaucracy that was more organised. In the summer of 1937, the monarchist general, Francisco Gómez Jordana, took over the presidency of the Junta Técnica del Estado, replacing another general, Fidel Dávila, who had been fairly ineffective during the months he had presided over this body, and whom the Falangists referred to as 'Don Fávila', after the ineffectual son of Don Pelayo, king of Asturias in the eighth century. Gómez Jordana, Count of Jordana, deplored the chaos and 'shambles'

---

[18] Quoted in Preston, *Franco*, p. 279.

that had been left and, together with Serrano Súñer, he tried to restore order to the administrative apparatus. They both believed that what rebel Spain needed was a proper government, not a *Junta Técnica*. And this is what they told Franco.

On 30 November 1938 Franco named his first government, based on suggestions from Serrano Súñer, if we are to believe what he himself claimed in his memoirs. As with all subsequent Francoist governments, the posts were carefully shared out between officers, Carlists, Falangists and monarchists – in other words, between all the sectors that joined forces to rise against the Republic in July 1936. Each sector controlled the area that it felt affinity to: the military and public order ministries for the officers; the trade union and 'social' ministries for the Falangists; the financial ministries for technocrats, lawyers and engineers; and education and justice for Catholics, traditionalists or ex-members of Acción Española. Not once in thirty-seven years of Francoist governments did a woman occupy a ministry. And what the Caudillo always required, above any other merit, was loyalty to the 'command'.

The principal political outcome of this new phase was the passing on 9 March 1938 of the *Fuero del Trabajo* (Labour Rights), a kind of mock constitution based on the *Carta del lavoro* in fascist Italy. The text represented a compromise between Falangism, represented by Dionisio Ridruejo, and Catholic traditionalism (the drafting of this part clearly being the work of Eduardo Aunós, of Acción Española); it struck a middle line between 'liberal capitalism and Marxist materialism', guaranteeing Spaniards 'the Fatherland, bread and justice in a military and devoutly religious style'.[19]

Fascism and Catholicism: these were the two cornerstones of the New State that emerged as the war progressed. On the one hand, the Caudillo was exalted like the Führer or Il Duce, with the straight-arm salute and blue shirts; on the other, rituals and religious displays made their appearance with processions, open-air masses and political-religious ceremonies in the medieval style. Rebel Spain became a territory particularly suitable for the 'harmonisation' of fascism, of the 'modern authoritarian current', with 'glorious tradition'.[20]

The radicalisation that fascism brought to counter-revolutionary projects and practices – its totalitarian potential, its ideological purity and exclusivity and the experience of the war of attrition that had been waged by the military rebels since July 1936 – was melded with the restoration

---

[19] Published in the *Official State Gazette* of 10 March 1938 and included in the publication of FET y de las JONS, *Doctrina e Historia de la Revolución Nacional Española* (1939).

[20] Julián Casanova, *La Iglesia de Franco*, pp. 332–5.

of this historical parallel between Catholicism and the Spanish national identity. Catholicism was the ideal antidote to the secular Republic, separatism and revolutionary ideologies. It became the perfect hook for all those who joined the rebel camp, from the most hardline fascists to those who had proclaimed themselves to be rightist republicans. And so, this civil war caused by a *coup d'état* became a religious crusade to save Christian civilisation, the protective cloak for the annihilation of the 'wicked Marxists' and the 'red rabble'.

Battlefields

In the three months following the July 1936 uprising, the war was a struggle between armed militias, which lacked the basic elements of a conventional army, and a military power that concentrated all its resources in authority, discipline, and the declaration of martial law, and almost from the start was able to employ the services of the well-trained troops of the Africa Army.

The Battle of Madrid, in November of that year, saw the arrival of a new form of waging war and transformed this group of militiamen into soldiers in a new army. After the failure of various attempts to take Madrid, between November 1936 and March 1937, Franco changed his strategy and chose to unleash a war of attrition, the gradual occupation of territory and total destruction of the republican army. His materiel and offensive superiority led him to his final victory two years later.

'Wars are lost in the rear', wrote General Vicente Rojo.[21] And this is what was happening to the Republic, where hunger created major conflicts as the war went on, and one defeat after another ended up by demoralising large sectors of the population that abandoned their commitment to the values and material interests they were fighting for. The air raids by the Italians and Germans on Madrid, Valencia and Barcelona also helped Franco to win the war. The outcome of the horrors of this war leaves no room for doubt: before its defeat, the Republic had been slowly battered, with battles that left its troops butchered and brutal repression after Franco's army entered any city it captured.

By the middle of October 1936, the rebel troops, now well equipped with Italian artillery pieces and armoured vehicles, had occupied most of the towns and villages around Madrid. The militiamen, cowed by the advance of the Africa Army, withdrew to the capital, and they were joined there by hundreds of refugees fleeing from the occupied localities. On

---

[21] Quoted in José Andrés Rojo, *Vicente Rojo: retrato de un general republicano* (Barcelona: Tusquets, 2006), p. 270.

29 October the first Soviet tanks and aircraft, sent by the Kremlin to counteract Italian and German aid, arrived in Madrid.

General José Enrique Varela, an *Africanista* and Carlist sympathiser, attacked with 25,000 men via the Casa de Campo and the university campus. General José Miaja, whom Prime Minister Largo Caballero, had left in charge of the Junta de Defensa of Madrid, and Lieutenant Colonel Vicente Rojo, the chief of the General Staff for the defence of Madrid, had 20,000 men at their disposal. Nobody in the government, least of all Largo Caballero and Prieto, was confident that Madrid could resist the attack of the military rebels. On 8 November the militiamen and the Moorish troops were engaged in hand-to-hand combat on the university campus. Two weeks later, Franco and Varela had to call a halt to the attacks.

While the popular hero of the defence of Madrid might have been General José Miaja, who was seen all over the city attempting to raise the people's morale, the technical and military aspects were in the hands of Vicente Rojo, an officer who remained loyal to the Republic because he believed that such was his duty; a few months after his appointment to the Junta de Defensa of Madrid, he became head of its army. He always defined himself as a 'Catholic, officer and patriot', and according to his grandson, José Andrés Rojo, he felt caught between the world of the *Africanista* officers who took part in the coup, with whom he did not identify, and that of the armed militiamen who defended the revolution and burnt churches. Between these two worlds, he took it upon himself to design a new strategy to organise an efficient force to confront the military rebels, and tried to establish the authority of professional officers like himself and the chain of command of this army.[22]

Vicente Rojo was born on 8 October 1894 in a small town in the region of Valencia, Fuente de la Higuera. He was two years younger than Franco and was not yet 42 when the war began. After the chaos caused by the military uprising, Largo Caballero's first government reorganised its General Staff and Rojo became number two there under the immediate orders of Lieutenant Colonel Manuel Estrada. On 25 October 1936, Rojo was promoted to lieutenant colonel 'for his loyalty', a few days before Miaja received the order to appoint him chief of the General Staff for the defence of Madrid. He was made colonel 'for his war service' on 24 March 1937, and in May Juan Negrín appointed him chief of the Central Staff of the Republic, a post he held until the end of the war. On 24 September that same year, he was promoted to general.

---

[22] *Ibid.*, p. 76.

One of the biggest drawbacks in the republican army set up by Largo Caballero's government was the shortage of professional officers. Of the 16,000 officers in the army who were serving before the military uprising, only about 20% stayed in the republican zone, and this, in the words of Gabriel Cardona, 'was totally inadequate for an army whose troop numbers increased five-fold in less than a year'. Very few of its officers had held high command before the war, and this shortcoming 'brought about the rapid promotion of officers who knew nothing about commanding large units'.

Thus, this improvisation of commands posed a serious problem, which intensified as one moved down the ranks, because most of the more junior officers were on the rebel side. Battalion and company commanders had to be appointed precipitately, and the army took in and commissioned the political heads of the militias and columns that were created in the days that followed the military uprising. In Cardona's opinion, 'while the republicans were on the defensive, these shortcomings were not so dramatic as when the major offensives started, in which a clear chain of command was required'.[23]

But it is worth pointing out that, as well as Rojo, there was a group of professional officers, including Juan Hernández Sarabia, Antonio Escobar, Francisco Llano de la Encomienda, José Fontán and Manuel Matallana, who remained loyal to the institutions of the Republic, yet they are now forgotten. In spite of the fact that many of them were the last to flee Spain, ultra-radical writers in exile, both anarchist and socialist, branded them as traitors, Francoists or mere Stalinist puppets. With the bitter taste of defeat, the Communists also joined in the chorus of invective, while they never warranted respect from the victors. On the one hand, there were officers, those who won the war, who are still remembered in the street names of many towns and cities in Spain, and there were others, those who lost, who today are complete unknowns.

At the beginning of 1937 the republican forces numbered almost 350,000 men, a figure very similar to that of Franco's army, although the latter boasted the priceless aid of almost 80,000 Italians in the CTV under the command of General Mario Roatta, and several thousand Germans who since November 1936 had been serving in the Condor Legion, as well as in anti-tank and artillery land units. In fact, it was the Italians who entered Málaga on 8 February 1937. Two days earlier, tens of thousands of people – men, women and children of all ages – had begun to swarm out of the city towards Almería, to escape the reprisals and pillaging of their

[23] Gabriel Cardona, 'Entre la revolución y la disciplina: ensayo sobre la dimensión militar de la guerra civil', in Enrique Moradiellos (ed.), 'La guerra civil', *Ayer*, 50 (2003), pp. 41–51.

subjugators. They were bombarded by aircraft and the warships *Cervera* and *Baleares*, and the road was littered with the dead and wounded, while many families lost their children in the flight.

Franco, meanwhile, had begun to prepare a new offensive against Madrid, via the Jarama valley, along the road from Madrid to Valencia. This operation was supposed to be completed with an attack by the Italian CTV troops from Sigüenza towards Guadalajara to catch Madrid in a pincer movement. Over three weeks in February, from 6 February to the end of the month, both sides lost thousands of men, and although the Francoists managed to advance their front a few kilometres, the battle of the Jarama was fairly unproductive. A few days later, on 8 March, General Amerigo Coppi's motorised division began its attack, but it was surprised by a heavy snowstorm and within a few days it suffered a crushing defeat, among other reasons because Franco failed to carry out his diversionary operation from the Jarama, and the republican troops, aided by the Garibaldi Battalion of the International Brigades and Soviet tanks, were able to concentrate all their efforts on halting the Italian advance.

The succession of failures to capture Madrid brought about a change in Franco's strategy, and from that moment on he opted for a long, drawn-out war of attrition to grind the enemy down. He said as much to Colonel Emilio Faldella, General Roatta's chief of staff, who was trying to convince him of the advantages of a *guerra celere* (lightning war): 'In a civil war, a systematic occupation of territory, accompanied by a necessary clean-up operation, is preferable to a rapid defeat of the enemy armies that will leave the country infested with adversaries.' And he said it again, in more detail, to Mussolini's ambassador, Roberto Cantalupo, on 4 April 1937: 'We must perform a painstaking task of atonement and pacification, or else the military occupation will be largely useless ... Nothing will make me give up this gradual programme. It will give me less glory, but greater internal peace ... I will take the capital not an hour before it is necessary: first I must have the certainty of being able to found a regime.'[24]

Franco held all the trump cards to apply this military strategy. He had plenty of men, made possible by the continuance of the traditional system of recruitment and by the large number of Moroccan volunteers swelling the ranks of the Africa Army. Since September 1936 he had two academies, in Burgos and Seville, to rapidly train university graduates as second lieutenants, and he also set up four establishments to train officers and non-commissioned officers. But above all he had the confidence given by

---

[24] Preston, *Franco*, pp. 222, 242.

the international prospect of German and Italian backing for his cause and that the isolation of the Republic by the western democracies was not going to alter. Thus, he was able to count on a large army and a guaranteed supply of materiel.

The Nationalists now concentrated their attention on the industrial and mining areas of the north, which were cut off from the rest of the republican zone. General Mola wanted to conquer these areas and teach the Basques a lesson: 'I have decided to finish the war quickly in the north . . . If submission is not immediate, I will raze Vizcaya to the ground, beginning with the industries of war.'[25] And the Germans thought that obtaining coal and steel from the north-west would help Hitler's aggressive rearmament programme. Mola began his campaign at the end of March with heavy bombing by the Condor Legion designed to shatter the morale of the civilian population and destroy ground communication networks. First it was Durango, on 31 March; then, Guernica on 26 April. On 19 June, 'the industrious city' of Bilbao was 'reintegrated into civilisation and order', in the words of the war dispatch of the occupiers for that day.

The 'united, great and free Spain' spread later to Santander and in October to the red zone of Asturias. With the fall of the industrial north, the balance of power began to tip clearly in favour of the Nationalists. Colonel Vicente Rojo, recently appointed chief of the General Staff of the Republic, organised a defensive strategy aimed at limiting the Nationalist advance as far as possible, given the material superiority of the enemy and the difficulties involved in consolidating a true republican army. This was the objective of the surprise diversionary offensives launched in Brunete in July 1937, to halt the Nationalist advance on Santander; at Belchite, in August and September, to slow down the conquest of Asturias; and in Teruel, in December 1937, to counteract the expected Nationalist attack on Madrid.

And indeed, now that he had occupied the north, Franco was planning to launch a new attack on Madrid, through Guadalajara, the same route that the Italians had taken unsuccessfully in March 1937. Vicente Rojo decided to launch a preventive attack against Teruel. He deployed some 40,000 men there, with some of the divisions fighting on the Aragón front, the 11th under Lister and the 25th under García Vivancos, as well as the Levante army, commanded by Colonel Juan Hernández Saravia. The attack, initiated by Lister on 15 December 1937, caught the limited Nationalist forces that were defending the city, under the command of Colonel Domingo Rey d'Harcourt, by surprise, and counter-attacks by

---

[25] *Ibid.*, p. 239.

Generals Varela and Antonio Aranda were hampered by extremely harsh weather conditions.

On 7 January 1938, the republican troops broke through Rey d'Harcourt's defence, and he signed the surrender document which he ended by requesting 'that the lives of civilian personnel be spared'. Teruel became the only provincial capital to be taken by the republicans throughout the war, although it was recaptured on 22 February by troops under the direction of General Juan Vigón, who deployed 100,000 men, including the Italian CTV. Thus ended one of the cruellest battles of the Civil War, with 40,000 Nationalist and more than 60,000 republican casualties. The two armies had the same number of troops mobilised at that time, almost 800,000 each, but the materiel superiority of the Nationalists was overwhelming. In just a few weeks, Teruel went from being the republicans' biggest victory, blown out of all proportion in their propaganda, to what Antony Beevor calls 'the biggest republican disaster in the whole war', because 'the Republic had set out to seize a city of no strategic value, which it could never have hoped to hold, all at a catastrophic cost in lives and equipment'.[26]

The truth was that the state of the republican troops following the Teruel disaster was worrying, and this was borne out just a few days later in the full-scale push begun by the Nationalists through Aragón and Castellón to the coast. On 9 March, some 150,000 men, backed up by hundreds of artillery pieces and aircraft of the Condor Legion and the Aviazione Legionaria, began their advance through Aragón. On 10 March, they recaptured Belchite, which they had lost the previous summer; on 14 March, Alcañiz, after several tonnes of bombs had been dropped on the town a few days previously; and on 17 March, the Morocco Corps and the 1st Division entered Caspe, which had been the headquarters of the Council of Aragón and was now that of the republican authority that replaced it, Governor-General José Ignacio Mantecón. There then followed two simultaneous actions: one, to the south of the Ebro, with the capture of Gandesa, in the province of Tarragona, on 1 April; and the other, to the north of the river, which saw Yagüe take Fraga on 27 March and Lérida on 3 April. The campaign ended on 15 April on the Mediterranean coast. 'The victorious sword of Franco', said the Seville daily, *ABC*, the following day, 'has split the Spain still held by the reds into two.'

Split into two, beset by a serious economic crisis and with its morale shattered, the Republic was in torment. Indalecio Prieto, who made no secret of his defeatism, left ('was driven out of' as he put it) the government

---

[26] Antony Beevor, *The Battle for Spain: The Spanish Civil War 1936–1939* (London: Phoenix, 2007; published in Spanish as *La guerra civil española* (Barcelona: Crítica, 2005)), p. 329.

of the Republic, which he had served both in peace and in war. On 29 March 1938, Prieto presented the cabinet with a devastating report on the situation. On the night of 29 to 30 March, Negrín decided to remove his intimate friend and collaborator from his post as minister of defence because, as he wrote to him later while in exile, 'you, with your suggestive eloquence, your habitual pathos and the authority of your office completely demoralised our government colleagues'. Prieto, on the other hand, always believed that Negrín had got rid of him in response 'to demands from the Communist Party'. In the government formed on 6 April 1938, without Indalecio Prieto, Negrín took on the national defence portfolio.[27]

Outside Spain, things were no better: on 20 February, Anthony Eden, the only minister in Neville Chamberlain's government who had not openly expressed any antagonism towards the Republic, resigned as foreign secretary. On 16 April his successor in the Foreign Office, Lord Halifax, signed an agreement with Italy in which once again the British turned a blind eye to the fascist intervention on Franco's side. In France, after a short-lived government led by the socialist, Léon Blum, which lasted only thirty days, the radical Édouard Daladier took over that same month, and in June he once again closed the border with Spain. Such was the harsh situation that the Republic found itself in, and the government began to reconstruct the Army of the East with all the units that had withdrawn to Catalonia. It had to defend itself, resist, and at least prevent a swift collapse that would almost certainly be accompanied by the likely unconditional victory of Franco, while all the time waiting for the international headwinds to change direction.

But Franco insisted on the idea of a long drawn-out war of attrition, in which he would conclusively crush the Republic. 'He had a vast army and could afford to be careless of his men's lives', writes Preston. Instead of launching a swift attack against Barcelona, as it appears his colleagues had asked him to do in view of the victorious Aragón campaign, Franco ordered Generals José Varela, Antonio Aranda and Rafael García Valiño to advance from Teruel to Castellón, which they took on 13 June.[28] The offensive against Valencia – the main objective of this campaign that was initiated a few days later – came up against an effective defensive response from the republicans. However, the Nationalist troops remained less than 50 kilometres from what had been the capital of the Republic for a year. Franco said that he would enter Valencia on 25 July, the feast day of Saint James the Apostle. And it was on that night, 24 to 25 July, that various units of the republican army, under the command of the Communist Juan

[27] Miralles, *Juan Negrín*, pp. 196–200.   [28] Preston, *Franco*, pp. 304–16.

Modesto, crossed the Ebro in rowing boats, following the plan outlined by General Rojo to relink the Levante with Catalonia. Thus began the Battle of the Ebro, the longest and harshest of the whole war.

Almost all the commanders in this ad hoc army of the Ebro were Communists. The commander-in-chief was Lieutenant Colonel Juan Modesto, and on his staff were Enrique Lister, who commanded the 5th Army Corps, and Lieutenant Colonel Manuel Tagüeña, a physics and mathematics student who had begun the war in the ranks and ended up commanding the 15th Army Corps. General Rojo told them, according to Tagüeña in *Testimonio entre dos guerras*, 'that he would answer for any decision we might take on the opposite shore if we found ourselves cut off and in a difficult situation'. They crossed the river in various locations, from Fayón in the north and Miravete in the south. The initial advance, as was normal in these republican actions, was considerable, but it was quickly halted, as was also normal. And Franco acted as he had done on previous occasions, in Brunete, Belchite and Teruel and began to take back the ground lost.

At first the battle looked like a tactical victory for the republicans, as they had halted the Nationalist offensive on Valencia, but almost throughout it was a defensive battle with the aim of tiring the adversary and forcing them to negotiate a victory that was less unconditional, rather than to defeat them, which was impossible. The battle – in which 250,000 men were involved – lasted for nearly four months, until 16 November. The Nationalists lost more than 30,000 men (dead and wounded) and the republicans double that number, although leading military historians disagree over the exact number of dead, some citing 13,000 in total, spread almost equally between the two sides. The Republic had lost the best of its army and soon afterwards lost the whole of Catalonia. The Republic by now seemed to have been defeated, particularly because the Munich Pact, signed at the end of September, allowing Hitler to advance freely on Czechoslovakia, ruined Negrín's resistance and showed that the democracies had no intention of changing their policy of appeasement of the fascist powers. On 7 November, Franco told the vice president of the United Press, James Miller, something that he had never tired of repeating throughout that year: 'There will be no negotiated peace. There will be no negotiated peace because the criminals and their victims cannot live side by side.'[29]

Rojo's opinion after the withdrawal from Teruel still held after the Battle of the Ebro: all they had was an 'outline' of an army, 'an embryonic

[29] *Ibid.*, p. 316.

organisation'.[30] The Civil War in the republican camp began with a revolution and ended with a desperate attempt by Negrín to introduce a democratic and disciplined alternative which would bring about a change in French and British policy, and which many people, particularly anarchists and the socialist left, saw as a communist dictatorship, because of the Republic's dependence on the Soviet Union for military equipment and because of the rise of communist militants in the republican army. This last plan of Negrin's was unsuccessful and the Republic lost the war.

The defeat of the Republic

The end of the Republic had already been a foregone conclusion since the Munich Pact and the outcome of the Battle of the Ebro, but its last three months were particularly painful. The whole of Catalonia fell to Franco's troops in barely a month, in the midst of patriotic and religious fervour. They entered Tarragona in the middle of January 1939 and Barcelona on 26 January.

The republican troops withdrew in a rabble to the French border. According to Manuel Azaña's description, 'the horde just kept on growing to immeasurable proportions. A crazed mob jammed the roads, and spilled on to shortcuts looking for the frontier. It was one solid mass of humanity stretching 15 kilometres along the road. Some women had miscarriages at the roadside. There were children who died from the cold or were trampled to death.'[31] Large numbers of people were killed or injured by bombing and machine-gun fire from Nationalist aircraft.

The retribution against red Catalonia rekindled the 'hot-blooded' terror, with on-the-spot firing squads without trial. Between the total occupation of Catalonia and the final victory of Franco's army there was a fifty-day orgy of anti-Catalan reprisal, in the form of beatings, acts of humiliation against women, looting and destruction of libraries, and killings of those whose 'hands were stained with blood' and could not escape. British diplomats, in an assessment made two years later, thought that the 'treatment received by the Catalans is worse than that suffered by the victims of the Gestapo and the OVRA [Italian secret police]'.[32]

---

[30] Report to Indalecio Prieto, Minister of Defence, 26 Feb. 1937, quoted in Andrés Rojo, *Vicente Rojo*, pp. 190–6.

[31] Manuel Azaña, 'Carta a Ángel Osorio', in *Obras completas*, 7 vols., ed. Juan Marichal (Mexico City: Oasis, 1967), vol. III, p. 539.

[32] Michael Richards, *Un tiempo de silencio: la guerra civil y la cultura de la represión en la España de Franco, 1936–1945* (Barcelona: Crítica, 1999), p. 228, n. 151 (English edition: *A Time of Silence* (New York: Cambridge University Press, 1998)).

With the fall of Barcelona and the total conquest of Catalonia, the Republic was in its death throes. The governments of Britain and France finally officially recognised Franco's government. Azaña, who had crossed over into France three weeks previously, resigned as president of the Republic. A few days later, a coup by Colonel Segismundo Casado made things worse.

Madrid, the anti-fascist city of resistance, the seat of the Junta Delegada de Defensa, had gradually become, according to Ángel Bahamonde and Javier Cervera, a passive city and above all the city of the fifth column, which, since 1938, used 'the tactic of infiltration into the apparatuses of republican power so that it could maintain a presence there and, over the long term, control their nerve centres'. Hunger, the black market and loss of morale were rife towards the end of 1938. The accumulated tensions were as big as or even bigger than those that had led to the bloody May of 1937 in Barcelona, and they had not emerged earlier because of 'the physical proximity of the enemy' and the 'pressing need to hold on'.[33]

Casado's coup was not only the culmination of a political conflict but also 'the rebellion of the officers' against the republican government, whose legitimacy they no longer recognised. It was also the embodiment of the idea that 'it would be easier to settle the war through an understanding between officers'.[34] It heralded a desperate, costly fratricidal struggle in this moribund Republic, with offshoots in other parts of the central zone and Cartagena, which achieved not an 'honourable peace' but an unconditional surrender, something which Franco, the officers, the civil authorities and the Catholic Church never tired of announcing – in other words, the annihilation of the republican regime and its supporters.

Still to come was the drama of Alicante. Some 15,000 people, between senior officers, republican politicians, combatants and civilians had been crowding together in the port since 29 March. At dawn the following day, Italian troops of the Vittorio Division, commanded by General Gaetano Gambara, arrived in the city before most of this assemblage was able to board French and British ships. Many of those captured were executed on the spot. Others preferred to kill themselves before becoming victims of Nationalist repression.

'Today, with the red army captured and disarmed, our victorious troops have achieved their final military objectives. The war is over', said the last official report issued by Franco's general headquarters on 1 April 1939, read by the broadcaster and actor, Fernando Fernández de Córdoba.

---

[33] Ángel Bahamonde and Javier Cervera, *Así terminó la guerra de España* (Madrid: Marcial Pons, 2000), pp. 247–56.
[34] *Ibid.*, pp. 349–404.

The war had lasted almost a thousand days, leaving long-lasting scars on Spanish society. The total number of dead, according to historians, was nearly 600,000, of which 100,000 deaths were due to the repression unleashed by the military rebels, and 55,000 due to the violence in the republican zone. Half a million people were crowded in prisons and concentration camps.

The Spanish Civil War was the first of the wars in the twentieth century in which aviation was used in a premeditated fashion in bombing raids behind the lines. Foreign intervention allowed Italian SM.81s and SM.79s, German He-111s and Soviet Katiushas to turn Spain into a testing ground for the major world war that was on the horizon. Madrid, Durango, Guernica, Alcañiz, Lérida, Barcelona, Valencia, Alicante and Cartagena were among the cities whose defenceless populations became military targets. According to the study by Josep María Solé i Sabaté and Joan Villarroya, bombing by the Nationalist, Italian and German planes in the republican zone accounted for more than 11,000 lives, more than 2,500 of which were in Barcelona, while deaths caused by republican and Soviet aircraft, if we accept the figures given by the winners themselves, numbered 1,088 up to May 1938. The intervention of Italian and German air power was a decisive factor in hastening the Nationalist victory. The majority of bombing raids had as their sole objective to punish and spread panic among the population, and many of them occurred in Catalan and Levantine cities from the end of 1938, when the war was as good as won.[35]

The exodus of the defeated population also left its mark. 'The withdrawal', as this great exile of 1939 was known, saw some 450,000 refugees fleeing to France in the first three months of that year, of whom 170,000 were women, children and the elderly. Some 200,000 returned in the following months, only to continue their living hell in the Nationalist dictatorship gaols. The three prime ministers of the Republic during the war died in exile: José Giral in Mexico in 1962; Francisco Largo Caballero in Paris, in 1946, having passed through the Nazi concentration camp of Orianenburg; and Juan Negrín died in the same city in 1956. Manuel Azaña, the president of the Republic and Spain's most important politician of the 1930s, died in Montauban, France, on 3 November 1940.

Many Spaniards viewed the war as a horror from the outset; others felt that they were in the wrong zone and tried to escape. There were distinguished figures of the Republic who took no part in the war, such as Alejandro Lerroux or Niceto Alcalá Zamora, dismissed as president of the Republic in April 1936, who was on a cruise in northern Europe when

---

[35] Josep Maria Solé i Sabaté and Joan Villarroya, *España en llamas: la guerra civil desde el aire* (Madrid: Temas de Hoy, 2003), pp. 9–10, 313–16.

the military uprising occurred. Having learnt about it in Reykjavik he went to Paris and Buenos Aires, where he died in 1949. There was also the so-called third Spain, intellectuals who were able to 'abstain from the war' as Salvador de Madariaga said of himself. But the war caught most of the Spanish population, millions of them, and forced them to take sides – although some would suffer more than others – and saw the beginning of a period of violence without precedent in the history of Spain, however much some historians see this war as a logical consequence of the Spanish ancestral tendency to kill one another.

From April 1939 onwards, Spain experienced the peace of Franco, the consequences of the war and of those that caused it. Spain was left divided between victors and vanquished. From before the ending of the war, the churches were filled with plaques commemorating those who had 'fallen in the service of God and the Fatherland'. On the other hand, thousands of Spaniards killed by the violence initiated by the military rebels in July 1936 were never registered nor even had an insignificant tombstone to remember them by, and their families are still searching for their remains today. The reformist project of the Republic and all that this type of government meant was swept away and the dust scattered over the graves of thousands of Spaniards; and the workers' movement, its organisations and its ideas were systematically wiped out, in a process that was more violent and long-lasting than that suffered by any of the other European movements opposed to fascism. This was the 'surgical operation on the social body of Spain', so vehemently demanded by the military rebels, the land-owning classes and the Catholic Church.

'Italy and Germany did a great deal for Spain in 1936 ... Without the aid of both countries, there would be no Franco today', said Adolf Hitler to Galeazzo Ciano, the Italian minister of foreign affairs and son-in-law of Benito Mussolini, in September 1940.[36] It is an opinion that sums up perfectly what many contemporaries believed then, and some studies have confirmed decades later: that the German and Italian intervention had been decisive in the defeat of the Republic and the victory of the rebel officers who rose against it in July 1936.

Other historians, however, believe that the international intervention was not so decisive, and the causes are to be found in the characteristics of the two armies – Franco's was better – and in their policies, which is usually summed up as the 'unity' of the National zone and republican 'discord'. Political, military and international causes would thus summarise the

---

[36] Quoted in Walther L. Bernecker, *Guerra en España 1936–1939* (Madrid: Sintesis, 1996), p. 45.

essence of complex explanations to answer the simple question as to why the Republic lost the war.

The international situation 'determined' the course and outcome of the Civil War. That is the conclusion of Enrique Moradiellos when he assesses all that he and other researchers, including Ángel Viñas, Robert Whealey, Paul Preston, Walther L. Bernecker, Gerald Howson, and Pablo Martín Aceña, have written on this subject.[37] Without the aid of Hitler and Mussolini, 'it is very hard to believe that Franco could have won his absolute and unconditional victory' and, 'had it not been for the suffocating embargo imposed by non-intervention and the resulting inhibition shown by the western democracies, it is very unlikely that the Republic would have suffered an internal cave-in and such a total and merciless military defeat'.[38]

The Republic was not short of money or weaponry. In fact, the Republic spent a similar amount of money in losing the war as Franco did in winning it – some $600 million on each side – but the war materiel it acquired using Bank of Spain gold reserves was inferior, both in quantity and quality, to that which the fascist powers supplied to the military rebels. And the most important aspect is that the Nationalists received this aid constantly, while the Soviet aid depended, among other factors, on the entente between Moscow and the western democratic powers. Thus, at the end of 1937 and in 1938, shipments were either interrupted or blocked at the French border. The expansionist policies of the fascist powers and 'appeasement', defended by Britain and supported by France, played a major role in the development and outcome of the Spanish Civil War.

Anthony Beevor attributes less importance to the foreign intervention and much more to the strategy followed by the Republic's High Command and the 'disastrous conduct of the war' by the Communist commanders and their Soviet advisers. Beevor feels that Hitler's decision to send Junkers 52 transport planes to help the Army of Africa to cross the Strait of Gibraltar was not decisive, because it would have happened sooner or later, in view of 'the incompetence and lack of initiative of the republican fleet' during the revolutionary chaos of the early weeks. And it was not the fascist and Nazi intervention that gave Franco victory in the end, although Beevor does believe that it 'cut short' the war considerably in his favour, above all because of the Condor Legion's actions in the rapid

---

[37] As well as the works cited by Bernecker, Moradiellos, Viñas and Preston, see also Robert Whealey, *Hitler and Spain: The Nazi Role in the Spanish Civil War, 1936–1939* (Lexington: University Press of Kentucky, 1998); Gerald Howson, *Arms for Spain: The Untold Story of the Spanish Civil War* (New York: St Martins Press, 1999); and Pablo Martín Aceña, *El oro de Moscú y el oro de Berlín* (Madrid: Taurus, 2001).

[38] Moradiellos, *El reñidero español*, pp. 61–2.

conquest of the north, enabling the rebels to 'concentrate their forces in the centre of Spain', and because of its 'devastating effectiveness' to counter the major republican offensives of the second half of 1937 and 1938. For Beevor, an expert in some of the great battles of the Second World War, it was not so much a case of Franco winning the war, as the senior republican officers losing it – a theory that supports what certain Francoist historians, such as Ramón Salas Larrazábal, had held in the last few years of the dictatorship.[39]

Other experts, such as Gabriel Cardona, maintain that the rebels won the war because from the very first shot they had an army, and all they had to do was to 'expand their military resources', while the Republic had to organise one 'practically from scratch'. On one side there were the militias and the whole interminable discussion over whether a regular army should be set up; and, on the other, the highly trained troops of Morocco. It is hardly surprising that, under Franco's command, they managed 'to arrive unbeaten at the edge of Madrid'. When Negrín, with Rojo advising him, embarked upon military reorganisation, he found himself with too many insurmountable problems, particularly 'the poor quality of many of the middle and junior command'. An army in action, adds Cardona, 'needs guaranteed supplies and the support of a solid rear'. Because the arms came to republican Spain by sea and depended on the policies of Stalin, naval monitoring by the Non-Intervention Committee and the vagaries of French politics as to whether to allow the shipments to go through or not, 'there were constant ups and downs in the supply line, and they could find themselves without arms or munitions at the most vital or critical moment'. Furthermore, the rear had enough on its plate what with hunger, air raids and military defeats.[40]

However, Michael Seidman believes that the rear could have done much more and that was where, in fact, the Republic lost the war. His categorical conclusion is that the Republic was incapable of retaining the 'commitment and devotion' of the urban population who at first defended it. Nor could it raise enthusiasm among the rural population, including the collectivists, who did not agree with price control. The initial activism and militancy gradually faded and commitment turned into unwillingness to sacrifice their own self-interest, and the 'struggle for basic survival'.

[39] Beevor, *La guerra civil española*, pp. 676–80; the discipline of Franco's army and the indiscipline of the republican army are also emphasised by this author on pp. 82–3, 193–5. One of best-documented works by a Francoist historian is Ramón Salas Larrazábal, *Historia del Ejercito Popular de la República*, 4 vols. (Madrid: Editoria Nacional, 1973).

[40] Gabriel Cardona, 'Entre la revolución y la disciplina: ensayo sobre la dimensión militar de la guerra civil', pp. 41–51. Cardona's detailed research into these subjects may be found in his book, *Historia militar de una guerra civil* (Barcelona: Flor del Viento, 2006).

Many citizens of the Republic were more concerned with their *patria chica*, their homes and families, than for 'larger entities, such as the state and the nation'.[41]

This emphasis on the personal aspect without doubt adds to the general vision of the war, but it cannot be set apart from the international rivalries, foreign aid received, the availability of a better army and the political disputes that characterise democracies, or those attempting to achieve this status, as against authoritarian ideas and practices.

After the First World War and the triumph of the revolution in Russia, no civil war could be said to be solely 'internal' any more. When the Spanish Civil War began, the democratic powers were trying at all costs to 'appease' the fascist powers, especially Nazi Germany, instead of opposing those who were really threatening the balance of power. The Republic found itself, therefore, at an enormous disadvantage in having to wage war on some military rebels, who, from the outset, were the beneficiaries of this international situation that was so favourable to their interests. Dictatorships dominated by authoritarian governments of a single man and a single party were at that time replacing democracy in many countries of Europe and, except for the Soviet Union, all of these dictatorships were based on the ideas of order and authority of the extreme right. Six of the most solid democracies on the continent were invaded by the Nazis the year after the Civil War ended. Consequently, Spain was no exception, nor the only country in which the ideas of order and extreme nationalism replaced those of democracy and revolution.

The two sides in Spain were so different from the point of view of ideas, of how they wanted to organise the state and society, and they were so committed to the objectives that led them to take up arms, that it was hard to come to an agreement. And the international context did not allow for negotiations either. Thus, the war ended with the crushing victory of the Nationalists, a victory that, from that moment onwards, was linked to all types of atrocity and violation of human rights. This exterminating violence had little in common with the repression and censorship used by the monarchist regime of Alfonso XIII or the dictatorship of Primo de Rivera. The dictatorships that emerged in Europe in the 1930s, in Germany, Austria, or Spain, had to face mass opposition movements, and to contain them they needed to implement new instruments of terror. It was no longer enough to ban political parties, impose censorship or deny people

[41] Michael Seidman, *A ras del suelo: historia social de la República durante la guerra civil* (Madrid: Alianza Editorial, 2003), pp. 26, 232, 349–55 (originally published in English: *Republic of Egos: A Social History of the Spanish Civil War* (Madison: University of Wisconsin Press, 2002)).

their individual rights. A group of murderers had seized power. And the brutal reality that resulted from their decisions was killings, torture and concentration camps. The victory of Franco was also a victory for Hitler and Mussolini. And the defeat of the Republic was also a defeat for the democracies.

Part IV

Franco's dictatorship

10   Franco's peace

The Spanish Civil War was followed by a long uncivil peace. Franco's dictatorship was the only one in Europe to emerge from a civil war, establish a repressive state from the ashes of this war, relentlessly persecute its opponents and mete out cruel and bitter punishment on the vanquished until the end. There were other dictatorships – some fascist, some not – but not one of them arrived as a consequence of civil war. And there were other civil wars, but not one of them followed a *coup d'état*, nor produced such a violent and long-lasting reactionary outcome.

In short, in Franco's long and cruel dictatorship lies the exceptional nature of Spain's twentieth-century history in comparison to that of other European capitalist countries. It is true that, unlike Finland and Greece, nations that also suffered civil wars in the first half of the century, Spain was never able to enjoy the benefit of an international democratic intervention that would block the authoritarian outcome at the end of a civil war.[1] But more than anything else it was the victors' commitment to revenge, with no pardon or reconciliation on offer, that should be emphasised along with their desire to hold on to the power that armed conflict gave them for as long as possible. For decades, the army, the Catholic Church and Franco made coexistence very difficult. It was their attitudes, and those of hundreds of thousands who supported them, that really made Spain different.

For years and years, the fate of the vanquished lay in the hands of the victors. Extermination of the adversary gave way to the centralisation and control of violence by the military authorities, an institutionalised terror sanctioned by the repressive legislation of the new state. This state of terror, a continuation of the state of war, transformed Spanish society, destroyed entire families and imbued daily life with intimidating and

---

[1] Julián Casanova, 'Civil Wars, Revolutions and Counterrevolutions in Finland, Spain, and Greece (1918–1949): A Comparative Analysis', *International Journal of Politics, Culture and Society*, 13, 3 (2000), pp. 515–37.

punitive practices. As several studies have shown, violence was the spinal cord of Franco's dictatorship.

Victors and vanquished

After the official conclusion of the war on 1 April 1939, the destruction of the vanquished became an absolute priority. That moment marked the beginning of a new period of mass executions, prison and torture for thousands of men and women, particularly in the provinces taken by Franco's army in the final three months of the war.

The collapse of the republican army in the spring of 1939 meant that hundreds of thousands of prisoners were sent to prisons and improvised concentration camps. In late 1939 and throughout 1940, there were more than 270,000 prisoners, a figure that constantly fell in the following two years because of the numerous executions and thousands of deaths from illness and malnutrition. At least 50,000 people were executed in the decade following the end of the war. Among the thousands of people who were shot, there were distinguished names – arrested in France and handed over to the Nationalist authorities by the Gestapo – such as Lluís Companys, first minister of the Generalitat, as well as Julián Zugazagoitia and Joan Peiró, republican ministers during the Civil War.

The main feature of the terror that was imposed after the war was the fact that it was organised from above, based on military jurisdiction, in trials and courts martial. Following the typical explosion of reprisals in the recently captured cities, the *paseos* and actions of autonomous powers, such as the squadrons of Falangists, gave way to the monopoly of violence of the new state, which implemented exceptional mechanisms of terror sanctioned and legitimised by laws. With the military jurisdiction holding sway, a cold, administrative and methodical terror was imposed. The courts martial, which tried tens of thousands of people between 1939 and 1945, were nothing more than procedural farces, with nothing to prove, because it had already been decided that the accused was a red, and therefore guilty.

The first manifestation of the revenge that was the basis of Francoism appeared on 9 February 1939. The Ley de Responsabilidades Políticas declared 'the political responsibility of any person or body' that since 1 October 1934 'helped to create or aggravate subversion of any kind of which Spain was the victim' and that since 18 July 1936 'has opposed or currently opposes the Movimiento Nacional with specific acts or passive resistance'. All the parties and 'political and social groups' that had made up the Frente Popular, its 'allies, the separatist organisations' and 'all those who have opposed the victory of the Movimiento Nacional', were 'hereby outlawed' and would suffer 'the full loss of their rights of all kinds and the loss of all their property', which would henceforth be 'state property'.[2]

The implementation of this repressive and commandeering mechanism devastated the defeated and the reds, signalling as it did open season on an arbitrary and extra-judicial persecution that in daily life often amounted to looting and pillage. Up to October 1941, 125,286 proceedings were opened, and a further 200,000 people suffered the 'judicial force' of this law during subsequent years. The law, which was partially modified in 1942, was repealed on 13 April 1945, but many of the cases that had been opened previously followed their course until 10 November 1966.

The punishments established by the act were extremely harsh, with Article 8 classing them under three types: 'restriction of activity', with absolute and special disqualification from exercising one's profession, which amounted to a thorough and selective purge; 'limitation of the freedom of residence', leading to deportation, 'relegation to our African possessions', confinement or exile; and 'economic sanctions', with total or partial loss of certain assets and imposition of fines. Falling foul of this law meant, in the words of Marc Carrillo, 'civil death'. Those affected, condemned by the tribunals and denounced by their neighbours, were left living in the most abject misery.[3]

Under the act, the instructing judge had to request reports on the accused from 'the mayor, head of the local division of the Falange Española Tradicionalista y de las JONS, parish priest and commandant of the Civil Guard post in the accused's place of residence or at his previous address'. The act described the powerful, omnipresent circle of authorities, their unlimited coercive and intimidatory power which, during the long years of Franco's peace, was to control Spaniards' property and lives, a fearsome triad of political, military and religious dominion.

The repressive procedural system implemented after the war, involving the surge of special jurisdictional bodies, was in force throughout the dictatorship. When a law was repealed, the new measure would repeat the repressive nature of its predecessor. This was the case, for example, with the Ley de Seguridad del Estado of 29 March 1941. It was repealed six years later, and replaced with the decree of 13 April 1947 for the repression of banditry and terrorism, maintaining the death penalty for

[2] *Responsabilidades Políticas (Ley de 9 de febrero de 1939, Comentarios, Notas, Disposiciones Complementarias y Formularios)*, by Rafael Díaz-Llanos y Lecuona (Zaragoza: Librería General, 1939).
[3] Marc Carrillo, 'El marc legal de la repressió de la dictadura franquista en el període 1939–1959', in Carrillo et al., *Noticia de la negra nit: vida i veus a les presons franquistes (1939–1959)* (Barcelona: Associació Catalana d'Expresos Politics, Diputació de Barcelona, 2001), p. 20.

various crimes. Another basic instrument of persecution, the Ley de Represión de la Masonería y el Comunismo of 1 March 1940, lasted even longer, reflecting Franco's and the victors' fixation in blaming those who fell within the broad scope of Masonry and communism for all Spain's ills. The Special Tribunal set up by this law was suppressed on 8 March 1964, although, in fact, many of its remits had been taken on since 1963 by the Tribunal de Orden Público (TOP). On the death of Franco, the TOP was still there, to be dissolved finally by an executive order of 4 January 1977.[4]

Keeping so many prisoners in gaol for such a long time, torturing them, letting them die of hunger and disease, was not – like the harsh post-war repression in general – inevitable. It was the necessary punishment for the defeated reds and, as such, legal niceties had no place. As Michael Richards has observed, the derogatory label of 'red' came to denote in the post-war years 'not just the left-wing political affiliation of other times, but also a sort of "dirtiness", the act of being different, of being an outcast'.[5] In 1943 there were still more than 100,000 people in gaol. Close to 16,000 people were serving their sentences in the 121 labour camps which, scattered all over Spain, used the inmates for reconstruction of roads and dams. In 1952 there were still prisoners of war in Spanish gaols awaiting sentence.

The system of remission through labour, which its principal promoter, the Jesuit José Antonio Pérez del Pulgar, attributed to a new 'extremely Christian' concept of the prison system favoured by the Caudillo, was also an excellent means of providing cheap labour to many companies and to the state itself.[6] In Asturias new gaols were built close to the coal mines so that the inmates could be exploited. In the mercury mines at Almadén and the coal mines in León and the Basque Country, a large number of prisoners were used to work exhausting hours that were too much for many of them. In the two decades that it took to build the Valle de los Caídos, some 20,000 prisoners were used, many of whom – particularly up to 1950 – were 'red' prisoners of war and political prisoners, exploited by the companies that had been awarded the various construction contracts, Banús, Agromán and Huarte. Gaol and factory, blessed by the same religion, were two sides of the same concept in the early years of Francoism and formed part of the same repressive system. Political

---

[4] *Ibid.*, pp. 22–3.   [5] Richards, *Un tiempo de silencio*, pp. 24–70.
[6] José Antonio Pérez del Pulgar, *La solución que España da al problema de los presos* (Valladolid: Librería Santarén, 1939). Explicit information on the Remission of Sentence Through Labour Board may be found in Martín Torrent, *¿Qué me dice Usted de los presos?* (Imprenta Talleres Penitenciarios de Alcalá de Henares), 1942.

prisoners were given work and 'free' workers were disciplined with patriotic propaganda and religion.

There were also victors and vanquished among the female population. In 1940 there were more than 20,000 female prisoners in Spain. At the beginning of that year, the women's prison of Las Ventas in Madrid, built to house 500 inmates, held between 6,000 and 8,000. In Barcelona, Las Corts prison, with room for 100 prisoners, had a steady population of around 2,000. There were countless cases of typhus and tuberculosis, according to the prison doctor, Enrique Fosar Bayarri, who would complain in meetings of the disciplinary board of the lack of medicines and sanitary material. In 1939 there were forty-four children under 4 years old in prison with their mothers.

Children were part of the closed-in world of women's gaols. Many of those who survived prison, after reaching the age of 4, were separated from their mothers and interned in homes and Church schools under the patronage of the Patronato Central de Redención de Penas por el Trabajo (Central Board for the Remission of Sentences Through Work), known as Nuestra Señora de la Merced. In 1942 there were 9,050 boys and girls under the care of this board. By the following year this number had risen to 10,675. As Ricard Vinyes has pointed out, there were many more girls than boys in care; they were interned in Church establishments with strict, austere rules, the ideal education for women in the eyes of many Francoists: correction and hardship for 'red' mothers, and more of the same for their daughters.[7]

They were under surveillance, re-educated and literally purged, with castor oil if necessary, to drive the demons out of their bodies. As reprehensible individuals, comments Michael Richards, they had their scalps shaved, a common sight in the 1940s, to make it even easier for the victors to identify 'la pelona' (the 'baldie').[8] The Sección Femenina and the Church took great pains to torment red women and wives of reds, submitting them to moral and physical hardships and plaguing them with symbols of moral womanhood in the form of the Virgin Mary, Isabella the Catholic and Santa Teresa de Jesús.

However, this mechanism of terror organised from above called for full 'popular' co-operation from informers and snoopers, whose number included not only the usual beneficiaries of the victory, the Church, the army, the Falange and life-long right-wingers. Naturally the purge was social as well as political, and the people of order and authorities in the

---

[7] Ricard Vinyes, *Irredentas: las presas políticas y sus hijos en las cárceles franquistas* (Madrid: Temas de Hoy, 2002).
[8] Richards, *Un tiempo de silencio*, pp. 58–9.

Figure 5 The prisons were one of the main components of the necessary punishment for the defeated 'reds'. In late 1939 and throughout 1940, there were more than 270,000 prisoners. The photo shows the Porlier prison in Madrid, with the director and inmates performing the fascist salute. © Agencia EFE

community used the opportunity to rid themselves of these 'undesirables', 'animals' and trouble-makers. But what this minority wanted found favour with many more who saw the political necessity of punishing their neighbours, against whom they made accusations, or whom they failed to defend when they were accused by others.

These were times of personal vendettas, accusations and silence. In Valencia, the authorities set up centres of denunciation from the very first day; long queues formed at the doors, made up of Spaniards either seeking revenge or desirous of avoiding the repression that might be unleashed on them, bearing in mind the warnings issued by the military government: 'Any person aware of the committing of a crime during the period of the red domination is required to denounce the fact ... so as duly to comply with the spirit of justice beloved of our Caudillo.'[9]

Collaborating through informing also meant being involved in the initiation of a whole series of investigative procedures that was set in motion by the victors. Hence the insistence on active participation: inaction was hunted down and punished. Denouncing 'crimes', revealing 'criminals', was the duty of 'good patriots' upon whom the 'New Spain' was founded. The informer thus became the first link in Franco's justice.

Hatred, revenge and resentment nourished the lust to seize the thousands of posts that killings and reprisals had left vacant in the state administration, town and city councils, and provincial and local institutions. A law dated 10 February 1939 institutionalised the purging of public servants, a process which the rebel army had begun without the need for laws in the summer of 1936. Behind this law, and in general, the whole process of purging was a two-fold objective: to deprive those 'hostile to the regime' of their employment and income, an exemplary punishment that condemned them to social exclusion; and, secondly, to ensure a post for everyone who had helped the Nationalists during the Civil War and demonstrated their loyalty to the movement. Therein lay one of the pillars of enduring support for Franco's dictatorship, the 'unswerving allegiance' of all those who had benefited from the victory.[10]

One year after the end of the war, the dictatorship set up and implemented a system of legal denunciation, a state mechanism to stimulate informers to come forward, something which not even Nazi Germany ever put into practice. The 'Causa General to inform on crimes and other aspects

[9] Vicent Gabarda, *Els afusellements al País Valencià (1938–1950)* (Valencia: Edicions Alfons el Magnànim, 1993), p. 36.

[10] The 'usefulness' of this terror is emphasised to good effect in Antonio Cazorla, *Las políticas de la victoria: la consolidación del Nuevo Estado franquista (1938–1953)* (Madrid: Marcial Pons, 2000), pp. 98–110.

of life in the red zone from 18 July 1936 to its liberation' was created by a Ministry of Justice decree on 26 April 1940. Its purpose was to 'investigate anything to do with crime, its causes and effects, procedures used in its commission, allocation of blame, identification of its victims and reparation of any harm caused, either material or moral, to individuals, property, as well as to the national religion, culture, art and heritage'.[11]

In practice, the Causa General achieved several goals. It disseminated and imprinted on the memory of many Spaniards the various manifestations of the 'red terror' during the Civil War. It redressed the families of victims of this violence, thereby underlining the social divide between victors and vanquished. And, above all, it became the instrument of denunciation and persecution of citizens who had had nothing to do with the alleged crimes. Research that has been conducted on this topic, particularly in Catalonia, Aragón, Castile-La Mancha and Andalucía, reveals the social support enjoyed by Francoism from the outset. To divert suspicion from themselves, many attempted to demonstrate that they were more patriotic than anyone else or denounced others. Many had to prove that they were not what they seemed, and bury their past, erasing any trace of dissidence or expression of liberty.

The families of victims of the 'red terror' played a major role in the repression of the vanquished. Conxita Mir has shown that in rural Lérida there were close 'blood ties' between the informants, men more than women, although the latter did not hold back, and many of them were young people who were ensuring their future. Presenting allegations – informing – became for many people their first political act of commitment to the dictatorship. This was a society 'under surveillance, silenced, almost immersed in mutual espionage, where ... collaboration was essential for effectively replacing popular politics with submission to power'.[12]

All these reports from the security forces, the clergy, Falangists, 'ordinary' people, the necessary guarantees and safe conduct to be able to live, testify to the degree of involvement of the population in this terror system. And, in short, this means that Francoism did not survive only on violence and terror, nor was it nourished exclusively by repression.

---

[11] Isidro Sánchez, Manuel Ortiz and David Ruiz (eds.), *España franquista: causa general y actitudes sociales ante la dictadura* (Albacete: Servicio Publicaciones de la Universidad de Castilla-La Mancha, 1993). The Causa General as a state tool for denunciation is discussed in Ángela Cenarro, 'Violence, Surveillance and Denunciation: Social Cleavage in the Spanish Civil War and Francoism, 1936–1950', in Clive Emsley, Eric Johnson and Pieter Spierenburg (eds.), *Social Control in Europe, 1800–2000* (Columbus: Ohio University Press, 2004), pp. 281–300.

[12] Conxita Mir, *Vivir es sobrevivir: justicia, orden y marginación en la Cataluña rural de posguerra* (Lérida: Milenio, 2000), pp. 265–7.

But for this public participation, the regime's terror would have survived merely through force and coercion. With the passing of the most violent years, what in fact was apparent was a system of auto-surveillance in which there was no incentive for disobedience, let alone opposition and resistance. As time went by, the violence and repression changed their aspect, the dictatorship evolved and 'diluted' its methods, and the lack of outside interference enabled it to relax and present a more kindly face, with a dictator who inaugurated hydro schemes and distributed Christmas hampers to the workers.

However, the terror continued to settle old scores, ensuring that this dictatorship, forged under a blood pact, remained firm. The vanquished were paralysed, cowed, unable to offer any response. In the words of Enrique Moradiellos, the repression was 'a social policy of "cleansing" and "purging" of enemies and dissenters that was remarkably fruitful for the Francoist dictatorship. Otherwise it is extremely difficult to understand how it became consolidated and survived for so long within widely varying international contexts.'[13]

To remind people of his victory in the Civil War, lest anyone forget their origins, Franco's dictatorship covered Spanish soil with sites of remembrance. This remembrance had begun even before the end of the war when a decree by the head of state dated 16 November 1938 proclaimed that henceforth 20 November would be a national 'day of mourning', in memory of the shooting of José Antonio Primo de Rivera on that date, and established, 'with the prior agreement of the Church authorities', that 'on the walls of every parish church there is to be an inscription with the names of the fallen, either in the present Crusade, or as victims of the Marxist revolution'.[14]

This was the origin of the placing in churches of commemorative plaques and inscriptions to those who had 'fallen for God and the Fatherland', which visitors can still see attached or carved on the old walls of distinctive Romanesque, Gothic or Baroque monuments in many places in Spain. And although the decree did not stipulate as such, most of these inscriptions were headed by the name of José Antonio, a sacred fusion of those who had died for political and religious causes, all of them 'martyrs of the Crusade'. As Aniceto de Castro Albarrán, the senior canon of Salamanca, wrote in his pamphlet *Guerra Santa: el sentido católico del Movimiento Nacional*, published in 1938, all victims of the 'Russian savagery' were religious victims, and not just the clergy: 'the most prominent Catholics,

---

[13] Enrique Moradiellos, *La España de Franco (1939–1975): política y sociedad*, Síntesis (Madrid, 2000), p. 237.

[14] Julián Casanova, *La Iglesia de Franco*, pp. 249–50.

the most pious figures, the most evangelistic right-wingers, in short, all those whose martyrdom exclusively involved religious hatred and persecution of the Church'.[15]

With the war over, during Franco's uncivil peace, the victors settled their scores with the vanquished, reminding them over decades who the patriots were and where the traitors were. Streets, squares, schools and hospitals in hundreds of villages and cities bore, from that moment on, and still do in many cases, the names of military rebels, senior or minor fascist figures and Catholic politicians. Some of the names appeared in many places, such as those of Franco, Yagüe, Millán Astray, Sanjurjo, Mola, José Antonio Primo de Rivera and Onésimo Redondo, one of the founders of the Juntas de Ofensiva Nacional Sindicalista (JONS), killed in action in the Sierra de Guadarrama on 24 July 1936, barely a week after the first shot in the conflict was fired, leaving him no time to consolidate his marginal fascist leadership.

However, the final consecration of the commemoration of the victors of the Civil War came with the construction of the Valley of the Fallen, 'the glorious pantheon of heroes', in the words of Fray Justo Pérez de Urbel, professor of history at the University of Madrid, an apologist for the crusade and Franco, and the first mitred abbot of Santa Cruz of the Valley of the Fallen. The monument was officially opened on 1 April 1959, after almost twenty years of construction work involving countless 'red detainees' and political prisoners. It was a majestic monument, built to defy 'time and oblivion', in homage to the sacrifice of 'the heroes and martyrs of the Crusade'. 'Our dead did not sacrifice their precious lives so that we could sit back and relax', declared Franco at the opening: 'They call on us to be faithful guardians of all that they died for.'[16]

It was a question of remembering the war, being constantly watchful of the enemy, changing nothing, always trusting in the armed forces who had served the nation so well, using the Catholic religion to screen the tyranny and cruelty of the dictatorship. The other dead, the thousands of reds and unbelievers who were killed during and after the war, did not exist, and they had to be remembered by their families in silence.

A few months after the end of the Civil War, the German invasion of Poland, in September 1939, marked the start of another war in Europe, the second in the twentieth century, which was to turn into a worldwide

[15] Aniceto de Castro Albarrán, *Guerra Santa: el sentido católico del Movimiento Nacional Español* (Burgos: Editorial Española, 1938), p. 33.

[16] Daniel Sueiro, *La verdadera historia del Valle de los Caídos* (Madrid: Sedmay Ediciones, 1976), in which he describes a long conversation with Fray Justo Pérez de Urbel in the summer of 1976 (pp. 207–22).

conflict after the Japanese bombing of the American naval base at Pearl Harbor on 7 December 1941. It was a global war, six years of death and destruction, which Franco and his dictatorship managed to avoid, although there were thousands of Spaniards who also took part in the struggle, against fascism or communism, representing Act II of a tragedy that they had recently left behind in their own country.

Fascism

Franco and his army controlled Spain from 1 April 1939 onwards and together they held sway, with hardly any cracks, for almost forty years. On 19 May 1939, 120,000 soldiers marched past their Caudillo as 'the victorious army and people's militia', in a triumphal political-military ceremony, in which Spain, as the following day's *ABC* reported, displayed 'to the world the might of the arms that had forged the New State', the 'second reconquest'. In the opinion of Paul Preston, the display served 'to identify Franco with Hitler and Mussolini, to associate him with the great medieval warrior figures of Spanish history and to humiliate the defeated republican population'.[17]

Franco, in military uniform with the blue shirt of the Falange and the Carlist red beret, occupied the dais erected on the Paseo de la Castellana. The march-past was led by General Andrés Saliquet. In a procession lasting five hours, all those who had helped to obtain victory and spill blood throughout Spain marched past: Italian blackshirts, Falangists, Carlists with their crucifixes, regular troops, the Foreign Legion and Moorish mercenaries. Bringing up the rear was General Wolfram von Richthofen of the Condor Legion. Overhead, various aircraft spelled out the letters '¡Viva Franco!' In his speech, Franco made it quite clear that he was determined to wipe the defeated political forces off the map and promised to be ever watchful against 'the Jewish spirit which permitted the alliance of big capital with Marxism'.

The day of the victory of 1939 was also honoured in every school with 'patriotic lectures' which, as stipulated by the Ministry of National Education, were required to focus on the 'need and significance of the Spanish Crusade', 'the highlights of the War of liberation' and 'on the Caudillo of Spain as the architect of Victory and the Saviour of the Fatherland'.[18]

The first government appointed by Franco after the war, on 9 August 1939, had officers in five of the fourteen posts including, as would be usual

---

[17] Preston, *Franco*, p. 329.

[18] Álvarez Bolado, *Para ganar la guerra, para ganar la paz*, pp. 399–400.

throughout the dictatorship, the newly created Ministries of the Army, the Navy and the Air. During the early post-war years, up to the defeat of the Axis powers in 1945, officers had a major presence in ministerial and administrative posts.

But the winds that were sweeping through Europe at the time were fascist winds, particularly from Nazi Germany, and this caused marked political tensions between the officers and the Falangist leaders. German and Italian intervention had been decisive in securing victory for Franco's troops against the Republic, and during the months between the end of the Civil War and the beginning of the Second World War, Nationalist foreign policy had aligned with the fascist powers, who in April had signed the Anti-Comintern Pact, an agreement between Germany, Italy and Japan to fight communism. However, when the German army invaded Poland, and Britain and France declared war on Germany, Franco issued a decree ordering Spanish subjects to observe 'strict neutrality'. It was a policy of apparent impartiality, at a time when not even Italy had entered the war, which would be hard to maintain in such a turbulent Europe.

The acid test for this neutrality came one year later, in the spring of 1940, with the Nazis' sudden and victorious invasion of the Netherlands, Belgium and France. Benito Mussolini felt that this was the right time for Italy to enter the war, enabling it to share in the spoils of victory, and Franco, who was also convinced of an inevitable fascist victory, prepared the way to participate as a belligerent nation in the share-out of the spoils at the expense of the democratic powers. In the words of Ramón Serrano, who shared Franco's diplomatic strategy, the intention was 'to enter the war at the moment of German victory, when the last shots were being fired'. While waiting to take this crucial step, Franco's government abandoned its 'strict neutrality' and declared its non-belligerence on 13 June 1940, imitating what Mussolini had done up to that moment, a formula explicitly acknowledging sympathy for the Axis camp.[19]

The problem was Spain's disastrous economic and military situation, barely a year after the end of the Civil War, and the ambitious demands that Franco claimed as a reward. The army was 'totally' unprepared to enter the world war, reported General Alfredo Kindelán in March 1940, and as Admiral Wilhelm Canaris, head of the German Military Secret Service, said a little later, Spain was experiencing 'a very bad domestic situation', with food and raw materials shortages, and would be more of a

---

[19] Useful accounts of this process may be found in Moradiellos, *La España de Franco*, pp. 63–9; Julio Gil Pecharromán, *Con permiso de la autoridad: la España de Franco (1939–1975)* (Madrid: Temas de Hoy, 2008), pp. 45–8; and much more extensively, in Preston, *Franco*, pp. 343–73.

burden than an aid: 'We would have an ally that would cost us dear.' And, furthermore, Franco asked Hitler for Gibraltar, French Morocco, the province of Oran (north-western region of Algeria) and a supply of food, oil and arms in exchange.[20]

The requests came to Hitler via a letter that General Juan Vigón delivered by hand in June and a visit by Ramón Serrano Súñer, the interior minister, in September. Joachim von Ribbentrop, the German foreign minister, made it quite clear that Germany did not see the advantage of Spanish belligerence, regarding it as an economic and military burden, and in addition the Germans wanted to establish military bases in the Canary Islands. Accordingly, the two diplomatic delegations agreed to discuss the basic points of negotiation in a meeting between the Führer and the Caudillo. The historic meeting took place in Hendaye on Wednesday, 23 October 1940. To prepare the security arrangements for this meeting, Heinrich Himmler, the architect of the SS and head of the Nazi police network, visited Madrid three days before. There he was welcomed with all the fascist paraphernalia by Serrano Súñer, whom Franco had just appointed minister of foreign affairs in place of Juan Beigbeder. Mussolini told Hitler that this change in Francoist diplomacy ensured 'that the tendencies hostile to the Axis are eliminated or at least neutralised', but repeated his 'conviction that Spain's non-belligerence is more advantageous for us than its intervention'.[21]

The meeting was held in the Führer's special train, and present were von Ribbentrop and Serrano Súñer, together with two interpreters. As Preston has said, 'in spite of the myth of Franco's bravado towards Hitler's threats', Hitler did not go to Hendaye to 'demand Spain's immediate entry into the war'. Hitler did not accept Franco's demands and Spain did not enter the war because it was unable to, in view of its disastrous economic and military situation, and because its intervention carried a price that was too high for Hitler and Mussolini, who held a meeting with Franco in Bordighera in February 1941, to accept. Hitler and Mussolini always saw Franco as the dictator of a weak country that had little influence on the international stage. Quite another thing is what the Francoist propaganda said, to the extent of creating a myth that is still bandied about today: that Franco, with his skill and good sense, mocked and resisted the Nazi leader's threats, seeing to it that Spain took no part in the Second World War. However, in view of how history turned out, this venture would have been disastrous for Francoism.

---

[20] Preston, *Franco*, p. 340.
[21] *Ibid.*, p. 392. What follows on the meeting between Franco and Hitler can be found *ibid.*, pp. 393–8.

Figure 6 The historic meeting between Francisco Franco and Adolf Hitler took place in Hendaye on Wednesday, 23 October 1940. The meeting was held in the Führer's special train. © Time & Life Pictures/Getty Images

The enthusiasm of Franco and the most fascist sector of his dictatorship for the Nazi cause and against communism could be seen, in spite of Spain's official non-belligerence, in the setting up of the División Azul (Blue Division). In June 1941, at the start of Operation Barbarossa when the German troops invaded the Soviet Union, thousands of Falangists, officers and ex-Civil War combatants saw an opportunity to continue the anti-Bolshevik crusade in Soviet territory. This division, commanded by the Falangist general Agustín Muñoz Grandes, saw almost 47,000 troops passing through its ranks, fighting on the northern Russian front and at the siege of Leningrad. They were paid a German soldier's wages, as well as an allowance that went to their families, and they were promised work on their return, although 5,000 of them died in combat on the eastern front.[22]

Fascist winds were also blowing in those years within the domestic policy of the dictatorship, which was experiencing the pinnacle of its fascistisation from its beginning in the Civil War with German and Italian intervention. This moment also marked the maximum height of power and glory for Ramón Serrano Súñer, the interior minister since 1938, a post he did not leave until May 1941, head of the Junta Política of the then influential Falange and minister of foreign affairs since 16 October 1940. Serrano Súñer also played a major role in the persecution of Spanish republicans who had fled to France, and he negotiated with Himmler close collaboration between the Gestapo and the Francoist police.

The invasion of France by the German troops, which began on 10 May 1940, brought about the capture of thousands of Spanish republicans who had fled to French territory after the conquest of Catalonia by Franco's troops and the end of the Civil War. Many of them ended up in Nazi concentration camps, particularly Mauthausen, and several thousand more fought their second war against fascism as members of French battalions. Serrano Súñer used his good relationships with Himmler and the Gestapo leaders to secure the identification and capture of notable authorities of republican Spain, such as Lluís Companys, Julián Zugazagoitia and Joan Peiró. They were handed over to the Francoist police by the Vichy regime without any extradition treaties or legal procedures, protected by the impunity afforded by the Nazi domination of Europe and the extraordinary terror measures sanctioned by the laws of the Francoist dictatorship.

Spain's disastrous economic situation had influenced Franco in his negotiations with Hitler and marked the lives of millions of Spaniards for more than a decade. Figures for the economic and social costs of this long post-war period are conclusive. Salaries remained below the pre-war

---

[22] A recent account appears in Jorge M. Reverte, *La División Azul: Rusia 1941–1944* (Madrid: RBA, 2011).

Figure 7 In the División Azul (Blue Division), set up in 1941, thousands of Falangists, officers and ex-Civil War combatants saw an opportunity to continue the anti-Bolshevik crusade in Russian territory. Volunteers from the Blue Division who had returned previously from Russia wait for their compatriots at the Norte Station in Madrid, 1942. © Agencia EFE

level throughout the 1940s. Prices increased, in inflationary spurts, between an average of 13% in the first half of the decade and 23% in 1950–1. This meant that in a city such as Barcelona, for example, the cost of living, according to official figures that did not include the black market, was 5.4 times higher in 1950 than in 1936. Per capita income barely changed up to 1950 and it was not until 1952 that the industrial sector production output once more achieved its maximum pre-war level. Francoism, as reliable research has shown, failed to bring in modernisation of the Spanish economy: on the contrary, it put a brake on the growth that had begun in the first third of the twentieth century. 'Comparisons reveal that in 1950 Spaniards were experiencing a larger gap between their average standard of living and that of the English, French and Germans . . . than in 1900, accompanied by a drifting apart between the Spanish and Italian incomes per capita to an unprecedented extent.'[23]

In a Spain of poverty, hunger, ration books, black marketeering and high death rates through disease, militarisation, order and discipline held sway over the labour market. A law issued on 29 September 1939 gave the Falange the assets of the 'former Marxist and anarchist trade unions'. Militants of the workers' movement, collectivists, revolutionaries and reds were stripped of their jobs, and they had to go on their knees to beg for reinstatement. The removing of the rights of association and strike action did away with what little was left of these trade union organisations. They no longer had any leaders (all were dead or in prison), premises to meet in or scope to protest.

As such, open protest was impossible. Firing squads in the cemeteries, prisons, concentration camps and exile sidelined the most active opposition from the struggle. Daily violence, hunger, the need to survive and control of the trade unions did the rest. There were no more legal processes, the UGT's favourite tactic, or direct action, the trademark of the CNT. The workers' movement was lifeless, or at least dormant, divided by still-resounding memories of the bitter disputes that had marked the political scene in the republican zone.

The defeat and persecution of the workers' movement cleared the way for the setting up of the Organización Sindical Española (OSE), 'an instrument for the structuring and control of the workers, the dissuasion of potential protest or demands, and repression if dissuasion is not effective'. The Francoist trade union apparatus, claim Carme Molinero and Pere Ysàs, was an essential component of the dictatorship which, by attempting to oppress the working class and eliminate class struggle, 'matched the nature

---

[23] García Delgado and Jiménez, *La historia de España del siglo XX: la economía*, pp. 15–27.

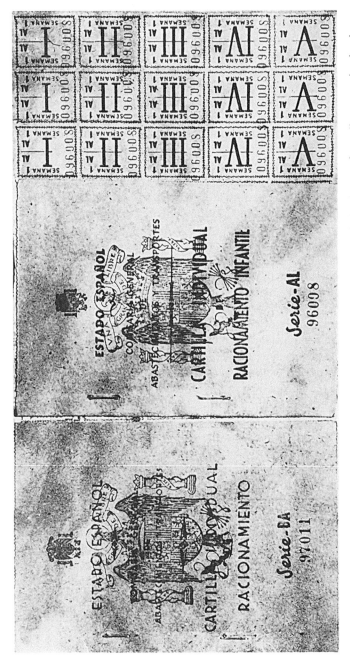

Figure 8 During the post-war period, in a Spain of poverty, hunger and high death rates from disease, ration books were part of everyday life. © Agencia EFE

and operation of trade union apparatuses of other European fascist regimes'.[24] The OSE was made up of twenty-eight employment bodies or vertical syndicates which brought together workers and employers by production sector, controlled by the Falangist bureaucracy.

In the early years of the fascistisation of the dictatorship, Serrano Súñer drew up a programme of indoctrination, propaganda and social mobilisation, which Franco supported while the Axis powers were garnering military success. The desire to control public opinion could be seen in the establishment of an extensive network of state-controlled newspapers and magazines (Prensa de Movimiento), radio stations and a documentary news bulletin (Noticiario Documental – NO-DO) to be shown in every cinema in the land. The 22 April 1938 Press Act, which remained in force until the 1966 act, made the media, as its preamble declared, vital bodies 'for the formation of popular culture and creation of collective awareness'.

Spain's single party, the Falange Española Tradicionalista y de las JONS, also known as the National Movement, went from having 240,000 affiliates in 1937 to almost a million in 1942. Its leaders, together with the military, occupied senior posts in the central administration, and many of the country's civil governors, mayors and city councillors were Falangists as well. The principal sections of the organisation – which before the Civil War, like the party in general, had barely any members – became state institutions. The Sindicato Español Universitario (SEU) was the mechanism used for controlling university students, who from 1943 onwards were required to become members. The Frente de Juventudes looked after the political and paramilitary education of thousands of young people. And the Sección Femenina, under Pilar Primo de Rivera, the sister of the Falange's founder, trained Spanish women in submission and subordination to men. After May 1940, every woman was required to take part in social work for a minimum of six months, to obtain a certificate that was essential for entering a profession, obtaining academic qualifications or applying for a passport.

The growing influence of the Falange in the state created tension with certain members of the military and was the cause of the only serious political crisis experienced by the dictatorship in its early years. On 16 August 1942, General José Enrique Varela, the minister of the army, an anglophile who had close links to the Carlists, presided over the annual ceremony held in the sanctuary of the Virgin of Begoña, in Vizcaya, in remembrance of the *Requetés* who had died during the Civil War. After the mass, there were some scuffles between the Carlists and a group of

[24] Carme Molinero and Pere Ysàs, *Productores disciplinados y minorías subversivas: clase obrera y conflictividad laboral en la España franquista* (Madrid: Siglo XXI, 1998), p. 10.

Falangists who had attended with arms and hand grenades. One of the Falangists, Juan Domínguez, the national inspector of the SEU, wounded several people with one of the grenades. Varela, backed up by Colonel Valentín Galarza, the interior minister, and by other senior military officers, claimed that the incident was an attack on the army and saw to it that, following an immediate court martial, Domínguez was executed. Franco, who had defended the Falangists, agreed to the execution, but he also dismissed Varela and Galarza for stirring up anti-Falangist feelings in the army.

Subsequent events were clearly dominated by Luis Carrero Blanco, a naval commander who since the previous year had been under-secretary for presidential affairs, and who after the crisis of August 1942 became Franco's most influential adviser. Carrero persuaded Franco, according to Preston, that there had to be 'both victors and vanquished' after the crisis and that, to balance matters, Serrano Súñer needed to be removed from power.[25] On 3 September Franco dismissed his brother-in-law as minister of foreign affairs. His replacement was the veteran General Francisco Gómez Jordana, while another general, Carlos Asensio Cabanellas, took over as minister of the army. The removal of Serrano Súñer was a triumph for the military, which also cleared the path for the taming of the Falange.

Although some generals were a source of friction for Franco during those years, particularly those who supported the return of the monarchy, the possibility of a serious plot to remove Franco from power was unthinkable. Together they had won the war and none of them was going to risk his career by starting a conflict that would never be supported by middle-ranking officers – those colonels, majors and captains who belonged to the generation that had attended the Zaragoza Military Academy when Franco was its director, between 1927 and 1931 – who displayed unconditional loyalty to the Caudillo as the saviour of Spain.

Furthermore, the tide of the Second World War was turning, and following the United States' alignment with the Allies in December 1941 and Germany's problems on the Soviet front, an Axis victory was now far from being a foregone conclusion. The Allied landings in Sicily on 9 July 1943, and Mussolini's downfall a few days later, thus putting an end to a Fascist dictatorship lasting two decades, made it advisable to abandon the non-belligerence of the previous three years, and Franco once more proclaimed Spain's 'strict neutrality' in the war and announced the withdrawal of the Blue Division from the USSR. From that moment on, in its desire to survive fascism in Europe, the dictatorship's propaganda began

[25] Preston, *Franco*, p. 468.

to present Franco as a neutral and impartial statesman who had managed to keep Spain out of the disaster that was the Second World War. It would have to remove the trappings of fascism and emphasise its Catholic base, the essential identification of Catholicism with Spanish tradition. The regime that came out of the Civil War had nothing in common with fascism, said Franco in an interview with United Press in 7 November 1944, because fascism did not include Catholicism as a basic principle. What there was in Spain was a Catholic 'organic democracy'.

Catholicism

Catholicism, which had brought together the various factions of the rebels during the Civil War, played a similar role afterwards. Isidro Gomá, Cardinal of Toledo and Primate of Spain, one of the architects of the conversion of the Civil War into a crusade, friend of Franco and staunch supporter of his authority, died on 22 August 1940. Before his death, he told the Vatican nuncio, Monsignor Gaetano Cicognani, that the ideal man to succeed him was Enrique Pla y Deniel. There was no man better than the Bishop of Salamanca to maintain the Church's partnership with Franco's regime. Pla y Deniel, the ideologue of the crusade, continued the Church's 'friendly accord', as he called it, with the New State. He was convinced – and he said as much on several occasions – that the Spanish Civil War had been an armed plebiscite, that the post-war repression was a 'surgical operation on the social body of Spain' and that, after the fall of fascism, nothing needed to be changed. Primate of the Spanish Church since October 1941, Pla y Deniel spent the post-war era explaining to whoever wanted to listen, both at home and abroad, the 'rationale of the war in Spain'. He died on 5 July 1968, almost thirty years after having written 'El triunfo de la Ciudad de Dios y la resurrección de España'.[26] Times were changing, with a new climate emerging from the Second Vatican Council. But the Spanish Church was still enjoying the fruits of the abundance of power that the hallowing of the war and its identification with the Francoist dictatorship had granted it.

A look back at these achievements and powers must necessarily begin with education, a vital field in which the Catholic element was marked since the early days of the Civil War. In his 1942 article, 'La hora católica de España', Pedro Cantero Cuadrado summarised the extent of this

---

[26] Pla y Deniel signed this pastoral on 21 May 1939, and it was reproduced in *Boletín Eclesiástico del Arzobispado de Burgos,* on 15 and 20 September the same year. See also Glicerio Sánchez Recio, *De las dos ciudades a la resurrección de España: magisterio pastoral y pensamiento político de Enrique Pla y Deniel* (Valladolid: Ámbito, 1994).

'Christian and Christianising' legislation in the field of education: 'Co-education in Secondary Schools and Teachers' Colleges has been abolished; orders have been issued for the reappearance of the Crucifix, the purging of public libraries, aid for Church universities and the construction of prayer rooms in our Middle Schools and Universities ... These, and other provisions show that the Ministry that was defended and nurtured by the Institución Libre de Enseñanza is no longer a haven for secularism, and is now at the service of Catholic Spain.'[27]

Cantero Cuadrado – who had been chaplain for the cavalry division during the war – was, in 1942, a national adviser for Auxilio Social, the Falangist institution set up by Javier Martínez Bedoya and Mercedes Sanz Bachiller, the widow of Onésimo Redondo. He had studied humanities, philosophy, theology and law, but all his academic skills went into serving Franco, as a deputy in the Cortes, councillor of the kingdom and member of the Regency Council. Not content with being Bishop of Barbastro (1952–4) and Huelva (1954–64) and Archbishop of Zaragoza (1964–77), Cantero, as a leader of Franco's Church, took his commitment further until he became steeped in the 'organic democracy' set up by the saviour Caudillo.

From Gomá to Cantero, not forgetting Pla y Deniel, the Church hierarchy was firmly committed to the aim of re-Catholicising Spain through education. They were helped in this by fascistised Catholic intellectuals, whom Franco rewarded with the Ministry of Education. In his first government, appointed on 30 January 1938, the post was given to Pedro Sainz Rodríguez, a university professor and extreme right-wing monarchist. With the war over, Franco formed his second government on 9 August 1939, with the education portfolio being given to José Ibáñez Martín. He held this post until 1951, and in those twelve years he had time to complete the purging of teachers' colleges started by the Culture and Education Committee – whose chairman had been José María Pemán since the end of 1936 – and to Catholicise schools and grant generous subsidies to Church schools. Ibáñez Martín also left as his legacy a whole host of anti-modernist declarations, glowing praise for the teaching methods of St Joseph Calasanctius and striking reflections regarding teacher training and the basic problems of education: 'How can a child's soul be moulded by a teacher who does not know how to pray?', he wondered in 1943: 'That is the fundamental problem of Spanish education.'[28]

[27] Quoted in Feliciano Blázquez, *La traición de los clérigos en la España de Franco: crónica de una intolerancia (1936–1975)* (Madrid: Trotta, 1991), pp. 49–50.

[28] José Ibáñez Martín, *La escuela bajo el signo de Franco (Discurso de clausura del Primer Congreso Nacional del SEM)* (Madrid: Imprenta Samarán, 1943), p. 7.

It is hardly surprising that, under Ibáñez Martin, education went from
strength to strength in those Catholic-influenced 1940s. In fact, he had a
fairly comprehensive background to recommend him for this post. During
the Primo de Rivera dictatorship he had been a member of the Unión
Patriótica, deputy mayor of Murcia and president of the Murcia
Provincial Council. Like José María Pemán, he had also been a member
of the Asociación Católica de Propagandistas, helped to set up Acción
Nacional at the beginning of the Republic, and was a CEDA deputy for
Murcia after the November 1933 elections. He held the chair of geogra-
phy and history at the Instituto San Isidro in Madrid, and spent the first
year of the war as a fugitive in a South American embassy until he
managed to escape to join the Nationalists.

To serve as two of the ministry's main department heads, Ibáñez Martín
kept on Tiburcio Romualdo de Toledo and José Permatín, two extreme
Catholics from Sainz Rodríguez's time, and he also introduced some 'old
hands' from the Falange, in just one more example of this mixture of
fascism and Catholicism that held sway in post-war Spanish society.
Romualdo de Toledo, head of the National Primary Education Service,
was a traditionalist whose idea of a model school was 'the western monastic
order founded by St Benedict', and José Permatín, in charge of higher
and intermediate education, had advocated 'careful and painstaking
purging – not punitive but unwavering' of primary schoolteachers and
training colleges.[29]

Between them they dismissed and penalised thousands of primary
schoolteachers, a vast purge well documented by Francisco Morente, and
turned Spanish schools into a spoil of war shared out among Catholic
families, Falangists and ex-combatants. Disqualification and penalties
also affected university lecturers, whose posts were shared out, under the
watchful eye of Ibáñez Martín, between Catholic propagandists and
Opus Dei.[30] One of Ibáñez Martín's fellow refugees in Madrid during
the first year of the war was José María Albareda, an Aragonese chemist
from Caspe, a member of Opus Dei and a colleague of its founder.
After the war, Ibáñez Martín appointed Albareda secretary general of
the Consejo Superior de Investigaciones Científicas (CSIC), set up on
24 November 1939. Albareda surrounded himself with Opus Dei members such as Alfredo Sánchez Bella and turned the CSIC into a nursery

[29] Biographical details for Ibáñez Martín and his collaborators are in Francisco Morente, *La escuela y el Estado Nuevo: la depuración del Magisterio Nacional (1936–1943)* (Valladolid: Ámbito, 1997), pp. 109–12.
[30] Opus Dei is an institution of the Catholic Church founded by the Spanish priest José María Escriva de Balaguer in 1928. Its members (now numbering some 90,000 world-wide) believe that everyone is called to holiness and that ordinary life is a path to sanctity.

for university professors. In 1959 he was ordained as a priest and the following year he was appointed rector of the University of Navarre, a post he maintained until his death in 1996.[31]

Nor were they content with just denouncing and persecuting republican teachers and cornering the best posts. They acted as censors, they imbued education – from primary to university level – with a religious morality that was strict and authoritarian, aimed, wrote Gregorio Cámara Villar, 'at training subjects who were acquiescent to, and respectful of, order and the social hierarchy'.[32] In the field of education, the Church was steadfast, said *Ecclesia*, the official journal of Acción Católica on 30 June 1945: 'Education is more the province of the family and the Church than of the state ... The Church can supervise the teaching and religious-moral education of its faithful even in private and state schools. In a perfect society such as this, the education it provides cannot, in all honesty, be sustained by private education.'

The Church was the soul of the New State, resurrected after its death at the hands of anti-clericalism. The Church and the Catholic religion pervaded all aspects of life: education, customs, the administration and centres of power. As Giuliana de Febo has noted, 'Baroque devotional models' were reimposed, 'based on devout Catholics' fascination – through the extraneous – with emotion and majesty, united with the militarisation of the religious, which in some cultures had a long tradition'.[33] Liturgical rites and displays, processions and open-air masses could be seen all over Spain, with the Roman salute – dubbed 'National' rather than fascist – side by side with the singing of Cara al Sol and the cult of the Jefe (leader), whose face appeared on coins with the inscription 'Caudillo of Spain by the Grace of God'.

As part of the prevailing re-Catholicisation of the time, the bishops spoke out against 'lewdness' and recommended women to 'employ the Spanish style of dress'. Isabella the Catholic's and Saint Teresa's 'Christian feminism' had to prevail at all times over the 'secular feminism' of co-education, divorce and women taking part in politics. Women were reduced to 'tasks befitting their sex', and were deprived of any legal, economic and cultural emancipation, as well as being condemned to obedience and sacrifice. The concern that religious censorship and the Acción Católica leadership showed for public morality, decency and

[31] Jaume Claret, *El atroz desmoche: la destrucción de la Universidad española por el franquismo, 1936–1945* (Barcelona: Crítica, 2006).
[32] Gregorio Cámara Villar, *Nacional-catolicismo y escuela: la socialización política del franquismo (1936–1951)* (Jaén: Hesperia, 1984), pp. 67–8.
[33] Giuliana di Febo, *La Santa de la Raza. Teresa de Ávila: un culto barroco en la España franquista (1937–1962)* (Barcelona: Icaria, 1988), p. 33.

chasteness was obsessive and was in marked contrast with the treatment meted out to reds, with their shaved heads and castor oil emetics.[34]

Spain was being re-Catholicised with rosaries, popular missions, campaigns against blasphemy, *Cursillos* (short courses on Christianity) and spiritual exercises. St Ignatius of Loyola's precept of isolation and detachment from the outside world was even taken to overcrowded gaols full of reds, as if they were not already isolated enough. According to *Ecclesia*, 100,000 young people had taken part in spiritual exercises organised by Acción Católica in the two years that followed the official end of the war. Seminaries and Church boarding schools were attended in large numbers by children and adolescents who were ready to absorb militant Catholicism, while at the same time providing an escape from poverty for a good many rural workers. The number of adult seminarists, 2,935 in 1942, tripled in the following few years. The bishops called for the 'fostering of ecclesiastical vocations' that had been devastated by the Republic and anti-clericalism.[35]

The Church was happy with this 'Catholic apotheosis', this 'religious inflation' that forced the vanquished, atheists and heathens to suffer the rigours of the sacraments, celebrations saturated with pomp and pageantry. For a long time religion and victory were inexorably linked, with the army, the social elite, Catholics, 'old hands' and upstarts enjoying the spoils.

Cardinal Francesc Vidal i Barraquer, the Archbishop of Tarragona who had refused to sign the collective pastoral issued by the Spanish bishops, and who was forbidden from returning to his see by Franco's government, perceived while in exile the risks of this abuse of 'exaggerated manifestations of Catholicism' by the victors, a 'belligerent' Catholicism stimulated by certain clergy who had exchanged 'the spirit of evangelical charity, gentleness and meekness for violence, reprisals and punishment'. He said as much in various letters to Pope Pius XII in 1939 and 1940. These external manifestations of worship were 'a political reaction to the persecuting secularity of times past, and so any results obtained will be short-lived, and therefore there is a risk of presenting an offensive image of religion to the apathetic and supporters of the previous state of affairs'.[36]

However, this was not how most of the Spanish Catholic clergy saw it, a clergy that was stuck in the past, steeped in extremism, with little

---

[34] On 'Christian feminism' and 'secular feminism', see *ibid.*, p. 102. For 'employment of the Spanish style of dress', see Ángela Cenarro, *Cruzados y camisas azules: los orígenes del franquismo en Aragón, 1936–1945* (Prensas Universitarias de Zaragoza, 1997), p. 230.

[35] The Archbishop of Burgos' call for the 'fostering of ecclesiastical vocations' is in *Boletín Eclesiástico del Arzobispado de Burgos*, 15 May 1939.

[36] Ramon Muntanyola, *Vidal Barraquer, el cardenal de la paz* (Barcelona: Estela, 1971), p. 422.

244 Franco's dictatorship

education and totally insensitive to social problems, a clergy that – thanks to the war and subsequent victory – became the powerful guardian of public morality, subject to the Caudillo and grateful for the many benefits obtained.

The forty-six bishops who were still in their sees at the end of the war had blessed the crusade, supported the extermination of the unfaithful and were enthusiastic partners in the construction of the New State. More than half of them died before the 1953 Concordat, during which time those who were to become prominent Church leaders in the golden years of Francoism – including Pedro Cantero Cuadrado, Ángel Herrera Oria, José María Bueno Monreal and Casimiro Morcillo – were made bishops. Almost three decades after the end of the war, 68% of the Spanish bishops were aged over 60, and the oldest, with Enrique Pla y Deniel at the head, still embodied the spirit of the crusade. For example, still in the same sees that they occupied during the war were Santos Moro Briz (Ávila) and Antonio Pildain (Las Palmas), while Marcelino Olaechea carried on in Valencia, Gregorio Modrego in Barcelona and Benjamín de Arriba y Castro in Tarragona.

The Church was stagnant in the first twenty-five years of Franco's peace, although it had had to share its power bases with Falangists, the armed forces and the old and new *caciques*, all of them Catholicised, fascistised and militarised until the passing of time enabled many of them to lower flags that were now faded.

This symbiosis between the Fatherland and Religion – National Catholicism – was forged after the military uprising of July 1936 as a binding agent for the heterogeneous groups on the rebel side, and came out of the war, in the words of Alfonso Botti, 'as a unifying, prevailing ideology' for this reactionary coalition that was centred around General Franco's authority. National Catholicism, as the perfect antidote to the secular Republic, separatism and revolutionary ideologies, held a special meaning for conservatives and landowners, the military and a broad sector of rural smallholders and the urban middle classes. It was an effective ideology for the mobilisation of all those groups who wished to resurrect social conflicts and provide them with a surgical solution.[37]

National Catholicism, said its champions, was historically deeply rooted in Spain, during the imperial era of the Catholic monarchs, the Golden Age and the Counter-Reformation. The subsequent decline was caused by the various foreign heresies – Protestantism, liberalism and

---

[37] Alfonso Botti, *Cielo y dinero: el nacional-catolicismo en España (1881–1975)* (Madrid: Alianza Editorial, 1992), pp. 89–90. See also José Casanova, *Public Religions in the Modern World* (University of Chicago Press, 1994), pp. 80–1.

socialism – that bad Spaniards had seized on. From Menéndez Pelayo at the end of the nineteenth century to the dyed-in-the-wool Catholics of the 1920s, this view was constantly to be found in school textbooks, religious publications, pastoral letters and sermons.

The experience and extent of the republican reforms, of the social conflicts and revolution unleashed by the military uprising, meant that the victory of Catholic Spain in April 1939 would not lead to a mere restoration of this historical matching of Catholicism and Spanish national identity. Furthermore, the radicalisation that fascism brought to counter-revolutionary plans and practices, its totalitarian potential, its ideological purity and exclusivity, and the experience of the extreme political violence implemented by the military rebels after July 1936, meant that the fascism of the victors was not restricted to external manifestations and symbolic paraphernalia.

For a time – until the defeat of the Axis powers – fascism and Catholicism were compatible, in declarations and daily life, in the projects that emerged within the rebel camp and in the form of government and way of life imposed by the victors. The combination of brand-new, modern elements and the traditional attributes of religiosity and rural populism apparently helped to place on the public stage major rhetorical, tactical and stylistic differences, but it never changed the anti-socialist principles and hostility towards republican democracy that had united the powerful reactionary coalition that emerged victorious from the Civil War. The army, the Falange and the Church represented these victors, and they occupied the senior posts in the government, both central and local, and the administration. After the fall of fascist regimes in Europe, the defence of Catholicism as a basic component of the history of Spain was used as a smoke-screen by the dictatorship at this crucial time for its survival. The Church leadership saw this as a unique opportunity to increase its power and consolidate its plans, and so it decided to partici-pate formally in the government and advisory bodies of the state. A key player in this initiative was Alberto Martín Artajo.

Martín Artajo, a former CEDA politician and deputy, was a 40-year-old lawyer, chairman of Acción Católica and a leading member of the Asociación Católica Nacional de Propagandistas (ACNP). He was a protégé of Ángel Herrera, founder of the ACNP and the Madrid daily *El Debate*, who had been ordained as a priest in 1940 and was to attain the office of cardinal in 1965. Martín Artajo offered Franco the collaboration of the Catholics. Herrera, Martín Artajo and the Primate of Spain, Enrique Pla y Deniel, were convinced that the time had come for Catholics to take on political responsibilities now that Spain and its regime were under-going difficult times. Martín Artajo had already said as much to Franco during a long conversation they had on 1 May 1945. He also knew Luis Carrero Blanco, under-secretary for presidential affairs and chief of the Naval General Staff. Martín Artajo and Carrero Blanco had taken refuge together in the Mexican embassy in Madrid in the 'red terror' months in the second half of 1936.

On 18 July 1945, nine years after the military uprising that led to the Civil War, Franco enlarged the presence of Catholics in his government. He kept Ibáñez Martín in education and appointed José María Fernández Ladreda minister of public works and Alberto Martín Artajo minister of foreign affairs. Fernández Ladreda had been elected the CEDA deputy for Oviedo in the February 1936 elections, but he played a much less significant role in the government than Martín Artajo. In these times of 'international ostracism' and with the need to get rid of the taint of fascism, relations had to be established with the outside world via the most direct route, selling Spanish Catholicism which, among other things, also meant selling Spain's tradition and anti-communism.[38]

Martín Artajo kept his post for twelve years and, as well as helping to clean up Francoism's image abroad, he did the same as the other Catholics at home: reject any possibility of a return to constitutionalism, to freedom of expression and the 'dogmas of liberalism'. As far as the vanquished in the war were concerned, they were in the right place, in prison, hounded, kept under guard, with no rights. So said Pla y Deniel a month after Martín Artajo joined Franco's government, and no one was going to argue with the head of the Spanish bishops. The bountiful harvest obtained from the Crusade – the 'armed plebiscite', as Pla y Deniel continued to call it many years later – needed to be looked after. It was one thing to cast off fascist ties and lessen the political ostracism that was beleaguering Spain, and quite another to dismantle the authoritarian structure, give up privileges and come to terms with the reds.

The Church leadership had begun to take part in the Francoist Cortes two years previously, and its presence was now plainly visible in senior state advisory posts. The primate was to find himself one of the three members of the Council of the Kingdom and, together with another bishop, the Council of State. Furthermore, as stipulated in the Ley de Sucesión en la Jefatura del Estado (Succession to the Headship of State Act), passed by the Cortes on 31 May 1947, the 'most senior and longest-serving prelate' was to be a member of the Regency Council should the headship of state become vacant. The prelate would be accompanied in

---

[38] Javier Tusell, *Franco y los católicos: la política interior española entre 1945–1957* (Madrid: Alianza Editorial, 1984), pp. 16–7, 36–8, 52ff.; and Guy Hermet, *Los católicos en la España franquista* (Madrid: CIS-Siglo XXI, 1985–6), vol. II, pp. 210–25.

the Regency Council by the Speaker of the Cortes and the longest-serving captain general of the army, navy or air force.

The Francoist Cortes initiated their own particular farce on 16 March 1943. Franco, making use of his prerogative as head of state to appoint the deputies, chose eight bishops, the cream of the Church of the Crusade: Enrique Pla y Deniel, Archbishop of Toledo; Manuel de Castro Alonso, Archbishop of Burgos; Tomás Muniz Pablos, Archbishop of Santiago; Leopoldo Eijo y Garay, Bishop of Madrid-Alcalá; Agustín Parrado García, Bishop of Granada; Carmelo Ballester y Nieto, Bishop of León; Gregorio Modrego, Bishop of Barcelona; and Pedro Segura, Archbishop of Seville.[39]

In spite of its natural rivalry with the Falange, the other great bureaucracy that supplied politicians, the Church never perceived major challenges to its power. The political exclusivity that emerged from the war prevented the survival of a great many organisations founded, promoted and controlled by the ACNP. The confessional syndicates – strictly speaking, religious organisations for workers and rural smallholders – were dissolved, but the new vertical trade unionism maintained the old Catholic principles of harmony and co-operation between classes, to which were added doctrinal, advisory and propagandist functions. This was confirmed in April 1941 by Monseñor Zacarías de Vizcarra, the secretary of the Acción Católica Central Committee, who during the years of the Republic wrote salient articles on Catholic political traditionalism: the apostolate was the perfect complement to 'the job carried out by the sword'.[40]

In brief, the former CEDA politicians and significant ACNP members were decisive factors in the institutionalising of the victors' New Spanish State. The political structure that emerged from the war 'harmonised' the best of Spanish tradition with modern forms of mass mobilisation characterised by the trappings and symbols of fascism and other methods arising out of this 'divine totalitarianism' – an expression coined by Cardinal Gomá – to be found in processions, schools, Acción Católica, the parishes, the pulpit and even in the gaols. The Church fully adapted to the dictatorship, fascist or otherwise, and throughout the development of Catholic regeneration, its discourse, its elite leadership and its associations survived.

With the fall of the Fascist regimes, Franco was still there, although his dictatorship was to undergo several years of international ostracism. On 19 June 1945, the inaugural conference of the United Nations

[39] José Manuel Sabín, *La dictadura franquista (1936–1975): textos y documentos* (Madrid: Akal, 1997), p. 300.
[40] Cited in Ángela Cenarro, *Cruzados y camisas azules*, p. 230.

Organization, held in San Francisco, carried a Mexican motion expressly vetoing Spain's entry into the new body. This veto was followed by various actions, including the closing of the French border and the withdrawal of ambassadors, but what a good many republicans in exile and in Spain hoped for never came to pass: that the democratic powers would drive out Franco for being a bloodthirsty dictator, one that came to power with the help of Nazi German and fascist Italian arms.

In fact, Spain did not – and could not – play a major role in international politics during those years and, according to Enrique Moradiellos, 'faced with the alternative of either tolerating an inoffensive Franco or provoking political destabilisation in Spain with an uncertain outcome, the democratic powers opted to put up with his presence as the lesser of two evils'.[41] Furthermore, however democratic these nations may have been, Franco's dictatorship always had the sympathy and support of a broad spectrum of Catholics and conservatives worldwide. Luis Carrero Blanco, the under-secretary for presidential affairs, was convinced that the great western capital powers would not take any strong military or economic measures against a Catholic and anti-communist Spain. He said as much to Franco in one of his frequent reports during those troubled times: 'The right formula for us can only be: order, unity and patience.' It was a formula that was to hold good for the next thirty years.

---

[41] Moradiellos, *La España de Franco*, p. 98, which also reproduces Carrero Blanco's report to Franco at the end of August 1945 (pp. 96–7) quoted below.

11 'The spiritual reserve of the world'

The Second World War was soon followed by the Cold War, the unarmed confrontation between the Soviet Union and the United States and their respective allies. Franco's anti-communism found favour among the American military, a recognition embodied in the Madrid Pacts, signed on 26 September 1953, the point of departure for the significant economic and military aid that the United States was to give Spain over the following years.

One month previously, Franco's government had managed to sign a new Concordat with the Vatican. Franco was keen to describe Spain as 'one of the world's great spiritual reserves'.[1] With the military, American aid and the blessing of the Holy See, the dictatorship was in no danger. Those who employed armed resistance, the *maquis* or guerrillas, were doomed to failure almost before they started their struggle. The mechanism of the dictatorship's power was stable despite undergoing major challenges at the beginning of the 1960s. Internal immigration, very important for the development of the Spanish economy, brought several million agricultural workers to the towns and cities during that decade. With the industrialisation and growth of the cities, the working classes recovered, or re-established, strike activity and their organisations, the two instruments of struggle that had been eliminated by the result of the Civil War. Hunger and poor working conditions gradually gave way to salaries improved by collective agreements and the demand for liberties. Change within order was the tonic during those golden years of Franco's dictatorship.

Order

The new order imposed by the Civil War victors went through more than a decade of hunger, shortages and extreme economic nationalism before it

---

[1] Speech given in the Cortes on 26 October 1953, in *Discursos y mensajes del jefe del Estado, 1951–1954* (Madrid: Publicaciones Españolas, 1955), p. 401.

was finally recognised by the United States and the Vatican. Bureaucrats, economists, industrialists and certain sectors of the military defended state intervention and autarky, which led to highly inefficient administration of the economy and disastrous consequences for most of the population. As Carlos Barciela has pointed out, the post-war administration aimed 'to replace the liberal and capitalist system with a sort of national-syndicalist economy' in which, by controlling the means of production, the state occupied a central position. In line with the barrack-room mentality of Franco – an ardent amateur economist – 'economists, duly incorporated within a single organisation controlled by the state, would obey the rules governing economic activity in the same way as soldiers obey orders'.[2]

This 'barrack room-style zeal for regulations',[3] to use an expression coined by José Luis García Delgado, set up a comprehensive system of intervention in the economy, leading to various bodies that monitored agricultural production (the Servicio Nacional del Trigo (wheat)), irrigation (Instituto Nacional de Colonización) and the transport and supply of food (Comisaría General de Abastecimiento y Transporte), and promoted industrialisation (Instituto Nacional de Industria, INI). The institute, the brainchild of naval engineer Juan Antonio Suanzes, was set up in September 1941 as a group of publicly owned companies, similar to the one developed in fascist Italy – the Istituto per la Reconstruzione Industriale (IRI). Suanzes, the son of the director of the Naval College at El Ferrol, which Franco attended in his youth, wielded a great deal of influence in the industrial policy of the early years of Francoism: he was president of the INI for more than twenty years, as well as minister of industry and trade from 1945 to 1951. Investment by the INI a few years after its foundation accounted for one-fifth of total public investment. Its principal sphere of action was energy, oil and petrochemicals, with significant companies such as ENCASO (Empresa Nacional Calvo Sotelo) and ENDESA (Empresa Nacional de Electricidad, SA). As those who have studied this topic have emphasised, these public companies were safeguarded by protectionist measures and enjoyed special privileges, meaning that they did not have to worry about costs or competition.[4]

But the main problem during these years was not how much iron or coal was being produced, but how to feed the population. Corruption and the black market dominated the long period during which most of the

[2] Carlos Barciela et al., La España de Franco (1939–1975): economía (Madrid: Síntesis, 2001), p. 29.
[3] José Luis García Delgado, 'La industrialización y el desarrollo económico de España durante el franquismo', in J. Nadal, A. Carreras and C. Sudri (eds.), La economía española en el siglo XX: una perspectiva histórica (Barcelona: Ariel, 1987), p. 69.
[4] Barciela et al., La España de Franco, pp. 122–3.

population had access only to those quantities of staple products that the authorities allocated to them in ration books. Producers who did not want to sell their products at the prices fixed by the government would use the black market to sell them at much higher prices. And consumers, both rich and poor, had to use the same illegal method to buy the basic staples – bread, cooking oil and milk – or, in the case of the wealthier, to obtain products that were not so necessary. While almost everyone was engaged in shady dealings on the black market in order to ward off hunger, at the risk of harsh punishment if they were caught, the large-scale black-marketeers, who included among their number politicians and civil servants of the Francoist state – people protected by power – amassed vast fortunes. Political influence provided large profits to landowners, industrialists and intermediaries who managed to evade regulation by monitoring bodies or who received exceptional orders from the state.

Hunger, the survival instinct, repression and social control meant that open protest was almost impossible. The dictatorship was in no danger, and even less so when, from the early 1950s onwards, it saw Spain being gradually integrated into international organisations. On 4 November 1950 the United Nations Organization repealed its 1946 resolution to isolate Spain. The year 1951 saw the return of ambassadors to Spain, headed by the representatives of the United States and Britain, and the country became a member of the World Health Organization. Following the Concordat with the Vatican and the Defence and Mutual Aid Pacts with the United States in 1953, Spain was finally admitted into the UN in December 1955.

Although the Democratic president Harry S. Truman – in power from 1945 until early 1953 – made no secret of his hostility towards Franco, US foreign policy with regard to the dictatorship began to change during 1949–50, under pressure from a small group of senators, members of Congress and senior army officers. The Francoist dictatorship's anti-communism and strategic considerations provided by the military eased this change. Although Spain was not included in the Marshall Plan and was not invited to join the North Atlantic Treaty Organization, founded on 4 April 1949, while the dictatorship lasted, the United States' posture was a key element in reducing the harsher aspects of international ostracism, even though certain European governments were less well disposed, and others, such as Mexico, still remained hostile.

Negotiations between Spanish and United States diplomats began in 1951 after the official exchange of ambassadors. The pact signed in September 1953 – by which time the Republican Dwight D. Eisenhower had replaced Truman – provided Spain with economic and military aid and the chance to acquire large quantities of American raw materials and surplus basic foodstuffs at reduced prices. The agreements were to last ten years and during that time economic aid amounted, according to official American figures, to $1,688 million, credits handled by the Export-Import Bank, which were mostly used to purchase American products. Military aid which, as Ángel Viñas, the authority on these pacts, points out, was aimed at modernising Spain's 'impoverished armed forces', was worth more than $500 million. During those years, in exchange for all this aid, the Americans built four military bases at Torrejón de Ardoz (Madrid), Morón (Seville), Rota (Cádiz) and Zaragoza.

Ángel Viñas says that this bilateral relationship, which became 'the backbone of Spanish foreign and security policy' over thirty crucial years of the twentieth century, facilitated 'the acquisition of extra resources which were channelled into the military and civil sectors' and got Spain out of the 'jam' it had been in since the end of the Second World War as a consequence of its 'original sin' – its alignment with the fascist powers.[5] When the economy started to become liberalised a few years later, US investment helped to maintain the pace of accelerated growth. The media celebrated the agreements and presented them as yet another of the Caudillo's triumphs. From that moment, Franco acquired 'the right to present himself publicly as the valued ally of the United States'[6] – that is to say, an ally – albeit lower-ranking – of the world's greatest power, based on the handing over of a large measure of its sovereignty.

The pact with the United States was completed at practically the same time as the new Concordat with the Holy See. Over the years following the Civil War, the Spanish Catholic Church had managed to recoup most of its institutional privileges. State financing of the Church – abolished by the Republic – was restored on 9 November 1939. On 10 March 1941, the state issued a decree committing it to reconstructing parish churches. There were also agreements between the dictatorship and the Vatican, in 1941, 1946 and 1950, regarding the appointment of bishops and other Church personnel, as well as the maintenance of seminaries and Church universities. Finally, fourteen years after the official end of the Crusade, a new Concordat ratified the confessional nature of the state, formally proclaimed Catholic unity and recognised Franco's right of presentation of bishops.

The negotiations – long and complicated because Franco constantly refused to give way on the basic matter of the state's right of

---

[5] Ángel Viñas, *En las garras del águila: los pactos con Estados Unidos de Francisco Franco a Felipe González (1945–1995)* (Barcelona: Crítica, 2003), pp. 189–207. For a detailed analysis of those years of the dictatorship, see Stanley G. Payne, *The Franco Regime 1936–1975* (Madison: University of Wisconsin Press, 1987).

[6] Preston, *Franco*, p. 624.

patronage – had been initiated five years earlier by Joaquín Ruiz Giménez, the Spanish ambassador to the Holy See between 1948 and 1951, supported by the minister of foreign affairs, Martín Artajo. The Concordat, signed on 25 August 1953 by Martín Artajo and Monsignor Domenico Tardini, the assistant secretary of the Vatican, confirmed this prerogative of presenting bishops that had been granted to the dictator in June 1941. Franco would submit six names to the pope to cover any vacant sees and finally appoint one from the three selected by the pope, ensuring in practice that the Church that had emerged from the victorious Crusade would remain loyal to the 'Caudillo by the grace of God'.

Chief among the many prerogatives and powers granted to the Spanish Church by the Concordat was the funding of the clergy and the obligation for all schools – state or otherwise – to adapt their teaching 'to the principles of the Catholic Church dogma and morality'. In exchange, Franco, as William J. Callahan points out, obtained substantial political benefits that underpinned the regime's legitimacy at home and abroad. The dictatorship propaganda saw it as much a triumph for the Church as for the State because, to quote Franco, there was no room 'in an eminently Catholic nation such as ours for a system of separation between Church and State, as advocated by liberal systems'.[7] The obsequious identification of the Catholic Church with Franco reached its peak at this time. Soon afterwards, Pope Pius XII granted him the Supreme Order of Christ, the University of Salamanca gave him the title of Doctor *honoris causa* in Canon Law and the Spanish bishops echoed the praise and unconditional support that they had given during the Civil War.

This Catholic dominance existed at all times alongside the shadow of the Falange, the other source of ideological inspiration to be found in the administrative and political apparatus of the dictatorship, in labour relations, discourse, iconography and the trappings of mass mobilisation. It is true that, after the defeat of the fascist regimes in the Second World War, the Falange went through years of contention between those who preferred to trade ideological principles for power and the minority of hardliners who still dreamt of a fascist revolution. But we should not underestimate the comprehensive network of influences wielded by what was known as the Movimiento, ranging from the press to the vertical syndicates, as well as labour relations and social services. Army officers and civil servants were automatically members of FET y de las JONS.

The Organización Sindical bureaucracy aimed to 'educate' the workers – 'producers', to use the national-syndicalist term – within a hierarchical

---

[7] William J. Callahan, *The Catholic Church in Spain 1875–1998* (Washington, DC: Catholic University of America Press, 2000).

structure and to provide them with a system of social benefits via what were known as *obras sindicales* (trade union services), the human face of the dictatorship, to bring about the integration of the masses previously affiliated with socialist or anarchist trade unionism. The chief component of this apparatus of social influence was the Obra Sindical 18 de Julio, the organisation for medical and hospital assistance which later evolved into the Social Security and Compulsory Sickness Insurance. The *obras sindicales* of Co-operation, Colonisation and Professional Training aimed to control everything from schools to co-operativism, while the Obra Sindical of Education and Leisure – a copy of the Nazi Kraft durch Freude and the fascist Opera Nazionale Dopolavoro – provided workers with leisure activities and cultural and recreational assistance. Most of these initiatives were implemented and consolidated during the long period in which José Antonio Girón de Velasco, a long-term follower of Onésimo Redondo, held the post of minister of labour, from 1941 to 1957.

This populist face of *nacionalsindicalismo* could never be disconnected from the use of violence and repression. Towards the end of the 1950s the dictatorship underwent its first major crisis, and a sector of society also began to display – albeit never on a massive scale – its first manifestations of resistance. In July 1951 Franco had carried out his first government reshuffle in six years. The Under-Secretariat of Presidential Affairs, occupied by Carrero Blanco, became a ministry, and a new ministry was created, Information and Tourism, run by Gabriel Arias Salgado, a supremely devout Catholic who displayed more loyalty to Franco than to Falangism. He surrounded himself with a group of reactionaries and Falangists in the General Directorate of the Press (occupied by the veteran member of FET y de las JONS, Juan Aparicio), in the General Directorate of Information (Florentino Pérez Embid) and the General Directorate of the Cinema and Theatre (José María García Escudero). The group stayed together, monitoring and imposing strict censorship on information, until 1962, when Arias Salgado was replaced by the Falangist Manuel Fraga Iribarne.

The new minister of education in this government, Joaquín Ruiz Giménez, was linked to the Asociación Católica Nacional de Propagandistas, although most of the collaborators he appointed came from the old intellectual sectors of the Falange. Ruiz Giménez had a policy of openness and innovation, thereby distancing himself from the most extreme Catholics who had hitherto maintained a large presence in the ministry under Ibáñez Martín, and from the more conservative pro-Francoist Falangists, and this created major tension with a sector of the Church leadership headed by Cardinal Segura, which rejected any state initiative to regulate education. However, it was in the run-down Spanish university system that Ruiz Giménez's reforms came up against most obstacles, beginning with his policy of reintegrating exiled lecturers. It was there that he encountered the rejection of the hardline Francoists and the extreme sectors of Opus Dei, which controlled the Supreme Council of Academic Research.

Ruiz Giménez's liberalising initiatives also created tension between SEU leaders linked to the Movimiento and small anti-Francoist dissident groups. The main setting was the University of Madrid. In January 1956, with the backing of Pedro Laín Entralgo, the rector appointed by Ruiz Giménez, some left-wing and radical Falangist students applied to hold a Young Writers' Congress in which, as Dionisio Ridruejo recalled many years later, 'young university students would be able to exchange ideas reasonably freely, giving them an opportunity for a dialogue that would enlighten them more than a silence that would poison them'. The Congress, backed by Ridruejo and Laín, was banned by the interior minister, Blas Pérez, and so the students, among whom were Enrique Múgica, Ramón Tamames and Javier Pradera, drew up a manifesto, which gathered 3,000 signatures, calling for a more representative syndicate. There were confrontations in the San Bernardo Law Faculty, with Falangists beating up students, and on 9 February a group of armed thugs belonging to the extreme right Guardia de Franco, who were returning from the celebration of the Day of the Fallen Student, in commemoration of Matías Montero – a Falangist who was killed in disturbances in 1934 – became embroiled in a fight with anti-Francoist students. One of the Falangists was wounded, possibly shot accidentally by a colleague.[8]

The Falangist press blamed communist agitators for the incidents. After a Council of Ministers meeting that day, the government imposed a three-month suspension of five articles of the pseudo-constitution known as the *Fuero de los Españoles*, closed the University of Madrid and dismissed Pedro Laín. A few days later, Franco dismissed Ruiz Giménez and the secretary general of the Movimiento, Raimundo Fernández Cuesta. The former lost his job because he had allowed seeds of left-wing dissidence to germinate in the university system; the latter, because he had failed to maintain the unity of the Movimiento, something which his loyal friend Girón had warned him about. A dyed-in-the-wool Falangist, Jesús Rubio García-Mina, replaced Ruiz Giménez. And to restore discipline in the Movimiento, Franco called on José Luis Arrese, a former Hedilla

[8] Dioniso Ridruejo, *Casi unas memorias* (Barcelona: Península, 2007), p. 221. On this early dissidence and the intellectual and political debate within the dictatorship, see Jordi Gracia and Miguel Ángel Ruiz Carnicer, *La España de Franco (1939–1975): cultura y vida cotidiana*, pp. 201–37; and Jordi Gracia, *La resistencia silenciosa* (Barcelona: Anagrama, 2004). The February confrontations are covered in Gil Pecharromán, *Con permiso de la autoridad*, p. 125.

supporter who since the events of April 1937 in Salamanca had begun to fawn on Franco in order to enjoy the privileges of power. Franco needed the Falange to counteract the pressure that was being placed on him to restore the monarchy.

These unforeseen, emergency government reshuffles aimed to turn the clock back, going back to basics, but they could not hide the appearance of a new opposition, as yet unorganised and separate from the resistance of exiled republicans, which included Falangist intellectuals who were beginning to distance themselves from the dictatorship, as well as young left-wing students, the sons and daughters of well-off Francoist families. All this was still very much in its infancy, the seed of a cultural activism that would be transformed into political resistance in the following decade.

These years also saw the dynamic emergence of Carrero Blanco's plan to disarm the Falange politically and create a new legislative framework that would permit the evolution of an authoritarian monarchy, a continuance of Francoism after the death of Franco. Carrero entrusted this task to Laureano López Rodó, a professor of administrative law and prominent member of Opus Dei. Autarky had led the Spanish economy to a desperate situation, with a considerable balance-of-payments deficit and galloping inflation and with no foreign reserves to pay for imports. The reform of the administration of the state and a change in economic policy would constitute the two main axes of action of the group of technocrats who joined Franco's government for the first time on 25 February 1957.

Changes

The new finance minister, Mariano Navarro Rubio, was a Catholic lawyer, a member of Opus Dei and a military justice official who had held senior posts in the Falangist syndicates. Also a member of Opus Dei was the new trade minister, the professor of economic history, Alberto Ullastres Calvo. Since López Rodó, the figure behind this change of tack, was also a member of Opus Dei, the idea began to spread – particularly among displaced Falangists – that this lay institute was a Catholic mafia plotting to usurp power within the political apparatus of Francoism.

After the Civil War, Opus Dei recruited young people from the upwardly mobile elites with a new message, in the words of José Casanova, of 'sanctification of professional work and ascetic dedication to personal professional vocation'. From 1957 until January 1974, these Opus Dei members occupied senior posts in the administration of the state, economic policy and development plans. They were the driving force behind an aggressive policy of export-oriented economic growth, 'rationalising the administration of the state and integrating Spain into the world capitalist system. Their gospel was rationalisation, development and efficiency, without political democratisation' and without ever abandoning the framework of authoritarianism. Naturally, they stood for the interests of capital and capitalist rationalisation, and since their legitimacy to control power lay in their economic and legal skills – they were all experts in economics and the law – they have gone down in history as 'technocrats'.[9]

The arrival of the technocrats in power was a pragmatic response to the bankruptcy and rundown political model that was afflicting the regime, particularly because the constant rise of imports required for industrialisation could not be paid for by modest exports, and international reserves had run out. And although Franco gave four portfolios to Falangists in the February 1957 government, it was clear that the arrival of the technocrats into government would mean giving up the ideas that Franco and the Falangists had shared since the end of the Civil War.

Problems with the public deficit, inflation and the balance of payments continued during the first few months of the government of technocrats. The leading economic organisations, led by the International Monetary Fund, recommended that an economic stabilisation plan be implemented. Despite the fact that Franco distrusted these recommendations and had no clue as to what this plan meant, he finally accepted it when Ullastres and Navarro Rubio told him that Spain was on the brink of bankruptcy. On 21 July 1959, the Executive Order for New Economic Planning, known as the Stabilisation Plan, was decreed.

According to Navarro Rubio, the main objective was 'the gradual liberalisation of imports and, at the same time, the liberalisation of their commercialisation in the domestic market'. This plan also authorised 'the convertibility of the peseta and a regularisation of the foreign exchange market', and implemented a set of measures to cut back on state intervention and give more flexibility to the economy. The official exchange rate was set at 70 pesetas to the dollar and limits to foreign investments were relaxed in a bid to promote the inflow of foreign capital and increase Spain's economic competitiveness.[10]

These measures were helped by the economic boom on the international front, and immediately bore fruit. The balance of payments recovered and a year later was in surplus. Gross domestic product experienced spectacular growth, rising from 0.5% in 1960 to 3.7% in 1961 and 7% in

[9] José Casanova, *Public Religions in the Modern World*, p. 82, and José Casanova, 'The Opus Dei Ethic, the Technocrats and the Modernization of Spain', *Social Science Information*, 22, 1 (1983), pp. 27–50.

[10] A detailed analysis in Barciela *et al.*, *La España de Franco (1939–1975)*, pp. 171–95.

1962. All experts agree that the Stabilisation Plan was the principal cause of the economic growth that began in the mid 1960s and lasted until the international crisis of 1973. It enabled the Spanish economy to benefit from the healthy economic development that the western capitalist nations had begun to experience from the early 1950s. The high social costs arising from these measures, particularly in terms of salary cuts and increased unemployment, found an escape valve in emigration to European countries which were then looking for labour.

The success of the Stabilisation Plan reinforced the standing of the technocrats. In January 1962, Franco, acting on a suggestion by Carrero Blanco, appointed López Rodó head of the new Development Plan Commissariat, the central planning body recommended by the World Bank advisers. Emulating the French planning model – the 'Monnet Plan' – the commissioner would represent the Ministry of Presidential Affairs in each of the economic ministries, with the power to set up inter-ministerial commissions. A few months later, on 10 July, Franco carried out a major government reshuffle. Another member of Opus Dei, the young marine engineer Gregorio López Bravo, became the new minister of industry, a sector where the policy of economic liberalisation would also be put into operation. This new government also saw the promotion to the political front ranks of Manuel Fraga Iribarne – a professor of political law and adviser to the Movimiento – whose mission, as minister of information and tourism, was to clean up the repressive image of the dictatorship.

The development plans were optional for the private sector but binding for the public sector, and they were based on a policy of industrial promotion through regional development. The first plan was launched in 1964 and the third, initiated in 1972, began to dwindle along with the dictatorship and the dictator, when it was clear that the plans had not achieved everything they aspired to. Most of the major economic decisions were adapted outside the planning framework, plagued as it was with defects, organisational difficulties and a great deal of propaganda, as economists and historians alike have pointed out. Nor did it reduce regional imbalances, precisely because the economic development model was typified by the high spatial concentration of population and economic activity: by the time a final assessment was carried out, in 1973, it was found that more than half the income was obtained in barely 10% of the Spanish territory.

However, in absolute terms, economic progress was remarkable during those years. During the post-war and autarky years, per capita income in Spain had fallen compared to the wealthiest countries in western Europe. However, between 1960 and 1973, the Spanish annual per capita growth rate stood at 7%, much higher than the rate achieved in those countries, and this enabled the Spanish economy to close the gap that separated them. Per capita annual income rose from $300 in 1960 to $1,000 a decade later.

As in the wealthier countries of Europe, Spanish economic growth was driven by improved productivity, with decisive structural changes, and by capital accumulation. One of the causes of this improved productivity was the major shift of labour from the agrarian sector to industry and services. More than 4 million people, mostly underemployed agricultural labourers, moved to towns and cities in the 1960s to meet the demand for employment in developing economic sectors. The primary sector – which in 1960 provided one-quarter of the GDP – accounted for just 10% in 1975. The proportion of the population employed in activities in this sector fell from more than 42% to less than 24%. Industry, on the other hand, employed 37% of the population at the end of the dictatorship, and services, which provided half of the GDP in 1975, became the economic activity with the most employees.

The opening of the Spanish economy to the outside world also served as a source of growth. The increase in exports was always lower than that of imports, but the cost of this imbalance was met by remittances sent by emigrants, foreign investment and foreign exchange generated by tourism. Emigration, mainly to France, Switzerland, Belgium and Germany – 3 million Spaniards moved to those countries to work between 1960 and 1975 – provided a major source of income – more than $7 million during that period – which financed over 50% of the trade deficit. Spaniards went to work in other countries and inhabitants of those same countries came to Spain as tourists. The annual number of foreign tourists increased eightfold between 1959 and 1973, from a little over 4 million to 35 million. And foreign currency income went up from $296.5 million in 1960 to more than $3,400 million in 1975, a sum which financed over one-third of the total import bill.

Following the marked trend since the early years of the twentieth century, industrial growth was concentrated in the Barcelona–Vizcaya–Madrid triangle, with far-reaching consequences for regional population distribution: these industrial areas and the cities of the Levante received hundreds of thousands of emigrants, while large areas in other regions, particularly Andalucía, the two Castiles and Extremadura, became depopulated. Spain's population rose by 10 million in the four decades of the dictatorship, from 26 million in 1940 to 36 million in 1975, due mainly to the sharp fall in the mortality rate, but the most significant factor was the massive population shift from the country to the city – what was known as the rural exodus – which transformed Spanish society.

Moreover, this remarkable economic growth was accompanied by far-reaching social changes. The rural exodus put an end to the comprehensive availability of manpower in the country, one of the distinctive features of Spanish agriculture before the Civil War. Traditional agriculture was in crisis as a result of a migratory process which basically affected day-labourers or full-time workers and small landowners. This population redistribution led to a marked increase in agricultural wages, forcing the owners to replace manual labour with machinery, which they were able to do thanks to improved technology and crop diversification.

The problem of land distribution, one of the basic issues of conflict during the Second Republic, disappeared. The days of the revolutionary-dream-filled struggles of agricultural day-labourers were over. With the Francoist dictatorship and repression, agricultural reform had disappeared from the scene, and what was now being offered to tens of thousands of these workers was the chance to find jobs in industries that were opening up on the outskirts of the big cities. The number of full-time salaried farm workers employed in 1960 – 2 million – fell to 1 million ten years later. The land-owning class lost its political power and influence, and without the power of this agrarian elite, whom Barrington Moore credited with playing an important role in consolidating authoritarian regimes, the path was clear for the industrial middle class to adopt democratic policies.[11]

The crisis of traditional agriculture, industrial growth and emigration from the country to the cities had major repercussions on the class structure. A new working class emerged which at first had to survive in miserable conditions with low pay, controlled by the Falangists and the vertical syndicates and subjected to intense repression, but which, from the early 1970s, was able to benefit from the new legislation on collective agreements to improve their contracts. The introduction of collective bargaining, a way of institutionalising class conflicts, brought about significant changes in the theory and practice of trade unionism, as it had done in other European countries between the two world wars. The aims of the workers' revolution were set aside in order to achieve other more immediate objectives related to wages, duration of contracts and the demand for freedoms.

The state was not the same as it was in the 1930s either. Its responsibilities increased and diversified. The army and the police force – essential tools for keeping the order conquered by arms in the Civil War – were expanded, but there was also an increase in the number of civil servants and public services. Naturally, it was not a 'welfare' state such as existed at that time in the west European democracies. However, it did leave an imprint on the population that was more permanent and further-reaching

---

[11] Barrington Moore, *Social Origins of Dictatorship and Democracy: Lord and Peasant in the Making of the Modern World* (Boston: Beacon Press, 1966).

than in previous stages of Spanish history, traces in the liberalisation and rationalisation of the mechanism of the capitalist market, social assistance and services, which would be of use to the population. Although it was a police, paternalistic and technocratic state, it was stronger and more efficient than the one that had enabled anarchists and revolutionary socialists to take up the fight in the early decades of the century.

This pattern of accelerated growth reached a crisis point in Europe in 1974, caused mainly by the sudden rise in oil prices imposed by the Arab nations the previous year, driving up raw material and food costs, and this hit Spain even more dramatically just when the transition to democracy was beginning; it hampered its consolidation and gave rise to the assertion, often heard at the time, that life was better under Franco. This was because, as Paul Preston has pointed out, Franco took all the credit for Spain's economic growth, in the same way as he had done with regard to the country's neutrality in the Second World War and survival during the Cold War.[12] The propaganda spread this myth, as if foreign investment, industrialisation, development and even preparing the ground for future democracy were the dictator's doing. In fact, both Franco and Carrero Blanco continued to believe in autarky at a time when the technocrats introduced liberalisation and integration into international economic organisations.

One of the great advantages that Franco's dictatorship enjoyed on the international stage, beginning in the 1950s, was that communism had replaced fascism as the enemy of the democracies. Franco's regime, which expressed its opposition to communism more than any other, appeared more attractive to western eyes. After more than a decade of economic hardship, the dictatorship was invited to rejoin the western capitalist system. In those years Spain was a fertile field for the penetration of foreign capital. With a subdued working class and a population under constant political vigilance by the Falange and repressive forces, it is hardly surprising that the Spanish economy, stimulated by American loans and the marked expansion of the European economy, began to take off again and attain hitherto unseen growth rates.

The Spain of the last fifteen years of the dictatorship straddled the line between tradition and modernity. There was a desolate and primitive Spain, a Spain of hunger and poverty, which has now disappeared – although not entirely – captured in the images of photographers, film directors and writers. And there was another Spain that was emerging, although it could not yet dominate and eradicate the old Spain. This

---

[12] Preston, *Franco*, pp. 706 and 785.

tension between tradition and modernity was a central theme of the cinema output of Carlos Saura, in *La caza* (The Hunt (1965)), Luis Buñuel in *Viridiana* (1965) and Luis García Berlanga in *El verdugo* (The Executioner (1964)). In *La caza* we know from the very beginning that the setting where the four characters go rabbit shooting is where many people died in the Civil War. The three older men, all of them pursued by their common past and whose present does not allow them to be happy, kill each other. Only the young man survives, we know not whether to keep remembering as a prisoner of the past, or as a hope for change: while the older men get ready for their confrontation, with their memories, conversations, reproaches and suppressed violence, the young man listens to modern music on the radio and dances the twist with the gamekeeper's niece. And in the last scene of *El verdugo*, after an execution by the garrotte, the cruellest and most primitive method of killing, we see some blonde foreign girls dancing the twist on a yacht.

However, during those years of development and economic growth, modernity was never able to forget history, the violent past, which constantly made its presence felt through personal reminiscences, repression and sites of remembrance. The same year that saw the implementation of the Stabilisation Plan, the U-turn in Francoist economic policy, also saw the inauguration of the Valley of the Fallen, the monument that twenty years after the end of the Civil War would honour the memory of the victors.

The gaols, executions and exile had placed the trade unions and political parties inside a tunnel from which they would take decades to emerge. Industrial growth and emigration also marked the beginnings of new forms of social protest. The final years of Francoism and the early days of the transition saw conflicts and mobilisations that bore certain similarities to the new social movements that were flourishing in the industrial countries of Europe and North America at that time. The dictatorship lasted long enough that there was time for a wide range of forms of resistance, from the armed struggle by guerrillas to student protests, as well as the new trade unionism of Comisiones Obreras (CC.OO.).

Resistance

The policy of violence and division between victors and vanquished, 'patriots and traitors' and 'Nationalists and reds' was imposed on Spanish society for at least two decades. The vanquished who managed to survive had to adapt to the norms of coexistence imposed by the victors. Many lost their jobs; others, particularly in rural areas, were forced to move to different cities or villages. Persecuted and denounced, the militants of republican political parties and trade unions came off worst. For those who were not so firmly committed, many of them illiterate, Francoism imposed silence in order for them to survive, forcing them to erase their own identity.

There were those who showed resistance to the dictatorship, the so-called *maquis* or guerrillas. Their origins lay in the *huidos* (fugitives), those who in order to escape repression by the military rebels had taken refuge at various stages of the Civil War in the mountains of Andalucía, Asturias, León and Galicia, in the knowledge that they could not return if they wanted to stay alive. Early resistance by these fugitives, and all those who refused to bow to the victors, gradually gave way to a more organised armed struggle that emulated the characteristics of the anti-fascist resistance which had been tried out in France against the Nazis. Although many socialists and anarchists fought in the guerrilla bands, only the PCE gave full support to this armed response. In the 1940s, some 7,000 *maquis* took part in armed activities in the various mountain areas that covered Spanish soil, and some 60,000 contacts or collaborators ended up in prison for giving their support. If Civil Guard sources are to be believed, 2,713 guerrillas and 300 members of the armed forces died in clashes.[13]

Up to the end of the Second World War, there was still hope for the guerrilla bands. Furthermore, a good number of former fighters on the republican side, both those defeated and those in exile, enrolled in the French resistance against Nazism, thinking that this was still their war, one which would put an end to all tyrants, the biggest of all being Franco, thus enabling them to return to their homes, their jobs and their land. The biggest operation in those war years was the invasion of the Valley of Arán, when between 3,500 and 4,000 men occupied various locations in the Pyrenees between 14 and 28 October 1944, until Vicente López Tovar, the leader of the operation, had to order a retreat, leaving behind 600 dead and 800 prisoners.

With the deaths of Hitler and Mussolini, the Axis powers were defeated, but Franco was still there. And he continued remembering the war and administering harsh punishment on those who had lost it. Over the next five years, between 1945 and 1949, scattered guerrilla groups maintained continuous clashes with the Civil Guard until their eventual defeat. But without help from the democratic powers, there was little they could do against the militarised, absolute might of the Francoist victors.

---

[13] Francisco Moreno, 'Huidos, guerrilleros, resistentes: la oposición armada a la dictadura', in Julián Casanova (ed.), *Morir, matar, sobrevivir: la violencia en la dictadura de Franco* (Barcelona: Crítica, 2002), pp. 197–295; and Secundino Serrano, *Maquis: historia de la guerrilla antifranquista* (Madrid: Temas de Hoy, 2001).

And the libertarians in Catalonia who had supported armed resistance fared little better. By 1949 the repression had finished with them as well. Some were shot down by the police and Civil Guard; others met their end in front of a firing squad. Among those who escaped this fate were José Luis Facerías and Francisco Sabaté ('Quico'), the last 'urban guerrillas', who over the following decade mounted strikes and skirmishes against the forces of order. Facerías was hunted down on 30 August 1957 in an ambush laid for him in a district of Barcelona. Sabaté met the same fate on 5 January 1960, in the town of Sant Celoni, near Barcelona.[14]

Armed resistance was only very occasionally involved with clandestine attempts to reorganise the trade union structure of the CNT and the UGT, and with occasional workers' protests which spontaneously and sporadically began to make their presence felt from the end of the 1940s in Catalonia and the Basque Country. Protests against low wages and rationing were the expression of pressure mounted to end hardship, but they had a political dimension in that they were a challenge to the Francoist author-ities. There had already been a major strike involving more than 20,000 workers on the Bilbao waterfront on 1 May 1947, although the most significant strike during those years was the one that began in Barcelona in March 1951 with a boycott of the trams, in protest at a rise in fares. The strike spread to other industrial sectors, and was also strongly backed in Vizcaya and Guipúzcoa. In those conflicts, and those of subsequent years, up to the early student mobilisations of 1956, it was already clear that the two traditional branches of trade unionism, socialist and anarchist, were finding it very hard to become involved with these protests while under cover, and that the Communists were starting to become the most active opposition force against the dictatorship.

The Communists began to make their presence felt particularly after the 1958 Collective Agreements Act, a law that was really trying to channel these protests and at the same time place negotiations on wage and work-ing conditions under the control of vertical syndicalism. And even if this control failed, and the dictatorship had the police and the penal code to fall back on, the introduction of collective bargaining gave rise to an undercover syndicalism, CC.OO., activated and guided by Catholic and communist groups, which tried to infiltrate the Francoist syndicates, negotiate with the employers as far as circumstances permitted, with patience, waiting for this official restrictive system to collapse one day.

It was a new trade union culture, consisting of 'indirect' action, which used the channels that the dictatorship provided, and which had very little

---

[14] José Luis Ledesma, 'Francisco *Quico* Sabaté', in Julián Casanova (ed.), *Tierra y Libertad: cien años de anarquismo en España* (Barcelona: Crítica, 2010), pp. 283–6.

to do with 'direct action', the type of action – as practised by the anarcho-syndicalists – that brought capitalists and workers, the authorities and the oppressed, into open confrontation, without intermediaries, thereby removing any possibility of these existing mechanisms of power being used to benefit the working class. Naturally, missing from the orchestra-tors of this new trade union culture – conflict negotiation – were the militants of the CNT, both those inside Spain and those who continued from abroad to analyse the Spanish situation in terms of the revolutionary experiences of the Civil War.

The Comisiones Obreras movement originated with the labour conflicts of the early 1960s, shortly to be joined, at first spontaneously, by groups of workers who were most active in the struggle against Francoism. The CC. OO. representatives aspired to act publicly and legally, and they managed it in some strikes, although in view of the fact that they were banned and harshly repressed, this new trade unionism always had to operate under cover. Their method of involving the workers was to propose basic demands with regard to wages and working conditions, but among their more hardline groups there were always demands that were more political in nature, such as trade union freedom and the right to strike. Since the strike movement of 1962 in the mines of Asturias, the presence of CC. OO. was inextricably linked to all the labour conflicts that spread through-out Spain until the death of Franco.

During those first twenty years of the dictatorship, the political opposi-tion to Francoism was lost in the wilderness. This is why the meeting held in Munich from 5 to 8 July 1962 of representatives from groups opposing the dictatorship made such an impact. Monarchists, Catholics and Falangists who at the time had distanced themselves from the authoritarian posture, led by Gil Robles and Dionisio Ridruejo, met socialists and Basque and Catalan nationalists. Although the meeting's final communiqué called for only moderate and gradual changes, the dictatorship considered it to be a serious attack against Spain – 'the Munich Conspiracy' – and arrested and sent into exile some of those who attended.

Also reds and dissidents in Franco's eyes were the teachers and students who questioned the rationale of a second-rate repressive university system, clergy who distanced themselves from a Church that was deferential to the dictatorship, and Basque and Catalan nationalists. The number of university students – barely 50,000 in 1955 – had tripled by 1971, and to deal with this considerable growth a body of contracted untenured teach-ers was set up who were openly hostile to the ideological and political principles of Francoism. Faced with this dissidence, involving students and some department professors, the dictatorship responded with repres-sion every time, particularly when these protests and acts of defiance found ways to eradicate the useless SEU, in theory the compulsory union for all students. In 1965, a year of conflicts, Professors José Luis López-Aranguren, Agustín García Calvo and Enrique Tierno Galván were dismissed from their universities for their backing of the student movement. That was also the year in which the Ministry of National Education changed its name to Education and Science and when the minister, Manuel Lora Tamayo, implemented the University Education Act, which was modified in 1970 under the General Education Act, brought in by his successor, José Luis Villar Palasi.[15]

Until then, the Catholic Church had wielded almost total power in education and the monitoring of ideology in textbooks. At the beginning of the 1940s, only one-fifth of secondary schools were run by the state, while almost all the rest belonged to religious orders, providing education to more than half of the nation's pupils. More than 8 million pupils attended seminaries in 1963, and 7,000 new priests were ordained that same year. One-third of the more than 100 daily papers published in Spain were Catholic, and there were several hundred publications edited by priests or by lay members of Catholic associations. And, as if that were not enough, in 1962 a new agreement with the state exempted Catholic publications from censorship, while Church officials continued to impose their own particular censorship as well as that of the state.

But these socio-economic changes that defied the dictatorship also brought about a thorough secularisation of society. The expansion of state education and growing number of public service teaching staff caused the Church to lose its monopoly on education and moral control of culture. In 1972 the number of seminarists had fallen to 2,700 and fewer than 300 new priests were ordained. Furthermore, nearly 4,000 left their ministries, as against the 167 who had done so in 1963, and a considerable number of priests began to speak out against the repressive measures taken by the dictatorship. Many of them came from the Basque Country and Catalonia, where young nationalists and priests denounced the absence of liberties and actively supported the workers' movements. In 1963, Joaquín Ruiz Giménez, dismissed by Franco from the Ministry of Education following the events of 1956, began to publish *Cuadernos para el Diálogo*, a mouthpiece for Christians and moderate Marxists who wished to construct a democratic political culture.

[15] On conflicts and changes in protesting, we adhere to the line taken by Carme Molinero and Pere Ysàs, *Productores disciplinados y minorías subversivas. Clase obrera y conflictividad laboral en la España franquista* (Madrid: Siglo XXI, 1988); for a discussion of intellectual dissidence, see Jordi Gracia, *Estado y cultura: el despertar de una conciencia crítica bajo el franquismo (1940–1962)* (Toulouse: Presses Universitaires du Mirail, 1996).

However, Franco and his armed forces were not prepared to yield one ounce of the power they had won as a result of the Civil War. On the one hand, they propagated their 'Twenty-Five Years of Peace' campaign, with the information minister, Fraga Iribarne, as the 'master of ceremonies', and, on the other, they were still torturing and executing people for crimes allegedly committed during the Civil War, as they did, for example, with the Communist leader, Julián Grimau, on 20 April 1963. A few months later, on 17 August, when protests were still ringing out over that execution, the anarchists Francisco Granados and Joaquín Delgado were executed by garrotte in the gaol at Carabanchel.

December of that same year saw the passing of the act setting up the Juzgado y Tribunal de Orden Público, the draft of which was presented by the minister of justice, Antonio Iturmendi, to Luis Carrero Blanco before the execution of Grimau. This was a special court which, during its twelve years of operation until it was abolished on 5 January 1977, tried thousands of 'crimes against interior security', including 'illicit association', 'illegal propaganda' and 'non-peaceful meetings or demonstrations'. This was how Francoism criminalised what in other democratic countries were legally authorised public political practices.[16]

The absolute control that the authorities were trying to impose on the public was no longer enough to stop social protests demanding liberties. Furthermore, the last few years of the dictatorship saw conflicts and mobilisations that were very similar to the new social movements to be found in the industrial sector in Europe and North America at the time. These years saw the burgeoning student movement, protesting not so much against the educational system as against a repressive and reactionary political regime; and nationalist movements, which attracted a high proportion of the political and cultural elite; and we should not forget other forms of action linked to pacifism/anti-militarism, feminism, ecology and local community collectives. Most of these movements left behind the revolutionary dream of structural change, preferring instead to advocate a democratic civil society. Their organisation was less hierarchical and centralised, and they attracted young people, students and public sector employees – in other words, people who no longer represented a particular social class (usually the working class) and therefore no longer reflected the interests and demands of that class alone.

In short, a lot of things seemed to have changed since 1939, in the three long decades since the defeat of the Republic in the Civil War. A new political and trade union culture had emerged. Negotiation had been

---

[16] Juan José del Águila, *El TOP: la represión de la libertad (1963–1977)* (Barcelona: Planeta, 2001).

imposed as a way of institutionalising conflicts. New social movements and new players had replaced those based on class, the working class which had been assigned the historical task of transforming society. Rural workers who had flooded the cities since the 1950s did so to join a wide range of industrial sectors, and not – as was the case in the 1920s – just construction and sectors that straddled agriculture and industry. The rural working class had decreased considerably and was no longer the driving force behind strike action. There had been a drastic reduction in illiteracy, which was now no longer, as the 1931 CNT Congress had stated, 'the blight . . . which has the people sunk in the greatest of infamies'.[17]

The environmental and cultural factors that in earlier eras had allowed for nostalgia concerning ancestral and messianic myths – easily recognisable in anarchism but also in other Marxist-inspired workers' movements – were now consigned to history. The old state, which had been weak, which had fostered the illusion and the dream that revolutions depended only on the revolutionary aspirations of workers and peasants, had been transformed into one that was stronger, more efficient and more interventionist, almost 'philanthropic'. Consumerism worked miracles: it enabled capital to spread and workers to improve their standard of living. With capitalism booming and workers who were leaving radicalism behind in the hope of tangible and immediate improvements, and who preferred cars and refrigerators to altruism and sacrifice for the cause, anarchism and its revolutionary options were flagging, to be seen no more. In fact, except for socialism – an ideology that had undergone major reform and could see itself mirrored in the more advanced countries – none of the historic pre-Civil War movements, such as republicanism and anarchism, managed to resurface after the death of Franco.

Some movements were past history, and others appeared just when the dictator was coming to the end of his days. Such was the case with ETA (Euskadi Ta Askatasuna, Basque Homeland and Freedom). Although it was founded in July 1959 with remnants of the youth organisations of the PNV, it began to hit the headlines in August 1968, when its propaganda and victimless bombs gave way to the murder in Irún of the police superintendent Melitón Manzanas. From then on, ETA terrorism became a serious public order problem and had great success in bringing about indiscriminate repression and anti-dictatorship reaction by a large sector of the Basque population. The trial in Burgos of sixteen people charged with having links to ETA, in December 1970, and the assassination of Carrero Blanco just three years later, accompanied the death throes of

---

[17] Cited in Julián Casanova, *Anarchism, the Republic and Civil War in Spain*, p. 163.

Francoism. But Franco went on killing, even on his deathbed. A few weeks before his death, he signed warrants for the execution of five suspected terrorists. In so doing, he left no one in any doubt as to what kind of dictatorship his was, from victory in the Civil War to his last breath in November 1975.

12 The death throes of Francoism

Franco died in his bed in 1975, putting an end to nearly forty years of a dictatorship that had been born from the ashes of a civil war. There followed a transition to democracy 'from above', instigated by authorities who had been active during Francoism, although it was negotiated in certain basic aspects with democratic opposition leaders. There are historians, such as José María Maravall and Julián Santamaría, who argue that the raw materials that brought about this particular mode of transition originated in the crisis that Franco's regime experienced from the mid 1960s onwards. Thus the comprehensive political and cultural transition that followed the dictator's death can only be judged in the light of the social changes that had begun fifteen years previously.[1]

Other historians go further. The traumatic memory of the Civil War, fear of the army and the Francoist right, and the desire to avoid a repetition of such a violent conflict were very much to the fore during the early years of the transition.[2] A dictatorship lasting forty years would have had a great influence on the period of transition from authoritarian domination to democracy, and this is what many of the experts have tried to explain and correlate.

But before studying the transition and authoritarianism's legacy in the new democracy, in this chapter we shall attempt to identify the crisis of

---

[1] José María Maravall and Julián Santamaría in 'El cambio político en España y la perspectiva de la democracia', in Guillermo O'Donnell, Philippe C. Schmitter and Laurence Whitehead (comps.), *Transiciones desde un gobierno autoritario*, vol. I, *Europa meridional* (Buenos Aires: Paidós, 1989), pp. 116–18. This line has been emphasised by Santos Juliá, 'Cambio social y cultura política en la transición a la democracia', in José-Carlos Mainer and Santos Juliá, *El aprendizaje de la libertad 1973–1986: la cultura de la transición* (Madrid: Alianza, 2000), pp. 16–17. The case for Spain as a transition 'from above' is made in José Casanova, 'Las enseñanzas de la transición democrática en España', in Manuel Redero San Román (ed.), 'La transición a la democracia en España', *Ayer*, 15 (1994), pp. 32–4.

[2] This thesis is developed by Paloma Aguilar Fernández, *Memoria y olvido de la guerra civil española* (Madrid: Alianza, 1996), subsequently reworked in her 'Justicia, política y memoria: los legados del franquismo en la transición española', in Alexandra Barahona de Brito, Paloma Aguilar and Carmen González Enríquez (eds.), *Las políticas hacia el pasado: juicios, depuraciones, perdón y olvido en las nuevas democracias* (Madrid: Istmo, 2002), pp. 140–2.

Francoism, its death throes and why this regime lasted so long. Firstly, let us look at the most important events of its final years and then examine the principal interpretations of its duration and final crisis.

Difficult years

The crisis and decline of Francoism may be considered to have dated from 1969, with a major acceleration point in December 1973 with the assassination of Luis Carrero Blanco. On 21 July 1969 Franco presented Juan Carlos as his successor to the Council of the Kingdom and a day later to the Cortes, which accepted the dictator's choice with 491 votes in favour, 19 against and 9 abstentions. On 23 July, the prince swore 'loyalty to His Excellency the Head of State and the Principles of the Movement and the Basic Laws'. His appointment finally settled the question 'after Franco, who?' and seemed to guarantee a continuance of the principles and institutions of the dictatorship.

Franco was 77 years old at the time and had already begun to display clear symptoms of ageing, aggravated by Parkinson's disease, which was borne out by his trembling hands, facial rigidity and faltering voice. In view of this, Carrero Blanco, who in September 1967 had replaced General Agustín Muñoz Grandes as deputy prime minister, accelerated his plan to tie the institutionalisation of the dictatorship to Franco's appointment of a successor with the title of king. Since the beginning of the 1960s, and having been subject to a great deal of pressure to appoint Don Juan, the son of Alfonso XIII and father of Juan Carlos, Franco discounted not only him as his successor, but also any member of the Carlist dynasty. It was Carrero Blanco who, particularly after January 1968, when Juan Carlos reached his thirtieth birthday – the age established by the 1947 Succession to the Headship of State Act for eligibility to reign – convinced Franco to take the decision to appoint the 'prince of Spain' as his successor, to head a 'Monarchy of the Movimiento Nacional which would permanently maintain its principles and institutions'.[3]

In fact, at that time it was Carrero Blanco, not so much the prince, who ensured this continuity. This was true particularly after the Matesa scandal and the formation of a new government in October 1969, the two most important events following the recognition of Juan Carlos as successor.

The Matesa (Maquinaria Textil, SA) affair suddenly broke out in the summer of that year and became the biggest scandal of the entire dictatorship. The company manufactured textile machinery in Pamplona and had

[3] Javier Tusell, *Carrero: la eminencia gris del régimen de Franco* (Madrid: Temas de Hoy, 1993), p. 461.

branches and subsidiary companies in South America. Its director, Juan
Vilá Reyes, with links to Opus Dei and to certain technocrats, managed to
obtain generous export credits, some 11 billion pesetas, for orders that either
did not exist or were highly inflated. The irregularities were denounced and
made public by the Movimiento press, with government help from Manuel
Fraga Iribarne and José Solís Ruiz, in an attempt to discredit the Opus
Dei ministers – yet another trial of strength in the bitter battle for power
between these two groups since the beginning of the 1960s.

The political effects of this scandal were immediate. Carrero Blanco
asked Franco for a complete government reshuffle, and on 29 October he
formed what has gone down in history as the 'monochrome government'.
Carrero continued as deputy prime minister, although with more power
than ever, and almost all the ministers in key posts were members of Opus
Dei or the ACNP, or identified with the reactionary technocratic line laid
down by López Rodó and Carrero Blanco. Fraga Iribarne and Solís Ruiz
were dismissed and, although Carrero Blanco was not yet prime minister,
he was the one who directed government policy.

This struggle for control of the political scene between Carrero Blanco
and Opus Dei on one side, and the 'blue' (conservative) sector of the
Movimiento on the other, was the catalyst for the crisis within Francoism.
In the opinion of Juan Pablo Fusi, Carrero Blanco and López Rodó
envisaged a strong government, with economic development, administrative reform and 'controlled and careful' continuation via the monarchy.
The members of the Movimiento, represented by Solís Ruiz, wanted to
make it and its National Council the only channel of the regime's political
representation, the base of the continuance of the political power that had
emerged from its victory in the 1936–9 Civil War.[4]

Power struggles among government members have been asserted as being
one of the fundamental factors for destabilising dictatorial regimes, even
more so than conflicts between rulers and the governed: various authors,
following Philippe Schmitter's classic explanation for the Portuguese dictatorship, have emphasised this aspect for the final years of Francoism. It was
a conflict between hardline Francoists ready to defend their privileges to the
end, always under the protection of the dictatorship, and those Francoists
who had become aware that their survival would be better assured with
gradual, moderate reform.[5]

---

[4] Juan Pablo Fusi, *Franco: autoritarismo y poder personal* (Madrid: Taurus, 1995 (1st edn,
1985)), p. 214.
[5] José Casanova dwells at length on this conflict over the distribution of power in 'Las
enseñanzas de la transición democrática en España', p. 23, a basic argument in the classic

But it was not only internal power struggles that made life difficult for the dictatorship in its final years. A particularly tense period was 1970. That year saw the highest number of labour conflicts of the decade, with almost half a million workers involved in disputes and 9 million man-hours lost. Many of these strikes evolved into confrontations with the police, and numerous strikers were tortured and imprisoned. Repression was particularly harsh in the Basque Country, where ETA had begun to defy the dictatorship's armed forces with assassinations, bank robberies and industrial extortion. This mixture of labour, student and terrorist unrest provoked a severe reaction from the military and extreme right-wing politicians who convinced Franco to respond with a show trial against sixteen Basque prisoners, including two priests. It began in December in Burgos, the headquarters of the military region that included the Basque Country, and concluded with the death penalty for six of the accused and a total of 519 years' imprisonment for the others.

Certain ministers, led by López Bravo, interceded before Franco. Franco's brother Nicolás wrote to him on 6 December recommending that he not sign the death warrants: 'It's not in your interests. I'm telling you because I love you. You're a good Christian and afterwards you will regret it. We're getting old. Listen to my advice, you know how much I love you.' In his end-of-year message on television on 30 December, Franco announced his magnanimous decision to commute the death sentences to prison terms. According to the dictator, this pardon was the best proof of the strength of his government: 'The firmness and the strength of my spirit will not let you down while God gives me life to continue ruling over the destinies of our *Patria*.'[6]

In spite of the reprieve, the whole process had extremely negative consequences for the regime. It witnessed a sector of society responding with strikes and demonstrations, Basque bishops pleading for clemency and the outside world protesting against Franco to an extent that had not been seen since just after the Second World War. The consequences were particularly dire in the Basque Country, where the Burgos trial, according to Fusi, 'was a true turning point in history, a salutary lesson for Basque national consciousness . . . It marked the beginning of a process which, in just a few years of unrest and repression, would end up by alienating Franco's regime from broad sectors of Basque opinion, generating a comprehensive feeling of acrimony and tension against the very idea of Spain.'[7]

reading by Philippe Schmitter of the Portuguese dictatorship crisis: 'Liberation by Golpe: Retrospective Thoughts on the Demise of Authoritarian Rule in Portugal', *Armed Forces and Society*, 2 (1975), pp. 21–2.
[6] Preston, *Franco*, pp. 752–3.   [7] Fusi, *Franco*, p. 227.

What followed were the most turbulent years of Franco's dictatorship. Certain members of the Church hierarchy, a hierarchy that had undergone marked renewal after the death of leading champions of the Crusade and National Catholicism, began to divorce themselves from the dictatorship. They were also responding to pressure from a good many priests and Christian communities which, particularly in Catalonia, the Basque Country and the large cities, were calling for a Church that was more open, and committed to social justice and human rights. In 1971, the First Joint National Assembly of Bishops and Priests presented a draft resolution asking for 'pardon because we were slow to act as true ministers of reconciliation among our people, a people divided by a war between brothers'. Two years later, in a document titled 'The Church and the Political Community', the bishops requested a review of the 1953 Concordat and the separation of Church and State. Things were stirring in this Church, which since 1972 had been under the direction of Cardinal Vicente Enrique y Tarancón, and which was attempting to adapt to the requirements of the Second Vatican Council and changes in Spanish society.[8]

The comprehensive transformation of Spain during this decade of development in the 1960s gave rise, as most experts have emphasised, to high levels of conflict that shattered the much-heralded peace of Franco. In 1973, there was a dramatic rise in the number of conflicts, with the province of Barcelona having the most strikes, as had been the case throughout almost all this period. In fact, from 1971 until the death of Franco, the conflicts spread to all the big cities and were radicalised by the repressive intervention of the police, which often led to deaths and injuries in strikes and demonstrations. Police violence also came to the universities, where protests intensified, with a growing number of tiny extreme left-wing organisations appearing on the scene. The response of the Francoist authorities, run by Carrero Blanco, was always a firm hand, repression and unshakeable trust in the armed forces to control the situation.

Public order had been a constant worry for Carrero Blanco from the very moment that he became Franco's right-hand man, although this worry intensified in the final years when the mushrooming of violent incidents harmed the image that had been created of a peaceful regime that always maintained order. On the day that he was killed, 20 December 1973, Carrero Blanco was going to present a document in cabinet in which he revealed his obsession with Francoist Spain's biggest demons, communism and Freemasonry. They were, as had been insistently repeated ever since the victory in the Civil War, the great enemies of Spain, and now, in times

[8] Rafael Gómez Pérez, *Política y religión en el régimen de Franco* (Barcelona: Dopesa, 1976), pp. 170–1.

of development and modernisation, they had infiltrated the Church and universities, the working class and the media.

They would always be met with 'the spirit of our Movimiento, virility, patriotism, honour, decency'. And the recipe Carrero Blanco offered for tackling the infiltration of communism in education was very similar to the one that had been so successful for the military rebels and Francoist authorities during the war and post-war years: 'We need to purge primary and university teaching staff of all enemies of the regime and separate all students who are instruments of subversion from the universities.'[9]

The assassination of Carrero Blanco – who had been prime minister since June of that year – intensified the dictatorship's internal crisis. A few days later, Franco chose Carlos Arias Navarro, the interior minister at the time of Carrero's assassination, as prime minister. He was a living symbol of Francoist repression, from his term as public prosecutor in Málaga after the conquest of the city by Franco's troops in February 1937, to the General Directorate of Security and Ministry of the Interior. Everything pointed to what was known as the 'El Pardo Clique' – with Carmen Polo, her son-in-law Cristóbal Martínez Bordiu, the Marquis of Villaverde, and Antonio Urcelay, Franco's aide – having intervened in the appointment of Arias. The recommendations made by this inner circle had a marked influence in the final years of the dictatorship, a clear sign of the irreparable breakdown of the internal balance of the governing coalition. According to Javier Tusell, the influence of Franco's family was 'a new political factor . . . which had hitherto been practically non-existent' and may be attributed to the 'physical decline of Franco'.[10]

Arias announced his government on 3 January 1974. He dispensed with López Rodó and the technocrats, thereby putting an end to more than fifteen years of Opus Dei presence in the principal ministries, and he called up Falangists from the Movimiento, led by José Utrera Molina. He discounted anyone who might be close to Juan Carlos. Antonio Carro Martínez, as under-secretary for presidential affairs, and Pío Cabanillas, the minister of information, were his right-hand men. Arias Navarro's promise of open government, embodied in his first speech to the Cortes on 12 February, what was called 'the spirit of February', was very soon swallowed up by the repression with which he had to confront the mushrooming of conflicts, the escalation of terrorism and the open defiance from a political opposition that was still too divided. And, as if that were

[9] This aspect is studied in Tusell, *Carrero*, pp. 428–33. In the same book, the author devotes an interesting section on Carrero's concern for public order and its influence on the policies of the final years of Francoism (pp. 377–89).
[10] *Ibid.*, pp. 398–9.

not enough, the desperate economic crisis that accompanied his government from the beginning put an end to the years of economic miracles and prosperity of the dictatorship.

Barely three months after the government was formed, its image was highly tarnished by the house arrest of the bishop of Bilbao, Antonio Añoveros, after his sermon defending the use of the Basque language, and the execution by garrotte of a Catalan anarchist, Salvador Puig Antich, and a Polish national, Hein Chez, accused of having killed a policeman and a Civil Guard. A little later came the Carnation Revolution in Portugal, which overthrew the dictatorship founded in the 1930s by António de Oliveira Salazar and served as a stimulus to the opposition to Francoism, although a revolution of this type, with the army as the main actor, could never occur in Spain. Terrorism hit hard in September that year, with twelve fatalities from a bomb placed in the Cafetería Rolando, close by the General Directorate of Security in the Puerta del Sol, Madrid, in what was ETA's deadliest bombing during the dictatorship.

The 'bunker' (as Franco's closest advisers were known) and the extreme right came down hard. August 1975 saw the passing of a new Anti-Terrorist Act which re-established summary courts martial and was applied retroactively to eleven members of ETA and FRAP (Frente Revolucionario Antifascista Patriótico), a small terrorist group with Marxist-Leninist leanings founded two years earlier, accused of the murder of three policemen. Figures for the proceedings initiated by the TOP, which had been set up in December 1963, clearly show the extent of the escalation of repression: in its final three years (1974, 1975 and 1976), with Arias Navarro in the government, 13,010 cases were processed, almost 60% of all cases during the thirteen years of its existence.[11]

The death sentences passed on these three ETA and eight FRAP members, including three pregnant women, provoked a significant general strike in the Basque Country, protests abroad and petitions for clemency from eminent figures such as Pope Paul VI, Don Juan de Borbón, Queen Elizabeth II and Leonid Brezhnev. Shut up in his bunker, Franco exercised his celebrated right of pardon on six of the condemned and approved the sentences of the other five, who were executed on 27 September 1975. Several governments recalled their ambassadors in protest. The regime's response was the normal one in the these cases: a mass rally in support of Franco in the Plaza de Oriente. In what was to be his last full-scale public appearance, the dictator, in his weak and trembling voice, announced what everyone in Spain saw on television, heard on the radio and can remember

[11] Del Águila, *El TOP*, p. 17. The TOP was operational from December 1963 to January 1977.

from the now historic sequences in the NO-DO report: 'All the evils that have beset Spain and Europe are due to a political Masonic–leftwing plot, in conspiracy with a social communist–terrorist subversion which, while glorifying us, debases them.'

Thirty-nine years had passed since Franco was elevated to the headship of state by his brothers-in-arms. Two months after ordering these executions, the dictator breathed his last. At 10.00 a.m. on 20 November, a few hours after Franco's death had been officially announced, Arias Navarro publicly read out his political testament, the testament of a 'faithful son of the Church' whose only enemies were 'the enemies of Spain'. It is not easy to summarise his legacy, and it is a subject of discussion among historians and the general public. He looked for and achieved the annihilation of his enemies – and if they were enemies of Spain, then there were truly many of them. He governed with terror and repression but he also enjoyed widespread popular support, active from the many who benefited from his victory in the Civil War, and more passive among those who had been conditioned into apathy by fear or from those who were grateful for rising living standards in the last fifteen years of his life.[12]

When he died, his dictatorship was crumbling. The disarray of the so-called reformists or liberalisers searching for a new political identity was now widespread. Many hardline Francoists, whether powerful or not, became lifelong democrats overnight. Most of the surveys conducted in the final years of the dictatorship revealed growing support for democracy, although it was not going to be easy after the dose of authoritarianism that had permeated Spanish society for so long. It was unlikely that Francoism would continue without Franco, but Arias Navarro and his government maintained the apparatus of repression and were able to count on an army that had an institutional memory of having fought in the Civil War, was honed during the dictatorship and was loyal to Franco. This 'unequal and unstable' balance between the authoritarian legacy of Francoism and the pursuit of democracy formed the background of the early years of the transition, which is dealt with in Chapter 13. Let us now examine why this dictatorship lasted so long, and analyse its final crisis.[13]

The dictatorship that lasted forty years

Franco's long and cruel dictatorship was the result of a civil war, and therein lies the exceptional nature of Spain's twentieth-century history

---

[12] A summary of this legacy can be found in Preston, *Franco*, pp. 779–87.

[13] The idea of this 'unequal and unstable' balance is taken from Maravall and Santamaría, 'El cambio político en España', p. 125.

in comparison to that of other European capitalist countries. It is true that Spain, unlike other countries, was not able to enjoy the benefit of an international democratic intervention to prevent an authoritarian outcome at the end of the war, but it is worth emphasising more than anything else the victors' commitment to revenge and their denial of pardon and reconciliation, as well as their willingness to cling on to the power that was won by arms until the last possible moment. As Paloma Aguilar pointed out, the Civil War was 'an event that laid the foundations of Francoism . . . and, as such, was overwhelmingly and obsessively in evidence' throughout the dictatorship.[14]

This myth of foundation, 18 July and the Civil War, Franco's victory and its exclusionary, ultra-nationalist culture of physical and economic repression, determined the identity and nature of Francoism, at least during the early decades, although this terror and violence – as several rigorous studies have shown – were not just a post-war or early-dictatorship phenomenon.

For years and years, the fate of the vanquished lay in the hands of the victors via the various mechanisms and manifestations of terror. Firstly, there was physical, arbitrary and retaliatory violence, with killings on the spot without a trial. It was a continuation of the 'hot-blooded terror' that had dominated the Francoist home front all through the war, and which soon disappeared, although there were still plenty of examples of it between 1940 and 1943. It gave way to the centralisation and control of violence by the military authorities, an institutionalised terror sanctioned by the repressive legislation of the new state. This state of terror, a continuation of the state of war, transformed Spanish society, destroyed entire families and imbued daily life with intimidating and punitive practices. Finally, there were what Conxita Mir calls the 'unaccounted effects' of repression, fear, surveillance, the need for guarantees and a good record, humiliation and exclusion.[15] Thus was established the Francoist state, and thus it continued, although it evolved, displaying kindlier, more selective and more accessible faces, right up to the end.

But for all its evolution and dilution of methods, the dictatorship never tried to rid itself of its bloody origins, the Civil War as its inaugural moment, which it recalled time and again in order to maintain the unity of this broad coalition of victors and to keep the vanquished in misery and humiliation. Repression was not something 'inevitable'. It was the victors who found it totally necessary and considered death and prison to be suitable punishment for the reds. The terror settled old scores, and

---

[14] Aguilar Fernández, *Memoria y olvido de la Guerra Civil española*, p. 64.
[15] Conxita Mir, 'Violencia política, coacción legal y oposición interior', in Glicerio Sánchez Recio (ed.), 'El primer franquismo (1936–1959)', *Ayer*, 33 (1999), pp. 137–9.

ensured that this dictatorship, forged under a blood pact, remained firm. The vanquished were paralysed, cowed, unable to offer any response. The repression was, in the words of Paul Preston, 'a kind of political investment, a bankable terror, which accelerated the process of Spain's depoliticization, pushing the mass of Spaniards into political apathy'.[16]

In addition, it is impossible to understand how the dictatorship lasted so long without taking into account the principal role played by the army – Franco's army – which had been built up in the middle of a civil war and subsequent victory, and which guaranteed the continuity of the dictatorship to the end. It was the Caudillo's generation that held the reins in this army, the ones who really won the war. But it was also a subsequent military generation, represented by Carrero Blanco, consisting of those who had been very young during the war, or who had joined in the immediate post-war years, a very active sector when Franco died, for whom he was 'the providential Caudillo sent by God, who was responsible for saving the *Patria* and who unfortunately', as Carrero wrote on several occasions, 'one day will no longer be with us'.[17]

This army, united around Franco, displayed no cracks. As Franco got older and whenever anyone expressed their concern for the future and his succession, the dictator's response was always the same: the army was always there to defend the regime and guarantee its continuity. He said as much to his cousin Francisco Franco Salgado-Araujo in 1969: 'I have the security of knowing that the three services will always defend the regime, which naturally will evolve to adapt to future world political situations, but will always maintain its essential principles intact.' He said the same when he was recovering from his serious illness in the summer of 1974 and the Falangist Utrera Molina warned him about the liberal threat: 'Don't forget that, in the final analysis, the army will defend its victory.' And Carrero Blanco, in a speech to the High Command in April 1968, warned 'let no one, from outside or in, harbour the slightest hope that they can alter the institutional system in any way, because although the people would never tolerate it, in the final analysis there are always the armed forces'.[18]

And so it was, although in September 1974, in the light of what had happened a few months previously in Portugal with the Carnation Revolution, a group of officers, three majors and nine captains, including

---

[16] Preston, *Franco*, p. 783.   [17] Tusell, *Carrero*, p. 453.

[18] Quoted in Preston, *Franco*, p. 830. The first quote is in Francisco Franco Salgado-Araujo, *Mis conversaciones privadas con Franco* (Barcelona: Planeta, 1976), p. 549. Utrera Molina's quote is in Preston, *Franco*, p. 770. Carrero Blanco's speech is reproduced in Moradiellos, *La España de Franco*, p. 156.

Luis Otero Fernández, Julio Busquets and Gabriel Cardona, founded the Unión Militar Democrática (UMD). They issued a manifesto that spoke of 'going beyond a political system that was born with the Civil War' and of creating a 'new Spain where we can all live in peace and where no one can acquire a monopoly on truth and patriotism, in the knowledge that the armed forces must collaborate in this positive and patriotic task'. The only incident of military dissidence during the dictatorship was unable to get very far. Its ringleaders were arrested the following summer and put on trial when Franco was already dead.[19] Franco's army, which survived him by a few years, complicating the transition to democracy, did not allow these democratic officers to return to their commands, and they were excluded from the October 1977 Amnesty Act, thus demonstrating, as Aguilar points out, 'the ability of the officers to defend their corporate interests even in the face of opposition from most of the political class'.[20]

Franco and his army also had to adapt to changes in the international situation. They dreamt of a new Spanish empire, but in fact, given its scant potential, they had to give up what little remained of it, the African territories, from the protectorate in Morocco to Sidi Ifni and Equatorial Guinea. One after another, they had been released from the mid 1950s onwards, until only the Spanish Sahara was left, a territory over which Spain engaged in open conflict with Morocco just as Franco was coming to the end of his life. Although the loss of the protectorate in 1956 had been a harsh blow for many Spanish officers who had served there, distancing itself from imperial ventures was, in the end, highly advantageous for Francoism, in that it did not experience the serious friction within the army that other dictatorships, such as Portugal, had as a result of colonial conflict.

In fact, the international situation was extremely advantageous for Francoism, from beginning to end. In 1939, with the Republic defeated, the international climate that favoured fascist regimes helped to consolidate the violent counter-revolution that had been initiated with the invaluable aid provided by those very same fascist regimes after the 1936 coup. With Hitler and Mussolini dead, the victorious democratic powers cared little for the fact that down in the south of Europe, in a second-rate country that counted for nothing in the foreign policy of those years, there was still a dictator sowing terror and flouting the most elementary norms of so-called international law. In the words of one senior British diplomat, Franco's

---

[19] Francisco Caparrós, *La UDM: militares rebeldes* (Barcelona: Argos Vergara, 1983); and Javier Fernández, *Militares contra Franco: historia de la Unión Militar Democrática* (Zaragoza: Mira, 2002).

[20] Aguilar, 'Justicia, política y memoria', p. 163.

Spain 'is a danger and inconvenience only to itself'.[21] This is why the most that the democratic powers did after the Second World War was to put pressure on Franco's government because, as Laurence Whitehead rightly pointed out in his study on the international aspects of democratisation, it was one thing to declare Franco a pariah and quite another to lose men in an attempt to overthrow him or provoke a civil war.[22]

Whitehead went on to say that after the Second World War, the west European governments got used to coexisting with a variety of non-democratic regimes and no longer intervened. As the Cold War went on, as long as these governments became reliable allies in the global struggle against the Soviet Union, no pressure would be put on them to become democratised.[23] Thus Franco and his regime were gradually rehabilitated, something that was fully borne out by the Pact of Madrid with the United States signed on 26 September 1953, the signing of the Concordat with the Vatican on 27 August that same year and Spain's entry into the UN in December 1955.

With no outside intervention, Franco's dictatorship, as we have tried to show, was ordained to last. The Catholic Church's contribution to this end was also significant. In no other authoritarian regime in the twentieth century, fascist or otherwise – and there have been a few of varying colour and intensity – did the Church take on such a transparent political or policing responsibility in the social control of the people, not the Protestant Church in Nazi Germany nor the Catholic Church in fascist Italy. And in Finland and Greece, after their civil wars, the Lutheran and Orthodox Churches signed co-operation pacts with the victorious right that defended patriotism, traditional moral values and patriarchal authority in the family. However, in neither of these two cases did they call for vengeance and bloodshed with the intensity and determination of the Catholic Church in Spain. It is true that no other Church had been persecuted with such cruelty and violence as the Spanish Church had been. But with the war over, the memory of so many martyrs reinforced bitterness instead of forgiveness, and encouraged the clergy to take revenge.

Three basic ideas sum up the relationship between the Church and the dictatorship in those decisive early years of Franco's peace. The first was that the Catholic Church became involved and was steeped in the 'legal' system of repression organised by Franco's dictatorship after the Civil

---

[21] Quoted in Javier Tusell, *La dictadura de Franco* (Madrid: Alianza, 1988).

[22] Laurence Whitehead, 'Aspectos internacionales de la democratización', in Guillermo O'Donnell, Philippe C. Schmitter and Laurence Whitehead, *Transiciones desde un gobierno autoritario*, vol. III, *Perspectivas comparadas* (Buenos Aires: Paidos, 1988), p. 30.

[23] *Ibid.*, p. 58.

War. The second, that the Catholic Church endorsed and glorified this violence not only because the blood of its thousands of martyrs cried out for vengeance but also, particularly, because this authoritarian outcome recovered at a stroke the important ground won by secularism before the military coup of 1936 and gave it more primacy and monopoly than it had ever dreamed of. The third idea was that the symbiosis between religion, the *Patria* and the Caudillo was decisive for the survival and maintenance of the dictatorship after the defeat of the fascist powers in the Second World War.

But, as we have seen, the Church hierarchy, Catholicism and the clergy did not remain impervious to the socio-economic changes that, at the beginning of the 1960s, challenged the political apparatus of the Francoist dictatorship. Catholicism had to adapt to this evolution with a series of internal and external transformations that have been analysed by various authors. In the opinion of José Casanova, 'the acute secularization of Spanish society that accompanied the rapid processes of industrialization and urbanization was viewed at first with alarm by the Church's hierarchy. Slowly, however, the most conscious sectors of Spanish Catholicism began to talk of Spain no longer as an inherently Catholic nation to be reconquered anew but rather as *a país de misión* [missionary country]. Catholic faith could no longer be compulsorily enforced from above; it had to be voluntarily adopted through a process of individual conversion.'[24]

This secularisation occurred at the same time as general trends of change that arrived from the Second Vatican Council. Catholic opinion and practice began to be more pluralistic, with young priests who abandoned traditional ideology, workers of the JOC (Juventud Obrera Católica, the Catholic Workers' Youth) and the HOAC (Hermandad Obrera de Acción Católica, Catholic Action Workers' Brotherhood) who militated against Francoism, and Christian sectors who, together with the Marxists, thought about a future society that would follow the defeat of capitalism.

There were priests and Catholics who talked about democracy and socialism and criticised the dictatorship and its most repressive aspects. All this was new in Spain, very new, and it is not surprising that it caused a reaction in broad Francoist sectors, accustomed as they were to a servile Church that kowtowed to the dictatorship. A confidential document of the General Directorate of Security, dated 1966, warned that of the three pillars of the dictatorship, 'Catholicism, the army and the Falange', only the second seemed to be 'solid, united with reality and expectations of continuity', while Catholicism showed signs of division over three problems: 'separatist

---

[24] José Casanova, *Public Religions in the Modern World*, p. 83.

clergy; the internal struggle between conservative and progressive priests; and certain clergy's attitude to the senior Church hierarchy'.[25]

Carrero Blanco called this dissidence of a part of the Catholic Church 'the betrayal of the clergy', because the protective blanket that the dictatorship had given the Church did not deserve this. And to demonstrate the service rendered, 'although it be only of a material kind', proof of how Franco 'wanted to serve God by serving His Church', Carrero Blanco gave some figures: 'Since 1939, the state has spent some 300,000 million pesetas on the building of temples, seminaries, charity and educational establishments, and the sustaining of worship.'[26]

Something was stirring in the Spanish Catholic Church in the final decade of the dictatorship, now that most of the bishops who had blessed the Crusade, and enthusiastically joined in the construction of the New State that rose out of the ashes of the Second Republic, were dead. Enrique Pla y Deniel, for example, the main architect, along with Gomá, of Franco's Church, died in 1968, just before his 92nd birthday. But it would be an exaggeration to conclude that the majority of the clergy, and the Bishops' Conference, set up in 1966, abandoned Francoism in its final years and embraced the cause of democracy. Enrique Vicente y Tarancón, Narcís Jubany and Antonio Añoveros, the Bishops of Madrid-Alcalá, Barcelona and Bilbao respectively, whom the General Directorate of Security classed as being 'the disaffected hierarchy', may have been members, but a great deal of weight in this Church was also carried by bishops such as José Guerra Campos and Pedro Cantero Cuadrado. José María García Lahiguera, the archbishop of Valencia in 1975, who had directed the spiritual exercises of Franco and his wife in 1949 and 1953, summed up in his sermon at Franco's funeral mass in Valencia the three main virtues of the Caudillo whom he admired so much: 'He was a man of faith; given to works of charity, in favour of everyone, since he loved everyone; a man of humility.'[27] And there were many bishops at the time who agreed with this description of Franco.

This is why it would be more correct to say, as Frances Lannon did some time ago, that the Spanish Church had discovered that its interests might have been better protected under a pluralistic regime than a dictatorship that was already showing major symptoms of crisis. The same idea has recently been put forward by William J. Callahan: it was a question

---

[25] Quoted in Carme Molinero and Pere Ysàs, *La anatomía del franquismo: de la supervivencia a la agonía, 1945–1977* (Barcelona: Crítica, 2008), p. 122.

[26] Tusell, *Carrero*, pp. 405–8.

[27] Manuel Garrido Bonaño, *Francisco Franco: cristiano ejemplar* (Madrid: Fundación Nacional Francisco Franco, 1995), pp. 143–52.

of reforming what was necessary but at the same time preserving everything that could be saved from the privileged relationship that the Church maintained with the regime.[28]

When the 'invincible Caudillo' died on 20 November 1975, the Spanish Catholic Church was no longer the monolithic block that had supported the Crusade and the blood-soaked vengeance of the post-war years. But the legacy it inherited from that golden age of privilege was, nevertheless, impressive in education, the propaganda apparatus and the media. What the Church did in the final years of Francoism was prepare itself for the political reforms and the transition to democracy that were on the horizon. Before Franco died, the Church hierarchy had, according to Callahan, drawn up a strategy based on the end of the official confessionality, the protection of the Church's finances and its rights in the matter of education, and recognition of the Church's influence in questions of moral order.[29]

Of course, the Church did undergo great change if we compare it to the other basic pillar of the dictatorship, the army, which identified with Franco and the regime without reserve and sustained it until the end. But in the long-term perspective of the forty years of the dictatorial regime, the Church did much more to legitimise it, to strengthen and protect it, and to cover up its many victims and human rights violations than to fight it. It provided Franco with the mask of religion to disguise his tyranny and cruelty. Without this mask and without the cult that the Church built up around him as *caudillo*, saint and supreme benefactor, Franco would have found it much harder to maintain his absolute power.

However, dictatorships do not rely only on the armed forces, repression or their legitimisation by the ecclesiastical powers to survive. To endure, they need popular support and Franco's long dictatorship, the result of a civil war, was no exception in this respect. Support for Francoism was widespread. It is hardly surprising that the rebels of July 1936, and subsequently the victors of the war, were supported by most of the clergy, the landowners and industrialists most under threat from the republican reforms and claims of the workers; after all, in previous years they had rehearsed various ways of destabilising the Republic. But together with all these people of order, grateful to Franco for re-establishing order and guaranteeing popular discipline, were poor and extremely poor rural

---

[28] Frances Lannon, *Privilegio, persecución y profecía: la Iglesia Católica en España, 1875–1975* (Madrid: Alianza Editorial, 1987), p. 266 (English edition: *Privilege, Persecution and Prophecy: The Catholic Church in Spain 1875–1975* (Oxford University Press, 1987)); and William J. Callahan, *La Iglesia católica en España (1875–2002)* (Barcelona: Crítica, 2002), p. 390.

[29] Callahan, *La Iglesia católica en España*, p. 422.

landowners, the middle classes and urban workers who did not seem to be on the right side of the social barrier.

Except for the most persecuted and repressed, people excluded and forgotten about by the dictatorship, the rest of those who had been on the losing side adapted gradually over the years, with apathy, fear and passive support, to a regime that defended order, authority, the traditional idea of the family, patriotism, belligerent hostility towards communism and inflexible Catholic conservatism. The fact that the Francoist regime lasted so long, wrote Juan Pablo Fusi fairly recently, was due 'to Spain's adjustment to Francoism. Adjustment means adaptation through expediency to a particular situation rather than emotional identification with it.' The 'Spanish people' were not, this author says, 'largely anti-Francoist'. Franco died in his bed 'and the transition to democracy after his death was a reform carried out within the framework of Francoist legality, and what is more it was led by men with Francoist backgrounds'.[30]

Modern states, as well as governing, need to administer societies and guide their economies. In the years following the Second World War, particularly in the 1960s, no regime in the world was impervious to the impulse of 'development'. The same went for the Francoist dictatorship, and the changes brought about by these development policies extended and transformed their social bases. Economic growth was presented as being the direct consequence of Franco's peace, in a campaign orchestrated by Manuel Fraga in the Ministry of Information and Tourism, and embodied in the 'Twenty-Five Years of Peace' celebrations in 1964, which reached every corner of Spain. Two years later, after it was passed by the Cortes, the people were asked to vote in a referendum to approve the Ley Orgánica del Estado, and once again Fraga filled the streets with propaganda and posters which read 'A "yes" vote is a vote for our Caudillo. A "no" vote is to follow the instructions of Moscow.' With all the typical irregularities of the political apparatus of the dictatorship, official figures state that there was a turnout of almost 89%, with 95.9% in favour and 1.79% against. The referendum was used as the most telling proof of popular support for Franco and his regime. Development and the relentless insistency that all this was the result of Franco's peace gave a new legitimacy to the dictatorship and brought about the support – or non-resistance – of millions of Spaniards.

Despite the challenges generated by the socio-economic changes and the rationalisation of the state and the administration, the dictatorship's political power apparatus remained intact, with order guaranteed by

---

[30] Fusi, prologue to the paperback edition of *Franco*, p. 11.

the armed forces, together with the help of Catholic leaders, the Church hierarchy and Opus Dei. In this, Franco's dictatorship was also successful, much more so than the fascist regimes defeated in the world war: it preserved the conditions under which it existed, based on repression and the denial of democracy until the end, until the dictator's final breath.

However, this 'development-obsessed' dictatorship was not able to 'successfully take on board the consequences of economic and social change' that it itself had induced. In other words, there arose a contradiction or split between the socio-economic structures, modified in the 1960s, and the political structure, which failed to become democratised. The socio-economic changes 'necessitated' changes in policy and this is what caused the final crisis, further 'aggravated', as José María Maravall and Julián Santamaría have pointed out, 'by the leadership succession crisis'.[31] Francoism did not end before it did because Franco, who was never prepared to give up his power, was still alive, because the army and the forces of law and order guaranteed his continuity, and because the political opposition, divided and with conflicting interests, was never able to organise a broad, decisive mobilisation against the dictatorship. However, because of these very changes that spread inexorably through Spanish society, it was clear, as many writers have pointed out, that Francoism could not survive Franco. Although the anti-Francoist opposition was incapable of creating a 'broad unitary platform', the conflicts and social movements of those years 'profoundly eroded the dictatorship', conclude Carme Molinero and Pere Ysàs.[32]

The Spain of 1939 was a completely different country from the Spain of 1975. A far-reaching economic and social transformation had brought about major changes in the middle and working classes, as well as in the administration. The trade unions were now no longer agents of social revolution but a vehicle for obtaining democratic freedoms. The Republic, anarchism and socialism disappeared from the list of demands, along with anti-clericalism, anti-capitalism and the problem of agrarian reform, all basic linchpins of social and political struggles in the 1930s. There could be no continuation of Francoism, says Stanley G. Payne, not so much because of the death of Franco as because of the disappearance of the structure of Spanish society and culture upon which it had originally been based in 1939. The traditional patterns of right-wing and left-wing society and culture were things of the past, superseded by modernisation. According to Santos Juliá, democratic values, which before the Civil War were of minority interest

[31] Maravall and Santamaría, 'El cambio político en España', p. 125.
[32] José María Marín, Carme Molinero and Pere Ysàs, *Historia política de España 1939–2000* (Madrid: Istmo, 2001), pp. 228–9.

among the working and middle classes, 'were, in the fifteen years preceding the death of Franco, adopted by them as their major concern'.[33]

There were further factors that made it impossible for Francoism to survive after Franco. The discontinuation of economic and cultural autarky was accompanied, says José Casanova, by the disappearance of 'the traditional and mostly Catholic resistance to Europeanisation'.[34] Integration in the European economy, including the vital tourism sector, became a necessity for the main banking and large business groups. A majority of Spanish people had displayed a 'growing predilection for a change that would lead to democracy without a breakdown of order' – in other words, they wanted neither the continuation of, nor a rupture with, Francoism.[35] Internal struggles between Francoist leaders and defection to the ranks of political reform by a good many of them meant that there could not be a united outcome to the death of Franco. Finally, Francoism survived the 'golden age' of European fascism by several decades, and when Franco died, fascist ideology – embraced by the most hardline sectors of the dictatorship – had lost all its attraction.

In substance, all these interpretations suggest that there was an anachronistic discrepancy between the political structure of the Francoist dictatorship and the values that had been prevalent in broad sectors of Spanish society since the mid 1960s. But these very same sectors of society that called for change were also so steeped in the alleged values of stability, order and peace – or fear, some would say – that they were unwilling to risk hastening the death of Francoism through violence. The dictatorship would end when Franco died. As in many other dictatorships, the presence of the leader was essential for the continuity of his system of control. Since Francoism could not be eliminated by a war, as was the case with Hitler and Mussolini, or by outside pressure, 'it gradually withered over many years'. With Franco barely in his tomb, many of his loyal followers changed their blue uniform for the jacket of democracy. Others wrote their memoirs to exonerate themselves of any personal involvement and, according to Gabrielle Ashford Hodges, to expose the regime's dirty linen, 'in their eagerness to avenge themselves, as it were, for the multitude of humiliations that they had to suffer during their prolonged association with the leader'.

---

[33] Santos Juliá, 'Cambio social y cultura política en la transición a la democracia', pp. 31–2. Payne's quote and the 'superseding' of the traditional patterns of left and right can be found in 'La política', in José Luis García Delgado (ed.), *Franquismo: el juicio de la historia* (Madrid: Temas de Hoy, 2000), p. 280.

[34] José Casanova, 'Las enseñanzas de la transición democrática en España', p. 28.

[35] The argument emphasised by Santos Juliá is based on information taken from Rafael López Pintor, *La opinión pública española: del franquismo a la democracia* (Madrid: CIS, 1982), p. 42.

No one who was really important, and who hoped to carve out a political future, was prepared to prop up the authoritarian edifice any longer.[36]

However, a seamless transition to democracy would not be so easy. More than one generation of Spaniards had grown up and lived with no first-hand experience of democratic rights or processes. Franco's army, united around him and not having suffered a military defeat, as had happened with other dictatorships, found it difficult to assimilate change. The rulers, with Arias Navarro at their head, preserved the political and repressive apparatus of the state almost untouched. Threats of a coup from above and terrorism from below were to make the years following Franco's death particularly difficult. As Preston concludes, 'inevitably, the most dramatic difficulties encountered by Spain's newborn democracy were the direct legacy of Franco's rule'.[37] And this is an idea that ties in with the premise defended in this book: that a prolonged authoritarian government has profound effects on a country's social and political structures, its individual values, and the behaviour and actions of its various social groups.

[36] Gabrielle Ashford Hodges, *Franco: retrato psicológico de un dictador* (Madrid: Taurus, 2001), pp. 352–3.
[37] Preston, *Franco*, p. 787.

Part V

Transition and democracy

13 The Transition

On 20 November 1975, the date of Franco's death, there was no script prepared, no pre-arranged path for an authoritarian dictatorship that had lasted almost four decades to turn peacefully into full democracy, recognised by every country in western Europe. Events followed their particular course but they could have been very different. The end result, at least from 1982 onwards, was a parliamentary monarchy based on a democratic constitution, with a large number of rights and freedoms, the consequence of a complex transition, riddled with conflicts, foreseen and unforeseen obstacles and problems, in the context of economic crisis and political uncertainty.

And all this occurred in barely seven years of history. In the first period, up to the 1977 general election, the political elites left over from Francoism went ahead with a legal reform of the institutions of the dictatorship, pushed from below by the forces of the democratic opposition and a broad social mobilisation of widely varying groups. A second phase was to run from the formation of a democratic parliament, with the power and willingness to draw up a constitution, until the approval of the text that had been agreed on among the main political parties in a referendum held in December 1978. Once the legal framework had been defined, the following years saw the beginning of the development of the rule of law and the organisation of autonomous territories amidst serious problems such as a military backlash, terrorism and the crisis of the party system. When the socialists came to power, following their landslide victory in October 1982, the Transition could be said to have concluded, and democracy was on the way to its consolidation.

Reform

At 12.35 p.m. on 22 November 1975, the strains of the national anthem announced the entrance of Prince Juan Carlos de Borbón y Borbón, dressed in the uniform of a captain general, into the debating chamber of the Cortes. Inside, on their feet, were the members of the government, the *procuradores* (parliamentary representatives) and councillors, and the guests who filled the upper gallery. After he had taken his place of honour on the rostrum, the Speaker of the Cortes and the Councils of the Kingdom and Regency, Alejandro Rodríguez de Valcárcel, proceeded to swear in the new king as set out in the Act of Succession of the Head of State: 'I swear by God and the Gospels to fulfil and uphold the Fundamental Laws of the Kingdom and to maintain loyalty to the guidelines of the National Movement.' Juan Carlos I then gave his first message to the nation in a speech of barely twelve minutes containing reassuring references. The monarch declared the beginning of 'a new stage in the history of Spain', expressed his desire to reach an 'effective consensus of national concord' and his intention to integrate 'all Spaniards', admitted the existence of 'regional anomalies', the need to carry out 'deep refinements', the 'recognition of social and economic rights' and the Crown's commitment to integration in Europe.

But these were not the most warmly applauded phrases. The report in *La Vanguardia* included the duration of the applause that was interspersed throughout the king's speech: thirty seconds when he recalled with respect and gratitude the figure of Franco, ten seconds after invoking the good name of his family and the monarchic tradition of duty and service to Spain, seventeen seconds when he emphasised 'national anomalies and political interests with which every people has the right to organise itself in line with its own singularity'. The longest applause, thirty-five seconds, came after the king referred to the struggle 'to restore the territorial integrity of our country', one of his firmest convictions. The last bout of applause was not for him. At the end of his speech, after the unanimous shout of '¡Viva España!', all the *procuradores* and councillors turned towards the guest gallery to offer an ovation lasting twenty seconds to Carmen Franco Polo, 'a final tribute to Generalísimo Franco'.

In the same newspaper, the cartoonist Máximo San Juan published a cartoon with a map of Spain in embroidered velvet, upon which lay the crown and sceptre, with a caption that was a fair summary of the hopes and concerns of those who, outside Parliament, hoped to find in the first words of the king signs that might be interpreted as being a commitment to change towards a democratic society. The cartoonist thought he noted muscular fatigue in the king's face from all the sleepless nights and the dark shadow of non-transferable responsibility, the 'weight of the purple'. He had been watching Juan Carlos I while he spoke, and the parliamentarians while they listened, all the time noting down the 'whens' and 'whats' of the applause and also the passages greeted with 'eloquent silence' by a chamber with a 'strange' atmosphere. He had hoped to hear 'signs which would herald innovations and words of a new era', the living and innovative 'dawn chorus' of reform and liberty. His article ended with a request for 'some agitation suggesting common expectation' and a little 'collective fortune and democratic niceties', and with the hope that Juan Carlos I 'will have success in being king of all Spaniards, including republicans, however theoretical their beliefs'.

But very few signs of change were to be seen in those days. Franco was still lying in state in the Hall of Columns in the Oriente Palace. According to newspaper reports more than 300,000 people had already filed past his coffin, and clothes shops in Madrid had sold out of black ties. The king's message to the armed forces, 'the safeguard and guarantee' of the Fundamental Laws, once more spoke of the 'virtues of our race' and promised the defence of Spain 'against the enemies of the Fatherland at all costs'. The following day, Sunday 23 November, in the state funeral, the Cardinal Primate of Spain and Archbishop of Toledo, Marcelo González, recalled the 'communion of the sword' that Franco once gave to Cardinal Gomá and the cross that was to be erected over his tomb, two symbols that had played a major role in 'half a century in the history of our nation', and he emphasised the duty to preserve 'Christian civilisation, which Francisco Franco willingly served, without which freedom is a dream' and that man dies 'choked by a vilifying materialism'. Among the foreign leaders, although no representative from the European democracies was present, was General Augusto Pinochet. The Chilean dictator lauded the 'Caudillo who has shown us the path to follow in the struggle against communism', against 'Marxism which spreads hatred and aims to exchange spiritual values for a materialistic and godless world'.

The memory of the Civil War was ever present in the Generalísimo's funeral. The funeral cortège proceeded from the Oriente Palace to the Arco de Triunfo in the Ciudad Universitaria, from where it continued its journey to the Basilica of the Holy Cross in the Valle de los Caídos. The crowd gathered on the esplanade outside sang the 'Cara al sol', 'Oriamendi' (the Fascist and Carlist anthems) and the anthem of the Legion, with a notable presence of groups of ex-combatants, who were to be received by the new king in his first official reception. Inside, behind the great altar, the open tomb was waiting alongside José Antonio's. At a quarter past two in the afternoon, a granite slab weighing one and a half tonnes was placed over the sepulchre, thus ending – in the words of *La Vanguardia* – an 'exceptional period in the life of Spain'. Exceptional, indeed, in terms of its length: almost four decades of dictatorship.[1]

---

[1] *La Vanguardia*, 22, 23 and 25 Nov. 1975.

Figure 9 Franco died on 23 November 1975. The crowd gathered on the streets to see the funeral cortège. Clothes shops in Madrid had sold out of black ties. © Getty Images

What was about to begin had no fixed course or concrete plans. There was as much hope and expectation as ambiguity and uncertainty. Everyone, inside and outside Spain, except those missing the spirit of 18 July (the date of the military uprising), recognised that a new era in history was about to open, in which, in the short or medium term, political change would be inevitable, but there was very little agreement as to how this process might be carried forward, and who its main players and what its scope and final result would be. Obviously, the hard core of the Francoist regime that wielded power showed no signs of embracing democracy and the new head of state did not offer the best reassurances. The PSOE was not surprised at the king's message in the Cortes: in their opinion he renewed his commitment to the dictatorship. In October the previous year, the party congress had emphasised its commitment to a republic. Santiago Carrillo, the leader of the PCE said that the new king would go down in history as Juan Carlos 'the brief'. At that time, the democratic opposition envisaged no scenario other than political rupture, social mobilisation and the forming of a government with no ties to the past.

In his proclamation speech, the king had based his legitimacy on three distinct principles: historical tradition, the fundamental laws of the kingdom and the mandate of the people. But in fact he did not come to the throne through royal succession – the right to the throne still belonged to his father, Don Juan, who was in exile – and the parliamentarians who were listening to him in the Cortes certainly did not represent the will of national sovereignty. So his only legitimacy at that time came from the political testament of the dictator, the Francoist legitimacy still in force. If he wanted to safeguard the monarchy, he had to use it to begin a process of reform, controlled by the institutions, that would bring about the seamless creation of a representative regime that would be acceptable within the European political framework. It would be a difficult balance between continuity and change.

The first step came on 3 December with the appointment of Torcuato Fernández-Miranda as Speaker of the Cortes and president of the Council of the Kingdom. A law professor familiar with the legal structure of the regime, he had been the king's tutor in the 1960s. In the early months of the new reign, he became the monarch's principal adviser, with the mission of promoting the reform of the rules of procedure of the Cortes and preparing the ground for the Council of the Kingdom to present the most suitable candidate for running a future reformist government. This was a role that would certainly not be played by the first prime minister of the monarchy, Arias Navarro, who in fact could easily be considered to be the last one of the dictatorship. His ratification as leader of the executive dashed the hopes of those who were expecting a more positive progressive policy. This was a logical disappointment bearing in mind his role, in previous years, in the persecution of the democratic opposition, the executions of September 1975 and the embarrassing withdrawal from the Spanish Sahara. Arias Navarro had not offered his resignation to the king after his proclamation, convinced that his appointment was for five years, and in his public statements even after the dictator's death he never pretended that he had modified his Francoist convictions. He had neither the will nor the skill to promote a coherent government policy, to specify somehow what he called a 'Spanish-style democracy', with his permanent obstruction to any change that would threaten the survival of the regime's political elite in power.

However, Arias Navarro's entrenched Francoism, with its overtones of the inflexibility of the bunker mentality, was a minor force in the cabinet appointed by the king on 12 December 1975. This cabinet was dominated by politicians who were more suited to the job and with clear reformist leanings, such as the second deputy prime minister and minister of the interior, Manuel Fraga; the minister of foreign affairs, José María de Areilza; justice, Antonio Garrigues; and cabinet affairs, Alfonso Osorio. They were joined by younger men who were to play a leading role in the political history of subsequent years: Adolfo Suárez as minister and secretary general of the Movement, Rodolfo Martín Villa in trade union relations and Leopoldo Calvo Sotelo in trade. The official announcement of 15 December was signed by Fraga. The executive declared its intention of extending citizen freedoms and rights via reforms in the laws governing meetings and assemblies and a new Trade Union Act, and the proposal to 'broaden the base' of the representative institutions by transforming essential parts of the Basic Organic Laws of the state, the Cortes and succession. The end result was the creation of a Cortes consisting of a Congress of 300 deputies elected by universal suffrage and a Senate of 285 seats, 4 for each province plus 25 by royal appointment, 20 from public corporations and another 40 permanent representatives. This programme of reform weakened the democratic potential of the Congress because it allotted to the Senate, with a long mandate of six years, any constitutional initiative and left the appointment of the prime minister as a prerogative of the king and the Council of the Kingdom.

As Ferran Gallego has pointed out, the proposals set out by Fraga and the rest of the reformist ministers, supported by the king, marked the clear limits of the offer of openness to 'all Spaniards'. The political class that had been trained in the administration of the state, with an authority that came directly from the previous regime, considered that it could dispense with the opposition in any situation other than the establishment of informal contact. It had in its hands the guarantee of the repressive apparatus of the system and the anticipated acquiescence of a large part of the public who had been taught to distrust political changes, identified with the values of security and order, and displayed a passive attitude in spite of the expectations of change nurtured by the timid political liberalisation of previous years.[2] Public opinion polls of those years show, as Aguilar has written, that the values that Spaniards considered to be most important, more important even than freedom and democracy, were peace and continuing economic development. She feels that the data show the success of Francoism when transmitting fears about public disorder, the far-reaching consequences of negative propaganda concerning political parties, and the wide-ranging concern that a return to party politics would reproduce the polarisation and violence experienced during the Second Republic and Civil War.[3]

Based on this 'sociological Francoism', the first government of this monarchy hoped to find the way clear to stable reform that would follow the political structures of the regime without the need for elections or dialogue with the opposition: all this, naturally, as long as it could side-step the misgivings of the most inflexible sectors still entrenched in the institutions and take a firm line against the social mobilisation that demanded democratic change. But six months later, at the end of spring 1976, it was clear that the obstacles from above and pressure from below were stronger than expected and the executive's original plan had reached a dead end.

Obstacles arose from above because Suarez's brainchild, the Joint Commission to negotiate the content of the reforms, made up of members of the government and the Movement's National Council, became bogged down in endless meetings that minimised the scope of Fraga's plan and disheartened the reformists. The Francoist implacability of figures such as the deputy prime minister and minister of defence, Lieutenant Colonel Fernando de Santiago, revealed the reactionary nature of the military establishment. In the Cortes, after many delays, the government managed to pass a restrictive Right of Assembly Act in May 1976 and a few weeks later, thanks to its being publicly championed by Adolfo Suarez, the draft bill governing meetings also went through Parliament. But 'totalitarian' parties (a clear reference to the Spanish Communist Party) remained outlawed, and a little later the representatives rejected the indispensable reform of the articles of the Penal Code that declared membership of

[2] Ferran Gallego, *El mito de la transición: la crisis del franquismo y los orígenes de la democracia (1973–1977)* (Barcelona: Crítica, 2008).

[3] Paloma Aguilar Fernández, *Memory and Amnesia: The Role of the Spanish Civil War in the Transition to Democracy* (Oxford: Berghahn, 2004).

political parties an offence. It was plain to see that the first government's unchanging attitude had peaked and that with Arias Navarro – distancing himself increasingly further from the king – at its head there was not going to be any progress as far as reform was concerned.

As far as pressure from below was concerned, Nicolás Sartorius and Alberto Sabio have emphasised that what really unblocked the situation, brought down Arias Navarro's government, and removed the obstacles that impeded the transition to a system of freedoms was the growing, powerful social pressure exerted by a not inconsiderable proportion of the Spanish population.[4] Opposition did not come just from the ranks of the workers' movement. Alongside the mobilisations that originated in the workplace, there were a great many actions carried out by social sectors, collectives and organisations of various types that had sprung up in the final years of Francoism: student organisations, residents' associations, the grass-roots sectors of the Church, intellectuals and professionals, agricultural labourers and smallholders, and other similar groups that represented new social movements such as feminism, pacifism or environmentalism. A decisive outbreak of democratic protest that in the early months of 1976 affected the whole of Spain. Official data from the Interior Ministry acknowledge that there were 17,455 strikes, 1,672 demonstrations and 283 sit-ins in the first quarter alone. The foreign minister, Areilza, spoke of 'squally gusts' to refer to the wave of strikes, demonstrations, sit-ins, assemblies, wage demands, petitions for political amnesty and freedom, and demands for regional self-government, with increasing presence in the media, that brought home to the elites who monopolised power, as well as the king, that the situation was slipping through their fingers and they might lose everything unless a more serious and decisive reformist programme was put into place.

In the universities, where there were over half a million students enrolled, there was an increase in the number of demonstrations, assemblies, solidarity campaigns with strikers, politically flavoured cultural and festive rallies, and sit-ins in favour of amnesty, which in many cases ended up with police baton charges, raids, house searches, disciplinary proceedings and the temporary closure of university premises. The PCE was the primary mover of this student unrest, with a notable influence in some universities of more radical activist groups with anarchistic, Trotskyite or Maoist leanings, such as the Movimiento Comunista de España (MCE), the Organización Revolucionaria de Trabajadores (ORT) or the Partido del Trabajo de España (PTE).

---

[4] Nicolás Sartorius and Alberto Sabio, *El final de la dictadura: la conquista de la democracia en España* (Madrid: Temas de Hoy), 2007.

There was evidence of the political influence of the PCE – in Catalonia's case, that of the PSUC – in many neighbourhood associations and *barrio* collectives too, but the citizens' movement was now spreading to women's associations, youth centres, cultural groups and professional bodies with a broader political profile. They were united over common issues such as the housing problem, the lack of public services, the environment or the cost of living. Urban protests, originating in the outlying areas, soon broadened their scope to include political issues such as demands for amnesty and democratic town and city councils. The neighbourhood movement acted as a political awareness platform that extended the social bases of the opposition and provided venues for meetings and militant activist groups. It was also an exceptional means of promoting political awareness among women, who were the key elements of the neighbour-hood association structure. As well as the protests against price rises and the problems of daily life in the *barrios*, there were mobilisations of a purely feminist nature, promoted by the Movimiento Democrático de Mujeres, which combined struggles for equality and an end to sex discrimination with campaigns supporting political prisoners and calls for amnesty.

It was in the *barrios* of the big cities that the *curas obreros* or 'anti-establishment' clergy, the bane of the Francoist regime in its final years, were to be found. Most of the Catholic Church hierarchy maintained the traditional conservative tenets that Franco, exalted since the first day of the Crusade in 1936, had benefited from and bestowed so many privileges upon. But in this self-same Church there was also a moderate liberalist sector, led by the Archbishop of Madrid and president of the Bishops' Conference, Cardinal Tarancón, and a smaller more progressive group, with leanings towards grass-roots organisations such as the HOAC and the JOC, which were motivated to move on from denouncing social injustice to demanding a transition to democracy. There were religious who became involved in amnesty commissions, condemning torture, protecting Comisiones Obreras and allowing Church property to be used for workers' sit-ins as well as in supporting agricultural action. This sector stood out for the collective actions of smallholders, who protested about agricultural prices and the absence of rural worker rep-resentation via local concentrations, road-blocks, tractor protests and marches on Madrid organised by the Comisiones Obreras del Campo, the Federación de Trabajadores de la Tierra-UGT and the Uniones de Agricultores y Ganaderos all grouped together within the Coordinadora de Agricultores y Ganaderos (COAG).

We see farmers, neighbourhood associations, grass-roots Christians, students and, above all, workers. As well as it being the right time politically, there were economic and structural factors that explain the framework of these labour mobilisations. In the winter of 1975 the first harsh effects of international economic recession caused by the 1973 oil crisis were beginning to be felt. The wage freeze and devaluation of the peseta did nothing to halt the galloping inflation that exacerbated even more a particularly delicate situation for workers, shortly before the negotiation and renewal of some 2,000 collective agreements. Labour disputes mushroomed from December 1975 onwards, not just because of the number of strikes and workers involved, but also because of the expansion of the protests throughout all production sectors the length and breadth of Spain. It was a social mobilisation that had not been seen for nearly forty years, basically structured around CC.OO., the most influential workers' organisation, with solid foundations in the vertical syndicalism of the regime and a broad network of representatives in all the major companies. The political authorities, civil governors and police were especially concerned that, along with labour demands and protests over the cost of living, other demands of a clearly political nature were emerging, such as the demand for free trade unions and rights of assembly, requests for the rehiring of sacked workers and the release of prisoners, sympathy strikes, symbolic strikes to protest against national events, hunger strikes and sit-ins in churches and sports halls, and the dissemination of information on how to organise assemblies, a breeding ground for the emergence of trade union leaders and a foretaste of democratic political culture.

A turning point was the escalation of strikes registered in Madrid in January 1976, which spread from the metal and building sectors to all public sectors, with more than 350,000 workers on strike. The strike phenomenon was particularly intense in Asturias, Catalonia, the Basque Country and Andalucía and in the urban areas of Aragón, Galicia and Valencia, involving sectors such as transport and construction which extended throughout Spain, to reach small cities and towns that had hitherto not taken part in social disputes.

Most of these collective protest actions, although usually without any violent incidents, were still not permitted by the legislation then in force. This was inevitable given a scenario with no rights of expression or assembly. In this respect, the policy of public order directed by Fraga was of a clearly discretional nature, with nods of tolerance to some rallies organised by the UGT and PSOE and implacable persecution of actions promoted by CC.OO. and the PCE, a deliberate strategy of the Interior Ministry aimed at isolating the communists and preventing their co-operation with the social democrats and other more moderate opposition groups. It has to be remembered that the repressive machinery of Francoism was still operating in all its facets. In Spain in 1976 there were more than 1,000 political prisoners, the members of the Brigada de Investigación Político-Social were working to full capacity, the TOP examined almost 5,000 cases carrying prison sentences, administrative penalties and heavy fines, and censorship was strictly imposed via government suspensions, newspaper seizures and disciplinary proceedings from the Dirección General de Prensa.

'The streets are mine', Fraga used to say, and the streets saw repeated police baton charges, the shutting down of business premises, mass arrests, arbitrary imprisonment, and ill-treatment and torture in the barracks and police stations – and machine-gun fire. A worker was killed in Elda in February, there were fatalities in Tarragona, San Adrián de Besós and Basauri and, most serious of all, there was the tragic outcome of the police charge on the Church of Saint Francis of Assisi in Vitoria: five workers killed and several dozen wounded. This massacre in Vitoria on 3 March unleashed a wave of protests all over Spain against the impunity and brutality of the repression and finally discredited the empty promises of Arias Navarro's government to introduce reform. The mobilisations of solidarity with political prisoners and victims of the violence also denounced the permissiveness, or even the connivance, of the police with the violence of right-wing extremist radicals such as the gangs of the Guerrilleros de Cristo Rey or the young militants of Fuerza Nueva. The bloodiest events took place in May on Montejurra, a mountain in Navarre, the traditional destination of Carlist pilgrimage, where a far-right group whose numbers were swelled by foreign gunmen, followers of the conservative extremists led by Sixto Borbón, opened fire on the followers of Carlos Hugo and his 'self-management socialism', killing two people and wounding thirty others.

By then, protests against repression and mobilisations calling for political amnesty had closed the gap between the ideas of the Junta Democrática led by the PCE and the Plataforma de Convergencia Democrática, headed by the PSOE, who since the end of March had come together under the name of Convergencia Democrática, popularly known as the 'Platajunta'. The situation was untenable for the government and also for the king, and in demonstrations, the recurring chant was 'Juan Carlos, listen to us.' Forced by circumstances, the king called Arias Navarro on 1 July to order him to resign and to form a new cabinet headed, to everyone's surprise, by Adolfo Suárez.

The president of the Council of the Kingdom, Fernández-Miranda, played a major role in helping Suárez to be included in the shortlist submitted to Juan Carlos I for the election of a new prime minister. Suárez was a young man, with no personal enemies or dark past, a Catholic Falangist with good contacts from his previous posts as head of Radio Televisión Española and secretary general of the Movement. He had no obvious affiliation with any sector of the regime and he possessed the necessary amount of courage, personality, pragmatism and clear-headedness to adapt to the circumstances, just the virtues needed to control the reformist elite of the regime ready to take up the reins of a process that was to be inevitable, a process that would simultaneously set the country on the road to democracy and give credibility to the monarchy.

And he wasted no time in taking the initiative. On 6 July, Suárez appeared on television to express his 'firm resolve to obtain a modern democracy' respecting 'the free will of the majority of Spaniards'. The military ministers continued to serve in his government, but they were joined by moderate young reformists with a Christian Democratic profile, who had been brought in from the second tier of the administration, such as Landelino Lavilla, Alfonso Ossorio, Marcelino Oreja, Fernando Abril and Leopoldo Calvo Sotelo. In mid July, the government programme promised dialogue, political pluralism and a commitment to hold a refer-endum to adapt 'the laws to the national reality' and to call a general election within a year. There was no time to lose. On 19 July, the Cortes passed the reform of the Penal Code that brought about the legalisation of certain political parties, and on 30 July the government issued a partial but significant amnesty decree and initiated contacts with leaders of the democratic opposition, including nationalists such as Jordi Pujol and socialists such as Felipe González and Tierno Galván, but not with the communists who were still considered to be 'inapplicable for legalisation'.

The short period between September and December 1976 was later seen as being highly significant, and the speed of events was a factor that clearly favoured the government's plans. By the end of August, the political reform draft bill was being discussed in cabinet. On 8 September Suárez presented it to the military establishment at a meeting from which the military high command, practically all of them with extremist right-wing leanings, emerged convinced the PCE would not be legalised. A week later, General Fernando de Santiago's marked opposition to the legal-isation of trade unions brought about his dismissal as first deputy prime minister and minister of defence and his retirement from the army. His post was occupied by General Manuel Gutiérrez Mellado, one of the few officers with liberal and reformist leanings, and Gutiérrez Mellado initi-ated a difficult policy of repostings and promotions in an effort to remove the most violent reactionaries from positions of responsibility in the forces of order.

Greater tolerance from the government enabled the celebration on 11 September in Sant Boi de Llobregat of the *Diada*, Catalonia's public holiday, with the three-fold demand for freedom, political amnesty and a statute of autonomy, and it also enabled most political and trade union groups certain freedom to operate throughout Spain. The most turbulent situation was to be found in the Basque Country, with serious confrontations between the police and demonstrators, mobilisations calling for political amnesty, a general strike that was called on the first anniversary of the shootings of 27 September and tension caused by the series of murders committed by ETA, twenty-six during that year. The most important political force, the PNV, was part of the Platajunta, which had changed its programme from 'democratic rupture' to 'an agreed rupture', two opposing concepts in theory which were misunderstood by the militants and local infrastructures that had been most involved in the anti-fascist struggle and in a period of open mobilisation after the death of Franco. The Platajunta's moderate strategy was concerned more with the conditions of future negotiation with the government than in maintaining protest actions, and these became fewer and less intense. Rapprochement with the rest of the democratic opposition groups became reality on 23 October with the signing of a pact with various regional co-ordinators of Catalonia, Valencia, Galicia, the Canary Islands and the Balearic Islands. The Plataforma de Organismos Democráticos that was hatched by this agreement called for the summoning of Constituent Cortes, a complete political amnesty, the legalisation of all parties and trade unions, the granting of statutes of autonomy and the dissolution of Francoist institutions. There was no longer any demand for a referendum to decide on the configuration of the state, a plebiscite on the continuity of the monarchy that would never again be proposed.

Naturally, Suárez was not prepared to lose the initiative in this process or the ability to establish the rhythm and rules; with him it was always 'from the law to the law', the maxim inspired by Torcuato Fernández-Miranda. The political reform draft bill was given its mandatory presentation to the National Council of the Movement, which issued a non-binding critical report and succeeded in eliminating the preamble. The debate in the Cortes began on 16 November, four days after the general strike called by the UGT, the Unión Sindical Obrera (USO) and CC.OO. The three trade union groups, which formed the Coordinadora de Organizaciones Sindicales (Co-ordinator of Trade Union Organisations) managed to call out between 1 million and 2 million workers to demand freedom, political amnesty and wage rises, but they failed to paralyse the country and cause problems for the government on the eve of the debate in which the Francoist deputies would be acquiescing to their own disappearance. And that is what they did. On 18 November, 435 of the 531 deputies voted in favour of the Reform Act. And for that reason, these Cortes were called the *hara-kiri* parliament, because they had willingly brought about their dismantling, as if they had agreed to commit collective political suicide.

But it was not to be. In order to overcome the first obstacle, the 183 deputies belonging to Alianza Popular (AP), the coalition of influential Francoists recently created by Fraga, the government had to accept significant modifications. The draft bill envisaged the setting up of a Cortes with two chambers, a Congress of Deputies with 350 members elected by universal suffrage and a Senate with 250 representatives, 41 of them appointed by the king and the rest coming from 'territorial entities'. After tough negotiations, AP managed to establish the province as the constituency unit, a minimum number of deputies per province and also a minimum percentage of votes to secure a seat. These measures favoured the creation of a two-party system and gave greater weight to the conservative vote in the smaller provinces as against more populated areas. Many deputies might have thought that they would return to Parliament elected by the provinces of origin, receiving the benefit of government support or as royally appointed senators. Others were convinced by promises of rewards, pledges and public office. As Martín Villa confessed to the historian Charles Powell, 'we did everything short of going to bed with them'. Beyond the pressures and personal handouts, the most sensible deputies took to heart Suárez's warning regarding 'the non-viability of a regressive posture', the risk that they were taking, if they rejected the project, of facing a far harsher proposal in the near future that would not give so much consideration to their Francoist past and would jeopardise their privileges and assets.[5]

This success in the Cortes was echoed at the polls a few weeks later in the referendum held on 15 December. The government's electoral slogan, 'To Silence Violence', attracted a large turnout from a population that still had the memory of a traumatic past, the Civil War, in their minds and underlined the merits of peace, order and stability. The high turnout, 77% – with the exception of the Basque Country, where it was only 54% – showed the limitations of the democratic opposition, which had campaigned for abstention. The 'yes' votes topped 94% of the poll, overwhelming support for the government that it needed to exploit in order to obtain a favourable result in the forthcoming general election set for June 1977. It would be playing with advantage, but with conditions that would need to be accepted by everyone, that would have international backing and would ultimately give democratic legitimacy to a political elite and a monarchy that were leftovers from the dictatorship.

[5] Charles Powell, *España en democracia, 1975–2000* (Barcelona: Plaza & Janés, 2001), p. 168.

In December 1976, the PSOE was able to hold its first congress inside Spain without any problem, and Santiago Carrillo, the leader of the PCE, ventured to call a press conference. His arrest, and almost immediate release, plus the government's refusal to negotiate with the *comisión de los nueve* (the 'commission of the nine', the delegation of the democratic forces) over the presence of a communist representative, revealed the government's hesitancy in taking the necessary steps to give legal approval to the existence of the PCE. The situation began to deteriorate as a result of what was called the *semana negra* (black week) in Madrid, between 23 and 28 January. During that week the Grupos de Resistencia Antifascista Primero de Octubre (the Anti-fascist Resistance Groups of 1 October – GRAPO), the armed wing of a communist splinter group, who had previously kidnapped the president of the Council of State, Antonio de Oriol, also kidnapped the president of the Supreme Military Justice Council, Lieutenant General Emilio Villaescusa, and they murdered three policemen. The week also saw the death of a student at the hands of a group of right-wing extremists, the subsequent death of a young woman hit by a smoke canister at a demonstration and some right-wing extremist gunmen bursting into the office of some labour lawyers linked to CC.OO., resulting in five dead and four seriously wounded. This massacre in the Calle Atocha had precisely the opposite effect to the one the perpetrators were pursuing. There was no clamour in army circles for a state of emergency, the government kept calm and the communists began to receive countless demonstrations of solidarity and public recognition for the order and calm they were able to display during the massive demonstration to mourn the murdered lawyers, with hundreds of thousands of marchers silently proceeding through the streets of Madrid, holding red carnations and with clenched fists in the air.

That afternoon of 26 January 1977, as Santos Juliá has remarked, the PCE's progress to legitimacy advanced more than in the previous two years put together. A sector of Spanish public opinion changed its perception of the Communists, and the government realised that a general election that did not include them, the party that was the most visible symbol of the struggle against the dictatorial regime, would cast an indelible shadow on the democratic nature of the poll and become a millstone around the neck of the government that would be taking power after the election.[6] The government therefore offered the PCE legality in exchange for increased legitimacy for itself. On 27 February, Suárez had a secret meeting with Carrillo and informed him of the possibility of legalisation in exchange for

[6] García Delgado and Jiménez, *La historia de España del siglo XX: la economía*, pp. 237–9.

acceptance of the Crown and the symbols of the state. On 9 April, during the Easter holidays, the government made use of an improvised opinion handed down by the judicial authorities to authorise the inscription of the PCE. The fearfully expected reaction from the military 'bunker' came two days later with the resignation of the minister of the navy, Admiral Gabriel Pita da Veiga, and a communiqué of disapproval from the Higher Army Council, accepting, however, that the legalisation of the PCE was a *fait accompli* on the grounds of 'national interests of a higher order'. Carrillo did not waste a second. In its first meeting as a legal party, the Central Committee of the PCE, despite the protests of certain Basque and Catalan communist leaders, voted by a large majority to recognise the parliamentary monarchy, and Carrillo appeared in a press conference in front of the flag 'of all Spaniards', promising to defend the unity of the 'common Fatherland'.[7]

With the first problem out of the way, the process of legal reform that was to conclude with the holding of a general election did not encounter too many obstacles. The government had already dismantled the TOP in January, published the decree permitting the inscription of political associations in February, and throughout March and the first few days of April passed other major provisions governing the right to join a trade union, with the immediate legalisation of CC.OO., the UGT and USO, and election regulations which recognised the proportional nature of the election of deputies to Congress but which favoured the theoretically more conservative rural provinces. As Miguel Herrero de Miñón, then the technical secretary of the Ministry of Justice, confessed in his memoirs, hectares had better representation than citizens.[8]

Nor was there any serious resistance to the dismantling of the regime's institutions. Between April and June, the 20,000 government employees of the Organización Sindical and the 7,000 in departments of the Movimiento were absorbed by the administration, with the retention of all their rights, and with no mention, naturally, of the possible purges. The final symbolic gestures occurred on 22 April, with the public declaration of the European Parliament's recognition that Suárez's promises of democracy had been kept; on 14 May, with Don Juan's official waiving of his dynastic rights; and on 21 June, when the last government-in-exile of the Republic, which no one remembered any more, decided to dissolve. The past was still an uncomfortable memory, but it was not an insurmountable obstacle. Everyone was looking to the most immediate future, the general election.

[7] Powell, *España en democracia, 1975–2000*, pp. 180–1.
[8] Miguel Herrero de Miñón, *Memorias de estio* (Madrid: Temas de Hoy, 1993).

Towards the Constitution

On 15 June 1977, 18.5 million Spanish men and women, aged 21 or over, 78.7% of the adult population, turned out to vote at the polls. Very few had remembered doing so freely before then. More than forty years had gone by since the last general election held in February 1936. Of the thirty or so political parties that had won seats then, only four were to be represented in the 1977 Cortes: the PSOE, PCE, PNV and ERC. Some historians have related the support for the PSOE in 1977 with the areas where the Frente Popular won in 1936, and the election majority for Suárez's Unión de Centro Democrático (UCD) with the regions in which the CEDA had held sway. Yet not too much should be read into these comparisons. Spanish society of 1977 had little in common with the society that existed on the eve of the Civil War, although the traumatic memory of that conflict was never absent during the years of transition. However, it is worth pausing a moment to analyse the 1977 election results because they began to set the pattern of Spanish democracy's party system and because the parliamentarians who were elected that day, although it was not preordained, were to be the ones responsible for debating and drafting a new constitution for Spain.

Javier Tusell has studied in detail the origin and progress of the political parties that sat in the chambers of the Cortes after election day. The majority, in percentage of votes, 34.4%, and number of seats, 165, was won by the UCD, led by Adolfo Suárez. It was really an 'archipelago party' formed five weeks before the election and made up of fifteen distinct organisations with fewer than 2,000 affiliates between them, and by politicians of widely differing origins. Almost half the candidates who stood, known as 'independents', came from moderate sectors of Francoism, the Partido Popular (PP) created by Areilza and Cabanillas and other smaller groups such as the Christian Democrats lumped together under Fernando Álvarez de Miranda, the Liberals under Ignacio Camuñas and Joaquín Garrigues, and Fernández Ordóñez's social democrats. The UCD votes came mainly from the rural zones and urban middle classes, the demographic that might be said to have been represented by 'sociological Francoism'. Suárez was able to count on the power of Televisión Española (TVE), with which he was very familiar, and on the control of civil and provincial governments and town and city councils.[9] But there is no denying that he was the politician with the highest rating in all the opinion polls, that he was

---

[9] Javier Tusell, *Spain, from Dictatorship to Democracy* (Chichester, UK: Wiley-Blackwell, 2011).

considered to be the king's man, and that in his desire to occupy the political centre he was aided by the reformist and moderate direction taken by his government.

The next most popular party was the PSOE, with 29.3% of the vote and 119 deputies. In December 1976, when it held its 27th Congress, it was a party with fewer than 10,000 militants that could not boast that it had been at the forefront of the anti-Francoist struggle, and that clung to a Marxist, anti-capitalist and republican programme. However, leaving aside any dogmatic and radical tendencies, the practical approach of its leaders, particularly Felipe González, had the adroitness and flexibility required for adapting to the government's reformist initiatives, gaining international backing, absorbing other socialist groups and winning the support of the majority of voters in the urban and industrial areas who identified the party with a commitment to liberty and social change.

To the left of the PSOE, the PCE obtained 9.3% of the votes and nineteen seats, disappointing results in view of their pre-election expectations, with clear support from the trade union and university sphere; these results would have been even worse had it not been for the solid implantation of the PSUC in Catalonia. Unlike the renovating image offered by the young socialist leaders, with no link to the Civil War generation, the old communist leadership seemed to be anchored in the past, without a realistic programme to tackle society's problems, and increasingly more alienated from the concerns and interests of its grass-roots membership, its militants.

To the right of the UCD was Alianza Popular, the party founded by Fraga to cater for the leading figures of the Francoist regime. AP won 8.8% of the votes and sixteen seats. Of these, thirteen were occupied by former Franco ministers. Arias Navarro stood for the Senate as the candidate for Madrid, but was not elected. It was the image of the past, which ill matched the democratic expectations aroused during the election campaign, and was too much of a millstone for Fraga's temperamental character to compete with the modern and open image displayed by Suárez.

The rest of the parties, with the exception of the Catalan and Basque nationalists, made no showing whatsoever in the election. Jordi Pujol's Pacte Democràtic per Catalunya obtained 2.8% of the vote and eleven seats, and the PNV gained 1.7% of the vote and eight deputies. The government's most pressing problem was going to be the situation in the Basque Country. Although the UCD was only the fourth party in terms of seats in Catalonia, it was able to envisage future agreements with broad sectors of moderates such as those represented by Pujol and with a figure like Josep Tarradellas, who possessed the historical legitimacy of his presidency of the Generalitat in exile. However, in the Basque Country the UCD failed to win any seat in Guipúzcoa, paying for Suárez's political error in refusing to legalise the *ikurriña* (the Basque national flag) and restore the autonomy agreements made with Vizcaya and Guipúzcoa. Ferran Gallego has rightly pointed out that the Basque problem had been 'festering' ever since the beginning of the Transition. ETA terrorism, responsible for twenty-eight deaths during 1977, was not the only problem. Suárez's government had lost the initiative in a setting of constant social mobilisation, labour disputes, demands for political amnesty and autonomy, and instances of police brutality – an initiative that it would never get back. As Gallego said, it was 'an issue that thirty years later may still be considered to be the principal cause of the failure of the reformist project'.[10]

The significant presence of the nationalist parties in the Cortes was to some extent due to the electoral system, which over-represented votes concentrated within the same constituency. But the parties that came out best from the election were undoubtedly the UCD and PSOE, which with 63% of the popular vote secured 86% of the seats, a marked deviation due to the strict proportionality-criterion correction mechanisms. Meanwhile, Tierno Galván's Partido Socialista Popular (PSP) failed to win a seat because it did not obtain the required provincial percentage even though it enjoyed wide popular support alongside other parties who did win seats, such as the PCE, AP and the PSP. The number of deputies assigned to each constituency gave priority to the vote in the small provinces – to be elected a deputy for Barcelona or Madrid it was necessary to have 100,000 more votes than in Soria, for example – and the D'Hondt electoral system favoured the formation of majorities. The electoral measures adopted at that time on a temporary basis became embodied and established as firm rules that clearly benefited the major parties which were well structured and financed and were subject to the closed-list system. It was a model that some people have called an 'imperfect two-party' system and others a 'polarised and plural' or 'multi-party with a bipolar tendency' system. Nevertheless, the UCD failed to win an absolute majority in the summer of 1977, and Suárez's new government, made up of the leading lights of the electoral coalition, had to govern in minority, forcing him to look for ad hoc alliances and negotiate a broad consensus in the light of the major problems and challenges facing him: agreement on a general amnesty law, channelling demands for autonomy from the various regions and nationalities, tackling the economic crisis and drawing up a constitution.

[10] Gallego, *El mito de la transición*, pp. 457–60.

The first issue, political amnesty, was addressed on the very day that the Cortes opened and was to dominate the first parliamentary debates. Most of the political forces shared the conviction that a general amnesty was an indispensable step towards the process of drafting of a constitution under conditions unfettered by the long shadow of the Civil War and dictatorship. The partial pardon granted by the king in November 1975 had been an isolated gesture that failed to put an end to the arrests and incarcerations. Just over six months later, in June 1976, the amnesty granted by Suárez's first government excluded any politically motivated act that might harm 'people's lives or integrity' and ruled out any reinstatement of condemned military personnel to their posts, a clear concession to army pressure to keep out UMD officers. The Amnesty Act passed on 15 October 1977 by all the parliamentary groups, except for the Alianza Popular, which abstained, included all politically motivated acts, 'whatever their result', and also 'any crimes or offences which might have been committed by the authorities, public servants and agents of public order during the investigation and prosecution of the acts included in this law'. ETA and GRAPO prisoners were released and the state renounced any future opening of judicial inquiries into, or holding anyone responsible for, 'crimes committed by public servants against human rights'.

The Amnesty Act, as Aguilar has pointed out, was the clearest and most explicit expression of the unspoken agreement that was made between the ex-Francoist elite and the opposition forces in order to prevent the thorniest of pasts from becoming the subject of political debate. This unwritten pact was founded upon an interpretation of the Civil War as being a fratricidal tragedy with collective responsibility, with heinous crimes on both sides, an insanity that must never be repeated. This idea, which began to take shape in the 1950s around the myth of national reconciliation, was shared by the majority of Spaniards, at least those who in December 1976 and June 1977 had advocated a moderate and cautious transition to democracy. The political culture of the people and public discourse of the parliamentarians were influenced by the traumatic memory of the war and the fear that a similar situation would be repeated in the middle of a process dominated by the uncertainty caused by the economic crisis, social conflict, terrorism and anxiety about threats of military involvement.[11]

It was a political pact of amnesia of the past, agreed on by the parliamentary elites, and a social and economic pact, also negotiated from above, signed by the leaders of the main parties in the Moncloa, the prime

[11] Aguilar Fernández, *Memory and Amnesia*.

minister's official residence. Since Franco's death, neither Arias Navarro's government, nor the subsequent one under Adolfo Suárez, dared, in the middle of a permanent climate of uncertainty and instability, to initiate an economic plan that would put a brake on the recession caused by the international oil crisis, aggravated in Spain's case by the structural deficiencies and fragility of its production system. Partial, temporary measures, such as subsidised energy consumption and wage rises, might have been able to alleviate popular unrest in the short term, but they merely accelerated the rise in prices, increased unemployment and the foreign deficit, unprotected due to the fall in foreign investment and the reduction of foreign exchange from tourism and emigration. Emigration abroad was no longer an option for the almost 700,000 workers who had left the primary sector between 1973 and 1977, and the Spanish industrial structure was unable to absorb this demand.

The summer of 1977 saw the foreign deficit continue to grow alarmingly, inflation was around 40%, and an unprecedented unemployment rate of some 7% was by now more than the OECD average. The government's economic policy, directed by an eminent university professor, Enrique Fuentes Quintana, combined a package of urgent measures, such as the devaluation of the peseta, with contacts with the social partners in a bid to obtain a far-reaching social pact. The misgivings of the trade unions and the recently constituted Confederación Española de Organizaciones Empresariales (Spanish Employers' Confederation – CEOE) led Suárez to make a change of contacts and to negotiate a political pact with the leaders of the main parties. After weeks of protracted meetings, what were called the Moncloa Pacts were signed on 25 October and were passed in Parliament soon afterwards. The agreements meant, in essence, the acceptance by the forces of the left of a policy of moderation and wage freezes to put a brake on inflation in exchange for a series of promises to initiate fiscal, legal, institutional and social reforms. These included the introduction of a property tax and the implementation of the Impuesto sobre la Renta de las Personas Físicas (income tax, IRPF), aimed at fiscal harmony with Europe, a reform of the financial system, the control of public expenditure, a review of the Military Justice Code, parliamentary control of the media, measures to put a brake on speculation and encourage house purchase, the extension of free education, an increase in unemployment benefit, the budgetary reinforcement of Social Security and the establishing of a new framework of labour relations via a Workers' Statute that would not be passed until 1980.

The Moncloa Pacts met two of the main objectives fairly quickly: a marked fall in foreign deficit and the swift reduction of inflation to 16% in 1978. However, unemployment was still rising (10% of the active population in 1978), there was no reduction in the number of strikes, and the upturn in the oil crisis in 1979 diminished some of the improvements that had been made. A worse fate was to befall the structural reforms that had been promised. Without the participation of the trade unions, which had been excluded from the negotiations, and with no body set up to oversee the promises, many of them were shelved until better times came along, and others suffered savage cuts. Fuentes Quintana resigned his post as deputy prime minister in February 1978, when he saw that the government was unwilling to implement the agreements reached or was prepared to undermine them in practice. A good example of this was the progressive nature of the IRPF, which was distorted by the reliefs on higher incomes and the limitations of the inspection service, which was incapable of discovering tax evasion or of controlling major fiscal fraud.

The success of the Moncloa Pacts, as Charles Powell has pointed out, was more a political than a social or economic one. The parties of the left accepted that in future all their claims would be 'bound by the constraints of the market economy'; meetings of the political leaders soothed old enmities, with informal contacts between Carrillo and former ministers of Franco; and the government obtained the legitimacy and consensus it needed to promote unpopular austerity measures and, perhaps most importantly at that time, enough stability and detente to embark on the drafting of a constitution.[12]

Another problem yet to be tackled, and which could not wait any longer, was the demands for autonomy from the Basque and Catalan nationalists. It was impossible to ignore the pictures of the impressive demonstration of 11 September 1977 in Barcelona, a *Diada* (Catalan national day) with around 1 million people taking part. The government had been holding meetings for months with Josep Tarradellas, the historical president of the Generalitat, conversations that were precipitated in order to disarm the initiative of the recently created Asamblea de Parlamentarios Catalanes, dominated by the forces of the left, which called for the re-establishment of the 1932 Statute and supported the concept of a federal state. On 29 September an executive order provisionally constituted the Generalitat, and on 23 October Tarradellas was able to pronounce in Barcelona his famous phrase, '*Ja sóc aquí*' ('I am here'), invoking the legitimacy that his past had given him. It was only a symbolic legitimacy because the new Generalitat, with very limited prerogatives, was based on the 1975 Ley de Régimen Local (Local Government Act) and not the republican statute. The government convinced Tarradellas to

---

[12] Powell, *España en democracia, 1975–2000*, p. 205.

recognise the unity of Spain, dismantled the *rupturista* alternative headed by the Catalan socialists and communists, and left the way clear for the constitutional process to define the guidelines for a future State of Autonomous Governments.

The government's strategy did not obtain the same result in the Basque Country. José María de Leizaola, the nationalist prime minister of the Basque government-in-exile, refused to negotiate with the government unless the Asamblea de Parlamentarios Vascos, which was in session in the Casa de Juntas in Guernica, was also involved. In December 1977 the Basque General Council was established, presided over by a veteran socialist leader, Ramón Rubial. PNV opposition intensified as a result of the refusal of most of the Navarran parliamentarians, belonging to the UCD, to join the Basque assembly. Yet to be dealt with, as well as the Navarran issue, were the re-establishing of economic accords for Vizcaya and Guipúzcoa, the calling of general assemblies and the unresolved problem of terrorism. The political amnesty had arrived late. Although there were no ETA prisoners left in gaol by Christmas 1977, all through 1978 they began to fill up again with activists, many of them accused of the sixty-eight murders committed by the group during the period of the drafting of the Constitution. Neither the terrorist organisation nor its political wing considered that the process of reforms during the Transition was anything other than the continuance of the Francoist regime, a belief that would have important social support during the following years.

Much easier was the task faced by the minister for regional relations, Manuel Clavero, in channelling the claims for self-government which, firstly in Galicia and Andalucía, and later in the rest of the regions, followed in the wake of the demands of the Basque and Catalan nationalists. What was dubbed as *café para todos* ('coffee for everyone', i.e. all regions would be treated the same) caused discontent among those who advocated that powers for a specific region should depend on those it had had in the past, and those on the left who warned that a more orthodox federal programme was gradually being edged out. The latter had a point. The fact that there were pre-Autonomous Government bodies all over Spain shaped the scope of the debate on the territorial restructuring of the state, a matter which was to be dealt with in the drafting of the Constitution.

The main role in this process was played by a report submitted by seven members of the Constitutional Commission created by Congress. There were three representatives from the UCD, Gabriel Cisneros, Miguel Herrero de Miñón and José Pérez Llorca; one from the PSOE, Gregorio Peces Barba; one from the AP, Manuel Fraga; one from the PCE-PSUC, Jordi Solé Tura; and a seventh representative, Miquel Roca, representing the Catalan and Basque nationalists, although the PNV very soon withdrew from the negotiations because they refused to waive their historical rights. The panel worked during the second half of 1977 and the first few months of 1978 on a draft report that was submitted to the Constitutional Commission at the beginning of May. There, the discussions continued and votes were taken on the various proposals, most of them put forward by the UCD and AP, which accounted for nineteen of the thirty-six members of the Commission. Because of this, the PSOE threatened to withdraw, and a series of extra-parliamentary negotiations between the government and the socialists was initiated, led by Fernando Abril Martorell and Alfonso Guerra.

The final agreement between the UCD and PSOE managed to heal the rift between them over issues such as territorial organisation, labour relations, education and the content of some of the fundamental rights from the long list proposed by the left. With concessions on both sides, and a calculated ambiguity in the drafting of the most controversial articles, the text passed by the commission was put before Congress and the Senate in the summer, where it received hundreds of amendments, and on 31 October it was put to a final vote in both chambers. In Congress there were 325 votes in favour, 6 against, 14 abstentions and 5 members were absent; in the Senate, 226 voted in favour and only 5 against, with 8 abstentions. The final result reflected the broad consensus reached between most of the parliamentary groups, with the exception of the AP, who had five deputies voting against, alongside the representative of Euskadiko Ezquerra, and three others who decided to abstain along with the members of the PNV.

The long period of drafting and discussing the Constitution and the length of the final text, with 11 chapters, 169 articles, and 9 transitional, 1 repeal and 1 final provisions, reveal the complexity of the process and the difficulties in reaching a consensus over the principles and limits of a 'social and democratic state subject to the rule of law' as proclaimed in Article 1. Chapter I, which set out the fundamental rights and freedoms, was one of the most discussed chapters. This was not so much because of the non-confessional nature of the state, which nevertheless recognised the social influence of the Catholic Church, but because of issues such as education, which concerned the public financing of private schools, the abolition of the death penalty and the right to life, with the problem of abortion lurking in the background. The passing of Chapter II, declaring that the political status of the state was a parliamentary monarchy, was less problematic than expected. The PSOE's vote for a republic in the Constitutional Commission was merely a symbolic gesture, and the Crown, an institution that preceded the Constitution, as Herrero de Miñón acknowledged, was incorporated with certain constraints which nevertheless gave Juan Carlos I two important prerogatives: the appointment of the prime minister and supreme command of the armed forces.

Subsequent chapters defined the legislative and executive powers, the structure of the public administration and the social and economic framework of the state. Some of the text's shortcomings can be seen in the cumbersome legacy of the Political Reform Act, which was influential in the maintaining of a two-chamber system which in practice relegated the Senate to a secondary role, keeping it apart from the national and federal political debate that it might have been involved in, and in the continuance of the electoral system, a precipitated agreement between the two political forces that benefited the most, the UCD and PSOE. It was much harder to reach a consensus over Chapter VIII, the territorial organisation of the state, almost certainly the section with the greatest amount of imprecision, and with ambiguities that allowed for widely varying interpretations. Earlier, in Article 2, the Constitution declared 'the indissoluble unity of the Spanish Nation, the common and indivisible homeland of all Spaniards' – one of the missions entrusted to the armed forces – and the right to self-government of 'the nationalities and regions of which it is composed'. The inclusion of the term 'nationalities' caused internal division in the UCD and the rejection of some AP parliamentarians, and it failed to persuade the PNV to join in the consensus of the majority. Nor was it made very clear how the prerogatives would be shared out between the state and the future Autonomous Communities, or how the various steps to self-government would be configured.

The positive and negative aspects of the constitutional process could be seen in the referendum held on 6 December 1978: 87% of Spaniards who went to the polls supported a constitution that was clearly democratic, the result of dialogue and the search for consensus, based on the principles of freedom, equality and pluralism, which eliminated all the laws of the dictatorship and defined a framework for civic coexistence comparable to that of the most advanced countries in Europe. However, participation was lower than expected, 67% of the electorate, and barely 45% in the Basque Country, where the PNV had called for abstention. Juan Carlos I's signature at the bottom of the Constitution did not represent the final act of the transition process. There were still no democratically elected town or city councils in Spain, the State of Autonomies was just an idea on paper, the general framework of social and labour relations was yet to be defined, and the fledgling democracy was facing serious problems such as the economic crisis, terrorism and the threat of military involvement.

BOLETIN OFICIAL DEL ESTADO
GACETA DE MADRID

Depósito Legal M. 1-1958   Año CCCXVIII   Viernes 29 de diciembre de 1978   Núm. 311.1

CONSTITUCION
ESPAÑOLA

APROBADA POR LAS CORTES EN SESIONES PLENARIAS
DEL CONGRESO DE LOS DIPUTADOS Y DEL SENADO CELEBRADAS
EL 31 DE OCTUBRE DE 1978

RATIFICADA POR EL PUEBLO ESPAÑOL EN REFERENDUM
DE 6 DE DICIEMBRE DE 1978

SANCIONADA POR S. M. EL REY ANTE LAS CORTES
EL 27 DE DICIEMBRE DE 1978

Figure 10 The Constitution that had been agreed among the main political parties was approved in a referendum held in December 1978. It established a democracy, presided over by a parliamentary monarchy, with a large number of rights and freedoms. © Agencia EFE

Consolidation problems

The March 1979 general election made no essential difference to the Spanish political map. The UCD won again, Suárez formed a new government without an absolute majority in the Cortes, and the PSOE, reinforced by the absorption of the PSP, established itself as the main opposition force and only alternative to government. Nor were there any surprises in April's municipal elections, the first to be held in Spain since the Second Republic, which renewed the local political elites and gave power to the left in the big cities, thanks to pacts between the socialists and communists. Worthy of mention here is the low participation, barely 60% in the municipal elections after the 67% in the general election, something which did not go unnoticed by the media; they began to speak of 'disenchantment', a vague term that, for some, indicated a certain frustration with the expectations of change generated by the transition process, at least among those who had played the biggest part in the struggle against the dictatorship.

Among the causes for this high rate of abstention, some historians have cited a certain weariness in the electorate brought on by five calls to the polls in just over two years, the apathy of young voters who were eligible to vote for the first time, and the influence, still visible in certain circles, of the political culture inherited from Francoism, which had bred distrust of party struggles and contempt for state institutions. Others ascribe it to the very nature of the democratisation process, based on transaction and negotiation by the political elites, causing gradual rejection by the public, and to the system of representation, with rigidly structured parties and closed lists which did little to favour membership and participation by civil society.

The election activities of the first half of 1979 delayed the processing of self-government plans which the parliamentary assemblies of the Basque Country and Catalonia had begun to draw up in the months preceding the proclamation of the Constitution. The two statutes had followed parallel paths, with many points in common. They were both passed in Congress, after relentless negotiations in a joint commission, and both were accepted by 90% of the vote in the referenda held on the same day, 25 October 1979, with a very low turnout, barely 60% of the electorate. The first Autonomous Government elections, held on 9 March 1980 in the Basque Country and 20 March in Catalonia, set up a political system of nationalist primacy, more evident in the Basque case, where Carlos Garaikoetxea's PNV obtained 38% of the vote, with a somewhat tighter result in Catalonia where the Convergència i Unió (CiU) coalition, led by Jordi Pujol, obtained 28% of the vote. Much later came the drafting of the Galician statute, endorsed in the referendum held in December 1980 and implemented in the Autonomous Government election in October 1981, in which the nationalists obtained a modest result compared to AP, with just over 30% of the vote.

By then, following in the wake of the three 'historical communities', the Andalucian political parties had achieved, by virtue of the referendum held in February 1980, access to self-government via Article 151 of the Constitution instead of treading the slower and more restrictive path of Article 143, which is what the government wanted. This, when added to the *derechos forales* (regional rights) belonging to Navarre and the special systems that had been granted to the Balearic and Canary Islands meant, in practice, the gradual extension of the maximum level of prerogatives envisaged by the Constitution to all regions. As Pere Ysàs has pointed out, the widespread granting of self-government statutes was the state's response to two complementary issues: political and administrative decentralisation, one of the remaining tasks in the process of consolidating democracy, and 'the structuring of a concept of Spain that would be compatible with the national identity of the Catalans, Basques and, to a lesser extent, Galicians'.[13]

The failure of this territorial policy in the Basque case calls for some clarification. Antonio Rivera has explained that democratic states, as well as being legal, need the legitimacy of their social partners and political forces, a prerequisite that was not met in Euskadi for various reasons. Firstly, the PNV, the majority party during the Transition, displayed very little support for the institutions. Its abstention in the constitutional referendum was the most visible sign of its defence of the Basque Country's traditional rights as a principle of legitimacy prior to the Constitution. Secondly, spring 1978 saw the emergence of another nationalist political force, Herri Batasuna (HB), backed by 19% of the vote in the following year's municipal elections, which not only called into question the legitimacy of the transition process, but even rejected it outright, and condoned the terrorist actions of ETA. Finally, the state was responsible, through what it did and did not do, for the failure of social legitimacy in the Basque Country. Examples of its inaction were holding back on the legalisation of the *ikurriña*, the short-sightedness of governments in failing to recognise in time the central role played by the nationalist primacy of the PNV, and in its belated granting of amnesty, when a mass movement opposing the reform process had already been initiated. What it did do was deploy the forces of order in its irrational response to the problem of violence and social conflict. The names of the young people killed by gunfire, allegations of torture or the images of the police action in Rentería and its

---

[13] Pere Ysàs, 'Democracia y autonomía en la transición española', *Ayer*, 15 (1994), pp. 77–108.

brutal intervention in the Pamplona bull ring, both occurring in the summer of 1978, were used by ETA and its political supporters as arguments to maintain that Francoism was not dead, to feed the traditional view of a Basque people that was 'occupied' and oppressed by Spain, and to justify terrorist violence as being an armed liberation struggle.[14]

The years of the proclamation of the statute and the first elections to the Basque Parliament, 1979 and 1980, marked the bloodiest period in ETA's history. This brief space of time saw the escalation of terrorist activity with a grim death toll of 167 victims. They included as many as twenty-one high-ranking military officers, a deliberate destabilisation strategy aimed at provoking an excessive reaction from the armed forces, an exaggerated response from the military and police command that would sorely test the democratic nature of political transition.

It is true to say that the wave of terrorist violence was, beyond a doubt, one of the leading factors in stirring up the 'bunker' mentality of the Francoist military and in sowing the seeds for a rebellion. Unrest among the officer class had been steadily growing since the spring of 1977, caused particularly by the legalisation of the PCE. The propaganda campaign waged by the extreme right-wing press – *El Alcázar, El Imparcial* and *Fuerza Nueva* – disseminated an image of a country torn apart by terrorist actions, the divisive demands of the nationalists, scorn for the flag and patriotic symbols and the weakness of a government which was doing nothing to get the country back on track and avoid plunging into the precipice of chaos. The butt of all this anger was General Gutiérrez Mellado. His strategy of professionalisation and modernisation of the army was seen as a direct affront to the top-ranking military who had played a leading role in the Civil War alongside Franco. And his controversial policy of promotions and appointments, aimed at separating the most hostile generals from positions of responsibility, garnered the enmity of his brothers-in-arms, who considered him to be a traitor. In military ceremonies, official receptions and funerals of military victims murdered by ETA, acts of indiscipline and jeers and insults directed against the government, as well as calls for military intervention, were a frequent occurrence.

Most of these acts of insubordination went unpunished. As Paul Preston has pointed out, instead of appeasing the extreme right-wing officers, which is what the government intended, this policy of leniency merely emboldened the most hardline of them to take the first step in putting an end to

---

[14] Antonio Rivera Blanco, 'La transición en el País Vasco: un caso particular', in Javier Ugarte (ed.), *La transición en el País Vasco y España: los inicios del proceso democratizador* (Bilbao: Universidad del País Vasco, 1998), pp. 79–82.

the democratic process.[15] There had already been a meeting in Játiva in September 1977 of generals who were ready to prepare a plot which would end up with the formation of a military government of salvation. Better known to the public was *Operación Galaxia*, named after the cafeteria in Madrid where the conspirators, in November 1978, planned an assault on the Palacio de La Moncloa (the prime minister's official residence) and the arrest of the entire government. Its ringleaders, Lieutenant Colonel Antonio Tejero, of the Civil Guard, and police captain Ricardo Sáenz de Inestrillas were arrested and sentenced to extremely light sentences of six and seven months of military detention, and nothing was done to shed light on the hidden workings of the coup or the units that were involved.

Not that the government could have expected much co-operation from intelligence services recently amalgamated into the Centro Superior de Información de la Defensa (CESID) but still made up of personnel inherited from Francoism, more inclined to investigate left-wing politicians than to inform the government of the movements of army officers. Discontent within the army establishment was intensified during 1979 due to the self-government negotiations, the wave of ETA violence, the anti-democratic pressure of the extreme right-wing press and government policy directed by Gutiérrez Mellado from the deputy prime minister's office and by Agustín Rodríguez Sahagún, the first civilian to head the Ministry of Defence since the republican era. From inside the Brunete Armoured Division another plot was being hatched under the leadership of General Luis Torres Rojas. His dismissal in January 1980, when he was sent to La Coruña, added to the indignation felt by the military commanders most inclined to head a coup.

Contact between the plotters began in the summer of 1980 and continued during the autumn and winter of that year. Finally, what many people had feared and others had urged in the pages of the extreme right-wing press and army headquarters, a *coup d'état*, materialised in the Cortes on the evening of 23 February 1981. The *Diario de Sesiones* of the Congress of Deputies reported that 'at approximately 6.20 pm, shots and cries of "Gunfire, gunfire!" and "Everybody down on the ground!" were heard in the passages. A large number of armed men in Civil Guard uniform burst into the chamber and, after placing themselves in strategic positions, threatened the Speaker's desk with force. After an altercation with the deputy prime minister, Lieutenant General Gutiérrez Mellado, they ordered everyone to get down on the ground to the accompaniment of bursts of machine gun fire. The session was adjourned.'

[15] Paul Preston, *The Politics of Revenge: Fascism and the Military in Twentieth-Century Spain* (London: Routledge, 1995).

Congress was holding no ordinary session that evening. The entry into the chamber of Lieutenant Colonel Tejero, brandishing a pistol, at the head of hundreds of Civil Guards, interrupted the second vote on electing Leopoldo Calvo Sotelo as prime minister. On 27 January, to the surprise of the majority of Spaniards and some of his ministers, Suárez had tendered his resignation to the king, who did nothing to dissuade him. In the less than two years since his victory in the spring 1979 election, his image had deteriorated to such an extent that the only solution was for him to resign. Behind the political paralysis and leadership crisis that caused his resignation were the growing discontent of public opinion over the economic downturn, with an unemployment rate of 12% in 1980, and the party's general fatigue caused by the spreading of the regional self-government process, with successive defeats in the elections held in the Basque Country, Catalonia and, most notoriously, Andalucía. But the determining factor was the internal division of the UCD, in which it was hard to separate ideological disputes from personal confrontations. Increasingly alienated from parliamentary procedure, Suárez saw that his presidential style was at loggerheads with pressure from the senior members of the party to accept the creation of a permanent commission in the shadow of the government, to carry out various cabinet reshuffles and to tackle, from a position of evident weakness, the attacks of the opposition, such as the motion of no confidence presented by the PSOE in May 1980. The internal disputes between the sectors of the UCD closest to social democracy, and the more conservative groups, backed by the Episcopal Conference and the CEOE (Employers' Federation), were aired in debates over economic policy, private education and the Divorce Bill, and irreversibly fragmented the parliamentary party.

The internal crisis of the governing party and Suárez's resignation gave the final nudge to the military commanders who were sounding out the possibilities of success in a *coup d'état*. The plotters' expectations were nurtured by the irresponsible attitude of the opposition leaders, including the socialists, who began to speculate about the need to adopt exceptional measures, including the possibility of setting up a government of national concentration to be led by a reputable army officer. It was what the historian Javier Cercas has called the 'placenta' of the coup, the atmosphere of confusion and political tension that preceded the 23-F (23 February) attempt.[16] Tejero's irruption into Congress was part of an operation directed by General Alfonso Armada, the deputy chief of the General Staff, with the firm collaboration of Milans del Bosch, at the head of the

[16] Javier Cercas, *Anatomía de un instante* (Barcelona: Mondadori, 2009).

captaincy general of Valencia. The plotters' plan envisaged the advance on Madrid of vehicles of the Brunete Armoured Division, subsequent support from the captains general in the various military regions, and the final intervention of Armada, the former general secretary of the Royal Household, to act in the name of the Crown and head a government of national salvation. It would be a monarchist coup against democracy.

Juan Carlos I's actions were decisive from the very beginning, when he refused to receive Armada in the Zarzuela Palace and began to telephone the captains general of the eleven military regions, ordering them not to follow the example of Milans del Bosch, who had declared a state of war in Valencia after bringing the tanks out on to the streets. The reaction of most of them, Francoist in ideology and patently hostile to the constitutional regime, wavered between doubt and apprehension. Those few who categorically decided to remain on the side of legality, such as Guillermo Quintana Lacaci, the captain general of Madrid, did so more through their sense of loyalty to the king, the supreme commander of the armed forces, than through their democratic convictions. But his loyalty, like that of General José Gabeiras, the chief of the General Staff, of Aramburu Topete, director general of the Civil Guard, and of José Antonio Sáenz de Santamaría, commander of the National Police Force, was a determining factor in the failure of the uprising in Madrid, and ensured that it did not extend to the rest of Spain. Tejero was isolated in Congress, the Brunete Armoured Division units that had managed to occupy the central studios of TVE returned to their barracks and, following long hours of confusion and uncertainty, at 1.20 in the early hours of 24 February, television sets throughout Spain broadcast a recorded message from the king: 'I have ordered the civil authorities and the Joint Chiefs of Staff to take all measures necessary to maintain constitutional order within the legislation in force.' The *coup d'état* had failed.

Paradoxically, as Powell has pointed out, the military rebels had unwittingly helped to consolidate the democratic regime that they had tried to overthrow by force of arms. The mass demonstrations held throughout Spain on 27 February, with several hundreds of thousands of citizens thronging the streets to support democracy and the Constitution, 'marked the end of the disenchantment which had seemed to dominate political life since the early days of 1979, giving way to a new phase that was characterised by hope in a political system which, despite its possible limitations, was undoubtedly preferable to the authoritarian alternative that the coup had intended to impose'.[17] This paradox may be extended to the Crown

---

[17] Powell, *España en democracia, 1975–2000*, p. 298.

as well. The ultra-conservative generals who had remained loyal to the king, mindful of the fact that he was the legitimate successor appointed by Franco, under whom they had served in the Civil War, unwittingly helped to reinforce the legitimacy of Juan Carlos I as a constitutional monarch and to increase his popularity as the guarantor of democratic principles. As Calvo Sotelo wrote in his memoirs, 'happily, it was Tejero's fault that the monarchy became entrenched'.[18]

Leopoldo Calvo Sotelo was 54 at the time. He had been a *procurador* in the Cortes during the final years of the Franco era, had close links with the business world, held solid monarchist convictions and had been a collaborator of Suárez during the transition years – minister of trade, public works, relations with the European Economic Community and deputy prime minister for economic affairs – until Suárez put his name forward in cabinet as his successor. On 25 February, two days after the coup attempt, he was elected prime minister thanks to the votes of the Fraga group and Catalan nationalists, but he rejected the option of a coalition government and formed a cabinet consisting entirely of leading UCD deputies, the first cabinet to have no military ministers.

The new government's first task was, of necessity, the normalisation of relations with the armed forces. The minister of defence, Alberto Oliart, proceeded with caution, renewing key posts in the military establishment, and placed a trustworthy officer, Lieutenant Colonel Alonso Manglano, at the head of the CESID. He also declined to launch a thorough investigation into the 23-F plot. In the end, the government's leniency meant that only thirty-two officers and one civilian were tried for open military rebellion in February 1982. Not one of the Civil Guards who threatened Gutiérrez Mellado was put on trial. As a result of the verdict of the Supreme Council of Military Justice, issued four months later, Tejero and Milans del Bosch were sentenced to thirty years in prison, but it was extremely lenient towards General Armada, who was sent to prison for six years, and towards the rest of the accused, most of whom were given prison sentences of less than three years, while others were acquitted. The government appealed the sentence in the Supreme Court, which finally raised Armada's punishment to match that of the other two ringleaders and markedly increased the prison sentences of the rest of the accused, while at the same time reaffirming the supremacy of civil power and marking the end of a long tradition of military interventionism.

One of the initiatives tackled by Calvo Sotelo was the policy of socioeconomic compromise, which enabled him to reach a National Accord on

---

[18] Leopoldo Calvo-Sotelo, *Memoria viva de la transición* (Barcelona: Plaza & Janés, 1990).

Figure 11 The entry into the Congress of Deputies of Lieutenant Colonel Antonio Tejero, brandishing a pistol, at the head of hundreds of Civil Guards, in February 1981, was the last and most important attempt to overthrow the Spanish democracy by force of arms. © Agencia EFE

Employment, signed in June 1981 by the government, the employers and the two major unions, CC.OO. and UGT, with the backing of Felipe González. The government promised aid to the trade unions and improved social protection against unemployment in exchange for a moratorium on wage demands. The agreement did not give the expected results – in 1982 inflation was at 14% and the unemployment rate had risen to 17% of the workforce – but it did bring about a downturn in labour conflicts and, perhaps more importantly, institutional recognition of the negotiating capacity of the social partners.

This understanding between the centrists and socialists was also to be found in another of the issues that were facing Calvo Sotelo, the full development of the State of Autonomies. The government's aim, said Rodolfo Martín Villa, the minister of territorial administration, was to 'reconduct' the process, to rationalise and harmonise those statutes that were already in force with self-government plans that were still being discussed in order to define a global model for territorial organisation that would be stable and permanent. Negotiations with the PSOE ended in the summer of 1981 with an agreement that those regions without self-government would continue along the lines laid down in Article 143 of the Constitution although, in the end, they would be subject to the same ceiling of prerogatives. Ten statutes were granted in the first few months of 1982, in July the Ley Orgánica de Armonización del Proceso Autonómico (Self-government Process Harmonisation Act – LOAPA) was passed in Congress, with the firm opposition of the PNV and CiU, which lodged an appeal in the Constitutional Court, and at the end of the summer, when the Cortes adjourned, the only statutes still to be ratified were those of Extremadura, the Balearic Islands, Madrid, and Castile and León, which would have no problem in concluding their processes at the beginning of the next legislature.

Along with the drawing of the self-government route map, compromise over social and labour relations and the restructuring of the armed forces, the Calvo Sotelo government's programme included another major challenge: coming out of international isolation and entering the European institutions, a necessary step for ensuring that democracy was consolidated. The foreign policy of the first transition governments had barely gone further than the narrow, secondary framework of traditional relations with South America and the Arab countries and an economic and military aid agreement with the United States, without any international political backing in return. When told of the 23-F coup attempt, the US secretary of state, Alexander Haig, went so far as to say that what happened was an internal affair for the Spanish. Furthermore, the formal opening of negotiations with the European Economic Community, begun in 1977 with

Calvo Sotelo becoming directly involved in 1978, came to a dead end two years later because of France's all-out opposition to Spain's entry. To salvage this situation, Calvo Sotelo decided to apply for Spain's membership of NATO, even though he did not have the support of the left. By joining the Atlantic Alliance, the government thought it would be able to obtain more favourable conditions when renewing the bilateral treaty with Washington, strengthen Spain's negotiating position in Brussels, narrow the rift with the United Kingdom over the Gibraltar question and, in passing, provide impetus for the modernisation and professionalisation of the Spanish army – in other words, taking Spain to Europe and bringing Europe to the army.

In October 1981, Congress passed the application for membership, thanks to the votes in favour from the right-wing and nationalist parties, and in May 1982 Spain became a member of NATO. This was despite strong opposition from the PSOE, which began a comprehensive campaign of social mobilisation with the slogan '*OTAN, de entrada no*' ('NATO, no from the outset'). They promised to call a referendum when they came to power, a possibility that they saw as being extremely likely after the beating taken by the UCD in the Autonomous elections in Galicia and Andalucía, with the socialists obtaining an absolute majority in the latter region.

The PSOE's landslide victory in the October 1982 general election was a result of the collapse of the UCD, a nosedive that Calvo Sotelo's government was unable to halt. Debates on the divorce bill, university autonomy and licensing of commercial television stations revealed the extreme fragility and disunity of a parliamentary group that was in self-destruct mode amidst internal struggles and personal squabbles over the sharing-out of power. The most critical groups eyed the right wing, seduced by Fraga's concept of the 'natural majority'; the social democrats supported the resignation of Fernández Ordóñez; and Adolfo Suárez left the party that he had created and led, to form a new one, the Centro Democrático y Social. When Calvo Sotelo dissolved the Cortes, in August 1982, the UCD held 168 seats; when Parliament reopened for the induction of Felipe González as prime minister, the centrists had only 12 seats. In barely three years their share of the vote had gone down from 35% to a meagre 7%, an exceptional case in European political history. The UCD, the party that had played the leading role in the Transition while in power, slumped not because it had now fulfilled its objectives, its historic mission, but because it had been incapable of creating a true party of the masses, a solid structure, a defined ideology and an unquestioned leadership. In fact, it had never been anything more than an unstable mix of factions and heterogeneous leaders, most of them relics of the Franco regime, all protected by the lucky star of Adolfo Suárez. Their decline would sooner or later be that of the party as well.

The practical disappearance of the UCD was in marked contrast to the indisputable victory of the PSOE, which obtained 202 seats and 10 million votes, 48% of the count in what was the election with the largest participation rate in the history of Spain's democracy, almost 80% of the electoral roll. This was no ordinary election. Industrial workers, professional sectors, young people voting for the first time and a large section of the urban middle classes and rural population went to the polls to give their support to a party with one hundred years of history but a young leadership, a party with a revolutionary name but a reform programme that promised stability and security, with all the weight of the traditional values of the left but promises that spoke only of the future and the electoral slogan 'Vote for change.' It was a political party that had a connection not with Francoism, but with the vanquished in the Civil War and repression, with four decades of exile and remaining underground. Many observers and most historians agree that the transition to democracy was concluded on the night of 28 October 1982, when Felipe González appeared at the window of the Hotel Palace in Madrid knowing that he was going to be the next prime minister, the first elected socialist prime minister in Spain's history.

14   Democracy

The PSOE's spectacular victory in the 1982 general election, with an unusually high turnout, enhanced the process of democratic consolidation. The exceptional result enabled Felipe González to head a strong government to tackle pending military, economic and social reforms. The socialists were in power for almost fourteen years, a long period of political primacy during which the pattern for regional self-government was developed, the welfare state was enlarged and Spain was integrated into European institutions. But they were also years of illegal activities in the fight against terrorism, corruption scandals, labour protests and an economic crisis that began in 1992, which had a severe effect on the Spanish economy leading to an exceptionally high unemployment rate.

By the time the twentieth century ended, Felipe González was no longer in power, nor even the leader of the PSOE, with the party steeped in a crisis from which it would take a long time to emerge. The 1996 election was won by the Partido Popular, under José María Aznar. Its first term was marked by spectacular economic growth and a moderate ideology that changed in 2000, when it won an absolute majority and implemented a right-wing neo-conservative programme that was dominated by a political confrontation strategy that was far removed from the climate of consensus during the Transition.

At the beginning of the twenty-first century, Spain was a modern, developed country, unrecognisable to any observer who might have spent several decades beyond its borders. The European dream of the regenerationist writers had come true, and society had left behind some of the historic problems that had caused it the most concern in the past. But it also inherited old, hitherto unresolved problems, such as the territorial organisation of the state and the continuation of terrorism, and new challenges such as immigration and the consequences of globalisation.

For change

'Partido Socialista Obrero Español, 202 seats'. It was late in the evening of 28 October 1982. The voice of Alfonso Guerra announced the provisional results of that day's election to the press that had gathered in the main hall of the Hotel Palace. It was the same place from where the developments of the 23-F coup attempt had been followed with nervousness and uncertainty. A year and a half later, the scene was quite different: 'Those present were stunned, left speechless. There was no applause from the guests. They were witnessing a victory that was so decisive that they were incapable of assimilating it. A few minutes later, there was an outburst of jubilation in the hotel; the streets all around began filling up with people and many of them drove round Madrid, sounding their horns and waving banners.'

And it was not surprising. A socialist victory had been expected, but no one had foreseen such an overwhelming majority. More than 10 million votes, 48% of those who had gone to the polls in a turnout of almost 80%: a sweeping victory. A long way behind came the AP with 106 seats, having gathered up some of the survivors from the UCD shipwreck. For the left, the PCE obtained just four seats, a disastrous result which led to the resignation of its long-established leader, Santiago Carrillo. Only the nationalists managed to hold their own, CiU with twelve seats and the PNV with eight. The far right had disappeared from the political map altogether. The 100,000 votes obtained by Fuerza Nueva were not enough for it to hold its single seat won in the previous parliament. It was one more indicator of the end of the Transition. The legislative chamber was to have just one colour, and the next government just one name that was announced in the special editions of the press: 'Felipe Prime Minister'.

In his memoirs, Alfonso Guerra recounts in great detail the emotions felt during the 'night at the Palace', the feeling of exultation, the blind enthusiasm of those who were there, those who found it impossible to interpret what they were experiencing, with an endless sequence of cheering, embraces and phrases 'that expressed the idea that "now" was just the beginning'. Victory was obtained under the leadership of a young lawyer from Seville, at the head of a group of colleagues who were tired of reading what was being written in Europe and of reorganising the party after sterile rows with the leadership in exile. It was their job 'to run a country, to solve serious problems, difficult problems that everyone else was trusting that they would be capable of fixing. From that moment on, we were the ones responsible for how Spain would turn out in the years to come.'

Felipe González was 40 years old. He had arrived in politics after taking part in student activism against the dictatorship. A member of the inner circle of the PSOE in 1966, he joined its executive in 1970 and four years later, in the famous Congress of Suresnes, he won the post of secretary general. At that time, he represented just over 2,000 members. By the beginning of 1976, this number had risen to 10,000. In the May 1979 Congress, it was more than 100,000. The PSOE had become the leading

Figure 12 Felipe González, the most charismatic leader of Spain's democracy, was in power for almost fourteen years, a long period of political primacy for the Socialist Party.

party of the left, relegating the PCE to a secondary position. But if the socialists aspired to present themselves as an alternative for government, they needed to look to the right for votes from the middle class, and to change their traditional ideology. Democracy would no longer be an inter-mediate stage in a transition to socialism, in the overcoming of capitalist society. From then on, the PSOE would define itself as being a moderate parliamentary party that aimed to carry out gradual social reforms within the legal framework of the Constitution and respect for institutions. It needed an ideological shift that involved abandoning its Marxist identity, removing the distinguishing feature that might be most awkward for cen-trist voters and the so-called factious powers. In other words, it needed to forget its revolutionary principles in order to win elections.

In the May 1979 Congress, Felipe González's strategy came up against the opposition of the most critical sector of the party, which disagreed with his reformist line. González resigned as secretary general and forced an internal debate which ended with an extraordinary congress held in September the same year, in which he was re-elected, this time with the backing of the delegates which was to prove unanimous – 100% of the votes – in the October 1981 Congress. As it had an undisputed leadership, a disciplined party strictly controlled by the executive committee, and a moderate social-democratic platform, all that remained was to wait for the decomposition of the UCD to take the leap to power.

A year later, on 30 November 1982, Felipe González was delivering his investiture speech to a Cortes dominated by the socialist deputies, the 'strong majority' he had asked for. It was a speech built around three basic principles: social peace, national unity and progress. The previous evening, Alfonso Guerra had told him that beyond what their electoral manifesto had said, it was necessary to make it clear what they wanted to do. Felipe's answer contained a good summary of the government's programme: 'Look, Alfonso, I would be fully satisfied if we achieve four clear goals: the con-solidation of democracy, so that Spaniards no longer worry that an army officer might attack the state; straightening out the economy, reducing galloping inflation and soaring unemployment; putting a brake on terrorism with a view to its disappearance in the medium term; and positioning Spain on the path to Europe and in its place internationally. These achievements would be a justification for government action over many years since it would represent the historical transformation the country needs.'[1]

It did, in fact, require many years. From 1982 onwards, and for at least a decade, Spanish politics was defined by the predominance of just one

---

[1] Alfonso Guerra, *Cuando el tiempo nos alcanza: memorias (1940–1982)* (Madrid: Espasa, 2004), pp. 339, 340, 342, 344–5.

party. In the June 1986 election, the PSOE managed to repeat its absolute majority without any problem, with 44% of the vote and 184 seats in parliament. Three years later, in October 1989, he won again with 175 seats and 39% of the vote. And again, in June 1993, when almost every one was forecasting the defeat of the government, Felipe González's personal charisma enabled the PSOE to obtain 38% of the vote and 159 seats. He formed a minority government with the support of the Catalan nationalists. Even in the March 1996 election, won by the PP under José María Aznar, the defeat of the socialists was deemed 'sweet'. The PSOE retained 141 seats with 37% of the votes, only 300,000 fewer than the PP. One year later, Felipe González resigned as secretary general of the party; he went down in history as probably one of the most important figures of the twentieth century in Spain. In all, he saw thirteen years in charge of Spanish politics, almost three times as long as the Second Republic had in order to implement their programme of democratic reforms, harassed as that government had been on all sides by inherited problems, deep conflicts and enemies willing to halt it; and almost twice as long as all the transitional governments put together, beset by economic crisis, political instability and the fear of military involvement.

The threat of a military coup had persisted until the eve of the October 1982 election, the date agreed on by a group of colonels to launch a violent assault on all the centres of civil and military power in Madrid. Although the plot was discovered, military unrest intensified on 8 November when ETA murdered General Víctor Lago, commander of the Brunete Armoured Division. On 8 December, five days before taking up his post as the new minister of defence, Narcís Serra went with Felipe González to visit the Division's headquarters on the occasion of the feast day of the patron saint of the Spanish infantry, the *Inmaculada*. It was a gesture that was warmly received when there was such a tense mood. A few days later, González ordered Serra to prohibit the Supreme Council of Military Justice from entering into any discussion of a possible release of those imprisoned for their role in the 23-F plot, a sentence still awaiting appeal in the civil court, which would end up by doubling their prison terms. The socialist government wanted to make it quite clear from the outset that it was not going to allow anyone to question the supremacy of the civil authorities and that the army was to keep clear of the struggle against terrorism, without responding to any provocations stemming from ETA activities.

A decisive step was the reform of the National Defence Act, passed in January 1984, which extended and legally defined the powers and duties of the prime minister and the minister of defence with regard to the armed forces. Then came various reshuffles in the leadership of the army, the reform of education programmes, the limiting of military justice to the military jurisdiction and a broad modernisation plan which, while increasing salaries and spending on resources, gradually reduced the number of senior posts.

The reduction in personnel was one of the aims of the military service reform enacted in 1984, which set the length of service at twelve months and established regulations for conscientious objection and alternative social service. The number of conscientious objectors increased from 1985 on, as did protests from anti-militarists who supported young men on trial for insubordination. A new law was passed in 1991, which again reduced the length of service to nine months. But these legislative changes were out of step with civil society which was manifestly against the maintaining of a compulsory call-up system. This was probably one of the socialists' most glaring errors. The incorporation of women into the armed forces, in 1988, and the beginning of international peace and humanitarian missions played a large part in improving the army's image in the eyes of Spanish society. But when the socialists lost power in 1996, they left behind two as yet unresolved issues: the conclusive creation of a professional armed forces model, which was tackled by the Partido Popular in its first term, and the permanence of the military nature of the Civil Guard, a question which has yet to be addressed. Nevertheless, by the end of the twentieth century the military problem, one of the most serious and persistent in the whole of contemporary Spanish history, may be said to have been resolved satisfactorily. The maintaining of public order was no longer a military issue, Spaniards were no longer obliged to devote part of their youth to armed service and, most importantly, a long tradition of *pronunciamientos*, rebellions and *coups d'état* had been brought to an end.

It was now a modern outward-looking army, firmly linked to the western defence system. The socialists' defence policy radically shifted at the end of 1983, when Felipe González began to express in public that he was in favour of continued membership of the Atlantic Alliance as an act of government responsibility. The PSOE's traditional stance was that of opposition to the maintaining of military blocs, a conviction expressed in its 1982 manifesto, with the promise to hold a referendum to decide on Spain's permanence in NATO. González waited until the end of his first term to call the plebiscite, following Spain's entry into the European Economic Community, and he posed a vague question which seemed to be tantamount to a vote of confidence: 'Do you feel it is advisable for Spain to remain in the Atlantic Alliance under the terms agreed on by the Government of the Nation?' The terms agreed on included keeping Spain out of the military structure, the banning of the importation of nuclear weapons into the country and the gradual closing down of US military bases. Uncertainty reigned up to the very day of the referendum, 12 March 1986. The right had asked for abstention, and all the political forces to the

Figure 13 Spain's successful entry into the European Economic Community on 1 January 1986 has been interpreted as the final step in the transition to democracy. The 'European dream' of many writers and intellectuals had come true. © Agencia EFE

left of the PSOE had campaigned for a 'no' vote. Rejection of NATO had become a catalyst for unrest among the organisations that had played a major role in the struggle against Franco and among the new social movements, particularly the pacifists and ecologists, who at the time were experiencing an upswing throughout Europe. In the end, with a very low turnout, just under 60% of the electorate, the government obtained its backing with 52% of the vote. Felipe González's gamble enhanced his personal power and left the way clear for a renewal of his absolute majority in the impending general election.

The anti-NATO platform was responsible for the birth of Izquierda Unida (IU), an electoral coalition made up of various parties and associations grouped around the PCE and its secretary general, Gerardo Iglesias, which obtained poor results in June 1986, less than 5% of the vote and just seven seats. Coalición Popular, the electoral platform designed by Fraga to try and improve on AP's results, obtained only 25% of the vote and lost two of the seats they had won four years earlier. Felipe González was at the height of his popularity. He had overcome the obstacle of the referendum, the worst of the economic crisis seemed to be over and Spain's successful entry into Europe on 1 January 1986 could be interpreted as the final step in the transition to democracy.

In 1982, inflation in Spain stood at 14%, more than 15% of the labour force was out of work, the government deficit was over 5% and annual growth barely exceeded 1%. The finance minister, Miguel Boyer, brought in a wide-reaching adjustment and recovery plan with the aim of achieving macro-economic stability. It was an orthodox plan, with the exception of the controversial expropriation of Rumasa, José María Ruiz Mateos' financial and business holding company. Measures such as the devaluation of the peseta, a restrained monetary policy and a pay freeze managed to reduce inflation and improve the foreign deficit. But unemployment continued to rise and the electoral promise to create 800,000 jobs was soon forgotten. The government also embarked on a financial recovery plan, increased taxes and stepped up its fight against fiscal fraud, reformed the National Energy Plan, privatised part of the public sector, restructured the INI, promoted measures to increase labour market flexibility and implemented a firm policy for industrial reconversion. This reconversion centred on the steel industry, shipbuilding and the textile and footwear sectors, involving hundreds of companies, leading to a reduction of almost 100,000 jobs and a cost to the state that exceeded 1.5 billion pesetas.

Economic recovery, which began in 1985, was helped by a fall in the prices of oil and raw materials, healthy international trade and a positive impact on investment and competitiveness arising from Spain's entry into the common market. Negotiations over entry into the EEC were long and complex, headed by the minister of foreign affairs, Fernando Morán. Once France had withdrawn its objection, the long-drawn-out negotiations of the first quarter of 1985 culminated on 12 June that year, with the signing of the Treaty of Accession of Spain and Portugal. The following years saw rapid, sustained economic growth, with an annual increase in the GDP of more than 4%, much higher than the European average, partly due to the constant inward foreign investment and also to the decisive impetus of public spending.

State investment in infrastructure was colossal. Starting in 1986, the General Highways Plan promoted the overhaul of thousands of kilometres of roads and the construction of a national network of highways and motorways, airports and the railway network, with the implementing of the first high speed train (AVE) line between Madrid and Seville, as well as the considerable work undertaken on hydro schemes, renovation of ports, coastline and environmental protection, housing and town planning. Foreigners visiting Spain in 1992 were able to appreciate the public works in Barcelona and Seville for the Olympic Games and the Universal Expo commemorating the 500th anniversary of Columbus' voyage to America.

There was also a dramatic increase in social welfare spending. Unemployment benefit conditions were improved, pensions were raised and the Social Security increased health spending. The minister of health, Ernest Lluch, brought in the General Health Act, passed in 1986, and the setting up of a National Health System that involved the extending of medical and hospital care to everyone. In education, the minister, José María Maravall, was responsible for the Ley de Reforma Universitaria (University Reform Act) in 1983 and in 1985 the Ley Orgánica del Derecho a la Educación (Right to Education Act – LODE). The reform was completed in 1990 with the Ley Orgánica de Ordenación General del Sistema Educativo (General Education System Planning Act), which raised the school leaving age to 16, thus increasing educational spending, 4.5% of the GDP in 1992, which was still below the European average.

With education, the legislators were tackling a sensitive issue because the Catholic Church owned a large number of primary and intermediate schools. The first serious conflict with the Bishops' Conference had arisen in 1983 with the debate on the Abortion Act, which depenalised termination of pregnancy under some circumstances. When it came to education, the government was indulgent with the Church's interests. The LODE recognised the existence of a public as well as private network of establishments, the latter also financed with state funding via a set of direct grants and educational covenants. Generally speaking, it is fair to say that the Catholic Church has been excellently treated by democratic Spain. The socialists were not willing to risk modifying the economic pacts signed with the Vatican in January 1979 – barely five days after the Constitution came into force – which involved the continuation of traditional privileges in public institutions, a great many tax breaks and public financing for religious service costs and clerical salaries. Subsequent governments have forgotten that the Church had made a commitment to move gradually to a situation in which it would be self-financing.

Public investment in education, health and other basic social services, such as unemployment benefit, child support and pensions, brought Spain closer to the welfare state model built up in western Europe during the second half of the twentieth century: economic development and social welfare by means of the partial redistribution of wealth. As well as social spending by the state, there was public investment by city councils and Autonomous Communities, which increasingly enjoyed more powers and services. Autonomous Government participation in total public sector expenditure went from 8% in 1983 to 18% in 1989 and 25% in 1992, still a lower percentage than in Germany and Switzerland but certainly much more similar to that of a federal state than to any other form of territorial organisation.

The autonomous map of Spain was completed in the early months of 1983 with the granting of the four statutes of autonomy pending from the previous legislature. That same year, the Constitutional Tribunal found for the Basque and Catalan nationalists in an appeal they had lodged, and declared part of the LOAPA unconstitutional. Henceforth, it was made clear that no government law could override the Constitution and the approved statutes, but in general the self-government model was not affected nor was the idea that, in the end, all the Communities would enjoy equal privileges. This was the beginning of the effective decentralisation of the state and the gradual devolution of powers, a troubled process plagued with appeals to the Constitutional Tribunal and tense negotiations between the national and regional authorities over the delay in transferring powers or because these powers were devolved without the financing they had asked for. Relations between the government and the 'historical' communities changed in 1993, when the PSOE lost its absolute majority in Congress and was forced to make a deal with the Catalan nationalists in exchange for the handing over of 15% of the income tax collected in the community, a percentage which was doubled in 1996 when Aznar came to power, also with a parliamentary minority; this percentage was later extended to the rest of the regions.

In general it is fair to conclude, as Antoni Segura has pointed out, that the development of the self-government model in the 1980s and 1990s was a success, that political debate on self-government aspirations was gradually giving way to an administrative debate on how far the state would be decentralised.[2] The thorniest issue at the end of the century was almost certainly that of the financing of communities and the demand for fiscal co-responsibility. In more centralist circles, the demands of the autonomous regions were seen as an affront from the nationalists and a danger to inter-territorial cohesion. On the other hand, in certain communities, particularly Catalonia, the overlying perception was that their contributions to the state were higher than the benefits obtained, that the more productive and dynamic regions were taxed more heavily but that their taxes were not used to close the gap with the poorer regions, despite the Inter-territorial Compensation Fund and the constant inflow of capital from the European Regional Development Fund. In Catalonia the negotiating process for powers clearly worked in favour of the leadership of Jordi Pujol, who was able to align the conservative and liberal vote with the nationalist feeling of a large proportion of the popular sectors; he was also able to identify his party, CiU, with the defence of the rights of Catalans against the central government's reluctance to grant greater autonomous powers and to extend tax collection powers.

It was a different case with the Basque Country. Nationalist rejection of the self-government model had nothing to do with the financing system, because of the fiscal regime enjoyed by both Euskadi and Navarre. The main objective of the PNV, the predominant force in the region, was the construction of a complete national community from the political, administrative and cultural point of view. But internal disputes in the PNV caused Garaikoetxea to resign as leader of the Basque government in 1984 and led to a split of the party's most critical sector to become part of Eusko Alkartasuna (EA). In 1986, the fragmentation of the party system forced the new Lehendakari, José Antonio Ardanza, to head PNV and Basque Socialist Party (Partido Socialista de Euskadi, PSE) coalition governments and to begin a stage of reduced confrontation and institutional tension. The result of this new political climate of greater collaboration was the signing of the Ajuria–Enea Pact in 1988. The political parties, except HB, were resolved to draw a line to separate not the nationalists from the non-nationalists, as had been the case up to then, but the democrats from the terrorists and their sympathisers who rejected the whole transition process and supported the 'armed struggle'.

And, indeed, ETA went on killing. There were more than 300 deaths during the thirteen long years of socialist government, with indiscriminate killings such as the bombing of the Hipercor hypermarket in Barcelona

---

[2] Antoni Segura, 'Un balance del Estado de las Autonomías en España (1976–2002)', in Rafael Quirosa-Cheyrouze Muñoz (ed.), *Historia de la transición en España: los inicios del proceso democratizador* (Madrid: Biblioteca Nueva, 2007), pp. 331–52.

and the Civil Guard married quarters in Zaragoza, both events occurring in 1987. The socialists' anti-terrorist policy combined police action – such as the Zona Especial Norte (ZEN) – and the first agreements with France over deportations and extraditions, with a view to putting an end to ETA sanctuary on the other side of the Pyrenees, with reinsertion measures to promote the laying down of arms. There were also the first attempts at negotiation with the terrorists, including what were known as the Algiers Conversations, held intermittently between the end of 1986 and the first few months of 1989. Successive ministers of internal affairs, José Barrionuevo, José Luis Corcuera, Antoni Asunción and Juan Alberto Belloch not only failed to put an end to the terrorist violence, but also left behind the dark shadow of the dirty war against ETA as one of the blackest marks in the entire socialist era.

From 1983 to 1987, while Barrionuevo was minister, what were known as the Grupos Antiterroristas de Liberación (GAL), made up of extreme right-wing gunmen and foreign mercenaries, were involved in more than forty terrorist incidents, killing twenty-eight people. From the outset, it was obvious that the GAL was linked to certain police chiefs and government authorities in the Basque Country, that government 'slush' funds were being used to fund the terrorists' activities and that the government was not willing to investigate these incidents. Several years later, between 1994 and 1996, investigations by the High Court and Judge Baltasar Garzón concluded with the imprisonment of Julián Sancristóbal, the former civil governor of Vizcaya; Rafael Vera, ex-secretary of state for security; Ricardo García Damborenea, secretary general of the PSE in Vizcaya; and the ex-minister himself, José Barrionuevo, who were all accused of being responsible for a 'terrorist plot' linked to the Ministry of Internal Affairs. Also arrested was the Civil Guard general, Enrique Rodríguez Galindo, for having ordered the murders of José Antonio Lasa and José Ignacio Zabala, two ETA activists kidnapped by the GAL in 1983, tortured and buried in quicklime in Alicante. Few images were capable of causing more harm to a state governed by the rule of law and a democratic government.

The first signs of the erosion of PSOE governments' political credibility began to appear at the end of their first term with the campaign against NATO and the American bases, led by the political and social forces of the left, and the beginning of the distancing of the trade unions for the harsh measures taken in the reconversion of industry. Labour conflicts and confrontation with the police took place at the blast furnaces in Sagunto and the Galician, Andalucian and Basque shipyards. In 1985 the UGT, which had followed a policy of moderation and restraint in its demands, began to draw closer to the more combative standpoint of CC.OO. The UGT leader, Nicolás Redondo, made no secret of his feeling of disillusion, bitterness even, with the government's measures, measures such as the reform of the public sector, the flexibilisation of the labour market, with the introduction of provisional contracts and the plan to modify the pensions system.

In 1988, in the midst of a general climate of economic recovery, the two trade union organisations agreed to embark on a series of mobilisations to demand a shift in the government's economic policy, directed by Carlos Solchaga in the Ministry of Economy and Finance. The presentation of a youth employment plan was the motive used by the unions for calling a 24-hour national strike for 14 December 1988. The success of the general strike was indisputable: it was a serious wake-up call to Felipe González's executive, more for its arrogance in government and lack of dialogue than for the scope and content of the reforms. The left's discontent was reflected in the October 1989 general election: the PSOE lost nine seats and barely maintained a parliamentary majority, while the relative rise of IU, led by Julio Anguita, with 9% of the vote, gave it seventeen seats in Congress.

As well as the labour protests and opposition of part of the left wing, the right and some of the media seized on the cases of corruption that were coming to light. At the end of 1989 Juan Guerra, the brother of the deputy prime minister, Alfonso Guerra, was accused of using an official position to devote himself to influence peddling for personal gain, although in the end he was found guilty only of tax fraud. Then, 1991 saw the exposure of Filesa, a company devoted to the illegal financing of the PSOE, and also involved in speculation in the purchase of land belonging to RENFE (Red Nacional de los Ferrocarriles Españoles). The following year it was a scandal involving cronyism and the receipt of illegal commissions in the adjudication of public works contracts in Andalucía. In 1994, Mariano Rubio, ex-governor of the Bank of Spain, and Manuel de la Concha, an ex-trustee of the Stock Exchange, were arrested for forgery and tax avoidance in the Ibercorp case. Almost at the same time came the flight from Spain of Luis Roldán, who had been director general of the Civil Guard, in order to avoid being tried for embezzlement and receipt of commissions. As if that were not enough, that same year saw the director general of the *BOE* (Official State Gazette) accused of embezzlement, the existence of colossal salaries being paid to senior figures at the Interior Ministry from slush funds, and the economic and political links of the financiers Mario Conde and Javier de la Rosa, who were found guilty and imprisoned for misappropriation, fraud and embezzlement.

The ongoing corruption scandals revealed the darkest facet of the expansive economic cycle of the previous years. Felipe González's government and the PSOE leadership, with Alfonso Guerra at the head, failed to put a brake on the spread of corrupt practices, widespread speculation and fraud, and the growth of lucrative private businesses funded by the public purse of the various administrations. And then the bubble burst. In the middle of the political storm unleashed by the wave of corruption cases, the scandals of the GAL trials, the internal disputes among the socialists between '*Guerristas*' and 'renovators' and the general climate of unrest and mistrust that reigned in public opinion, the first effects of the 1992 international economic crisis hit Spain. It was a brief recession, lasting barely two years, but it had a harsh effect on the Spanish economy, bringing about as many as four devaluations of the peseta in that period. The fall in production bottomed out in 1993, with negative GDP growth, a 7% public deficit and unemployment that hit 24% of the workforce. The labour market was unable to absorb the baby-boomers of the 1960s, who were now coming of age, and the growing incorporation of women into the workforce.

By 1995, the economy was showing marked signs of improvement, but the positive indicators of inflation, GDP and job creation were unable to reduce the tensions caused by political debate, a veritable headache for the last government under González, who was being pilloried daily by the scandals in the courts, and submitted to a campaign of harassment and aggravation in the media and in Congress, where the socialist parliamentary minority was sustained by the votes of the Catalan nationalists. The revelation of the CESID 'papers', some documents stolen by Colonel Juan Alberto Perote, with recordings of illegal phone taps that allegedly revealed the responsibility of leading socialists in the GAL case, precipitated the resignation of the minister of defence, Julián García Vargas, and Jordi Pujol withdrawing Catalan support in Parliament. The only thing left to do now was to call an early election for March 1996 and wait for the defeat of the government that would put an end to a long decade of socialist primacy.

Towards a new century

The coming to power of the Partido Popular to some extent ended the process of consolidation of democracy. By 1996 there was little doubt that Spain was a modern, developed country, well integrated into the European Community, with a solid welfare state, legitimate institutions and a stable political system; a country that had relegated the problem of the military to the past, consigned the religious question to a secondary role, and that had legal channels and peaceful ways for resolving social conflicts. Yet to be resolved in 1982 were the problems of unemployment, territorial organisation and terrorism. And there was one more: the creation of a conservative party that would be able to cast off the shackles that linked it to Francoism and to obtain enough popular backing to form a government.

Election results in the 1980s had made it quite clear that neither Manuel Fraga nor the old generation of Alianza Popular, both with links to the dictatorship, were able to represent an alternative that would be supported by the majority of the electorate. The crisis that affected the party after the 1986 election ended three years later with the AP being refounded as the Partido Popular and the political rise of José María Aznar, who led the party into the October 1989 election. That year it only obtained 25% of the vote, the ceiling reached by Fraga, but in 1993 it reached 37% and, finally, in 1996, 38%, barely 1 percentage point more than the PSOE, but enough for Aznar to try to form a government with the support of the Basque and Catalan nationalists. Aznar, who had been first minister of the Junta de Castilla y León since 1987, was not part of the generation that had played a role in the Transition. His public declarations had evolved from the questioning of the Constitution to the defence of the political legacy of the late UCD, by claiming the 'reformist centre' space, as the Partido Popular defined itself in its statutes. Aznar was able to renew the senior posts, create a tightly disciplined structure and transform the PP into an electoral party, with new symbols and communications techniques and an effective organisation.

Aznar's first term, between 1996 and 2000, was marked by the pact with CiU and the PNV. The government's parliamentary minority forced the party to display flexibility over some of the nationalists' claims, to restrain its ideological discourse and to moderate its social and economic policies with a willingness to engage in dialogue and the negotiation of agreements with the unions. To a great extent, this was made possible by the boom years of the international economy, a cycle of sustained growth that had begun in 1995 and which was to reign for more than a decade until well into the twenty-first century. The measures adopted by Rodrigo Rato, the finance minister, managed to lower interest rates and reduce inflation and the public deficit, the convergence criteria designed years earlier by the Treaty of Maastricht for entering into monetary union. The dynamism of its exports and the boost in investment and private spending enabled the Spanish economy to grow more than that of the rest of Europe, over 4% for several years running. By the beginning of the twenty-first century, Spain's per capita income stood at 83% of the European Community's average, the highest it had ever been, and the unemployment rate had gone down to 11%.

The economic boom, the image of competition, careful spending and efficient management, social dialogue, successful anti-terrorism actions by the police and the courts, and the internal crisis of the PSOE, accompanied by the abstention of certain sectors of the left, go a long way to explaining the absolute majority obtained by the PP in the 2000 general

Figure 14 Prime Minister José María Aznar (second from left) with former prime ministers Leopoldo Calvo Sotelo (left), Adolfo Suárez (second from right) and Felipe González (right) in 1997 at Moncloa Palace. The most notable features of the Spanish Transition have been the willingness to reach consensus along with established democratic institutions that allow for political rotation. © Agencia EFE

election, with 44% of the vote and 183 seats. From then on, as Javier
Tusell has pointed out, the new government forgot its spirit of dialogue
and centrist moderation and revealed 'a Spanish nationalist ambition, an
overinflated ego and contempt for the opposition, especially the nationalist opposition'. Aznar became 'a sort of moralist reformer, dogmatic and
prophetic, who acted wholly independently of the existing social conditions and the consensus that it had been necessary to build up in order to
take decisions that were truly designed to endure'.[3]

It was not a sudden change. Already during his first term he had shown
signs of this idea of power in aspects such as the control of the public
media, the imposition of an education policy, meddling in the judiciary,
the strategy of privatising public companies, appointing political cronies
to run them, measures designed to reinforce the privileges of the Catholic
Church or the withdrawal of the Immigration Bill, which brought about
the resignation of the minister of labour, Manuel Pimentel. But it was in
2001 that the true nature of the neo-conservative project became more
evident. Some of the controversial aspects of this second term which did
most to harm the government's image included university reform, the
rupture of dialogue with the unions, regional conflicts caused by the
National Hydrological Plan, the refusal to accept any political responsibility regarding the sinking of the *Prestige* tanker off the coast of Galicia
which led to a disastrous oil slick, the Yak-42 air crash in Turkey which
cost the lives of more than sixty military personnel, and the incident with
Morocco when the latter seized the tiny island of Perejil.

But without a doubt, Aznar's gravest error in the eyes of the public was
the direction taken by his foreign policy, which favoured and narrowed
relationships with the United States, particularly after the Twin Towers
attack in September 2001. The government's enthusiastic support for the
American invasion of Iraq – as seen in the famous photo of Bush, Blair
and Aznar in the Azores – meant that protests against the war turned into
massive demonstrations, such as the ones in February 2003, when millions of citizens took to the streets all over Spain. However, despite the
significant loss of popular support, the PP was expecting no outcome for
the general election on 14 March 2004 other than victory. And then, just
three days before polling, came the Islamist terrorist attack on various
suburban trains in Madrid, with 192 dead and more than 1,500 injured,
making it the most lethal in Spain's history. The government's reaction,
which attributed the terrorist attack to ETA, seen by many as a clear

[3] Javier Tusell and Javier Paniagua, *La España democrática* (Madrid: El País, 2008), p. 307.

manipulation of information, caused hundreds of thousands of voters to go to the polls to show their disapproval of the way the crisis was handled. The PSOE received 42% of the vote with 164 seats compared to the 148 seats retained by the PP, and José Luis Rodríguez Zapatero was set, with the support of the IU and the ERC, to become the fifth prime minister of democratic Spain after the passing of the 1978 Constitution. This saw the beginning of a new socialist government and a new political cycle which no longer forms part of twentieth-century Spain.

By the turn of the century, most of Spain's long-established problems seemed to have been consigned to the past. Perhaps the two most important issues that had yet to be resolved were the territorial organisation of the state and the persistence of ETA terrorism. After twenty-five years of existence, the State of Autonomous Governments seemed to be fully consolidated, with stable operation, broad legislative and executive powers, and a significant ability to run the policies that were most important for the quality of life of their citizens, health, education, social services, housing, public works and culture. The first goal of the self-government model, the regional decentralisation of power, seemed to have been met. The self-government powers of the seventeen Autonomous Communities were more far-reaching than those of most European regions.

But as well as administrative decentralisation, the 1978 Constitution had another goal, the structuring of an idea of a more pluralistic and heterogeneous Spain, a plan of coexistence that would allow for the various identities, languages and cultures of the state, a common framework that would overcome the nationalist conflicts that had left their mark on a century of its history. Twenty years later, in July 1998, the Bloque Nacionalista Gallego, the Partido Nacionalista Vasco and Convergència i Unió reminded the government that, in their opinion, the 'structuring of the Spanish state as pluri-national' was still unresolved. The parties that signed the Declaration of Barcelona complained of having 'suffered a lack of legal-political recognition, as well as of social and cultural acceptance of our respective national realities within the state', and they proposed acting outside the autonomous framework to press their claims regarding language, culture, institutions, public funding and presence in the European Union.[4]

That same summer, in the Basque Country, a secret agreement between the PNV, EA and ETA, which was to be the foundation of the Pact of Lizarra, was signed with HB in September. For the PNV it marked the end of a decade of collaboration with the PSOE and the beginning of

---

[4] 'Declaración de Barcelona', El País, 23 Jul. 1998.

a sovereignist policy within the 'Basque decision-making context'.[5] The moderate nationalists were breaking their pacts with the mainstream national parties and beginning to tread a path that was supposed to lead to self-determination in the territories of the Basque Country. In exchange, ETA undertook to end their violence. In the two previous years the terrorists had committed eighteen murders, including that of the professor of law and historian Francisco Tomás y Valiente in February 1996, and the execution of Miguel Ángel Blanco, a town councillor in Ermua, captured ten days after the police liberated Ortega Lara, a prison officer who had been kidnapped and held for more than a year. The murder of the town councillor in July 1997 brought millions of people throughout Spain on to the streets in protest. Public revulsion against terrorism was accompanied by successful police operations and legal actions against the political and financial structure close to ETA.

The terrorist ceasefire led, in May 1999, to a meeting in Switzerland with representatives of the Spanish government and measures to make the prison policy more flexible. But at the end of the year the hard line was restored and the 'armed struggle' taken up again. In January 2000, ETA once more started to murder members of the police, politicians, journalists and academics such as Ernest Lluch and, although the terrorists were unable to jeopardise the stability of democracy, they were able to threaten and extort a great many people who were deprived of their basic freedoms and the minimum conditions for exercising their political rights. The PP and PSOE signed the Pact for Liberties and Against Terrorism, and agreed on a common strategy to fight ETA on all fronts, from the prosecution of acts of urban violence, known as *kale borroka*, to the banning of HB and any other organisation that did not expressly condemn terrorism. Meanwhile, the PNV continued its commitment to sovereignty and presented its Proposal for a Political Statute for the Community of Euskadi, known as the Ibarretxe Plan after the Lehendakari at the time, Juan José Ibarretxe, which was a project to set up an associated free state to be ratified via a referendum in a non-violent scenario. The Lehendakari's plan was passed by the Basque Parliament but in February 2005 was rejected in Congress as being unconstitutional. The absence-of-violence condition has never been complied with. Zapatero's socialist government began a new round of talks with ETA, in which the latter declared a 'permanent ceasefire' in March 2006, which was kept only until 30 December, when a car bomb exploded in the Barajas airport parking lot, killing two young Ecuadorians. Democracy is still suffering the blight of the 'party of death'

---

[5] Tusell and Paniagua, *La España democrática*, p. 290.

as denounced by Ernest Lluch, and 'the crude reality of the hand, the gun and the back of the neck', as lamented by Tomás y Valiente shortly before he became another victim of terrorism.[6]

Without the menace of arms, Catalonia's situation at the end of the century was completely different. In 1998, the Catalan Parliament, with the support of CiU and ERC, passed a resolution in favour of the right of self-determination of the Catalan people. The political change that came about in 2003, with the coming to power of the socialist Pasqual Maragall, put an end to two long decades of Jordi Pujol's nationalist government, but not to the debate over moving beyond the framework of the 1980 Statute of Autonomy. Maragall proposed an asymmetrical federalism that would distinguish the regions from nationalities, a question which was on the agenda in the discussion of the new Statute of Autonomy passed in the Catalan Parliament and later reformed in Congress. The new statutes of Valencia, the Balearic Islands and Aragón also use the term 'historic nationality', Andalucía's talks of a 'national reality' and Castile and León's is defined as a 'historic and cultural community'.[7] The early years of the twenty-first century have brought the challenge of defining a cohesive pluri-national democracy, the co-ordination of inter-territorial relations and the construction of a consensus regarding the principles of equality and recognition of diversity and difference. And all this within a new context of Europeanisation and globalisation which calls for a rethink on the concept of sovereignty above and below the parameters of statehood.

In other words, a new scenario for a different country. The first thing to strike Giles Tremlett, *The Guardian*'s Spain correspondent, in his book of travels through Spain at the beginning of the twenty-first century, was its capacity for transformation, the dizzying speed at which it had changed over the previous three decades. There was little or nothing left of the romantic and adventurous view of foreign travellers who, even as late as the middle of the twentieth century, saw Spain as a pre-industrial territory on the fringe of Europe, inexorably backward and firmly introspective. Tremlett describes a modern country which is progressing at a remorseless rate, with motorways and high-speed trains that count distances in hours, with expanding cities that compete to be the home of vast modern buildings, and with far-reaching social changes that have astounded sociologists. In his opinion, the most evident symptom of Spain's success is the phenomenon of immigration: 'A country from which people once

---

[6] Ernest Lluch, 'Euskadi, tierra seductora', *La Vanguardia*, 15 Feb. 1996; Francisco Tomás y Valiente, 'Muerto de un tiro en la nuca', *ABC*, 15 Feb. 1996.
[7] Tusell and Paniagua, *La España democrática*, p. 453.

fled has now become a beacon of hope for those looking to improve their lives.'[8]

There has been a phenomenal change from one century to the next. In 1996 there were barely 500,000 foreign residents in Spain. A decade later, after three different immigration acts and a series of regularisations of immigration status, there were more than 4 million, nearly 10% of the population. The massive influx of immigrants has changed the demographic basis of Spanish society. In the final quarter of the twentieth century the natural population growth slowed due to the rapid fall in the birth rate, from 19 per 1,000 in 1974 to under 10 per 1,000 by the end of the century. In the same period, fertility fell from 2.8 children per woman to just 1.1, one of the lowest rates in the world. In 1998 there were almost as many births as deaths. It is fair to say that Spain was coming to the end of its demographic transition, the result of long, far-reaching processes of social, economic and cultural transformation that had brought the country in line with the rest of the developed nations. The average life expectancy was around 80, above that of most OECD countries, leading to concerns about a top-heavy pyramid of elderly people that jeopardised the future of the pensions system, public health and welfare services.

But in the first few years of the twenty-first century, the figures have experienced an unexpected shift. Because of immigration, the 40 million inhabitants figuring in the 2001 census numbered 46 million in 2008, an increase in barely seven years that is almost the same as that registered in the last three decades of the twentieth century, a growth rate unprecedented in Spain's history. The fertility rate had risen to 1.3 in 2003, with more than half the children born to foreign women. Workers from Africa, Latin America and eastern Europe were employed mainly in building, catering, domestic service and seasonal agriculture, usually taking the less skilled jobs that Spaniards were apparently not willing to fill. Spain has ceased to be an agricultural country. In 1975 agriculture was still providing one job in five. By the end of the century, it was one in twenty. Industry, not counting the construction industry, employed less than 20% of the working population while the service sector accounted for 65%.

De-agrarianisation and the development of the services economy have been accompanied by the growth of the new middle classes and an increasingly qualified labour force. This is due, in large measure, to the expansion of the educational system. Illiteracy and child labour have all but disappeared. Public spending on education, barely 1% of the GDP in the 1960s, was around 5% by the end of the century. In that time, the number of

---

[8] Giles Tremlett, *España ante sus fantasmas: un recorrido por un país en Transición* (Madrid: Siglo XXI, 1996), p. ix.

universities doubled and that of university graduates increased five-fold, to almost 5 million in 2004. More women than men were participating in higher education, one of the traditional factors in sex discrimination. Women played the undisputed leading role in this rapid process of social change. They joined the workforce, reduced their fertility and started behaving differently in the realm of daily and family life, with informal relationships that were gradually moving outside the model of the patriarchal family. The younger generations were more tolerant of homosexual relationships, divorce and child-bearing outside marriage, as they were less and less influenced by religious and traditional norms. Practising Catholics, six out of ten Spaniards in 1975, accounted for barely a third of the population by the end of the century. Society had become secularised, one of the most common signs of the advance of modernity.

The problems that most concern the Spanish are unemployment, the temporary nature of employment, and housing. The same concerns are felt by immigrants, living in worse conditions on lower wages, who have problems in adapting culturally and socially, and whose legal status is obscure. However both groups value positively the security afforded by the welfare state, the pensions system, education and health, the pillars with which democratic societies protect their citizens from the risks and shortcomings of the market economy, the most valuable legacy of the social conquests of the twentieth century. There are also global challenges that will need to be addressed in the twenty-first century, such as the alarming rate at which the environment is being destroyed, or the lot of the most disadvantaged in an unequal, unfair and uncompassionate world, a situation largely ignored by civil and government initiatives in development co-operation.

Within Spain, for a foreign observer like Tremlett, there are still two issues to be resolved. The first one, at the heart of the political agenda, is whether citizens with different identities are willing to coexist within the same frontiers, and under what conditions, and to discuss what they have in common and what separates them. The second has to do with the past, with the traumatic memory of the twentieth century that is still open to debate: 'Spaniards made a supreme effort to find consensus. That effort was driven, to a large degree, by the Civil War ghosts still haunting so many Spanish households. The divisions now visible in Spain have much to do with the release of those historic constraints. How Spaniards deal with them will be the ultimate test of that *Transición*.'[9]

---

[9] Giles Tremlett, *Ghosts of Spain: Travels Through Spain and Its Silent Past* (London: Faber, 2007), p. 387.

Transition and democracy under discussion

Thirty-five years have gone by since the promulgation of the 1978 Constitution. The transition to democracy is now part of history. It is a topic studied in university research projects, in conferences and academic publications, and in secondary education syllabuses. But it is also a subject of political controversy and public debate, used as an instrument and argument to define and pass judgement on the virtues and failings of Spain's democracy. As Carme Molinero has noted, the Transition has a strong presence in daily life, and at each phase it is reinterpreted 'in the light of current projects'. Some, who cling to an idealised vision of the period as a perfectly designed plan, functioning like clockwork, see the pacts and consensus reached as being set in stone. They reject any modification of the institutional framework and decry any balanced criticism as being an attack on the spirit of coexistence and reconciliation. Others, however, consider that a 'second Transition' is essential, one that sets right the political acts of back-tracking and betrayal, the shortcomings of the process, as if the events of those years were responsible for their personal frustrations and 'all the unresolved problems and all the vices – real or imaginary – of the democracy of today'. There are too many platitudes, too many commonplaces and biased conclusions. And, concludes Molinero, there is too much distance between academic research and socialised debate, a space which needs to be occupied by historians in order to ensure that knowledge of our recent past reaches society by offsetting 'media noise and self-serving interpretations'.[10]

The first to address the study of the Spanish democratic transformation were sociologists and political scientists. At the end of the 1960s, in the midst of the Transition, the change that was affecting Spain aroused the interest of social scientists all over the world. And this was only natural. The transition processes in Portugal, Spain and Greece represented the earliest examples of what was later to be called the third wave of democratisation. Nothing like it had occurred since the years immediately following the Second World War. The same path was taken in the 1980s by a dozen Latin American nations which threw off the shackles of their authoritarian regimes. And at the end of the decade, after the fall of communism, it was the countries of eastern Europe and the former Soviet republics in a movement that spread to other areas of the world, as seen in the case of the disappearance of apartheid in South Africa. Democracy, which at the

---

[10] Carme Molinero, 'Treinta años después: la transición revisada', in Molinero (ed.), *La Transición, treinta años después: de la dictadura a la instauración y consolidación de la democracia* (Barcelona: Península, 2006), pp. 9–26.

beginning of the twentieth century was merely a possibility discerned in some places and which in the inter-war years was sidelined by totalitarian ideologies, by the end of the century seemed to come out as the most common form of government in the world. Things are more difficult and complex than many people thought they would be and the result has not always been satisfactory, but the magnitude and depth of the change are undisputable.

The Spanish Transition drew the attention of social and political theorists, and also political players in other countries immersed in similar situations, for its pioneering nature, the surprising speed of the negotiations regarding democratisation and its undeniable success obtained with practically no violence. The democratic opposition and the reformist leaders of eastern and central Europe and South America thought that they could draw practical lessons and useful analyses for their own countries. If not an exportable model, Spain provided at least an encouraging example.

José Casanova has conducted a comparative analysis of democratic transitions, distinguishing three types of exit from authoritarian regimes: 'from outside, from below or from above'. In his opinion, the Spanish case belongs to the last group because the decoupling from Francoism was a pact negotiated by the sectors that had been involved in the dictatorship and because the form that was adopted, a legal-constitutional reform, was what finally led to a real break with the old order. The negotiations came afterwards, the result of a situation in which none of the leading players, Francoists or the democratic opposition, were strong enough to impose their own solution. It was not a simple process. The economic climate was clearly unfavourable, there was no party or big name to symbolise the consensus of the opposition, there were nationalist movements that called the unity of the state into question, the authoritarian regime still controlled the administration and the means of restraint, and the army top brass, almost without exception, were profoundly Francoist.[11]

There were uncertainties, risks and setbacks that had to be dealt with in a relatively short period of time until a final result was reached that most experts have agreed was successful and a motive for collective pride according to the opinion polls. The most notable features of the Spanish Transition have been the willingness to reach consensus, the commitment to go beyond party interests and the ability to enter into long-lasting pacts and agreements. Thanks to all this, Spain has become a country that is

---

[11] José Casanova, 'Las enseñanzas de la Transición democrática en España', *Ayer*, 15 (1994), pp. 15–54.

clearly European, with an open and renewed economy, free of the threat of military power, with established democratic institutions that allow for political rotation and ensure a broad set of citizen rights and freedoms comparable to those of more advanced countries. The political, social, economic and cultural evolution of the final quarter of the twentieth century represents, without doubt, the longest period of stability and liberty in Spanish contemporary history. It would be unfair to present an overall balance that did not show clearly positive signs.

But it would be equally unfair to show a complacent image free of errors and setbacks, grey areas and aspects requiring improvement. The critical function of historical knowledge cannot be diluted, as Julio Aróstegui has remarked, when faced with an 'official' account that has been 'toned down', a rose-coloured description of an exemplary past free of any dark spots, the 'Immaculate Transition' as José Vidal Beneyto called it disparagingly.[12] It should be stressed again that Francoism was not a necessary antecedent of democracy but a fascist-inspired authoritarian regime that followed a military uprising and a bloody civil war that was remembered and celebrated for four decades. In the final years of the dictatorship, the reformist elites did not concentrate their energies on drawing up a perfect plan to ensure society made a peaceful transition to democracy, as some people claim, but on negotiating the least number of changes possible to enable the regime, or at least the bases of social order and social and economic privileges contained therein, to continue. Naturally, the profound socio-economic and cultural changes of the 1960s forced Francoism into an inevitable crisis. But the dictatorship did not come to an end suddenly just one day, 20 November 1975, when Franco died in a hospital bed. And what happened next was not the result of a plan preconceived from above independently, directed only by figures such as Adolfo Suárez or Juan Carlos I, who has been called the 'engine' or 'pilot' of the change.

The Transition, as Tomás y Valiente remarked, 'was a choral symphony without a score, which was performed in a concert without an audience, because everybody was on stage', a concert without a written score and without a conductor: 'There was not just one man with the baton in his hand. Not even the King.'[13] It was an irregular and problematic process, made up as it went along, admittedly the result of negotiations between the representatives of the class that had governed the country and politicians from the opposition, but also the coercions and threats from various factions and the pressure exerted from below by the social movements.

---

[12] Julio Aróstegui, *La Transición (1975–1982)* (Madrid: Acento, 2000), and José Beneyto, *Memoria democrática* (Madrid: FOCA, 2007).
[13] Francisco Tomás y Valiente, *A orillas del Estado* (Madrid: Taurus, 1997), p. 205.

The dictatorship died in the streets, say Nicolás Sartorius and Alberto Sabio, and 'Spanish democracy was not a democracy that was granted, but one gained with obvious effort and plenty of risk and sacrifice.'[14]

And some of the virtues of the Transition can be today be perceived as shortcomings of the democracy that Spaniards enjoy without necessarily discrediting the process or calling the legitimacy of Spain's political model into question. In this respect, we might mention the unfairness of the electoral system or the ambiguity and vagueness of the Constitution in defining a pluri-national reality. Josep M. Colomer adds another short-coming, the restrictive nature of certain democratic institutions that concentrate too much power in the leaders of the two main parties, weaken the channels of communication between the state and society and keep citizens out of the decision-making process. Javier Tusell also focused on the disadvantages of the cautionary measures adopted by the Spanish political class to achieve a stable democracy, a sort of guardianship over the population that alienates the political system from the 'lifeblood of the populace', as borne out, for example, in the low membership of the political parties and voluntary organisations.[15]

A quarter of a century has gone by since the end of the Transition. The Spanish political system is firmly entrenched and is able to embark on changes and reforms to improve the quality of its democracy and reinforce citizen participation. Gone are the fear and instability of the late 1970s. Also gone is the dread of a violent confrontation that might bring about a repetition of the Civil War or a return to a dictatorship. At that time there was an unspoken agreement among the political class not to convert the thorniest aspects of the past into a subject of parliamentary debate, or to hold anyone responsible. The controversial, much discussed 'pact of forgetting' or 'pact of silence' was observed by all parties during the Transition, and in the following decade the socialist governments, which enjoyed ample majorities, did not dare to break it either. But at the beginning of the twenty-first century there is a new generation of post-Transition Spaniards, who are adding their support to a widespread campaign in favour of historical memory and political, legal and moral redress for the victims of the war and the dictatorship. An unfettered look back to the traumatic experiences of the twentieth century is arousing debates on the complex relationships between history and memory, and also passionate public opinion and media discussions, a major feature of which is

---

[14] Sartorius and Sabio, *El final de la dictadura*, p. 778.

[15] Josep M. Colomer, *La transición a la democracia: el modelo español* (Barcelona: Anagrama, 1998); and Javier Tusell, *La transición a la democracia (España, 1975–1982)* (Madrid: Espasa-Calpe, 2007), pp. 281–2.

rejection from those who feel most uncomfortable with the memory of violence. But to address the need for a public memory policy, as has been done in other countries, does not mean sowing the seed of discord or jeopardising peaceful coexistence. It is simply evidence of the maturity of a democratic society that is deciding to confront the ghosts of its past without fear.

Conclusion: the balance sheet of a century

The twentieth century in Spain was exceptionally varied. Many Spaniards were born during a monarchy, that of Alfonso XIII, lived through two dictatorships, a republic and a civil war, and died with the grandson of Alfonso XIII, Juan Carlos I, as head of state. But their experiences were very different depending on whether they had always supported traditional order, won the war and lived quietly and contentedly during the dictatorship of their Caudillo; as opposed to those of another type of Spaniard, one who dreamt of the Republic, saw it come to fruition, fought for it until he was defeated, and never knew peace under Franco.

However, it is not the historian's job to choose the part of the film that suits him best. The twentieth century ended in a better state than when it began, and Spain in 2000 was a much more prosperous, democratic and less violent country than in the middle decades of the century, although any satisfactory balance sheet would also need to look at the misery and fear that was left behind on the way. For the historian taking stock, the twentieth century is a complete unit, and the history of Spain cannot be separated from that of the rest of Europe.

Seen from this comparative perspective, the distinctive feature of the history of twentieth-century Spain was the long duration of Franco's dictatorship after the Civil War. It was not a parenthesis in the history of Spain in that century but the central element that dominated the scene absolutely for almost four decades. The century's dividing line in Europe was, as Mark Mazower suggests, the 1940s, when 'the Nazi utopia reached its zenith, and then as swiftly collapsed'.[1] In Spain, everything happened a little before, in the 1930s, with democracy and revolution defeated in the Civil War by an authoritarianism that did not fall in 1945 and that for three decades survived the fascism that had done so much to help it.

The Cold War, the struggle between communism and the capitalist democracies, a phenomenon that occurred over a long period in other

---

[1] Mazower, *Dark Continent*, p. x.

parts of the world, did not affect Spain, which at that time was anchored in something that had disappeared in the rest of Europe, except for Portugal. From a European perspective, the 1980s were crucial, with the overthrow of the Soviet empire in 1989 and the end of the ideological rivalries that had flourished in the inter-war period. In Spain, these rivalries had ended a decade earlier, during the years between the death of Franco and the arrival of democracy. It is no coincidence that most of the studies carried out by Anglo-American Hispanicists, the most solid tradition of historical research conducted outside Spain, concentrate on this period between 1931 and 1982, and particularly between 1931 and 1939, the periods with the most international coverage in Spain's history. But these years do not explain the whole picture.

The democracy that emerged at the end of the 1970s was just one of the possible results, and today we know it was positive, that the consolidation of democracy changed Spain's position in Europe, integrating it fully – one of the dreams of the Spanish intellectual elites since the end of the nineteenth century. No longer was just one side described as representing the true Spain, and democracy brought comprehensive liberties and the status of European citizens. Also in Spain, as had occurred in part of Europe and North America, democracy was associated with the triumph of capitalism, which was no longer under fire from revolutionary forces. One of these forces, anarchism, which had been so evident in the first four decades of the century, and had seemed so exceptional and remarkable to foreign observers, such as Gerald Brenan, Franz Borkenau and George Orwell, disappeared with the arrival of this democracy, which had managed to avoid any temptation to include republican tendencies. The new Spanish democracy, which emerged from the elections of June 1977, broke off any link with the Second Republic, because it was administered from above by former Francoists and accepted from below as free from the stereotyped past of the Civil War and fratricidal divisions.

Looking back at the end of the twentieth century, we note that the leap that Spain made from 1900 onwards was spectacular, particularly as far as economic indicators are concerned. In the opinion of José Luis García Delgado and Juan Carlos Jiménez, who have undertaken some of the most solid research of the last three decades, the first third of the century represented 'a moderate but determined acquiring of prosperity'; and the period between 1936 and 1950, 'savage discontinuity, a slump, a catastrophic cutback'; while the growth in per capita income in the second half of the century reached an average of 3.8%, 'almost a four-fold increase to that of a hundred years earlier and the first third of the nineteen-hundreds'. If we draw up a balance sheet of a century, conclude these authors, we see that Spain travelled the same route as the most

advanced countries in Europe, and left behind a financial situation that
clearly did not favour its economy but which had pertained while the rest
of Europe strengthened its liberal revolutions and industrial society.[2]

During the twentieth century Spain was transformed from an agricultural and rural society to one that was industrial and urban. The almost
60% of the active population that worked in agriculture in 1900 had
decreased to less than 7% by the end of the century, although the sharpest
fall occurred between the mid 1950s and the beginning of the 1960s. The
definitive crisis in traditional agriculture – which with a surplus of manpower produced little – changed the soul of Spanish society and relegated
the primary sector to playing a minuscule role, around 3% at the end of the
century, in a production structure now dominated by industry, building
and, above all, services.

The high death and infant mortality rates, malnutrition and periodic
epidemics clearly show the hardships suffered by a population of almost
19 million inhabitants in 1900. The population went up to 40 million over
the century, despite the fact that the Civil War and exile accounted for
750,000 people, mostly male, and more than 2.5 million Spaniards emi-
grated to the Americas and Europe between 1950 and 1974. However,
everything evened out over the century as a whole. By 2000, infant mortality, malnutrition, poor hygienic and sanitary conditions, and the absence
of running water in the home was history, a memory for the older generation only.

If anything typified the European democracies that became consolidated after the Second World War, it was the commitment to provide a
welfare state, social services, for the majority of the population. One of the
great challenges facing Spain's democracy over the past quarter of a
century has been to catch up with the rest of Europe in terms of public
amenities, infrastructure and welfare systems. Public spending accounted
for less than 10% of the gross national income in 1900, went up just a few
points in 1960, was less than 25% at the time of Franco's death, and yet it
was around 50% in 2000, similar to that of more advanced countries in
Europe. Fairer distribution of wealth, the drastic fall in illiteracy, widespread schooling until the age of 16 and growing professional skill, with
more than 1.5 million university students, are unmistakeable signs that
modernisation has been realised.

But not everything was perfect in this century of conflicts, paradoxes and
contrasts. For more than four decades, what has been called the century of
the masses, of the citizenry, of civil and social rights, was deprived of free

[2] García Delgado and Jiménez, *La historia de España del siglo XX: la economía*, pp. 15–27.

elections with universal suffrage. The person most responsible for this state of affairs, Francisco Franco, was not a criminal madman who, together with his brothers-in-arms, insisted on taking a different path to the one taken by the western democracies. Today, European democracy and civilisation may appear superior to many Spaniards, but for years and years they supported the situation and allowed themselves to be organised under strict authoritarian rules, while forcing dissenters to comply.

War was a momentous experience in the lives of millions of Europeans during the first half of the twentieth century. Spain had not taken part in the First World War, and therefore had not undergone the upheaval that this war had caused, with the fall of empires and their subjects, the demobilisation of millions of ex-combatants and massive debt caused by the vast spending on the war effort. But it did share the division and tension that accompanied the process of modernisation between those supporters of order and authority who feared Bolshevism and the various manifestations of socialism, and those who dreamed of this new, egalitarian world that would arise from the class struggle.

Two world wars with a 'twenty-year crisis' in between marked the history of Europe in the twentieth century. It took only three years for Spanish society to undergo a wave of violence and an unprecedented disdain for the lives of others. Despite all that has been said about the violence that preceded the Civil War, in an attempt to justify its outbreak, it is clear that the *coup d'état* of July 1936 marked a watershed in twentieth-century Spanish history. Furthermore, for at least two decades after the end of the Civil War in 1939, there was no positive reconstruction such as had occurred in other countries in western Europe after 1945.

The climate of order, *patria* and religion overrode that of democracy, the Republic and revolution. In short, in Franco's long and cruel dictatorship lies the exceptional nature of Spain's twentieth-century history in comparison to that of other western capitalist countries. After the deaths of Hitler and Mussolini, Franco carried on. The darkest side of this European civil war, that ended in 1945, was to live on in Spain for a long time yet.

Spain's democracy tried to erase the most uncomfortable memories of Franco's dictatorship, and when in recent years they have reappeared and the state has implemented, albeit gingerly, public memory policies, remembering the past in order to learn from it, not to punish or condemn, a large section of society has come out against the measure. The past has become the present, time to draw down the curtain, in a political and cultural battlefield, where opinions are voiced more strongly than ever in books, documentaries and tributes to the survivors and victims of those traumatic experiences.

We are in the 'age of memory', which makes many people feel so uncomfortable. It is a social construction of memory, which evokes with other instruments, and at times deforms, what we historians uncover. We do not know what will be left of all this for future generations' knowledge of history. We historians are obliged to continue shedding light on the lives of men and women in the past. And we do so in a present no longer bound by some of the conflicts and uncertainties that beset our predecessors.

In spite of the existence of ETA, a legacy of the dictatorship that democracy has been unable to eliminate entirely, violence is no longer a vehicle of political action in Spain. That is the great success story after so much strife. Farewell to militarism, to violence. Farewell to arms. Will this hold true for what is left of the twenty-first century?

Guide to further reading

GENERAL WORKS

English-speaking readers who wish to have a view of the entire Spanish contemporary era should read Raymond Carr's classic study, *Spain 1808–1975* (Oxford: Clarendon Press, 1982), or a later version, *Modern Spain, 1875–1980* (Oxford University Press, 2001). But there are other more recent works summarising this period, equally as commendable, such as José Álvarez Junco and Adrian Shubert (eds.), *Spanish History Since 1808* (New York: Oxford University Press, 2000); Mary Vincent, *Spain, 1833–2002: People and State* (Oxford University Press, 2007); Charles J. Esdaile, *Spain in the Liberal Age: From Constitution to Civil War, 1808–1939* (Oxford: Blackwell, 2000); Christopher J. Ross, *Spain Since 1812* (London: Routledge, 2009); or the collection of studies edited by Nigel Townson, *Is Spain Different?* (Eastbourne: Sussex Academic Press, 2013). The transition from the nineteenth to the twentieth centuries is summarised in the article by José Álvarez Junco, 'History, Politics, and Culture, 1875–1936', in David Gies (ed.), *The Cambridge Companion to Modern Spanish Culture* (Cambridge University Press, 1999), pp. 67–85.

THE RESTORATION AND THE DICTATORSHIP OF PRIMO DE RIVERA

For an introduction to the complexity of the Restoration, between 1875 and 1930, see a standard Spanish text, Ramón Villares' and Javier Moreno Luzón's general overview of the period, in *Restauración y Dictadura* (Barcelona: Crítica and Marcial Pons, 2009), vol. VII of the *Historia de España* whose overall editors are Josep Fontana and Ramón Villares. To learn more about the political system of the Restoration and the complex issue of *caciquismo*, see José Varela Ortega (ed.), *El poder de la influencia: geografía del caciquismo en España (1875–1923)* (Madrid: Marcial Pons, 2001).

With regard to the end-of-century crisis, special mention should be made of the work edited by Juan Pan-Montojo, *Más se perdió en Cuba: España, 1898 y la crisis de fin de siglo* (Madrid: Alianza, 1998). The best account of the colonial conflict may be found in the book co-authored by Antonio Elorza and Helena Hernández Sandoica, *La Guerra de Cuba (1895–1898)* (Madrid: Alianza, 1998). As far as books in English are concerned, an essential reference is Sebastian Balfour, *The End of the Spanish Empire, 1898–1923* (Oxford University Press, 1997). The Spanish colonial system is covered in Christopher Schmidt-Nowara, *The Conquest of*

History: Spanish Colonialism and National Histories in the Nineteenth Century (University of Pittsburgh Press, 2006). For the War of 1898, see David F. Trask, *The War with Spain in 1898* (Lincoln: University of Nebraska Press, 1996), and Louis A. Perez Jnr and Louis A. Perez, *The War of 1898: The United States and Cuba in History and Historiography* (Chapel Hill: University of North Carolina Press, 1998). The situation in Spain during these years is covered in José Varela Ortega, 'Aftermath of Splendid Disaster: Spanish Politics Before and After the Spanish American War of 1898', *Journal of Contemporary History*, 15, 2 (Apr. 1980), pp. 317–44.

The reign of Alfonso XIII is very effectively introduced in works by Javier Moreno-Luzón, *Modernizing the Nation: Spain During the Reign of Alfonso XIII, 1902–1931* (Brighton: Sussex Academic Press, 2012), and 'Political Clientelism, Elites, and Caciquismo in Restoration Spain (1875–1923)', *European History Quarterly*, 37, 3 (2007), pp. 417–41; as well as in the essay by Morgan C. Hall, *Alfonso XIII and the Failure of the Liberal Monarchy in Spain, 1902–1923* (New York: Columbia University Press, 2003). The question of the political elites is well presented in works compiled by Sebastian Balfour and Paul Preston (eds.), *Spain and the Great Powers in the Twentieth Century* (London: Routledge, 1999), and by Frances Lannon and Paul Preston (eds.), *Elites and Power in Twentieth-Century Spain: Essays in Honour of Sir Raymond Carr* (Oxford University Press, 1991). For an introduction to the entrepreneurial classes, see the book by Mercedes Cabrera and Fernando del Rey Reguillo, *The Power of Entrepreneurs: Politics and Economy in Contemporary Spain* (New York and Oxford: Berghahn Books, 2007).

An examination of the political discourse and republican culture can be found in José Álvarez Junco, *The Emergence of Mass Politics in Spain: Populist Demagoguery and Republican Culture, 1890–1910* (Brighton: Sussex Academic Press, 2002). The same author is a good guide for discovering the process of the construction of the state and the difficult coexistence of various national identities: Junco, 'Spain: A Product of Incomplete Nation-Building', in Louk Hagendoorn, György Csepeli, Henk Dekker and Russell Farnen, *European Nations and Nationalism: Theoretical and Historical Perspectives* (Aldershot, UK, and Brookfield, VT: Ashgate, 2000), pp. 183–214. See also the essays in Jo Labanyi (ed.), *Constructing Identity in Twentieth-Century Spain: Theoretical Debates and Cultural Practice* (Oxford University Press, 2002). For another perspective, see Carolyn P. Boyd, *Historia Patria: Politics, History, and National Identity in Spain, 1875–1975* (Princeton University Press, 1997).

The problem of militarism is examined in Stanley G. Payne's classic book, *Politics and the Military in Modern Spain* (Stanford University Press, 1967). Also essential is Carolyn P. Boyd's analysis in *Praetorian Politics in Liberal Spain* (Chapel Hill: University of North Carolina Press, 1979). The conflict between clericalism and anti-clericalism is discussed in the comprehensive studies by Frances Lannon, *Privilege, Persecution, and Prophecy: The Catholic Church in Spain 1875–1975* (Oxford University Press, 1987), and William J. Callahan, *Church, Politics, and Society in Spain, 1750–1874* (Cambridge, MA: Harvard University Press, 1984), and Callahan, *The Catholic Church in Spain, 1875–1998* (Washington, DC: Catholic University of America Press, 2000). See also the detailed analysis by

Joan Connelly Ullman, *The Tragic Week: A Study of Anticlericalism in Spain, 1875–1912* (Cambridge, MA: Harvard University Press, 1968).

An overview of the living conditions of the popular classes can be found in Adrian Shubert, *A Social History of Modern Spain* (London: Routledge, 1990). A general introduction to the situation of women and the gender issue in Victoria Lorée Enders and Pamela Beth Radcliff (eds.), *Constructing Spanish Womanhood: Female Identity in Modern Spain* (Albany: State University of New York Press, 1999).

Readers who wish to learn more about the history of social movements in the early decades of the twentieth century should consult the studies by Angel Smith, *Red Barcelona: Social Protest and Labour Mobilization in the Twentieth Century* (London: Routledge, 2002), and Smith, *Anarchism, Revolution and Reaction: Catalan Labour and the Crisis of the Spanish State, 1898–1923* (Oxford: Berghahn, 2007); Pamela Radcliff, *From Mobilization to Civil War: The Politics of Polarization in the Spanish City of Gijon, 1900–1937* (Cambridge University Press, 1996); Richard Purkiss, *Democracy, Trade Unions and Political Violence in Spain: The Valencian Anarchist Movement, 1918–1936* (Brighton: Sussex Academic Press, 2011); Paul Heywood, *Marxism and the Failure of Organised Socialism in Spain, 1879–1936* (Cambridge University Press, 2003); Chris Ealham, *Class, Culture and Conflict in Barcelona, 1898–1937* (London: Routledge, 2004); Gerald Meaker, *The Revolutionary Left in Spain: 1914–1923* (Stanford University Press, 1974); Temma Kaplan, *Anarchists of Andalusia, 1868–1903* (Princeton University Press, 1977); and Kaplan, *Red City, Blue Period: Social Movements in Picasso's Barcelona* (Berkeley: University of California Press, 1992).

For the final years of the Restoration, between the general crisis of 1917, the disaster of the war in Morocco and Primo de Rivera's *coup d'état*, recommended texts are the works of Francisco J. Romero Salvadó, *Spain 1914–1918: Between War and Revolution* (London: Routledge, 1999); Romero Salvadó, *The Foundations of Civil War: Revolution, Social Conflict and Reaction in Liberal Spain, 1916–1923* (London: Routledge, 2010), and the set of studies co-ordinated by Angel Smith and Francisco J. Romero Salvadó (eds.), *The Agony of Spanish Liberalism: From Revolution to Dictatorship 1913–1923* (Basingstoke: Palgrave Macmillan, 2010). The evolution of conservative thought in the studies compiled by Alejandro Quiroga and Miguel Ángel del Arco, *Right-Wing Spain in the Civil War Era: Soldiers of God and Apostles of the Fatherland, 1914–1945* (London: Continuum, 2012). The importance of the war in Morocco for Spanish history in subsequent years is shown in Sebastian Balfour, *Deadly Embrace: Morocco and the Road to the Spanish Civil War* (Oxford University Press, 2002). Finally, for the years of the dictatorship, see Alejandro Quiroga, *Making Spaniards: Primo de Rivera and the Nationalization of the Masses, 1923–1930* (Basingstoke: Palgrave Macmillan, 2007), and a complete and updated summary in Spanish by Eduardo González Calleja, *La España de Primo de Rivera: la modernización autoritaria* (Madrid: Alianza, 2005).

THE SECOND REPUBLIC AND CIVIL WAR

It was foreign historians, particularly British and North American, who were the first to challenge the version of history told by the victors of the Civil War, and they did so with general summaries that were finely crafted and elegantly written that are still useful today. The best examples are Gabriel Jackson, *The Spanish Republic and the Civil War* (Princeton University Press, 1965); Hugh Thomas, *The Spanish Civil War* (London: Eyre & Spottiswoode, 1961); and Raymond Carr, *Spanish Tragedy: Civil War in Perspective* (London: Weidenfeld & Nicolson, 1977).

The thought and constant search for accuracy that marked these early works are still the distinguishing features of these British and North American Hispanists. Paul Preston is currently the bridging point between this first generation and the new British historians, at whom his books are usually directed. Chief among his extensive output are *The Coming of the Spanish Civil War: Reform, Reaction and Revolution in the Spanish Republic* (London: Routledge, 1994), and the revised and expanded version of *The Spanish Civil War* (London: Harper Perennial, 2006), which also includes a comprehensive bibliography. Preston's book and the recent work by Antony Beevor, *The Battle for Spain: The Spanish Civil War 1936–1939* (London: Weidenfeld & Nicolson, 2006), are the two most complete and updated summaries of the war, although one should not forget the contribution of Ronald Fraser, *The Blood of Spain: Experience of the Civil War* (London: Viking, 1979), which is still valuable for its highly imaginative approach.

Concise, although evocative, is the work by Helen Graham, *The Spanish Civil War: A Very Short Introduction* (Oxford University Press, 2005). See also Graham, *The War and Its Shadow: Spain's Civil War in Europe's Long Twentieth Century* (Eastbourne: Sussex Academic Press, 2012). In the United States, a constant output is being maintained by Stanley G. Payne, and we should emphasise two works: *Spain's First Democracy: The Second Republic, 1931–1936* (Madison: University of Wisconsin Press, 1993), and *The Collapse of the Spanish Republic, 1933–1936: Origins of the Civil War* (New Haven, CT: Yale University Press, 2006). Francisco J. Romero Salvadó's *The Spanish Civil War* (New York: Palgrave Macmillan, 2005) is useful. Another significant work is Burnett Bolloten, *The Spanish Civil War: Revolution and Counterrevolution* (Chapel Hill: University of North Carolina Press, 1991). See also my recent contribution on the whole period in Julián Casanova, *The Spanish Republic and Civil War* (Cambridge University Press, 2010).

Less prolific has been the output from French Hispanists. Pierre Broué and Emile Temime have made their contribution with the two volumes of *La revolución y la guerra de España* (Mexico City: FCE, 1974). A briefer synthesis appears in Pierre Vilar's *La guerra civil española* (Barcelona: Critica, 1986). More recent and more extensive, although not the work of a specialist, is Bartolomé Bennasar's *El infierno fuimos nosotros: la guerra civil española (1936–1942)* (Madrid: Taurus, 2005). The German Hispanist, Walther L. Bernecker, has given us a good analysis, particularly useful for the international dimension of the war: *Krieg in Spanien, 1936–1939* (Darmstadt: Wissenschaftliche Buchgesellschaft, 1991). A sound and thorough summary has recently been provided in Italian by Gabriele Ranzato, *L'eclissi della democracia: la guerra civile spagnola e le sue origini 1931–1939* (Turin: Bollati Boringhieri, 2004).

Many politicians, republican and otherwise, have written their memoirs about those years. The most useful are Niceto Alcalá Zamora, *Memorias*

(Madrid: Planeta, 1977); Miguel Maura, *Así cayó Alfonso XIII* ... (Barcelona: Ariel, 1966); Alejandro Lerroux, *La pequeña historia: apuntes para la historia grande, vividos y redactados por el autor* (Madrid: Afrodisio Aguado, 1966); José María Gil Robles, *No fue posible la paz* (Barcelona: Ariel, 1968); Joaquín Chapaprieta, *La paz fue posible: memorias de un político* (Barcelona: Ariel, 1971); César Jalón, *Memorias políticas: periodista, ministro, presidiario* (Madrid: Guadarrama, 1973); Diego Martínez Barrio, *Memorias* (Barcelona: Planeta, 1983); Manuel Portela Valladares, *Memorias: dentro del drama español* (Madrid: Alianza, 1988); and Manuel Azaña, *Diarios completos: monarquía, república, guerra civil* (Barcelona: Crítica, 2000).

Various socialist, anarchist and communist leaders have also left valuable testimonies. See, for example, Francisco Largo Caballero, *Mis recuerdos* (Mexico City: Ediciones Unidas, 1976); Indalecio Prieto, *Convulsiones de España* (Mexico City: Oasis, 1967–9), 3 vols.; Juan Simeón Vidarte, *Las Cortes Constituyentes de 1931 a 1933* (Barcelona: Grijalbo, 1976), Vidarte, *El bienio negro y la insurrección de Asturias* (Barcelona: Grijalbo, 1978) and Vidarte, *Todos fuimos culpables* (Mexico City: FCE, 1973); Julián Zugazagoitia, *Guerra y vicisitudes de los españoles* (Barcelona: Tusquets, 2001); Juan García Oliver, *El eco de los pasos* (Barcelona: Ruedo Ibérico, 1978); Diego Abad de Santillán, *Memorias, 1897–1936* (Barcelona: Planeta, 1977); and Santiago Carrillo, *La Segunda República: recuerdos y reflexiones* (Barcelona: Plaza & Janés, 1999).

There is a comprehensive body of work dealing with the reforms undertaken by the republican–socialist coalition government and the protests they generated, the theme of Part II. For the land problem, an essential resource is Edward Malefakis, *Agrarian Reform and Peasant Revolution in Spain* (New Haven, CT: Yale University Press, 1971). The military question is well presented in Michael Alpert, *La reforma militar de Azaña (1931–1939)* (Madrid: Siglo XXI, 1982), and Gabriel Cardona, *El poder militar en la España contemporánea hasta la guerra civil* (Madrid: Siglo XXI, 1983). The handing over of public order to the military is clearly explained in Manuel Ballbé, *Orden público y militarismo en la España constitucional (1812–1983)* (Madrid: Alianza, 1985). Santos Juliá has examined the performance of the socialists during the Republic and the Civil War in *Los socialistas y la política española, 1879–1982* (Madrid: Taurus, 1996).

A summary of the methods of protest, strikes and insurrections by the anarchists during the Second Republic may be found in Julián Casanova, *Anarchism, the Republic and Civil War in Spain: 1931–1939* (London: Routledge, 2005). On the peasant conflict, see Manuel Tuñón de Lara, *Tres claves de la Segunda República: la cuestión agraria, los aparatos del Estado, Frente Popular* (Madrid: Alianza, 1985). The basic work on the insurrection in Casas Viejas is by Jerome R. Mintz, *Los anarquistas de Casas Viejas* (Diputación Provincial de Cádiz, 1994).

The opposition to the Republic by employers, right-wing politicians and the Catholic Church is to be found in all the summaries cited previously. The hostility towards social reforms and collective bargaining appears in Mercedes Cabrera, *La patronal ante la II República: organizaciones y estrategia (1931–1936)* (Madrid: Siglo XXI, 1983). The dealings of the right in general are covered in Richard A. H. Robinson, *The Origins of Franco's Spain: The Right, the Republic and Revolution, 1931–1936* (Newton Abbot: David & Charles, 1970). A synthesis study on the monarchists appears in Julio Gil Pecharromán, *Conservadores subversivos: la derecha autoritaria alfonsina (1931–1936)* (Madrid: Eudema, 1994). Good analysis on the Carlists can be found in Martin Blinkhorn, *Carlism and Crisis in Spain 1931 to 1939* (Cambridge University Press, 1975). On the fascist right, see Sheelagh Ellwood, *Spanish Fascism in the Franco Era, 1933–1983* (Basingstoke: Macmillan, 1987); Joan Maria Tomàs, *Lo que fue la Falange* (Barcelona: Plaza & Janés, 1999); and Julio Gil Pecharromán, *José Antonio Primo de Rivera: retrato de un visionario* (Madrid: Temas de Hoy, 2003).

For the tense relations between the Catholic Church and republican institutions, see the documents included in *Archiu Vidal y Barraquer: Esglési i Estat durant la Segona República Espanyola 1931–1936* (Barcelona: Publicacions de l'Abadia de Montserrat, 1971). Various useful studies deal with the same issue in Frances Lannon, *Privilege, Persecution and Prophecy: The Catholic Church in Spain 1875–1975* (Oxford University Press, 1987); William J. Callahan, *The Catholic Church in Spain, 1875–2002* (Washington, DC: Catholic University of America Press, 2003), and in the first chapter of Hilari Raguer, *Gunpowder and Incense: The Catholic Church and the Spanish Civil War* (London: Routledge, 2007). On anticlericalism, see Maria Thomas, *The Faith and the Fury: Popular Anticlerical Violence and Iconoclasm in Spain, 1931–1936* (Brighton: Sussex Academic Press, 2013).

The best analysis of the Partido Radical during the Republic and also of the second republican biennium is provided by Nigel Townson, *The Crisis of Democracy in Spain: Centrist Politics Under the Second Republic, 1931–1936* (Brighton: Sussex Academic Press, 2000). The final months of the Republic in peace which followed the elections of February 1936, analysed in Chapter V, are amply covered in Stanley G. Payne, *The Collapse of the Spanish Republic, 1933–1936: Origins of the Civil War* (New Haven, CT: Yale University Press, 2006), also noted above. A very different viewpoint is offered in the recent work by Rafael Cruz, *En el nombre del pueblo: república, rebelión y guerra en la España de 1936* (Madrid: Siglo XXI, 2006).

The military uprising was recounted in detail some time ago by Luís Romero, *Tres días de julio* (Barcelona: Ariel, 1968). I have written about the breakdown of order and the violence engendered by the uprising in Julián Casanova, 'Verano sangriento', in Santos Juliá (ed.), Julián Casanova, Josep Maria Solé i Sabaté, Joan Villarroya and Francisco Moreno, *Victimas de la guerra civil* (Madrid: Temas de Hoy, 1999).

The crushing of the opposition and different expressions of political violence have been summarised, based on a large number of local, provincial and regional monographs on the subject, by Paul Preston in his exhaustive *The Spanish Holocaust: Inquisition and Extermination in Twentieth-Century Spain* (London: Harper Collins, 2011).

A wealth of information on the dark world of arms trafficking appears in Gerald Howson, *Arms for Spain: The Untold Story of the Spanish Civil War* (New York: St Martins Press, 1999).

A summary on the international dimension of the war can be found in Michael Alpert, *A New International History of the Spanish Civil War* (London: Palgrave Macmillan, 2003). A good compilation of articles on the topic is in Paul Preston and Ann L. Mackenzie (eds.), *The Republic Besieged: Civil War in*

Spain 1936–1939 (Edinburgh University Press, 1996). For the Republic at war, the most meticulous and detailed study is Helen Graham, *The Spanish Republic at War 1936–1939* (Cambridge University Press, 2002). I have analysed the positions and practice of anarchism in Julián Casanova, *Anarchism, the Republic and Civil War in Spain: 1931–1939* (London: Routledge, 2005). For communism, see Stanley G. Payne, *The Spanish Civil War, the Soviet Union, and Communism* (New Haven, CT: Yale University Press, 2004). For socialism, see Helen Graham, *Socialism and War: The Spanish Socialist Party in Power and Crisis, 1936–1939* (Cambridge University Press, 1991).

For Nationalist Spain, there is a wealth of well-organised information in Paul Preston, *Franco: A Biography* (London: Harper Collins, 1993). For the home fronts, Preston has also made insightful contributions in *Doves of War: Four Women of the Spanish Civil War* (London: Harper Collins, 2003). The best summary on women on the republican home front is by Mary Nash, *Defying Male Civilization: Women in the Spanish Civil War* (Denver: Arden Press, 1995). A social history, which places emphasis on the personal aspect and internal affairs of the Civil War, while giving less importance to international influence, is the work by Michael Seidman, *Republic of Egos: A History of the Spanish Civil War* (Madison: University of Wisconsin Press, 2002). Significant works reflecting a new approach to the Civil War include Chris Ealham and Michael Richards, *The Splintering of Spain: Cultural History and the Spanish Civil War, 1936–1939* (Cambridge University Press, 2005). See also Julián Casanova, *A Short History of the Spanish Civil War* (London: I. B. Tauris, 2012).

FRANCOISM

A personal dictatorship that takes the name of its founder and lasts for four decades explains the importance of the leader's biography. The essential reference is still the magnificent book by Paul Preston, *Franco: A Biography* (London: Harper Collins, 1993). English-speaking readers may also be interested in the works by Gabrielle Ashford Hodges, *Franco: A Concise Biography* (New York: Thomas Dunne Books, St Martin's Press, 2002); and Antonio Cazorla-Sánchez, *Franco: The Biography of the Myth* (London: Taylor & Francis, 2013).

The most comprehensive and recent monograph on this period in Spanish history is probably Borja de Riquer, *La dictadura de Franco* (Barcelona: Crítica and Marcial Pons, 2010), vol. IX of *Historia de España* edited by Josep Fontana and Ramón Villares. Also in Spanish, see Enrique Moradiellos, *La España de Franco (1939–1975): política y sociedad* (Madrid: Síntesis, 2000). An overview in English is Javier Tusell, *Spain: From Dictatorship to Democracy, 1939 to the Present* (London: Blackwell, 2007). See also Stanley G. Payne, *The Franco Regime, 1936–1975* (Madison: University of Wisconsin Press, 1987). Daily life in the dictatorship in the work by Antonio Cazorla-Sánchez, *Fear and Progress: Ordinary Lives in Franco's Spain, 1939–1975* (Oxford: Wiley Blackwell, 2009).

For information on the early years of the dictatorship, with issues such as the construction of the political regime, the misery of the post-war period and the cruelty of repression, see the studies by Michael Richards, *A Time of Silence: Civil War and the Culture of Repression in Franco's Spain, 1936–1945* (Cambridge University Press, 2006), and Richards, *After the Civil War: Making Memory and*

Re-Making Spain Since 1936 (Cambridge University Press, 2013). Also of interest are the works by Peter Anderson, *The Francoist Military Trials: Terror and Complicity, 1939–1945* (London: Routledge, 2009); Dacia Viejo-Rose, *Reconstructing Spain: Cultural Heritage and Memory After Civil War* (Brighton: Sussex Academic Press, 2011); Olivia Muñoz-Rojas, *Ashes and Granite: Destruction and Reconstruction in the Spanish Civil War and Its Aftermath* (Brighton: Sussex Academic Press, 2011); and Ronald Fraser, *In Hiding: The Life of Manuel Cortés* (London: Verso Books, 2010).

For the international situation in the context of the Second World War, see the books by Christian Leitz, *Nazi Germany and Francoist Spain* (London: Routledge, 2004); Richard Wigg (ed.), *Churchill and Spain: The Survival of the Franco Regime, 1940–1945* (London: Routledge, 2012); and Stanley G. Payne, *Franco and Hitler: Spain, Germany, and World War II* (New Haven, CT: Yale University Press, 2008). The issue of gender and women's organisations in the regime are covered in Kathleen J. L. Richmond, *Women and Spanish Fascism: The Women's Section of the Falange 1934–1959* (London: Routledge, 2003); and Inbal Offer, *Señoritas in Blue: The Making of a Female Political Elite in Franco's Spain* (Brighton: Sussex Academic Press, 2010).

The later years of Francoism, the 1960s and 1970s, are effectively addressed in the book edited by Nigel Townson, *Spain Transformed: The Late Franco Dictatorship, 1959–1975* (Basingstoke: Palgrave Macmillan, 2007). The influence of the Church is analysed in Joan Domke, 'Education, Fascism, and the Catholic Church in Franco's Spain: 1936–1975' (Ph.D. dissertation, Loyola University, Chicago, 2011, ecommons.luc.edu/luc_diss/104). The role of the army is considered in Paul Preston, *The Politics of Revenge: Fascism and the Military in Twentieth-Century Spain* (London: Routledge, 1995). The political evolution of the regime is analysed in Cristina Palomares, *The Quest for Survival After Franco: Moderate Francoism and the Slow Journey to the Polls, 1964–1977* (Brighton: Sussex Academic Press, 2004).

For more information on the social and political conflicts of the time, and to learn about the evolution of anti-Francoism, the following works are recommended: Joe Foweraker, *Making Democracy in Spain: Grass-Roots Struggle in the South, 1955–1975* (Cambridge University Press, 2003); Pamela Beth Radcliff, *Making Democratic Citizens in Spain: Civil Society and the Popular Origins of the Transition, 1960–1978* (Basingstoke: Palgrave Macmillan, 2011); Sebastian Balfour, *Dictatorship, Workers, and the City: Labour in Greater Barcelona Since 1939* (Oxford University Press, 1989); and Andrew Dowling, *Catalonia Since the Spanish Civil War: Reconstructing the Nation* (Eastbourne: Sussex Academic Press, 2013). The relationship between social change and the political end of Francoism in a comparative view is provided by Guillermo O'Donnell, Philippe C. Schmitter and Laurence Whitehead (eds.), *Transitions from Authoritarian Rule: Comparative Perspectives* (Baltimore: Johns Hopkins University Press, 1991).

THE TRANSITION AND THE CONSOLIDATION OF DEMOCRACY

Three and a half decades after the death of Franco, the Spanish political transition and the process of the consolidation of democracy are currently receiving a great deal of attention from historians. A chronological account of the political events between 1975 and 2004 may be found in Javier Tusell, *Spain: From Dictatorship to Democracy, 1939 to the Present* (Oxford: Blackwell Publishing, 2007). In Spanish, there is a good overall introduction in the summary by Charles Powell, *España en democracia, 1975–2000* (Barcelona: Plaza & Janés, 2001). In English, we have solid, well-crafted accounts such as those by Sebastian Balfour, *The Politics of Contemporary Spain* (London: Routledge, 2004); Richard Gunther and José Ramón Montero, *The Politics of Spain* (Cambridge University Press, 2009); Omar G. Encarnación, *Spanish Politics: Democracy After Dictatorship* (Cambridge: Polity Press, 2008); Paul Heywood, *Politics and Policy in Democratic Spain: No Longer Different?* (London: Routledge, 1998); and Paul Preston, *The Triumph of Democracy in Spain* (London: Routledge, 1987), and Preston, *Juan Carlos: Steering Spain from Dictatorship to Democracy* (London: Harper Perennial, 2005).

The Spanish Transition, from a comparative perspective, is scrutinised in the studies by Ronald H. Chilcote, Stylianos Hadjiyannis, Fred A. III Lopez, Daniel Nataf, and Elizabeth Sammis, *Transitions from Dictatorship to Democracy: Comparative Studies of Spain, Portugal and Greece* (London: Taylor & Francis, 1990); and Juan J. Linz and Alfred Stepan, *Problems of Democratic Transition and Consolidation: Southern Europe, South America, and Post-Communist Europe* (Baltimore: Johns Hopkins University Press, 1996). Spain's incorporation into the European institutions in Paul Christopher Manuel and Sebastian Royo, *Spain and Portugal in the European Union: The First Fifteen Years* (London: Routledge, 2004); and Julio Crespo MacLennan, *Spain and the Process of European Integration, 1957–1985* (London: Palgrave Macmillan, 2000).

The conflict of the various identities existing in the Spanish state in the works by Sebastian Balfour and Alejandro Quiroga, *The Reinvention of Spain: Nation and Identity Since Democracy* (Oxford University Press, 2007); and Xosé Manoel Núñez Seixas, 'A State of Many Nations: The Construction of a Plural Spanish Society Since 1976', in Christiane Harzig and Danielle Juteau (eds.), *The Social Construction of Diversity: Recasting the Master Narrative of Industrial Nations* (New York and Oxford: Berghahn Books, 2003), pp. 284–307, and Seixas, 'Regions, Nations and Nationalities: On the Process of Territorial Identity-Building During Spain's Democratic Transition and Consolidation', in Carlos H. Waisman and Raanan Rein (eds.), *Spanish and Latin American Transitions to Democracy* (Brighton: Sussex Academic Press, 2005), pp. 55–79. An introduction to the evolution of Basque and Catalan nationalism is given in the studies by Montserrat Guibernau, *Catalan Nationalism: Francoism, Transition and Democracy* (London: Routledge, 2012); and Diego Muro, *Ethnicity and Violence: The Case of Radical Basque Nationalism* (London: Routledge, 2011).

A critical view of the Transition can be found in the analysis by Ferran Gallego, *El mito de la transición: la crisis del franquismo y los orígenes de la democracia (1973–1977)* (Barcelona: Crítica, 2008). The controversial issues of the 'pact of forgetfulness' and of the Transition, and the debate on historical memory all have their own indispensable interpretations in the works of Paloma Aguilar, *Memory and Amnesia: The Role of the Spanish Civil War in the Transition to Democracy* (Oxford: Berghahn, 2002); and Alexandra Barahona de Brito and Carmen González Enríquez, *The Politics of Memory: Transitional Justice in Democratizing*

Societies (Oxford University Press, 2001). Also useful is the analysis by Diego Muro and Gregorio Alonso, *The Politics and Memory of Democratic Transition: The Spanish Model* (London: Routledge, 2010). Francisco Espinosa Maestre offers a different interpretation in *Shoot the Messenger? Spanish Democracy and the Crimes of Francoism: From the Pact of Silence to the Trial of Baltasar Garzón* (Brighton: Sussex Academic Press, 2013). A British observer's view can be found in Giles Tremlett's travel book, *Ghosts of Spain: Travels Through Spain and Its Silent Past* (London: Faber, 2007).

Index of names and authors